ENTREPRENEURSHIP AND THE MARKET PROCESS

A theory of entrepreneurship is crucial to a theory of the market process. Mainstream economics has failed to tackle adequately the problem of how economic agents improve their knowledge in a disequilibrium setting.

This book redresses this need by developing a dynamic theory of entrepreneurship. The author applies Karl Popper's ideas, developed in the context of the growth of scientific knowledge, to economic behaviour. The work:

- explores the implications of the growth of knowledge approach for entrepreneurship and learning behaviour;
- discusses the role of the market in screening entrepreneurial ideas;
- examines the philosophy and practical difficulties confronting entrepreneurs in interpreting market evidence;
- characterizes the market as an interpersonal problem-solving process;
- analyses the continuity and coherency of market processes.

The methodological approach successfully applies Popper's philosophy to the problem of how entrepreneurs learn in the light of experience and feedback from the market. As such, it provides a valuable new view of the market process as a learning procedure for generating and testing entrepreneurial ideas.

David Harper currently holds an advisory position with the New Zealand Treasury.

FOUNDATIONS OF THE MARKET ECONOMY

Edited by Mario J. Rizzo, *New York University* and Lawrence H. White, *University of Georgia*

A central theme of this series is the importance of understanding and assessing the market economy from a perspective broader than the static economics of perfect competition and Pareto optimality. Such a perspective sees markets as casual processes generated by the preferences, expectations and beliefs of economic agents. The creative acts of entrepreneurship that uncover new information about preferences, prices and technology are central to these processes with respect to their ability to promote the discovery and use of knowledge in society.

The market economy consists of a set of institutions that facilitate voluntary cooperation and exchange among individuals. These institutions include the legal and ethical framework as well as more narrowly 'economic' patterns of social interaction. Thus the law, legal institutions and cultural or ethical norms, as well as ordinary business practices and monetary phenomena, fall within the analytical domain of the economist.

ENTREPRENEURSHIP AND THE MARKET PROCESS

An enquiry into the growth of knowledge

David A. Harper

Routledge
Taylor & Francis Group

LONDON AND NEW YORK

First published 1996
by Routledge
2 Park Square, Milton Park, Abingdon, Oxfordshire OX14 4RN

Simultaneously published in the USA and Canada
by Routledge
711 Third Avenue, New York, NY 10017

Reprinted 1999, 2002

Transferred to Digital Printing 2006
First issued in paperback 2014

Routledge is an imprint of the Taylor & Francis Group, an informa business

Typeset in Adobe Garamond
by Keystroke, Jacaranda Lodge, Wolverhampton

British Library Cataloguing in Publication Data

A catalogue record for this book is available from the British Library

Library of Congress Cataloging in Publication Data

Harper, David A.
Entrepreneurship and the market process : an enquiry into the growth
of knowledge / David A. Harper.
p.   cm.
Includes bibliographical references and index.
ISBN 978-0-415-13048-6 (hbk)
ISBN 978-0-415-75658-7 (pbk)

1. Entrepreneurship. 2. Popper, Karl Raimund, Sir, 1902–
— View on entrepreneurship. I. Title.
HB615.H335   1996
338′.04—dc20   95-22510
CIP

ISBN 978-0-415-75658-7 (pbk)

Publisher's Note

The publisher has gone to great lengths to ensure the quality of this reprint
but points out that some imperfections in the original may be apparent

For Derek

CONTENTS

Part III   Agenda and conclusions

FIGURES AND TABLES

FIGURES

TABLES

PREFACE

This book has something new and important to say. It is finally
dawning on the economics profession that entrepreneurship is a
central concept in economic theory, and not just a peripheral subject
somewhere between economics and sociology. A key issue in
twentieth-century economics has been the operation of the market
system, in its many different guises – labour markets, product
markets, capital markets, and so on. Economists have been slow to
realise, though, that they need to explain not only how a given system
of markets works, but also how the market system emerges in the first
place. To do this properly it is necessary to recognise that the market
system is a special kind of economic institution - one that is designed
to encourage people to reveal their true valuation of different goods
and services, and to facilitate the reallocation of goods to those who
value them most. The institutional framework of the market system
evolves continually, creating new markets (and closing down old
ones) in response to newly expressed demands and newly available
supplies. The evolution of the system is driven by profit-seeking
entrepreneurs. In the final analysis, it is entrepreneurship which
explains why we have the configuration of markets that we have, and
not some other configuration instead.

But how do entrepreneurs know what new markets to set up?
They don't – if to know means to believe with certainty what is
actually true. Do they just make guesses, then – is entrepreneurial
success just a matter of luck? It is David Harper's thesis that entrepreneurs, though they are less than certain, do more than just
guess. Entrepreneurs act on the basis of hypotheses. Just as scientific
investigators formulate hypotheses which they test out experimen-
tally, so entrepreneurs formulate hypotheses which they test out in
the market environment. Precisely how they conduct these tests, and

xi

how they learn from these tests, is the central theme of this book. Speaking rather naively, hypotheses that are not falsified normally lead to successful market innovations. Hypotheses which appear to be falsified may be associated with short-run failure: but something is learnt when a hypothesis is falsified which may prove of inestimable value later on. The hypothesis may be refined, and a more sophisticated version may lead to an innovation of a more fundamental type. This is one reason why pioneers themselves do not always benefit as much from their efforts as those who follow along behind and learn from their mistakes.

The view of entrepreneurship presented by David Harper has the particular strength that it embeds the study of entrepreneurship within the wider issue of the growth of knowledge. Entrepreneurial activity accumulates knowledge of human wants, and of human productive capacities, according to much the same principles as scientific research accumulates knowledge of nature. There are important differences, of course, as the author makes clear. In particular, human subjects who know what others know about them can choose to act in an unpredictable way, thereby defeating attempts to control them. Nature, on the other hand, is more naive. But this difference should not obscure the fact that we learn about the behaviour of people in the aggregate in much the same way that we learn about nature – by constructing hypotheses, by acting on these hypotheses, and by appraising the results. Embedding the study of entrepreneurship within this wider context affords the range of insights which appear throughout the book.

So far as the economics profession is concerned, however, the most important point is a more specific one. The concept of learning employed by David Harper is far more sophisticated than the concept of learning employed in more conventional models. Conventional models of learning, based, for example, on Bayes's Rule, are usually concerned with the routine accumulation of ever-increasing amounts of data on the same subject, rather than with the imaginative synthesis of data on different subjects. They are usually concerned with refining the estimates of an economic parameter whose relevance is already established, rather than with testing hypotheses about which particular parameters are relevant and which are not.

David Harper's concept of entrepreneurial learning is far closer to the kind of learning that drives the evolution of the market system than is the conventional concept. His work therefore not only identifies an issue which has been seriously neglected by the economics profession, but also provides the conceptual apparatus with which it can be analysed in a more relevant way.

This book is based on David Harper's PhD thesis. As most academics are aware, the supervision of a PhD can be a long and painful process for both the supervisor and the supervisee. That is why it is important for scholars to choose PhD candidates with care. David Harper's PhD was somewhat unusual in two respects. For a start, he had written a large amount of it on his own initiative before finally registering for a PhD at Reading. Rather than us choosing him, it seems that he chose us as a suitable institution to help him finish off his work. This in turn produced the unusual scenario of someone completing their PhD ahead of schedule. Second, the process of supervision was unusually enjoyable, so far as I am concerned, at least. At the risk of repeating what (in other contexts) has become a cliché, I am sure that I learnt as much from him as he did from me. The PhD was like other PhDs in one respect, however – namely that when submitted it was a truly colossal work. It was so weighty, when finally bound, that it could be classified as an offensive weapon as well as a piece of research. No doubt the publisher is as much relieved as I am that the thesis has now shrunk to a size at which it can be offered to a wider readership. It is still a fairly substantial tome, but its content is equally substantial. Each page will therefore repay careful study.

Mark Casson
University of Reading

ACKNOWLEDGEMENTS

Writing acknowledgements is a welcome task, not least because it signals the fulfilment of what has been in this case an intensive endeavour. It also presents an opportunity to recall people and places connected with the preparation of this book.

I would like to express my deep gratitude to Mark Casson, my PhD supervisor, for his constructive advice and detailed feedback on successive drafts. The many letters he wrote in response to my papers are testimony to his patience and sagacity. He has also demonstrated to me that the entrepreneurial spirit is alive and well in academia.

I have also been lucky to receive insightful criticism from Tony Endres and Peter Earl. The fertility of their suggestions has been a constant spur to explore new directions. Valuable comments and assistance were obtained from Donal Krouse, Kevin Lang, Stephen Littlechild, Brian Loasby, David Mayes, Alan Musgrave, Robert Nola and Lawrence H. White. Naturally, I take full responsibility for any errors and shortcomings that remain.

The foundations from which this book is based would not have been possible without the splendid infrastructure provided by two institutions – the New Zealand Institute of Economic Research, Wellington, and the Lehrstuhl für Allgemeine und Industrielle Betriebswirtschaftslehre (Institute for Business Administration), Technische Universität, Munich. In particular, I would like to thank Alan Bollard and Arnold Picot for their practical encouragement. This book is very much the outgrowth of ideas formulated during my stimulating stay in Munich, a city for which I retain much fondness.

In completing the final stages of this book, I was also fortunate enough to spend some time at the Economics Department of New York University. The climate provided by the weekly Austrian Economics Colloquium and the fine company of Israel Kirzner, Mario Rizzo and Peter Boettke provided an added impetus to bring this work to completion. I am especially grateful to Mario for his encouragement (and sound guidance on where to dine out in the Big Apple). If only I could have stayed longer!

Furthermore, I would like to acknowledge the generous financial support awarded over the years by the Sarah Scaife Foundation, the Austrian Economics Program at New York University, Deutscher Akademischer Austauschdienst (German Academic Exchange Service), the Reserve Bank of New Zealand, the Social Sciences Research Fund Committee, the Goethe Institute, and the administrators of the travel fund under the Science and Technology Co-operation Agreement between the Federal Republic of Germany and New Zealand.

I also gratefully acknowledge permission from JAI Press to publish material which first appeared in my paper, 'A new approach to modeling endogenous learning processes in economic theory', in P.J. Boettke, I.M. Kirzner and M.J. Rizzo, *Advances in Austrian Economics*, 1, Greenwich, Connecticut: JAI Press.

In addition, I would like to thank Rachel Chan, Douglas Jenkin, Margaret Malan, Geraldine Sellens, Rhonda Taylor, and Christine Tether for helping out in producing typescripts, compiling the bibliography, and interloaning reading material.

Finally, my partner, Derek Arnold (to whom this book is dedicated), deserves a special mention for selflessly putting up with my long hours in the office and bolstering my tenacity to see this venture through to completion.

David A. Harper
Wellington
April 1995

Part I

BACKGROUND AND INTRODUCTION

1

INTRODUCTION

Beliefs are part of the fabric of economic life, woven into it in such a way that they cannot be taken out without disintegration of the cloth.

(Bacharach 1986: 178)

1.1 WHY DO WE NEED A THEORY OF ENTREPRENEURSHIP?

The objectives of this work are to explain entrepreneurial learning and to make some first steps in accounting for the 'endogenous' dynamics of the market process. In order to explain the disequilibrium process through which markets move, it is necessary to have a theory of entrepreneurship. Entrepreneurship is here defined as profit-seeking activity aimed at identifying and solving ill-specified problems in structurally uncertain and complex situations. It involves the discovery and creation of new ends–means frameworks, rather than the allocation of given means in the pursuit of given ends (see Chapter 3 for a more detailed description of entrepreneurship). It has been shown convincingly elsewhere that the market process cannot function, even within the market for a single commodity, if all market participants are assumed to be non-entrepreneurial maximisers who react mechanically to changes enforced upon them by external circumstances over which they have no control (Hayek 1949: ch. 5; Kirzner 1962a, 1973). Such an approach leaves the market process unexplained. This book aims to address this problem by laying the groundwork for a dynamic theory of how entrepreneurs learn. A theory of entrepreneurial learning is a prerequisite to any explanation of sequential entrepreneurial decision-making, and thus to any theory of the dynamics of the market process. It is crucial for

3

explaining the revision over time of people's knowledge, expectations, decisions and plans – changes which form the basis of the competitive market process. Indeed, it has been claimed that a theory of market dynamics is necessarily a theory of learning (Gordon and Hynes 1970: 377; White 1978: 4).

Given the failure of 'mainstream' economics (i.e. the prevailing neoclassical research programme) to examine entrepreneurship, it is necessary to turn to other approaches. It has been argued for some time that theories of the growth of (scientific) knowledge can provide significant insights into how markets operate and how economic agents learn from their experiences within the market.[1] Modern theories of the growth of science provide much scope for human imagination and experimentation, so that these approaches warrant investigation as a means of equipping economic agents within economic theories with entrepreneurial qualities. Boland (1982, 1986b) and Wible (1984) have independently argued that there is a need for a growth-of-knowledge conception of economic agents, which could lead to a more dynamic view of economic learning and to an alternative conception of economic rationality which goes beyond the narrow 'mainstream' view of rationality as typified by a maximising behavioural postulate. Theories of scientific development provide valuable insights which are useful for explaining the broad pattern of scientists' behaviour in particular situations. By extending the scope of these theories, science can be taken as a generalised model of sophisticated decision-making in structurally uncertain and complex problem situations. Applied to the context of entrepreneurship, this model shows promise of providing a basis for a theory of entrepreneurial learning and of market processes.

Consequently, the theory developed in this book draws upon the abundant literature in the philosophy of science. In particular, it applies Popper's critical rationalism and, to a lesser extent, Lakatos's methodology of scientific research programmes. Popper's theory of the growth of knowledge is chosen because it was the first *non-justificationist* philosophy in the history of the philosophy of science: it is non-justificationist in that it divorces knowledge from certainty, proof and 'hard' facts (Bartley 1964: 23). This conception of knowledge implies that there is no supreme, infallible method available to us for acquiring knowledge which can guarantee us the truth. Lakatos was convinced that Popper's philosophy represents 'the most advanced philosophy of our time', an accomplishment 'in the tradition – and on the level – of Hume, Kant or Whewell' (Lakatos 1974: 263). In his opinion, 'philosophical progress can only be based ... on its achievements' (1974: 263). The significance of Popper's philosophy of science arises from its vindication of the problems of the *growth* of scientific knowledge. It employs a dynamic, evolutionary concept of knowledge, rather than a structural concept. Many philosophers in the growth-of-knowledge tradition (including Lakatos) have accordingly adopted Popper's work as the starting point of their analysis (Caldwell 1982: 37).

This work represents the first major investigation into entrepreneurship (and, to a lesser extent, the market process) within a growth-of-knowledge (GK) framework.[2] It explores the implications of the GK approach for entrepreneurial learning and behaviour, the screening of entrepreneurial ideas, market adjustment and its continuity, and the coherence of the market system. This approach casts new light onto how economic agents in markets acquire, use and disseminate knowledge as they initiate and respond to change, and it highlights how agents must apply entrepreneurial imagination to generate their new conjectures. More specifically, the approach aims to develop a theory of how Popperian-style entrepreneurs improve their knowledge in a disequilibrium setting.[3] The tentative and conjectural nature of entrepreneurial knowledge is emphasised, and so too is the consequent need for an interpersonal process by which knowledge is constantly communicated, acquired, tested and improved.

The commonalities of scientific progress and the market process are exploited to the utmost. Like scientific enterprise, entrepreneurship is described essentially as a problem-solving activity which must be conceived in terms of human ends and purposes. Like science, the market is regarded as an inter-subjective and pluralistic process for generating conjectures, exchanging and promoting ideas and attempting to refute them. Both learning processes require conventions, many of which have evolved spontaneously, to facilitate the efficient production, coordination and criticism of knowledge (Loasby 1989: 164–166).

Explaining entrepreneurship and market processes in terms of these philosophical theories of the evolution of ideas is not simply to rely upon metaphor, however. It is a direct *application* of modern theories of the growth of knowledge to the twin problems of entrepreneurship and the market process: '[W]hat I wish to emphasise here is that the relationship between scientific and market processes is not just that of analogy, for the growth of knowledge is the subject of both' (Loasby 1989: 163).

1.1.1 What problems does the new theory attempt to solve?

The entrepreneurial function is the major driving force of the market economy. The entrepreneur is an agent who seeks to break outside the range of established routines and the existing framework of ideas. The imaginative, intuitive component of this activity is well-recognised (e.g. Schumpeter 1934, 1947, 1950; Shackle 1970, 1979a, 1979b). But previous theories have tended only to emphasise the non-rational, intuitive faculties required of an entrepreneur (e.g. Kirzner 1973, 1979b, 1982c, 1992). This perspective needs to be bolstered by emphasising in addition the rational and critical aspects of entrepreneurship which are a prerequisite to acquiring new knowledge. Though necessary, imaginative freedom and the generation of novel ideas are not sufficient for the evolution of knowledge. In attempting to solve market problems at a profit, the entrepreneur must also apply critical methods of error elimination: the entrepreneur's creative imagination must be subject to critical control. Reconstructions of the process of entrepreneurial learning which fail to stress the role of criticism are thus inadequate.

Consequently, the central problem addressed by this book is to explain the growth of knowledge at the level of individual entrepreneurs: how entrepreneurs learn in the light of experience and feedback from the market, how they may retain some part of their systems of knowledge while modifying the rest, and how they may even devise entirely new systems to replace their original ideas and strategies. Explaining the nature, causes and effects of entrepreneurial error also falls within the ambit of this work. Similarly, I seek to account for the methods by which entrepreneurs may test their own hypotheses (before, during and after commercialisation) in order to identify and to learn from their mistakes. Moreover, I hope to explain the difficulties which entrepreneurs encounter in interpreting market evidence, in deciding whether their ideas have been effectively refuted and in determining whether to abandon a failing venture. Another goal is to provide an explanation of why entrepreneurs in similar circumstances may behave differently.

The solution of these problems requires the development of a more sophisticated theory of (entrepreneurial) learning than has hitherto been put forward in economics. It calls for a theory which analyses entrepreneurial knowledge as a dynamic, evolving system rather than as a static or stationary structure; a theory which depicts the growth of knowledge as a series of revolutions which overturn old ideas, rather than as an incremental, cumulative process of improvement; and a theory which characterises entrepreneurial learning as a process of discovery rather than as a procedure of imitation or of inductive instruction through repetition. In particular, what is needed is a theory which portrays all learning of new market 'facts' as a sequence of continuous conjecture and refutation.

A theory of entrepreneurial learning (viewed *ex ante*) cannot be a theory of *ex post* successful learning. Success depends upon many factors, including luck (cf. Popper 1976c: 47). An adequate theory of learning cannot exclude human fallibility which can manifest itself in entrepreneurial error, losses and failure. On the contrary, genuine uncertainty, the unpredictability of the future growth of knowledge and the potential for entrepreneurial mistakes and losses must all be emphasised. In summary, the required type of theory of entrepreneurial learning is critical rather than dogmatic, dynamic rather than static, deductivist rather than inductivist, Darwinian rather than Lamarckian, and fallibilist rather than justificationist or positivist.

In addition to examining how entrepreneurs operate within the market system, this book also seeks to tease out implications of the GK approach for the competitive process as a whole, that is, problems at the level of markets. The new research programme outlined in this chapter aims in the long term to provide a theoretical framework for analysing dynamic market processes taking place over time. It should be noted at the outset, however, that the immediate objectives of the specific theory presented in this book are far more modest. Analysis at the level of market processes is given much less emphasis. The present work seeks only a very partial explanation of such phenomena, a first step towards a more adequate theory. At this stage of theoretical development, I confine my attention to only a few aspects of the market process: namely, the pattern of organisation of conjecture and refutation within the market economy; the criteria by which markets screen entrepreneurial conjectures; the origins of the competitive market process and their implications for the nature of this learning mechanism; the comparative performance of the market process in generating and screening new entrepreneurial conjectures; and how the market process can be perpetuated by endogenous forces (i.e. forces within the system, as opposed to external shocks).

1.2 ENTREPRENEURSHIP AS A LACUNA IN MAINSTREAM ECONOMIC THEORY

> One lesson to be learned from the history of economics is that the problem of the place of entrepreneurship in economic theory is not a problem of theory *per se*, it is a problem of method.
>
> (Hébert and Link 1989: 48)

The absence of a neoclassical theory of the entrepreneur has been investigated at length within the economics literature and will not be discussed in detail here.[4] At this juncture, it is sufficient to mention that the modern Walrasian theory of perfect competition (e.g. Arrow and Hahn 1971; Debreu 1959) cannot explain market processes – the way in which market forces bring about adjustments in prices and quantities and the introduction of new products and processes. At best, neoclassical theory describes the conditions for competitive equilibrium, without explaining adequately if or how equilibrium may be reached.

Of course, neoclassical models of market adjustment to equilibrium do exist, but they are unsatisfactory.[5] In this section, emphasis is placed upon models of price adjustment. (Indeed, in the neoclassical literature all the adjustment seems to concern prices and/or quantities. There is little in relation to other elements of the marketing mix that entrepreneurs might see worth adjusting, such as the product or promotion methods.) The following discussion is extremely selective, being limited to two distinct lines of research within the neoclassical research programme: analyses of the stability of (mostly general) competitive equilibrium; and partial-equilibrium models of equilibrium price dispersion in markets with imperfect and costly information. Lack of space precludes an examination of alternative concepts of equilibrium (such as temporary general equilibria and rational expectations equilibria) which have been developed in response to a growing dissatisfaction with the original Arrow–Debreu model of general equilibrium.

1.2.1 Analyses of adjustment to competitive equilibrium

The seminal study within the neoclassical programme is that of Samuelson (1941, 1942, 1947: 257–349) who provided the first description of the price adjustment process in terms of a system of differential equations. Following Samuelson's path-breaking contribution, the first neoclassical models of price adjustment were tâtonnement models in which no actual exchange occurred outside of equilibrium (see Arrow and Hurwicz 1958 and Arrow, Block and Hurwicz 1959). The tâtonnement process was not the only model to be offered of price adjustment in a competitive economy, however. Negishi (1961) was the first to show the stability of a non-tâtonnement process which does permit trading to take place out of equilibrium. These processes are generally more stable than tâtonnement processes. Two major types of non-tâtonnement models have been distinguished in the literature: those which model the Edgeworth process (Hahn 1962; Uzawa 1962) and those models based on the Hahn process (Hahn and Negishi 1962). The Edgeworth process assumes that trade will take place if and only if at least one individual gains in utility by exchange at current prices and no individual loses. In contrast, the basic assumption of the Hahn process is that markets are sufficiently orderly that after trade the goods that are in excess demand (supply) for a given agent are also in excess demand (supply) by the market as a whole. In other words, the Hahn process postulates that potential buyers and potential sellers can identify each other, so that at any time after trade there is not simultaneously both unsatisfied effective demand and unsatisfied supply for the same good (Fisher 1974: 472, 477; 1983: 31).

A major shortcoming of all these early models is that they failed to explain price changes as the result of rational decisions by individual market participants, because all economic agents were assumed to be price-takers. Thus, it was not explained who changes prices and why (Arrow 1959: 43; Koopmans 1957: 179). Price changes arose inexplicably as the consequence of a mythical auctioneer who sets and adjusts prices to their unique equilibrium levels or as a result of 'impersonal forces of the market'[6] (an auctioneer in disguise). The pricing rules of the auctioneer were not linked to the maximising actions of economic agents, actions which are supposed to constitute the basis of neoclassical theory. The price adjustment mechanism thus violated the requirements of methodological individualism (see Boland 1986b: 142; Hahn 1987: 137). 'The auctioneer, of course, is not a market actor but a *deus ex machina*. The appearance of the auctioneer is a methodological ruse, an attempt to lend plausibility to the Samuelsonian formulation by providing an "agent" whose behavior it describes' (White 1978: 10).

Consequently, in these models knowledge is the outcome of some fictional process rather than the product of actual learning by individual economic agents. This epistemological flight of fancy is highlighted by the extremely severe knowledge requirements of the Edgeworth process. Unlike the Hahn process, the Edgeworth process requires that whenever the conditions for beneficial exchange exist, trade will in fact take place. Each market participant is required to be aware of all opportunities to personally gain through trade. In reality, of course, without an auctioneer, 'exchange may fail to occur because knowledge is imperfect, in spite of the presence of the conditions for mutually profitable exchange' (Kirzner 1973: 216). In addition, the Hahn process does not address the entrepreneurial element involved in the decision to trade.

Following Arrow's (1959) criticism of Samuelson's mathematical statement of price adjustment, some later non-tâtonnement models distinctly located the task of price adjustment with individual economic agents, rather than a fictitious auctioneer. Such adjustment processes have been termed models of atomistic price adjustment (Hey 1974: 484). In this connection, the most notable series of contributions was by Fisher (1970, 1972, 1973). Some models of atomistic price dynamics (e.g. Fisher 1972), however, specified implausible decision rules which, although guaranteeing convergence to a competitive equilibrium, do not reflect the thoroughgoing pursuit of self-interest by the price-adjusting agent. Such models could not explain why economic agents should adopt the specified price-adjustment rule; their pricing behaviour was not motivated. The price-adjustment rules in other models (e.g. Fisher 1973) may have been consistent with profit maximisation but were based upon logically impossible knowledge requirements (Rothschild 1973: 1285; White 1978: 4, 24, 28).

From the point of view of the growth of knowledge, the gravest defect of the foregoing adjustment models is that they persistently assume that individuals fail to recognise that they are in disequilibrium during the adjustment process. At every moment in time, agents are required to act as if they naively believe themselves to be in competitive equilibrium. Market participants never learn from experience, even though their conjectures are continually refuted:

> [T]he agents . . . are remarkably stupid, always expecting prices to remain constant and transactions to be completed, when their constant experience tells them that this is not so. A model that hopes to explain how *arbitraging* agents drive a competitive economy to equilibrium can hardly afford to assume that

agents do *not* perceive the very arbitrage opportunities that characterize disequilibrium.

(Fisher 1987: 28; emphasis added)

Fisher's (1981, 1983: Part 2) next class of models was an ambitious endeavour to redress these shortcomings. As in earlier atomistic models, prices are set by individual agents – though the precise process by which agents make and accept price offers is not explained. A distinguishing feature of this type of 'disequilibrium' model is that the agents are more sophisticated than in previous models. Most importantly, agents understand that they are not in equilibrium, a recognition described as 'disequilibrium consciousness or awareness'. They have point (i.e. single-value) expectations of prices and may expect prices to change. Their expectations about future prices may also differ. They also contemplate the possibility that they may not be able to costlessly complete all their planned transactions. With disequilibrium awareness also comes the ability of agents to exploit arbitrage opportunities (Fisher 1987: 28).

Fisher's general strategy for allowing agents to recognise disequilibrium situations (and to make corresponding adjustments in their behaviour) is referred to by him as the assumption of 'No Favourable Surprise'. This assumption states that in the course of trading, agents perceive that opportunities to trade are gradually becoming less and less. Like the assumption of rational expectations (which is a special case of Fisher's), the assumption of 'No Favourable Surprise' is extremely restrictive: it precludes the discovery of any unsuspected, *favourable* opportunities for trading, including those which may appear in the process of adjustment to prior exogenous disturbances. The only unexpected changes allowed are those which make agents worse off than before. As a result, entrepreneurial initiatives which expand agents' opportunity sets – such as the introduction of new products and methods of production, the discovery of new markets and sources of supply, and the pioneering of new ways of organising – are excluded if they had not been envisaged (by whom – the agents or the analyst?) in the first place. Individuals are limited to adjusting to disequilibrium (namely, the disappointment of their expectations) by doing something wholly within the range of existing practice. It is proved that if 'No Favourable Surprise' prevails throughout the process of adjustment, then the process will converge to equilibrium (though not necessarily to a Walrasian equilibrium). As old opportunities disappear through arbitrage, this clockwork economy winds down inexorably towards some equilibrium which is characterised by the execution of previously planned transactions at correctly foreseen prices.[7] Consequently, convergence to equilibrium and proof of stability are bought at the expense of ruling out creative, entrepreneurial responses to economic change.

For the GK theorist, this class of models generally provides few, if any, favourable surprises. Fisher's 'disequilibrium' approach is not truly dynamic in the market-process sense (Ikeda 1990). The GK theorist emphasises that learning processes in real time will never converge to an equilibrium. Consequently, the assumption of 'No Favourable Surprise' itself appears to be a product of theoretical convenience, specified simply because it ensures a proof that the model will converge to some equilibrium. The assumption demands an *ad hoc* restriction on agents' knowledge, their expectations, change in expectations and their actions. Why should all agents expect that their situation (utilities, profits) will not improve in the course of the adjustment process? Why not 'No Unfavourable Surprise' instead? Furthermore, the presumed theory of knowledge that underlies the model is not tenable. Agents are assumed to have certain knowledge of their preferences and of all technology and are presumed to hold their expectations with certainty (although they do revise them) (Fisher 1981: 280, 309). This viewpoint is consistent with justificationism, an inadequate theory of knowledge that defines knowledge exclusively as something which is believed to be certain and proven true (see section 2.1).

Fisher provides a cogent discussion of the problems of modelling disequilibrium behaviour and recognises the crucial theoretical importance of how agents act when their plans are frustrated and their conjectures refuted. With his emphasis on methodological individualism, 'disequilibrium awareness' and the change over time in expectations, Fisher makes a significant step forward in the neoclassical theory of market-adjustment processes (and inadvertently proposes a model which superficially has some Kirznerian elements).[8] However, Fisher appears unprepared to make that radical leap which requires acknowledging the structural uncertainty of the human situation and going beyond single-exit methods of economic analysis based on the calculus of maximisation. As Boland (1986b: 110) notes, 'disequilibrium awareness' is not sufficient: how individuals respond to perceived disequilibria (i.e. to the failure of their plans) must also be explained. This in turn requires a more sophisticated approach to the knowledge and learning of economic agents. It must be recognised that the major limitation of Fisher's model as a characterisation of actual market processes is the absence of rivalrous entrepreneurship, entrepreneurial imagination and entrepreneurial learning.

1.2.2 Search-theoretic models of price dispersion in competitive markets with imperfect information

One common difficulty with the models discussed so far is that equilibrium is typically restricted to a single unchanging price.[9] Many models even insist that a given commodity be sold at the same price (i.e. that the law of the single price prevails) throughout any disequilibrium period of adjustment. Yet an important aspect of markets in the real world is a dispersion in prices at any one time – a phenomenon which originally spurred Stigler (1961) to formulate his now classic model on optimal consumer search. Inspired primarily by Stigler's work, some search-theoretic models have been extended to situations in which market equilibrium is not a uniform price but a distribution of prices for a homogeneous commodity (e.g. Grossman and Stiglitz 1976, 1980; Salop and Stiglitz 1977, 1982; Stiglitz 1989).[10] An important result in this literature is that even when there are no exogenous shocks in demand or supply and even when all individual consumers have identical and positive search costs (for all searches including the first), the only possible equilibrium is characterised by price dispersion. 'The Law of the Single Price is repealed' (Stiglitz 1989: 773).

Much of the neoclassical literature on adjustment has been at the general equilibrium level. In contrast, search-theoretic work on adjustment is generally of the nature of partial analysis or even 'partial partial-equilibrium analysis': it sometimes explains only *one* side of *one* market at a time.[11] Similarly, the imperfections of knowledge may emerge solely on one side or in one part of the market and even then it is conventionally assumed that the uninformed participants have rational expectations (e.g. Grossman and Stiglitz 1976, 1980; Salop and Stiglitz 1977, 1982). Search-theoretic models of price dispersion typically do not consider the structural uncertainty or knowledge problems confronting real-world entrepreneurs who set prices in disequilibrium situations. For example, Salop and Stiglitz's (1982) 'theory of sales' depicts price-setting agents as enjoying an empirical basis of certain knowledge when it comes to their (expected) demand curves: in taking competitors' prices as given, each agent knows with certainty the optimal pricing policy to adopt. Each firm is able to derive with certainty its profits as a function of the price that it sets. For there to be an equilibrium price distribution, firms must in addition know with certainty that their profit functions have multiple maxima and that the maxima represent exactly the same level of profits. Firms thus have complete knowledge of the environment in which they act. Yet how this knowledge is acquired remains unexplained within the logic of the model.

From the standpoint of modern theories of the growth of knowledge, a major problem with search-theoretic models is that they presume an inductive or conventionalist theory of knowledge and of learning: it is assumed that agents (including arbitrageurs) learn only by collecting more information. Learning activity is assumed to be undertaken in precisely the same manner as any other economising activity. Given that there are costs associated with the acquisition of information, it is claimed that agents search up to the point at which the net benefits of information acquisition are maximised: they thereby tolerate an optimal degree of parametric uncertainty. True knowledge about all arbitrage opportunities can only be obtained by collecting an infinite amount of information, which is too costly (Boland 1986b: 127; Kirzner 1979b: 141ff).

For example, in Grossman and Stiglitz's (1976, 1980) models of market adjustment arbitrageurs incur costs obtaining the information they need to perceive the price differentials which arise in a competitive market buffeted by random demand or supply shocks. In equilibrium, the marginal individual who purchases information finds the increment in expected utility from becoming informed equal to the cost of the information. Uninformed agents have no incentive to purchase the information required to identify arbitrage opportunities. Because arbitrage is costly, the market never completely adjusts to exogenous shocks: the competitive arbitrage process is 'imperfect' and some price differences will persist. There is an 'equilibrium degree of disequilibrium' (1980: 393).

In addition, search-theoretic models of adjustment rest on the mistaken assumption that economic actions are only based on knowledge which has been deliberately acquired.[12] It is not recognised that entrepreneurs can acquire fallible knowledge of profit opportunities by means other than planned search (e.g. by having a spontaneous flash of insight, by dreaming about them or by forming their ideas by accident). Furthermore, search theory does not acknowledge that, even with unlimited information acquisition, entrepreneurial conjectures cannot be proven true (even if they are true).

Finally, search-theoretic models of adjustment often ignore the interpersonal nature of the learning process inherent in market activity (e.g. word-of-mouth communication). Consequently, they may fail to explain why market information is not disseminated. It is sometimes found necessary to resort to such defensive devices as assuming that price setters pursue mixed strategies (i.e. random pricing policies) in order to prevent customers learning of the best buys.

In spite of recent developments, therefore, a major lacuna in the neoclassical research programme still remains: the absence of a coherent theory of how economic agents learn from experience in a disequilibrium environment of structural uncertainty and of how they act when their conjectures are refuted. This lamentable state of affairs in mainstream economic theory can aptly be described as the 'poverty of formalism'.[13] Economic agents are restricted to the calculus of optimisation based upon some set of certain or probable knowledge. They are devoid of imagination and other entrepreneurial qualities. The dimensions of the neoclassical agent's problem situation are so specified as to prohibit any possibility of entrepreneurship (see section 3.1.1). New modes of analysis are needed, rather than an incessant extension of equilibrium techniques to different contexts. The great preoccupation with the mathematical properties of equilibrium end-states must be supplanted by an investigation of the processes of competition.

1.3 PREVIOUS THEORIES OF ENTREPRENEURSHIP

Several theories of the entrepreneur and of the market process are to be found in the economics literature.[14] The two most significant recent contributions are Kirzner (1973, 1979b, 1982c, 1985, 1992) and Casson (1982). Kirzner's and Casson's theories can be judged to be important advances upon neoclassical theory because they contribute to our understanding of market *processes* rather than equilibrium states. Following Mises (1949, 1980), Hayek (1937, 1945) and Knight (1964), Kirzner and Casson emphasise the process of change that characterises real-world markets. For Casson and Kirzner, the driving force of the market process is assumed to be the movement towards equilibrium. They explain the operation of equilibrating forces within and between markets. Equilibration is explained as the product of entrepreneurial discovery and competition. The process of adjustment to equilibrium arises as the result of the activity of entrepreneurs who recognise exogenous changes in economic circumstances, discover gaps in the coordination of market participants' decisions and actively adjust prices to new market conditions. By their actions to capture arbitrageurial profits, entrepreneurs unwittingly bring prices towards their new equilibrium levels and switch resources over to the new equilibrium configuration defined by the new data.

Kirzner's and Casson's perspectives are lucid and insightful contributions and go some way to explaining the entrepreneurial character of the market process. Their theories provide a vehicle for progressing beyond the limited neoclassical problem of economising in the allocation of given means to achieve a set of given ends.

However, from the point of view of theories of the growth of knowledge, they do not provide adequate explanations of the market process. Kirzner and Casson explain the actual movement of the market process strictly in terms of movement toward a new equilibrium which the market is tending to create (but which it will never actually reach owing to continual exogenous disturbances). Since the market is regarded as a fundamentally equilibrating process, they must treat forces that create disequilibrium as exogenous to the market system and, therefore, as not amenable to economic analysis.

This conception of the scope of the market process is too narrow. The market is explained as a process involving only one type of economic change: equilibrating processes in response to exogenous disturbances. Thus, the market process consists of nothing more than adaptive responses to changes in the data – that is, to shifts in preferences, changes in resources and the invention of new technologies (Loasby 1984a: 78; 1985: 24). By treating disequilibrating events as exogenous developments, Kirzner and Casson simply abandon any attempt to predict them or to explain where these changes come from. These changes are an integral feature of the market process and provide it with an endogenous momentum. Thus, Kirzner and Casson do not explain adequately the nature of the forces which propel the market process:

> A conception of the market as a process which only equilibrates is incomplete at best; at worst it can distort our vision of the market by presenting as exogenous, forces that are really endogenous.
>
> (High 1986: 113)

16

Furthermore, although emphasising that the market is a process of continuous change, Kirzner and Casson fail to analyse adequately the conditions required to keep this process in motion. Their account of the continuity of the market process is incomplete because to perpetuate the market process, they must supply a continuing sequence of disequilibrating events which has taken place outside the economic system. Before market participants are able to adjust fully to an exogenous change and thereby establish a final equilibrium, another unexpected change in the data must be introduced so that the market must again veer towards some other final equilibrium point. Only by means of such a theoretical makeshift are Kirzner and Casson able to continually frustrate the equilibrating tendency of the market. In the hypothetical absence of exogenous disturbances, their version of a market economy would eventually converge to a final equilibrium position, and the market process would grind to a halt.[15]

Their conceptions of the market process – with their 'neat self-regulating' properties (Loasby 1985: 23) – are based upon inadequate justificationist theories of learning which they implicitly attribute to entrepreneurs. Their failure to endogenise disequilibrating economic changes is partly the result of the 'cumulative' rather than 'revolutionary' theories of knowledge inherent in their approaches. Once accepted as a basis for action, entrepreneurial conjectures are never refuted during the execution of the entrepreneur's plan. Kirzner's and Casson's conception of entrepreneurial knowledge is thus not truly dynamic: an entrepreneur's knowledge of market data does not change as decisions are made in the course of exploiting a particular profit opportunity.

Kirzner and Casson presume that there is some intuitive learning process by which the entrepreneur can always acquire true knowledge of market data (i.e. the givens). Kirzner describes alert entrepreneurs as discovering profit opportunities by 'opening their eyes' and noticing facts staring them in the face – a perceptual metaphor (see too Böhm 1992: 100–101). Casson (1982: 146–148) portrays entrepreneurs as synthesising knowledge but he does not discuss what is involved in the synthesis. Changes in consumer tastes, technological possibilities and resource availabilities are simply known by the alert and astute entrepreneur, although this knowledge may not be widely dispersed among other market participants who might find it useful. (Other market participants are assumed to overlook information or to be short of the information required to effect a synthesis.) Not only are price differentials and the true values of inputs known by entrepreneurs, they are also known with absolute certainty once they are recognised (Casson 1982: 201; Kirzner 1973: 38). Entrepreneurs know that their knowledge of basic market data is true. Before committing themselves to action, Kirzner's entrepreneurs can thus establish beyond doubt that their profit opportunities are genuine (i.e. their knowledge of a profit opportunity is proven true or justified) (Kirzner 1982c: 149). Entrepreneurs do not need to conduct market research with the express goal of testing their hypotheses about consumer preferences.

However, the infallible empirical basis of hard facts, upon which Kirzner's and Casson's entrepreneurs are presumed to act, does not in reality exist and its establishment is logically impossible. Kirzner and Casson assume that entrepreneurs can perform with complete logical certainty the recognition of past errors, the correction of misguided business decisions and the exploitation of profit opportunities. In order to faultlessly improve the coordination between the decisions of market participants, entrepreneurs are required to know more than they can possibly know: the truth of their knowledge (regarding changes in market data and consequent profit opportunities) which they have inexplicably acquired. In fact the susceptibility of entrepreneurs to make mistakes is excluded to such an extent that entrepreneurs are depicted as possessing epistemic knowledge, rather than tentative conjectures or theories. Kirzner and Casson do not recognise the tentativeness of the 'facts' possessed by the entrepreneur. Fallible background theories are involved, in the light of which the entrepreneur interprets the facts. Changes in market data and their implications are not as unambiguous as they assume. Information (on a change in technology, for instance) only becomes economically significant within a conceptual framework, such as a set of theories of latent demand and of production. Entrepreneurial conjectures about tastes, technology and resources are neither provable nor conclusively disprovable – that is, they can neither be proved true from experience nor can they be eliminated by hard, conclusive refutation (cf. Lakatos 1970: 98–99). Knowledge of market data is always conjectural: entrepreneurs can only ever have *theories* of what consumer preferences are, together with *conjectures* about what new uses for an input are possible and what new technologies might achieve.

Kirzner's and Casson's theories of the entrepreneur are thus explanatorily inadequate with respect to knowledge and its acquisition.

These theories have failed to tackle adequately the problem of how entrepreneurs improve their knowledge in a disequilibrium setting, even though these theories differentiate the entrepreneur in terms of knowledge. It is presumed that all entrepreneurs are working with the correct theoretical framework. As a consequence, their entrepreneurs do not face structural uncertainty, they do not make mistakes, they do not make losses, their businesses do not fail, they do not disrupt plans and their actions are never disequilibrating.

Their views about knowledge thus result in a distinct lack of symmetry in their treatments of entrepreneurship: only *ex post* successful entrepreneurship is considered and explained (Loasby 1982b, 1984a). Consequently, their theories only emphasise the role of profits and ignore entrepreneurial losses. This is a grave limitation, given that empirical research has suggested that most innovative entrepreneurial ideas do actually turn out to be mistakes. The scope of application of Kirzner's and Casson's theories is thus limited by their failure to include uncertainty and the possibility of entrepreneurial error and losses.

1.4 THE SPECIFICATION OF THE GROWTH-OF-KNOWLEDGE (GK) RESEARCH PROGRAMME

Previous sections have commented briefly on the inadequate treatment of knowledge in theories of market adjustment and entre-preneurship. One of the aims of this chapter is to advocate a new Lakatosian scientific research programme which introduces a more sophisticated approach to knowledge in economic theory. The theory of the entrepreneur presented in this book belongs to this proposed new research programme. Indeed, it is possible to regard this new research programme as a collection of rules that we are going to use for thinking about entrepreneurship, market processes and economic change. The GK research programme has its origins in the work of Agassi (1975), Boland (1982, 1986a, 1986b), Loasby (1976, 1983, 1986b, 1989, 1991, 1994) and Popper (1959, 1960, 1963, 1972, 1976a). However, these writers should *not* be held accountable for the interpretation that has been placed upon their contributions in developing this proposal for a GK programme.

The GK research programme is characterised by its hard core and its heuristics. Because scientific research programmes are dynamic, and because the GK programme is still very much at the embryonic stage, the following description of the programme should not be regarded as definitive. As Weintraub (1985b: 140–141) remarks in his appraisal of general equilibrium analysis, the hardening of a programme's hard core is a process that takes place in time: the hard core is not a static concept.[16] In addition, the positive heuristic (i.e. the concrete strategy for dealing with apparent refutations) cannot be articulated in detail at the outset of a programme; it has to be developed piecemeal as the programme itself unfolds (Musgrave 1976: 471–472). Thus, it is not possible to specify fully the hard core and heuristics of the GK research programme at this early stage. The following discussion must therefore be regarded as only a *prospectus* for a long-term research strategy and absolutely not as a retrospective theoretical appraisal. (A retrospective evaluation of the GK programme would require judging its theoretical progressiveness and the empirical success or failure of theories constructed in accordance with its hard core and heuristics.)

1.4.1 The hard core of the GK research programme

The programme is organised around the following hard-core propositions, which are to be treated as irrefutable by protagonists of the programme.

HC1　Only individual economic agents have aims, conjectures and preferences, and only individuals can make decisions (Agassi 1975; Boland 1982: 177; cf. Popper 1960).

HC2　Economic agents face objective problem situations, and an objective reality exists which is independent of the conjectures and preferences of individual economic agents. However, the objective problem situation is not automatically known by, or given to, the economic agent. Individual economic actors must attempt to define and to interpret the situations in which they find themselves. Of course, the problem situation as the economic agent sees it can be vastly different from the problem situation as it is (i.e. the economic agent can have false knowledge of the objective situation) (cf. Popper 1972: 179).[17]

HC3　There is no infallible method by which economic agents can acquire true knowledge. Economic agents can never know that they have found the truth even if they have found it. Economic agents thus do not have proven true (i.e. justified)

20

knowledge of their problem situations. The knowledge of economic agents is essentially theoretical and conjectural, and their knowledge of the objective situation is very often false (Boland 1978: 251). Because economic agents may unknowingly base their practical actions upon false theories about the world, their actions often produce unintended consequences (Popper 1972: 21–23; Boland 1982: 185). Consequently, all economic agents are fallible (i.e. prone to error).

HC4 Economic agents form their tentative solutions (i.e. conjectures) to problems in a world of structural uncertainty, complexity, and real time. There is real originality, real possibility and thus real indeterminism in the world of the economic agent.

HC5 The conjectures of economic agents are potentially objective (i.e. they can become conscious and can be articulated), and they can potentially be exposed to interpersonal criticism (Boland 1978: 251–252; Musgrave 1974b: 574; Popper 1972: chs 2, 3; 1983a: xxxv).

HC6 Learning is a logical and scientific process, rather than an internal psychological or sociopsychological process. There is no difference of kind between the methods of science and the methods of hypothesis-selection in everyday life. Like scientists, economic agents use deductive logic in the evaluation of their hypotheses.

HC7 Although economic agents do not possess proven true knowledge, they can still make rational decisions (Popper 1972: 265; Boland 1982: 185). Economic agents behave in a way appropriate to their situations (the rationality principle): specifically, they prefer the best alternatives given their tentative knowledge of the situation and the means at their disposal (cf. Latsis 1976c: 22; Langlois 1982: 80).[18] Rational decision-making involves evaluating rival schemes of action in the light of logic *and* experience.[19]

HC8 Although learning in the market context involves a critical feedback process of successive adjustments, feedback is rarely, if ever, optimal or perfect (and hence neither is learning). Entrepreneurial actions do not necessarily coordinate individual behaviour within and between markets. The interaction of individual entrepreneurs does not yield a unique and determinate outcome. Entrepreneurship is characterised by 'multiple-exit' problem situations.

1.4.2 The positive heuristic

The positive heuristic contains the long-term research policy of the programme, that is, instructions for developing the programme (Lakatos 1970: 135). The positive heuristic of the GK programme may be described in terms of the following maxims.

PH1 Explicitly ascribe non-justificationist (especially Popperian) theories of learning to the economic agents in economic theories.

PH2 In any explanation of economic phenomena (especially dynamic economic processes), progressively upgrade those aspects which pertain to the growth of knowledge and the theories of learning with which economic agents approach their problem situations. In particular, try to reduce as much as possible the inductivist and justificationist elements in agents' learning methodologies and theories of knowledge (e.g. by replacing dogmatic versions of falsificationism with a sophisticated variant).

PH3 Only construct theories and models which are consistent with the principles of methodological individualism, that is, which explain economic events as the consequence (often unintended) of the intelligible actions of individual economic agents.

PH4 Construct models in which only rational decision-making plays a part in the explanation (Popper 1983c). This assumption of rationality means that economic agents are disposed to learning from their mistakes. They are to be depicted as solving problems by the critical method of trial and the elimination of error. (The GK conception of rationality is explained in detail in Chapters 2, 4 and 6–8).

PH5 Construct dynamic models which explicitly recognise the relationship between real time and knowledge. That is, construct models employing a dynamic conception of economic agents' knowledge, according to which the acquisition of knowledge (i.e. learning) is a real-time irreversible process (Boland 1978: 240–242). Develop models which treat economic agents' knowledge and learning processes as endogenous rather than as exogenously fixed or exogenously variable (Boland 1978: 249–250; Boland and Newman 1979).

PH6 Construct multiple-exit decision models, that is, models in which economic agents face an environment which is situationally open, in the sense that it does not uniquely determine any optimal course of action (Latsis 1976c: 21).

1.4.3 The negative heuristic

The negative heuristic consists of propositions that immunise the hard core and reinforce the positive heuristic. Among the most important propositions within the negative heuristic of the GK programme are:

NH1 Do not construct theories or models which treat the knowledge or learning processes of economic agents as exogenously or statically given.

NH2 Do not develop theories which assume irrational behaviour.

NH3 Do not develop theories in which agents (especially entrepreneurs) can only optimise subject to constraints.

1.4.4 Discussion of the GK programme's features

Having outlined the GK programme, we are now in a position to examine the heterodox nature of the programme in more detail. The discussion is limited to major points of clarification. Afterwards, I compare the proposed GK programme with a number of established programmes in economic theory.

An important heuristic postulate of the GK programme is methodological individualism (HC1, PH3). Methodological individualism requires that all explanations of social phenomena (such as the market process) must be grounded in the objectives, perceptions, expectations, plans and actions of individuals. Accordingly, a theory of decentralised market processes must be built upon a theory of individual entrepreneurship. It must be based upon the actions of individual market participants and especially upon rational decision-making by individual entrepreneurs.

Methodological individualism is, of course, by no means new. However, the GK programme rejects a particular form of methodological individualism which is commonly associated with neoclassical economics: psychologistic individualism (Agassi 1975: 148; Boland 1982: 30–35). This version of methodological individualism attempts to reduce all explanations of economic phenomena to natural givens and exogenous psychological states (i.e. utility functions) of individual decision-makers.

In contrast, the GK programme adheres to a non-psychologistic form of individualism which explains behaviour in terms of the problem situations identified by, and the aim structure of, individual decision-makers. The GK programme adopts Popper's definition of the agent's problem situation. As used by Popper, the term 'situation' does not include irrational beliefs or unconscious motives, but it does include the agent's goals, theories, knowledge and information – even false theories, false knowledge and misinformation (Latsis 1972: 223–224; Popper 1972: 178; 1976a: 103).

In explanations of rational individual behaviour, the GK programme gives a more fundamental role to the knowledge and learning methodology of the individual decision-maker (HC5, PH1, PH2, PH5). It represents a more ambitious pursuit of the principles of methodological individualism by prescribing a more detailed and individualistic treatment of economic agents' knowledge and learning.

In order to explain the novelty of the GK programme, it is first necessary to distinguish between two levels of discourse: level I, the *object* level of economic theory; and level II, the *metatheoretical* level of economic methodology (Birner 1985: 216; cf. Popper 1972: 176–8).[20] Level I contains economic theories that have been proposed concerning a large range of economic phenomena, such as the theory of value and its associated theory of distribution, the theory of monopoly, the theory of the entrepreneur and of the firm.

Level II contains the various methodologies of science or theories of scientific method. These theories constitute theories of knowledge acquisition or of learning. Methodologies are 'said to be about, or to have as their subject matter, substantive scientific theories at level I' (Nola 1987: 445). Economists themselves apply second-order theories of scientific method to appraise their first-order economic theories. There has been a proliferation of second-order critical methods within economics: apriorism, positivism, instrumentalism, operationalism and falsificationism (Blaug 1980; Caldwell 1982; Stewart 1979).

Typically, methodology is used in economics at the meta-theoretical level (i.e. level II) rather than at the theoretical level (i.e. level I). In other words, methodology is usually regarded solely as a second-order discipline for adjudicating between first-order theories of economic phenomena. Methodology does not usually play a theoretical role in economics (Boland 1986a: 30).

In contrast to neoclassical orthodoxy, the GK programme aims to

24

integrate theories of learning (i.e. methodologies), which are typically at level II, into economic theories at level I. That is, it intends to build methodology into the *content* of theories of economic processes, in order to help economists explain how economic agents acquire the knowledge upon which they base their decisions (PH1, PH2, PH5, NH1). Thus, in discussing learning methodologies in this book I am *not* concerned with the level II methodologies used by economists themselves to expound their own first-order theories to other economists. Rather, I am concerned with the learning methodologies that economic agents in level I economic theories apply in order to obtain knowledge required for decision-making.

Consequently, in the GK programme, an adequate explanation of rational decision-making must formally introduce explicit conjectures about the individual decision-maker's second-order learning methodology (PH1, PH2):

> [A]ny economic theory which recognizes the need for knowledge in decision making must in some way imply a role for methodology, because as Hayek explicitly said in 1937, to explain a decision the economist must also explain the 'acquisition' of the knowledge needed to make that decision.
>
> (Boland 1986a: 30)[21]

Thus, any economic theory which seeks to explain entrepreneurial behaviour and the endogenous dynamics of the market process must specify the entrepreneur's learning methodology in addition to including assumptions about the entrepreneur's (conjectural) knowledge. More specifically, the GK programme proposes that microeconomic research into entrepreneurial decision-making can receive substantial input from non-justificationist (and especially Popperian) theories of the growth of knowledge, which incorporate real time seriously (PH5) and which are within the rationalist tradition (PH4, NH2). (On these theories of learning, see sections 2.2 and 2.3.)

1.4.5 Comparison of the GK programme with established research programmes in economics

Several scientific research programmes have been identified in the literature on economic methodology. These programmes can be termed neoclassical or neo-Walrasian, Keynesian, post-Keynesian, new Keynesian, Austrian, neo-Marxian, institutionalist, behavioural and evolutionary.[22] The last two programmes are still at relatively early stages of their development (Weintraub 1985b: 144). Nelson and Winter's evolutionary programme can in fact be conceived as an unorthodox perspective within the behavioural programme.

Table 1.1 outlines the differences between the proposed GK programme and three established programmes in economic theory. The following brief discussion is restricted to major points of comparison between their respective hard cores and positive heuristics, so as to differentiate the GK programme from its predecessors.[23] Such a cursory comparison is itself conjectural and runs the risk of misrepresenting each programme. It certainly does not constitute an assessment within a Lakatosian framework, which in the case of the GK programme would be extremely premature.

The GK programme and the other three programmes considered in Table 1.1 each assume that economic agents are rational, that is, teleologically oriented. This is, however, the only feature shared by all four programmes.

The GK programme has least in common with the neoclassical programme. Their respective hard cores contradict each other almost totally. The primary difference between their hard cores concerns assumptions made about the nature and scope of economic agents' knowledge. Neoclassical theories implicitly attribute justificationist philosophies of knowledge to economic actors. As mentioned above, justificationism asserts that knowledge is not knowledge unless it is proven true, or in its weaker form, probable to a proven degree (see section 2.1). The result is that economic decision-makers are depicted as having true actuarial knowledge of the past, present and future. Economic agents in a neoclassical world do not face structural uncertainty, and they do not decide and act in real time.

In contrast, the GK programme repudiates the proposition that decision-makers generally have correct (or probabilistic) knowledge of the relevant features of their problem situations. In particular, the GK approach strongly contends that economic actors do not, and cannot, have proven true knowledge of the future (including knowledge of the future consequences of each of the alternatives between which they are deciding).

Yet another distinguishing characteristic of the GK hard core – which differentiates it from the Austrian hard core too – relates to the degree of coordination attainable within a market economy. The neoclassical and Austrian programmes assume that the market system possesses an inherent tendency toward equilibrium, although the

Austrian camp clearly has its dissenters (High 1986; Lachmann 1971b, 1977, 1986). In contrast, proponents of the GK programme believe that economic structures do not necessarily exhibit strictly coordinated behaviour, and so they do not regard disequilibrium as simply the result of exogenous shocks. The GK programme rejects the notion that, given a sufficiently long time period and no extraneous disturbances, the economic process would reach full equilibrium. In this respect at least, proponents of the GK programme side with the post-Keynesians.

The positive heuristics of the GK and neoclassical programmes are also at odds with each other. The GK programme rejects cavalier neoclassical prescriptions requiring that economic agents' knowledge be treated as exogenous and static.[24] Neoclassical models often assume that knowledge is included among the data, together with tastes and resources (Lachmann 1976a: 55). In contrast, the GK programme emphasises the endogeneity of knowledge acquisition and adopts a dynamic conception of knowledge. For the problems within its domain, the GK programme also rejects situational determinism (in the sense of single-exit conditions) and its associated analytical methods.

The GK programme shares a great deal in common with Austrian and post-Keynesian economics because they also attribute a more strategic and sophisticated role to knowledge and learning in explanations of economic phenomena. They all seek to analyse economic change over real time and consequently stress economic processes rather than economic states. Similarly, they emphasise structural uncertainty, human fallibility, the imperfect dispersion of knowledge between economic agents, and the incompleteness and uncompletability of human knowledge.

However, the characterisation of economic agents' knowledge and learning (as specified in their respective hard cores) differs between the GK programme and the other two programmes. The post-Keynesian and Austrian programmes both make justificationist assumptions regarding the knowledge base of economic actors in their models. Each emphasises the tacit nature of economic knowledge and learning (a result of justificationist psychologism). The justificationist standards of economic rationality implicit in the post-Keynesian programme are also indicated by its hard-core assumption which postulates that perfect or probabilistic knowledge is a precondition for 'rational' decision-making on the part of economic agents (although it is emphasised that this precondition is

Table 1.1 Comparison of the GK programme with established research programmes in economics

Component of programme	Neoclassical	Post-Keynesian	Austrian	GK
Hard-core propositions				
Decision-makers have perfect or probabilistic knowledge of the relevant features of their economic situations	yes	no[a]	no	no
Economic agents' decisions are not necessarily correct in an objective sense	no	yes	yes	yes
Economic agents act in a world of structural uncertainty	no	yes	yes[b]	yes
Decision-makers are 'rational' in the sense defined by the respective programme	yes	yes	yes	yes
Even if decision-makers are 'rational', they cannot behave 'rationally' unless they have perfect or probabilistic knowledge	yes	yes	no	no
Economic agents can have the knowledge required for 'rational' behaviour	yes	no	yes	yes
Economic agents' conjectures are potentially objective	yes	*ex ante*: no *ex post*: yes	no	yes
There is a strict tendency towards the coordination of economic activities	yes	no	yes	no

Positive heuristics

Develop models which treat economic agents' knowledge and its acquisition as endogenous	no	no	no	yes
Construct dynamic models in which learning is a real-time, irreversible process	no	yes	yes	yes
Explicitly ascribe (non-justificationist) theories of learning to the economic agents in economic theories	no	no	no	yes
Construct theories and models which are consistent with the principles of methodological individualism	yes	not usually[c]	yes	yes
Construct single-exit situational models, that is, models which yield a determinate equilibrium	yes	no	no	no
Translate the situation into a mathematical constrained maximisation problem and apply the procedures of the calculus	yes	no	no	no

Sources:
Boland and Newman (1979: 71–75), Brown (1981: 115–127), Langlois (1982: 78–82), Latsis (1976c: 22–23), Rizzo (1982: 57–65).

Notes:
[a] As post-Keynesians, Bausor would probably be surprised to see 'No', whereas Shackle and Paul Davidson would not.
[b] O'Driscoll, Rizzo – yes; an exception is Kirzner's entrepreneur (1973, 1979b).
[c] Kalecki, Kaldor, Robinson – no; Shackle – yes.

seldom, if ever, met in the course of everyday economic activity) (Brown 1981: 116–117, 125).

In contrast, the GK hard core states that economic agents' knowledge is essentially theoretical and that it is thereby potentially objective (Boland 1978: 251–252). The GK programme also rejects justificationist notions of economic rationality without having to resort to irrationality (i.e. justificationist scepticism). It proposes a new conception of rationality which consists of critically appraising conjectures (including conjectures on the ends worth achieving and the means available) in the light of logic and experience – particularly, experience of error. Hence, rational decision-making is considered possible in the absence of proven true or probable knowledge.

According to the positive heuristics of the Austrian and post-Keynesian programmes, new knowledge (regarding technology, resources and tastes) is largely introduced exogenously and hence it is unexplained (although limited endogeneity of some new knowledge is recognised). For instance, in commenting upon the treatment of knowledge in Kirzner's theory of entrepreneurship, Böhm (1992: 100) notes that 'arising from a change in some data, new knowledge is injected into the economy'. However, Austrians and Post Keynesians do not treat economic knowledge as a fixed parameter as in neoclassical analysis (Boland and Newman 1979: 72, 74). Although exogenous, knowledge is permitted to change and can be extremely volatile. (In Boland and Newman's terminology, knowledge is assumed to be 'exogenously variable' rather than 'exogenously fixed'.) The GK programme, on the other hand, treats knowledge as endogenous to the economic system and as continually changing over time.

Although their positive heuristics advocate different ways of approaching economic problems, all three programmes (Austrian, PK, GK) take issue with the neoclassical emphasis upon determinate equilibrium models and dispute the wholesale application of single-exit methods of analysis (including the construction of functions to which calculus can be applied). The positive heuristic of the post-Keynesian programme is further distinguished by the fact that it does not advocate methodological individualism – unlike the proposed GK programme and the other schools of economic thought under consideration. As a result of their specialisation in explaining macroeconomic phenomena (such as income distribution), post-Keynesians have in general not emphasised the role of individual choice processes in their investigations (Earl 1983b: 2).

1.5 THE SCOPE OF THE INQUIRY

The theory which is developed in the following chapters presents a largely *cognitive-logical* perspective on the rationality of the entrepreneur, on entrepreneurial learning and on the character of the market process. The cognitive-logical dimension is defined to focus upon the logical, methodological, epistemological and metaphysical aspects of a phenomenon or activity. The cognitive-logical dimension is thus much wider in scope than the definition of logic which is current among formal logicians.[25] Like logic in its pure sense, however, the cognitive-logical dimension does not pertain to practical questions of how individuals think or reason. Just as the rules of logic do not constitute the laws of thought, so too the GK theory does not describe the entrepreneur's actual mental operations or inferential processes. That is the task of empirical psychology. The most that a cognitive-logical inquiry of entrepreneurship can achieve is to investigate the latent structure of rationality behind entrepreneurs' problem-solving efforts. Indeed, the way in which entrepreneurs learn from their mistakes constitutes the GK conception of entrepreneurial rationality. This entrepreneurial learning methodology is developed in Part II.

1.5.1 The psychological context of discovery

The GK theory does not profess to provide a complete account of the market process. As with the growth of scientific knowledge, the actual market process cannot be entirely rationally reconstructed from a logical point of view. The GK model can provide only a *logical skeleton* which accounts for the essential, fundamental character of the competitive market process. Thus it is not denied that, even if logic is interpreted in its wider sense, characterising entrepreneurs as Popperian decision-makers and the market process as a Popperian learning procedure neglects important extralogical forces which affect market processes, market decisions and market outcomes. In particular, the GK theory does not encompass psychological, sociological, cultural-anthropological, historical or political aspects of entrepreneurship.

The exclusion of extralogical factors is a direct consequence of applying Popper's critical philosophy of science. The Popperian programme takes the realm of logic and methodology (i.e. the context of justification) as the appropriate domain for philosophical analyses of the process by which knowledge grows (see section 2.2.2). It does not take into account psychological, sociological and historical factors (i.e. the context of discovery). The framework of the *logic* of scientific discovery is adopted as a basis for the rational reconstruction of the growth-of-knowledge process.

Just as Popper's philosophy does not concern itself with the manner in which scientific results are discovered (i.e. the context of discovery) but only with the way in which they are evaluated by the scientific community (i.e. the context of justification), so too the GK theory of entrepreneurship does not concern itself with the mental processes by which entrepreneurial discoveries of profit opportunities are made. (In addition, it does not claim any power to explain how entrepreneurs learn their learning methodologies.) The GK approach focuses exclusively upon the ways in which entrepreneurial ideas are critically evaluated by entrepreneurs themselves and by other transactors in the market process, such as consumers and venture capitalists. The actual mental processes by which entrepreneurs generate their business ideas is a subject belonging to the domain of psychological economics.

The GK approach is not concerned with the entrepreneur's private psychological motivations or psychological processes but with the outcome of these mental activities, namely, the entrepreneur's conjectures and plans. Lachmann similarly once suggested that explanations of social phenomena should be in terms of human plans (i.e. the outcomes of human cognition):[26]

> Such analysis of observed phenomena in terms of *pre-existent plans* has nothing to do with psychology. We are here concerned with purposes, not motives, *with plans, not with the psychic processes which give rise to them*, with acts of our conscious minds, not with what lies behind them. As soon as our thoughts have assumed *the firm outline of a plan* and we have taken the decision to carry it out over a definite period of future time, we have reached a point outside the realm of psychology, a point which we can use either as the starting point or as the goal of our enquiry. . . . In neither case are we trespassing on the domain of psychology.
>
> (Lachmann 1977: 155; emphasis added)

In concerning itself with the products rather than the processes of thought, the GK programme implicitly assumes that the entrepreneurial context of justification is independent from the entrepreneurial context of discovery. That is, it assumes either that (i) there is no relationship between the ways entrepreneurs generate business ideas and the methods by which they and other market participants evaluate them; or that (ii) any connections that may exist are irrelevant for explaining how entrepreneurs learn (cf. Amsterdamski 1975: 52–57). These assumptions are tenable if the entrepreneur applies the same learning methodology to all problem situations and if the entrepreneur's methodology is constant over time.[27]

These assumptions of the GK theory constitute a severe limitation if the capacity of entrepreneurs to discover profit opportunities and their ability to process information about them are indeed connected in some significant and relevant way. For example, historical connections will emerge if entrepreneurs' methodological rules for testing conjectures change over time with advances in their knowledge of the business world and specific markets.

1.5.2 The sociological and cultural contexts

The GK theory disregards other extralogical factors besides psychological ones. For instance, at least at this stage, its explanation of entrepreneurial behaviour and the market process does not invoke principles which are irreducibly sociological, and sociology is, as Kuhn reminds us, 'a field quite different from individual psychology reiterated n times' (Kuhn 1970b: 240).

In line with the GK programme's heuristic postulate of methodological individualism (HC1, PH3 – see section 1.4), the unit of analysis of the GK theory is the individual entrepreneur, not the entrepreneurial team or firm or any other sociological group (nor is it the entrepreneurial event or transaction).[28] The individual entrepreneur is the personification or embodiment of a particular economic function, type of act or market role:[29]

> Economics, in speaking of entrepreneurs, has in view not men, but a definite function. This function . . . is inherent in every action and burdens every actor. In embodying this function in an imaginary figure, we resort to a methodological makeshift.
> (Mises 1949: 253–254)

The individual entrepreneur is thus a special device introduced into the analysis in order to simplify the GK theory of market processes. This is an admissible limitation for developing a line of economic analysis and it is consistent with a piecemeal strategy. Developing the theory in terms of a single decision-maker enables me to abstract (for the time being) from two important and complex problems: how the internal 'architecture'[30] of a business enterprise affects the acceptance and rejection of entrepreneurial hypotheses and enterprising activity; and how members of an entrepreneurial team may have to modify their individual theories in order to work together (e.g. prior to any entrepreneurial action being undertaken). Thus, unlike Wu (1989), I do not examine the internal decision processes of businesses and the ways that decisions are implemented in firms managed jointly by many cooperative entrepreneurs (1989: 151–184).[31] At a later stage, the GK theory of entrepreneurship can be extended to entrepreneurial teams and complex intra-firm decision-making structures.

Furthermore, although in real-world markets entrepreneurial functions are frequently performed by groups, focusing on the individual entrepreneur does at least to some extent find its parallel in the actual market process.[32] It is granted that in assessing proposals, most venture capitalists evaluate the calibre and functional balance of the management team (e.g. MacMillan, Siegel and Subba-Narasimha 1985; Timmons 1981). But according to my own exploratory fieldwork, which included personal interviews with over a dozen venture capitalists (Harper 1992), venture capitalists also require that there be a single, outstanding entrepreneur-leader within the team (typically the chief executive officer [CEO]): the rationale being that the better the quality of the CEO of a venture, the more talent he or she will attract and hence the better the venture team that can be established. This is the key person who is the 'spark plug of the team and who makes it function effectively' (Waite 1982: 122).

It must also be noted that the GK approach does not focus attention upon the cultural aspects of entrepreneurship, either at the national level or at the corporate level. It examines neither the social status which culture gives to entrepreneurs, nor the function which entrepreneurship fulfils within culture. Nor does it analyse how cultural dynamics affect the kind and degree of cooperation within and between entrepreneurial teams and firms.[33]

1.5.3 A clarification on the complementarity of GK and psychological approaches

At the outset it is important to clear up a potential misunderstanding arising from my discussion of the GK programme, as I do not wish to alienate those economic theorists (including behaviouralists) who seek to add more psychology to economic theory. When I say that the present version of the GK theory does not encompass the context of discovery, the point I am making is simply that psychological and sociological explanatory principles do not form part of the GK methodology. The GK programme advances independently of these approaches.

However, the discussion is very definitely not intended to imply that behavioural economics and the like should be abandoned. I acknowledge that psychological, sociological and other extralogical factors are prevalent and clearly influence entrepreneurial behaviour and the operation of markets, so that they are worthy of investigation. Elsewhere I (and a co-author) have argued that economists should pay closer attention to psychological and sociological theories of the supply of entrepreneurship as this would enable them to endogenise, and hence explain, variables which have usually been treated as exogenous, and hence as unexplained (Hamilton and Harper 1994; see too Harper 1994b). Casson's (1991) analysis of the social dimension of morality is an example of this. Thus, I do not share Popper's and Boland's open hostility towards psychology and sociology (see, for example: Boland 1982: ch. 2; Popper 1970: 57–58).

Indeed, I would like to stress the potential complementarity of the GK and psychological approaches to economics, and where possible I highlight the parallels between the two. For instance, both proponents of the GK programme and behaviouralists in economics (not to be confused with behaviourists in psychology!) are involved in research activities which are similar from the point of view of economic modelling. In attempting to build the internal structure and decision processes of economic agents into their models, behaviouralists sometimes end up with specifications similar to the prescriptions of the GK programme: occasionally their models specify the theories of knowledge with which economic agents are supposed to confront their problem situations.[34]

The relation between the GK and behaviouralist programmes is a division of labour or a partition of domains of inquiry. Although they share related objectives, they do not ask the same questions or anticipate comparable answers. In general, each addresses questions to which the other is *a priori* unsuited.

In any event, both the GK and behaviouralist programmes reject the neoclassical, behaviouristic approach because it treats the psychological states of the economic agent as static and exogenous.

Moreover, they both avoid single-exit, deterministic methods of analysis which turn the economic agent into a cipher.

1.6 OUTLINE OF THE BOOK

This book is divided into three main parts. Part I constitutes the introduction and background. It outlines the GK methodology, describes the most basic assumptions upon which the new theory is built, defines key terms, and explains the concepts which are applied in later chapters.

Chapter 2 briefly reviews Popper's non-justificationist philosophy of science and some later developments within the Popperian programme. The Popperian approach is distinguished from the received view of justificationism within the philosophy of science. The chapter also highlights the aspects of Popper's evolutionary theory of the growth of knowledge which are most relevant to studying entrepreneurship and market processes.

In Chapter 3, a typology is developed for characterising the major dimensions of the entrepreneur's problem situation. This typology is used for defining entrepreneurship precisely and for contrasting it with other categories of human action, such as neoclassical economising and satisficing. The implications of two key dimensions for entrepreneurship are highlighted. Far from having perfect or probabilistic knowledge of their decision situations, entrepreneurs are pictured as possessing very tentative knowledge of the market, knowledge which may be refuted at any time. They face *structural uncertainty* about the future which they cannot eradicate completely. Their problem situations are particularly ill-defined, and unique and determinate solutions are seldom, if ever, forthcoming. Furthermore, the problem-solving efforts of entrepreneurs are undertaken in a world of irreversible *real time.*

According to the GK research programme, the problem situations of entrepreneurs also include the specific goals which they are seeking to attain, any relevant theories that they hold, and their learning methodology. The aim structure of entrepreneurs is elaborated in Chapter 4. The GK theory assumes that entrepreneurs aim to predict, to explain and to control economic and market events in the pursuit of economic gain. Chapter 5 elaborates on the character of entrepreneurial theories. Entrepreneurs need to construct theories in order to fulfil their basic aims of explaining the world in which they operate and of effecting changes within it.

Part II focuses on how the entrepreneur acts within the market system and it develops some implications of the GK approach for how the market process operates. The four chapters comprising Part II represent the body of the GK theory of entrepreneurship. The treatment of economic actors in this theory contrasts sharply with the portrayal of agents within the neoclassical research programme. Entrepreneurs are depicted as being sophisticated in their decision-making, not unlike practising scientists. The first chapter in Part II, Chapter 6, introduces and develops the idea of 'sophisticated falsificationist' entrepreneurs, who learn from their mistakes (as well as their partial successes). This chapter investigates the general characteristics which distinguish this type of entrepreneurship from others. It also closely examines the specific principles and methodological rules which falsificationist entrepreneurs adopt to promote the growth of their knowledge and to avoid immunising failing ventures against refutation.

Chapter 7 analyses in detail the kinds of deliberate critical tests to which falsificationist entrepreneurs subject their ideas during the new venture development process. It also identifies the 'testing environments' in which entrepreneurs can conduct their critical tests. It is argued that falsificationist entrepreneurs use the market as an educative tool – questioning the usual neoclassical assumptions that market outcomes reflect behaviour which is already well-informed. In addition, Chapter 7 explores the outcomes of testing – i.e. corroboration or refutation – and the speed with which different types of falsificationist entrepreneurs respond to refutations of their ideas. The epistemic returns and economic costs of testing are also taken into account. The discussion culminates in an evolutionary conception of the entrepreneur's learning process.

Continuing at the level of individual entrepreneurs, Chapter 8 inquires into the causes of refutation and the philosophical and practical difficulties which entrepreneurs encounter in deciding whether their theories have been effectively refuted. Apart from internal inconsistency and unexpected exogenous changes, the major cause of refutation of an entrepreneur's theory is its incompatibility with the theories of other economic agents and entrepreneurs. However, the entrepreneur can never pinpoint with certainty the source of a refutation. The Duhem–Quine irrefutability thesis emerges as the most important and comprehensive problem in this regard. The thesis argues that a single hypothesis can never be falsified conclusively, because it is necessary to test the hypothesis in combination with additional premises. The implications of the thesis and how falsificationist entrepreneurs cope with it are the subject matter of later sections in this chapter. Practical examples are provided to illustrate the points made.

Chapter 9 explains how the market process operates and the functions it performs, and it emphasises the centrality of the entrepreneur in this process. In line with the characterisation of entrepreneurship as a problem-solving activity, the market is portrayed as a problem-solving process (or an institutional learning mechanism), and not just as a system for the (static) allocation of resources. The market process is regarded as a continuous sequence of conjecture and exposure to refutation, a learning procedure for generating and testing entrepreneurial ideas.

Chapter 9 begins with a discussion of the organisation of conjecture and refutation in the modern market economy. The market process involves testing entrepreneurial ideas by exposing them to the critical appraisal of consumers, resource owners and competitors. This chapter identifies the criteria by which the market screens entrepreneurial conjectures. The role of entrepreneurial profits and losses in the market process is viewed from the perspective of Popper's theory of the growth of knowledge. In particular, *ex post* entrepreneurial loss is considered to be the important criterion by which the market system eliminates inferior tentative solutions to perceived market problems (i.e. entrepreneurial theories which are relatively poor approximations of consumers' latent demands). It is argued that the competitive market process largely owes its comparative success and continued existence to its ability to perform this function better than other institutions. In addition, given that most entrepreneurial conjectures are likely to be false, the proliferation of entrepreneurial ideas generated in the course of the competitive process also increases the chance that at least one tentative solution will survive for a time. I also discuss the implications of the market's spontaneous origins for generating and testing entrepreneurial conjectures, and I draw out some initial insights provided by the GK approach for the continuity of the market process.

Finally, Part III sets out the agenda for further empirical and theoretical development. Chapter 10 describes a potential empirical test of the GK theory of entrepreneurship. In particular, it specifies a possible test of the prediction that sophisticated falsificationist entrepreneurs perform significantly better than entrepreneurs who adhere to other learning methodologies (such as conventionalism).

A key feature of this empirical test is the application of the novel *Entrepreneurial Learning Methodology Inventory* for determining the learning methodologies of individual entrepreneurs.

Chapter 11 makes recommendations for developing subsequent theories within the GK research programme. This chapter suggests developing the theory in three different directions: at the level of individual decision-making, the level of the entrepreneurial team or firm, and the level of public policy. I close the discussion with some thoughts on the fruitfulness and prospects of the programme.

NOTES

1 See: Boland (1978, 1982, 1986a, 1986b); Choi (1993); Earl (1984, 1986a, 1986b, 1987); Langlois (1986d); Loasby (1976, 1983, 1986b, 1989, 1991, 1994); O'Driscoll and Rizzo (1985: 37); Rutherford (1984); and Wible (1984, 1984–85). See too Denzau and North (1994) for a related position.

2 In this work, I choose not to refer to the approach as 'the *non-justifica-tionist* research programme'. Although this is more correct technically, such terminology is cumbersome and is likely to represent a marketing obstacle. I therefore refer to it as the 'growth-of-knowledge approach', or the GK approach for short.

3 Of course, the identification of individual rationality with the methods of science is not new and has been popular in cognitive and social psychology and in one branch of personality theory. For example, attribution theorists, such as Kelley and Heider, claim that individuals arrive at their causal explanations of actions and events just as naive (inductivist) scientists do (Bacharach 1986: 197; Van Raaij 1985). In addition, Kelly's (not to be mistaken for Kelley) theory of personality, known better as personal construct theory, characterises people as if they were scientists in the general sense who test hypotheses and who learn by an empirical process. However, these psychological theories imply a conception of rationality different from that developed in the GK programme.

4 For example, see: Barreto (1989); Baumol (1968); Casson (1982); Kirzner (1962a, 1973, 1979b); Latsis (1972, 1976c); and Loasby (1989).

5 For surveys of neoclassical models of market adjustment to equilibrium (but excluding game-theoretic developments), see: Arrow and Hahn (1971); Boland (1986b); Fisher (1976; 1983: Part 1; 1987); Gordon and Hynes (1970); Kirzner (1979b: 16–20); Rothschild (1973); Stiglitz (1989); Thomsen (1992); and White (1978).

6 The wording is Scitovsky's (1952).

7 To be fair to Fisher, one must acknowledge that he sees the assumption of 'No Favourable Surprise' as being of heuristic value rather than as a plausible assumption about the real world (1981: 306). He emphasises that his principal convergence result shows the necessary conditions for instability:

The proper way to look at this result is not as stating that no optimistic surprise provides a sufficient condition for stability. Rather it is as stating that optimistic surprise is necessary for in stability. If all that is happening is that old opportunities are disappearing through arbitrage, then the system will be stable. It is the perception of new opportunities that keeps the system moving.

(1981: 281; original emphasis)

8 Unlike Kirzner, however, Fisher sees the perception of new, previously unforeseen opportunities as maintaining instability rather than as an equilibrating force:

There is no way in which stability can be guaranteed if agents can always wake up with a new idea on which to act. It makes no difference whether such ideas are realistic or mistaken; the perception and pursuit of new opportunities, however mistaken, will tend to keep things moving.

(Fisher 1981: 281)

9 But Fisher (1983: Part 2) did discuss price dispersion as an activity consistent with 'No Favourable Surprise'. The persistence of price dispersion in equilibrium was an issue Fisher placed upon his comprehensive agenda for further research.

10 For a survey of models with equilibrium price distributions, see: Rothschild (1973: 1298–1301); Salop and Stiglitz (1977: 508–509); and Stiglitz (1985; 1989: 807–817). For a market-process critique of Grossman and Stiglitz's work, see too Thomsen (1992).

11 This criticism was originally directed by Rothschild (1973: 1288) at Stigler's (1961) investigation of price distributions. See too: Butters (1977: 465); and Stigler (1983: 539).

12 Kirzner (1979b: 142, 148–149) has been the most vocal proponent of the view that an essential characteristic of entrepreneurial knowledge is that it is spontaneously learnt: it is prior knowledge acquired entirely without deliberate, cost-conscious search for information. However, in describing entrepreneurial knowledge as acquired at zero cost, Kirzner makes one caveat:

To describe [spontaneously acquired] knowledge . . . as having been costless or a free good is somewhat misleading. To be sure, the spontaneous learner has incurred no cost or sacrifice through his learning. But this is not so much because the knowledge was costlessly available as because the knowledge was simply not sought deliberately.

(1979b: 143)

Although there are aspects of Kirzner's conception of entrepreneurial knowledge which I find contentious, I concur with his criticism of search-theoretic approaches to learning activity. For further discussion on the differences between deliberate search and Kirzner's notion of entrepreneurial alertness, see Reekie (1984: 93–100).

13 For striking expositions on this subject, see Lachmann (1971b: 38–39; 1977: 33–38) and Mises (1949: 251, 257, 347–354).

14 Theories of the entrepreneur not included in this discussion are: Cantillon (1931); Casson (1990a); Knight (1964); Mises (1949, 1980: esp. ch. 9); Schumpeter (1934, 1947, 1950, 1954); Shackle (1970, 1972, 1979a); and

Wu (1989). For a review of most of this literature, see: Casson (1990b); Hébert and Link (1982, 1989); Reekie (1984); and Ricketts (1987a). Although more recent, Casson's (1990a, 1991) subsequent contributions on enterprise are less directly comparable with the GK theory than is his earlier (1982) work, and so they are not discussed here. For similar reasons, Wu's (1989) theory is also not examined because it applies to a different domain of inquiry.

15 Even with extraneous disturbances, if the speed with which economic agents adjust fully to exogenous changes was high, then it is also possible within Kirzner's and Casson's theoretical systems that equilibrium could be established temporarily before the next unexpected change occurs in the data (cf. Lachmann 1971b: 48).

16 On the dynamic nature of research programmes, see too Remenyi's (1979) work on core–demi-core interaction.

17 I desist from putting the hard core in entirely subjective terms. A purely subjectivist version of this hard-core assumption could be stated as follows:

> HC2 Economic agents subjectively believe themselves to face objective problem situations, and they subjectively believe that there is an objective reality which is independent of their conjectures and preferences.

I refrain from the purely subjectivist position because social events which come about as unintended consequences can sometimes not be explained in purely subjective terms (Latsis 1972: 222–223).

18 As applied in the GK research programme, the rationality principle does *not* imply single-exit methods of analysis. Thus, it is to be distinguished from Popper's version of the 'rationality principle' for explanations in the social sciences, which implies that a *unique* action is a rational response to the logic of the situation (Hands 1985a: 86; Latsis 1972: 224). For Popper's method of situational analysis, including the rationality principle, see Popper (1960: 149, 152–158; 1966b: ch. 14; 1972: ch. 4; 1976a: 102–103; 1983c); and also Blaug's (1985) commentary; Caldwell (1991: 13–22); Hands (1985a); Koertge (1979); Langlois (1982: 84; 1986d: 233); Latsis (1972: 222–229; 1976c: 4–5; 1983).

19 The possibility that economic agents will make mistakes does not contradict the rationality principle. '(Unintended) consequences are not evidence of the actor's so-called irrationality; rather, they are evidence that some of the actor's knowledge is false' (Boland 1982: 185). In this context, rationality is a purely formal relationship between the economic agent's behaviour and the agent's ranking of ends; it does not depend upon the truth status of the individual economic agent's knowledge (Kirzner 1982c; Rizzo 1982: 58). A decision can be mistaken but still be rational if, in the light of the agent's false knowledge of the relevant features of the problem situation, the decision is consistent with the agent's goal (see too Langlois 1982: 80).

Boland (1982: 185) would add another requirement for rational economic decision-making: the falsity of the agent's knowledge must be unknown to the actor at the time of the decision. However, even if an economic agent knew that his or her theory were false, and provided no

41

superior rival theory were available to the agent, Popper would maintain that it would still be rational for the economic agent to apply that knowledge as a basis for action until a better theory is developed (see section 2.2).

20 A third level may also be added: that of meta-methodology, which involves distinct rules or principles for critically evaluating competing methodologies at level II and for deciding between them (Nola 1987: 446–447). However, the third level is not germane to the present discussion and will not be pursued further.

21 In particular, Hayek stresses that to explain the behaviour of economic agents, an economic theory must explain how agents acquire knowledge of the givens or constraints if the givens are to play a role in their decision-making (Boland 1982: 176, 180, 184–187; Hayek 1937: 39).

22 On the neoclassical or neo-Walrasian programme, see Latsis (1972, 1976a, 1976c) and Weintraub (1979, 1985a, 1985b, 1988). On the Keynesian and post-Keynesian programmes, see Brown (1981); Eichner and Kregel (1975); and Weintraub (1979, 1985b). On the Austrian school, see Boettke (1994); Bosch *et al.* (1990); Caldwell and Böhm (1993); Dolan (1976); Groenveld *et al.* (1990); Kirzner (1980; 1994b: xviii–xx); Langlois (1982); Rizzo (1982); Vaughn (1994) and White (1984). On the neo-Marxian programme, see Baran and Sweezy (1966) and Brewer (1990). On the institutionalist programme, see Dugger (1979); Fusfeld (1980); Samuels (1989) and Wilber and Harrison (1978). On the behavioural and evolutionary approaches, see Latsis (1972); Nelson and Winter (1982); and Winter (1986).

For comprehensive collections of readings within most of these research programmes, see the ten-part series published by Edward Elgar: *Schools of Thought in Economics* (ed. Mark Blaug). Apart from Littlechild (1990) which is in this series, the reader interested in a sampling of Austrian work should consult Ebeling (1991) and Kirzner (1994a).

23 For further detail, see section 3.1 which compares the different characterisations of economic agents' problem situations within competing research programmes. It is of course the positive heuristic of a programme which largely prescribes the way in which agents' problem situations are to be specified in economic theories.

24 Ever since the emergence of adaptive expectations models, however, neoclassical economics has admitted the endogeneity of a small subset of economic agents' knowledge – namely, their expectations of given economic variables (Bacharach 1986: 178–179).

25 Logic, in the narrow sense of the word, pertains only to the (strictly logical) relationships between statements (Amsterdamski 1975: 79, 94).

26 In later years, however, Lachmann appeared to depart from his earlier views. For a survey of Austrian views on the relationship between psychology and economics, see: Coats (1976; 1983: 92–93); Runde (1988) and the comment by Endres (1988).

27 See section 10.3 on the *Entrepreneurial Learning Methodology Inventory*. If we adapt the nomenclature developed by Argyris and Schon (1983) for a somewhat different context, we can describe the GK model at this stage as postulating a single- rather than a double-loop model of

entrepreneurial learning. In single-loop learning, no change occurs in the criteria of theory-choice (i.e. the standards of rationality). Double-loop learning on the other hand involves a change in the criteria of evaluation.

28 The individual entrepreneur is also the unit of analysis in the theories developed by Casson (1982) and Kirzner (1973, 1979b, 1982c). In this respect, these theories and the GK approach can be distinguished from other theories of entrepreneurship and of innovation, including Nelson and Winter (1982) and Wu (1989), which focus upon enterprising activity and economic change at the firm level rather than at the level of the individual entrepreneur.

It should also be noted that Casson's later work (1990a) emphasises the nature and role of social groups in entrepreneurship. A similar shift occurred in Schumpeter's work. In his earlier writing (1934), Schumpeter depicted the entrepreneur as a particular type of individual, a person with exceptional creative ability and pioneering vision (at least on occasion, therefore, Schumpeter's entrepreneur accords with what Mises (1949: 255–256) called 'a promoter', which is a narrower concept than Mises' personified carrier of a pure entrepreneurial function). In a paper published somewhat later, Schumpeter appears to have extended the scope of his earlier thinking: '[T]he entrepreneurial function need not be embodied in a physical person and in particular in a single physical person. Every social environment has its own ways of filling the entrepreneurial function' (1965: 51). He even accepted that the entrepreneurial function may in fact be performed collectively, by both private and public corporations: 'With the development of the largest-scale corporations . . . aptitudes that no single individual combines can thus be built into a corporate personality' (1965: 53). In particular, the entrepreneurial function is allocated between professional managers and teams of research technicians (O'Donnell 1973: 212; Schumpeter 1950: 132).

29 On this point, see Aitken (1965c: 24), Kirzner (1973: 43; 1979b: 172) and Mises (1949: 252–256). Mises considers that the entrepreneur of economic theory is an economic or 'catallactic' category, which is a concept radically different from the entrepreneur in economic history who is an ideal type: 'The economic categories we are concerned with refer to purely integrated functions, the ideal types refer to historical events' (Mises 1949: 253). Cantillon (1931) was the first to stress the economic function rather than the personality or social status of the entrepreneur (Hébert and Link 1989: 42).

30 'The architecture . . . describes how the constituent decision-making units are arranged together in a system, how the decision-making authority and ability is distributed within a system, who gathers what information, and who communicates what with whom' (Sah and Stiglitz 1986: 716).

31 Indeed, Wu's (1989) theory is noteworthy in that it depicts firms as coalitions of entrepreneurs. These coalitions emerge as a result of entrepreneurs seeking to obtain simultaneously the benefits of both specialisation and diversification (1989: 115–118; 127–150). The multi- entrepreneur firm is argued to be a 'viable production institution' because it enforces the contracts entered into by the entrepreneurs: 'In short, the firm has the capability of curbing opportunism, thus enabling the entrepreneurs to

attain a superior cooperative outcome which the market fails to provide'
(Wu 1989: 118).

32 For further discussion of the importance of individual entrepreneurship in
innovation, see Quinn (1979: 19–23) and the references therein.

33 For an approach which does combine economic and cultural determinants
of entrepreneurship into a single theoretical framework, see Casson
(1990a). The reader is also referred to Berger (1991) which contains interdisciplinary work on the subject of the culture of entrepreneurship by
social scientists outside of economics. For selected readings on cultural
factors in economic development, with special reference to immigrant
groups, social mobility, religion and the state, see Casson (1990b: Part III).

34 Cf. Langlois (1986d: 233–234). For example, in their exploration of the
psychological and sociopsychological foundations of firms, Nelson and
Winter (1982: esp. chs 4, 5) employ Polanyi's (1958) concept of scripts
and tacit knowing to describe the knowledge possessed by economic
agents. Their evolutionary theory of economic change is not, of course,
within the GK programme because tacit knowing delves into the context
of discovery.

2

A BRIEF REVIEW OF POPPERIAN THEORIES OF THE GROWTH OF KNOWLEDGE

By way of introduction to this chapter, it is appropriate to discuss why indeed a short survey of Popper's philosophy is warranted at all, given that Popperian ideas are supposed to be so popular and widely disseminated within the economics profession. A review of Popper's work is considered necessary for two main reasons. First, commonly held and influential misinterpretations of Popper abound in the philosophy and history of science. For example, Ayer, followed by many other philosophers holding a justificationist theory of rationality, misread Popper and attributed a *dogmatic* form of falsificationism to him, in spite of the fact that Popper's *Logik der Forschung* is one of the most devastating attacks ever launched against dogmatic falsificationism (Lakatos 1970: 181; Settle 1974: 744). The pseudo-Popperian theory of dogmatic falsificationism is a mere myth that these philosophers have invented and criticised. Similarly, in alluding to Popper, Kuhn has offered a highly 'simplistic stereotype of falsificationism' and of the logic of scientific discovery (Popper 1983a: xxxii–v). Lakatos (1970: 93, 179) rebuked Kuhn for identifying Popper's basic position solely with *naive* falsificationism and for thereby overlooking Popper's sophisticated falsificationism and the novel philosophical research programme that he started.

The second reason why Popper's ideas deserve to be an urgent topic for discussion is that there are many misunderstandings and disagreements in the literature of economics, economic methodology and the history of economic thought about the content of Popper's philosophy of science:

> Popper is the most likely to be misinterpreted by those not well acquainted with his work . . .
>
> (Loasby 1984b: 407)

[S]ome methodological writers – economists among them – have recounted a naïve version of 'falsificationism' which is a vast oversimplification of what Popper actually said.

(Stewart 1979: 76)

As de Marchi notes in his own chapter (1988b) . . . , Popper was never really understood by economists; what practical economists took from Popper was the position that Lakatos called 'naive falsificationism' . . .

(Weintraub 1988: 225)

Popper's ideas are known (albeit imperfectly), referred to, often appealed to in disputes about 'right' practice, yet not deferred to in the actual doing.

(de Marchi 1988a: 10)

This chapter is first and foremost a sketch of some aspects of Popper's philosophy that are most relevant to the problems addressed by this book, namely, explaining entrepreneurial learning and market processes. The goal of the chapter is to explain and to clarify Popper's position: in particular, his methodology of science, his theory of knowledge and his critical rationalism. It does not intend to provide a comprehensive critical assessment of Popper's views but rather aims to clear up the most frequent confusions that exist about Popper in the economics literature.[1]

This chapter is limited to Popper's non-justificationist philosophy and to some developments of his programme. No attempt is made to detail a chronology of the evolution of Popperian philosophy. Furthermore, this chapter does not embrace more recent non-justificationist philosophies which have been advanced in the literature, such as that of Richard Rorty (1979). However, as a background to a better appreciation of Popper's contribution, it is appropriate to begin the discussion with an analysis of the 'received view' in the philosophy of science, namely, justificationism. Indeed, a critique of justificationism is one of the central pillars of Popper's philosophy.

2.1 THE RECEIVED VIEW: JUSTIFICATIONISM

Justificationism is the methodological doctrine which asserts that a theory cannot be accepted as genuine knowledge unless it can be positively justified, that is, proven true.[2] '[A] genuine statement must be capable of *conclusive verification*' (Schlick 1931: 150). Consequently, justificationism only identifies knowledge with certain knowledge, thereby demanding very high epistemological standards (Lakatos 1971a: 108). According to justificationism, 'conjectural knowledge was a contradiction in terms' (Lakatos 1968a: 321).

There are many divergent and competing brands of justificationism which share little in common other than the above assertions. Different justificationist methodologies recognise different foundations of knowledge. For example, classical intellectualists, such as Descartes and Spinoza in the seventeenth century, believed that the truth could be proved by the power of the intellect. The intellectualists were apriorists concerning the nature of the justification of scientific knowledge, that is, intellectualists attempted to justify their beliefs by appealing to *a priori* or self-evident truths. They extolled intelligence above empiricism but did not deny that knowledge of sorts could be gained from the senses. In contrast, classical empiricists (i.e. positivists and sensationalists) claimed that knowledge must be justified by the evidence of the senses.[3] Both acknowledged that *deductive* logic could only transmit truth and not establish truth, but they disagreed amongst themselves about how the truth of first principles or axioms could be justified and thus about what could be accepted as axioms.

Logical positivism was a dominant philosophy of science which was intrinsically justificationist. The positivists believed that scientific knowledge was the paradigm case of human knowledge because of its greater certainty. They wanted to demonstrate that a secure foundation for scientific claims existed which was provided by the rigorous standards scientists applied in recording observations and gathering data (Ackermann 1976: 1–2).

2.1.1 The logical problem of the justification of induction

The classical empiricists believed that the justification of scientific theories required an *inductive* logic, as opposed to the deductive logic of the classical intellectualists. As justificationists, they also assumed that inductive inference itself requires justification, i.e. proof that induction yields valid knowledge. However, an attempt at such a proof is fraught by Hume's logical problem of the justification of induction, which asks:

Are we justified in reasoning from (repeated) instances of which we have experience to other instances (conclusions) of which we have no experience?

Hume's answer ... is: No, however great the number of repetitions.

(Popper 1972: 4)

The inductive procedure involves learning the truth of a general law from observing numerous particular examples. One collects facts about some members of a set (e.g. observing the price of a good at a particular time and place) and then with the aid of the rules of induction, one draws the conclusion that some generalisation about the whole set is true (e.g. about the behaviour of that good's price over all time and wherever it is sold).

Inductive inferences, however, are not logically conclusive because there is no guarantee that what has been experienced in the past will persist in the future. Demonstrative (i.e. compelling) logical arguments are characterised by the fact that true premises necessarily imply true conclusions. Although deductive inferences possess this character, inductive inferences are non-demonstrative, because it is not the case that if the premises of an inductive argument are true, then the conclusion must always be true. The conclusions are not entailed by the premises. Even if the premises are true, it is logically possible for the conclusion of an inductive argument to be false (Blaug 1980: 14–17; Chalmers 1982, ch.2). Inductive learning cannot be logically justified: no amount of finite evidence about the singular elements of an infinite set can prove that such a set has specific general properties.[4] Indeed, a universal law goes essentially beyond an infinity of observations or repetitions (Popper 1972: 7).

Having demonstrated conclusively the impossibility of justifying induction, Hume still maintained that even though induction is not logically valid or rationally justifiable, it is still the universal method by which we all acquire our expectations and beliefs:

Hume's understanding of the problem of induction includes a psychological evaluation: though induction cannot be rationally justified, reasonable people still expect the future to resemble the past; put another way, though we cannot *prove* universal theories to be true, we still believe them to be true. That the origins of such beliefs are 'habit and custom', and ultimately based on an individual's *experience*, was Hume's thesis; and empiricists ever since have emphasized that observations of the phenomenal world are the source of theories.

(Caldwell 1982: 43; original emphasis)

This brings us to a discussion of the psychologism inherent in the justificationist position, which began with Hume's accommodating response to the problem of induction.

2.1.2 Justificationism's retreat to psychologism

The justificationist conception of knowledge as justified true belief leads to psychologism.[5] If the statements of science are to be justified on the basis of logic, then statements can only be justified by other statements (which have already been justified). But the justification of one statement by another leads to an *infinite regress* of proofs, so that classical empiricists resorted to psychologism, which Popper defines as the doctrine that statements can be justified not only by statements but also by perceptual experience (Popper 1959: 94). According to psychologism, sense experience represents immediate knowledge whose truth can be guaranteed subjectively. Perceptual experience produces immediate feelings of conviction by which one can establish the truth status of an observation statement. The rest of one's knowledge can be justified by reference to this immediate knowledge. Perceptual experiences justify observation statements, and all other scientific knowledge must be logically inferred (usually inductively, but also deductively) from such justified observation statements (Musgrave 1974b: 568, 582). For the classical empiricists, therefore, the narrow empirical basis of science consisted of a small set of propositions expressing hard facts, whose truth was established by experience.

What Popper terms the 'bucket theory of the mind' is an example of a psychologistic theory of knowledge. This theory takes as its starting point the idea that to know anything about the world, one must first have had perceptions or sense experiences (Popper 1972: ch.2, appendix 1). Hume's empiricist psychology was a version of this theory of knowledge.

Most justificationist theories of knowledge which recognise the senses as a source of knowledge assume implicitly that sensations are unimpregnated by theory and that a distinction between observational and theoretical terms is possible. They rely upon a psychology of observation which prescribes the right state of mind for observing the truth. For instance, classical empiricists claimed that the right mind was a clean slate from which all innate ideas and theoretical prejudices had been wiped (Lakatos 1970: 99). (By way of qualification, however, it must be recognised that some brands of justificationist empiricism do not distinguish so starkly between observational and theoretical terms. For instance, Margenau (1966) argues that there are varying layers of theory or degrees of abstraction. He emphasises that data in the domain of protocols – or p-domain – have no organisation of their own, that they must have organisation imposed upon them by the observer. The observer interprets observations of events in the p-domain in terms of low-level ideas in the domain of constructs, or c-domain.)

2.1.3 Other versions of justificationism

Justificationism was superseded by neojustificationism (or probabilism) when it was recognised that no scientific theory is provable, and that all theories are equally unprovable. Neojustificationism asserts that though equally unprovable, scientific theories have different degrees of probability (in the sense of the calculus of probability) in the light of the available empirical evidence (Lakatos 1970: 95). A proposition is therefore scientific if it is probable to a proven degree.[6] Neojustificationists believe that even if absolute certainty is an unattainable goal, science must still produce the next best thing: near-certainty. They water down the ideal of proven truth to 'probable truth'.

Neojustificationism was founded by intellectualists. However, philosophers also tried to construct an empiricist version of neojustificationism (Lakatos 1970: 95; 1968a: 367, 361). This approach culminated in Carnap's logical empiricism – Lakatos (1968a: 324) prefers the term neoclassical empiricism – which relied upon *confirmation* as a means for judging the acceptability of hypotheses. Its primary objective was the *partial* justification of theories: theories had to be at least partially proved, that is, confirmed by the facts to a certain degree. Being a more sophisticated form of logical positivism, it was thus one of the most justificationist philosophies ever to explore the nature and rationality of scientific inquiry.[7]

Given that all scientific theories are equally unprovable, logical empiricists attempted to distinguish scientific knowledge from ignorance by means of a probabilistic inductive logic, which could specify the probabilities – and hence the relative strengths – of competing hypotheses according to the available evidence (see Suppe 1977a: 624–632). Consequently, the probability of a hypothesis was supposed to represent the degree of rational belief in the truth of that proposition which could be logically supported by the evidence.

Neojustificationists search for (provably) highly probable theories, but exactly how highly probable is never clarified:

> A rational individual will therefore always choose hypotheses with higher probabilities over those with lower probabilities. As evidence accumulates the balance may tip to alter the probabilities of competing hypotheses, and the rational individual will alter his convictions according to the shift in probabilities.
> (Rutherford 1984: 378)

If the mathematical probability of a particular theory is high, it qualifies as scientific in the eyes of the neojustificationist. If its probability is low or even zero, it is rejected as unscientific. Neojustificationism thus provides a continuum ranging from poor theories with low probability to good theories with high probability: rather than a dichotomous demarcation between science and pseudoscience (Lakatos 1978: 3).

However, even neojustificationism is beset with difficulties. Its adherents failed to find even a probabilistic solution to the problem of induction.[8] Whereas the classical justificationists had failed to justify the inductive procedure needed to prove theories from facts, the neojustificationists failed to justify the inductive principles required to prove even the probability (i.e. the degree of confirmation) of hypotheses (Lakatos 1968a: 367).

Scepticism and conventionalism have been argued to be the only avenues open to the justificationist. Scepticism does not deny justificationism, since it assumes that knowledge, if it exists, must be justified true belief. It claims only that proven knowledge cannot be attained and that we have therefore no knowledge at all, everything is uncertain (Lakatos 1970: 94). Scepticism first conflates knowledge with certainty and then argues in effect that because certainty eludes us, so does knowledge (Coddington 1982: 484). Scepticism is thus the result of a tacit belief in justificationism. It is not a separate position but a variant of justificationist epistemology (Bartley 1964). Furthermore, sceptics regard rationality as impossible: if rational action presupposes proven or probable knowledge, and if such knowledge is not attainable, then neither is rational action. All in all then, these sceptics are *disappointed* justificationists: they are hopelessly resigned to the futility of rational, positive justification of their knowledge.

Conventionalism is one of the most sophisticated forms of justificationist scepticism. It can be defined as 'the justification of belief by deduction from contingent claims of truth associated with criteria for desirable theoretical statements (e.g., simplicity, testability)' (Brennan 1984: 132). Although not subscribing to conventionalism, Popper (1959: 451) even concedes that it is 'a system which is self-contained and defensible' and that 'attempts to detect inconsistencies in it are not likely to succeed' (see too: Popper 1959: sections 19–20; and Lakatos 1971a: 94–96). Whereas the inductivist believes that genuine (proven or probable) theoretical knowledge is possible and tries to glean it from a narrow empirical basis of hard facts, the conventionalist is far more street-wise, having fathomed that genuine theoretical knowledge of the world is not possible given the justificationist definition of knowledge. Conventionalism accepts that it is impossible to prove the truth of a theory inductively. In accepting that theories go beyond sense experience, conventionalism claims that a theory is neither empirical nor factual, but is rather an accepted way of classifying particular facts (Agassi 1966: 4–5). Accordingly, a theory is considered by the conventionalists to be simply a convenient catalogue system for filing facts and generalisations; the system is not regarded as proven true but only as true by convention (or possibly even as neither true nor false) (Boland 1982: 177; Lakatos 1971a: 95). In spite of its coherence, conventionalism still represents a rather negative position: theory-change does not constitute increasing truth-content; it merely involves replacing 'an unordered or an arbitrarily ordered heap of information by an elegantly ordered yet not richer stock of information' (Agassi 1966: 5).

Instrumentalism is closely related to conventionalism and shares the justificationist prejudices of the latter.[9] It is a methodological strategy which asserts that theories are best regarded as practical instruments for making predictions. A justificationist mistake underlies many versions of instrumentalism: it is assumed that only that is real which can be known with certainty (Popper 1963: 117). From its justificationist assumptions, instrumentalism thus draws rather anti-realist conclusions: it denies ontological status to theoretical concepts, that is, it rejects the claim that these concepts describe or correspond to anything in reality.

Both instrumentalism and conventionalism agree there is no direct solution to the logical problem of the justification of induction. Like conventionalism, instrumentalism eschews a theory's truth or falsity. However, the differences between the two methodologies have been acutely stated by Lakatos:

> Conventionalism rests on the recognition that false assumptions may have true consequences; therefore false theories may have great predictive power. . . . On the other hand some conventionalists did not have sufficient logical education to realise that some propositions may be true whilst being unproven; and others false whilst having true consequences, and also some which are both false and approximately true. These people opted for 'instrumentalism': they came to regard theories as neither true nor false but merely as 'instruments' for prediction. Conventionalism . . . is a philosophically sound position; instrumentalism is a degenerate version of it, based on a mere philosophical muddle caused by lack of elementary logical competence.
>
> (Lakatos 1971a: 95)[10]

Rather controversially, Boland (1982: 143–146) claims the major methodological difference between conventionalism and instrumentalism is that the former searches for a criterion to substitute for truth, whereas the latter searches for short-run criteria which provide immediate predictive success, no claim being made that these criteria are truth substitutes. According to Boland, conventionalism denies the possibility of solving the original problem of the justification of induction, but it accepts the necessity of reformulating the problem into one that can be solved: namely, the search for criteria and the establishment of acceptance rules that can be used in choosing between competing theories. In contrast, Boland argues that instrumentalism *dismisses* the problem of induction. It 'solves' the problem of induction by ignoring it. It does not try to justify theories because the truth of theories is not necessary for practical success. Boland's interpretation of instrumentalism is thus that it is in some sense a non-justificationist methodology.

Yet another dominant methodology which is consistent with justificationism is *dogmatic* falsificationism (as defined by Lakatos 1970: 95–103). Dogmatic falsificationism accords with the central tenets of justificationism: it assumes that the truth-value of observational propositions can be proved from facts; it also assumes that there is a natural demarcation between proven, observational propositions on the one hand, and theoretical propositions on the other; it asserts that theories can be tested against this absolutely firm foundation of authoritative facts and that it is possible to produce a hard, conclusive disproof of a theory under test; it also assumes that once theories are tested, they can be instantly assessed, and that if they are refuted, they are eliminated immediately. It also shares with justificationism the view that science evaluates one theory at a time, that is, it represents a monotheoretical model of assessment.

However, unlike many other variants of justificationism, dogmatic falsificationism refuses to accept that the infallible foundation of empirical knowledge can be used as the basis for inductive inference: it denies that theories can be arrived at by induction from facts and accumulated generalisations. It thereby rejects the cumulative theory of the growth of knowledge. Thus, it is argued that the certainty of the empirical basis cannot be transmitted to scientific theories. All theories are admitted by the dogmatic falsificationist to be equally fallible, unprovable and improbabilifiable. Hence, apart from justificationist scepticism, dogmatic falsificationism is the weakest form of justificationism (see too section 2.2.4).

There is a host of other methodological and philosophical doctrines which can be shown to be justificationist at heart. At this juncture it suffices merely to mention them in passing: pragmatism, operationalism, behaviourism, phenomenalism, existentialism and the hermeneutic and dialectical approaches. All these doctrines are brands of justificationism. The rejection of justificationism *per se* necessarily implies the rejection of each of these methodologies.

2.1.4 The justificationist conception of the growth of knowledge

To the justificationist or neojustificationist, learning or the acquisition of knowledge involves cautiously building up a store of proven or probable knowledge. Justificationist conceptions of knowledge are closely, but not strictly, linked with the thesis of intertheoretic reduction which maintains that all successor theories are simply amplifications of their predecessors, which they never contradict:

> science establishes theories which, if highly confirmed, are accepted and continue to be accepted relatively free from the danger of subsequent disconfirmation. The development of

science consists in the extension of such theories to wider scopes
... the development of new highly confirmed theories for
related domains, and the incorporation of confirmed theories
into more comprehensive theories. ... Science thus is a cumulative enterprise, extending and augmenting old successes
with new successes; old theories are not rejected or abandoned
once they have been accepted; they are just superseded by more
comprehensive theories to which they are reduced.

(Suppe 1977b: 55–56)

The growth of knowledge is thus conceived as the gradual unilinear
accumulation of eternally valid facts, empirical generalisations and
theories of higher levels of universality. 'According to this school
then, ... the growth of knowledge is the growth of proven knowledge ...' (Lakatos 1978: 193). Once knowledge is justified (i.e.
proven true), it stays so for all time.[11] To the justificationist, the
growth of knowledge is continuous and coherent in the sense
that consistency must always be maintained between all (scientific)
theories in all domains. Perceived unity in the growth of knowledge
arises from the justificationist notion that science progresses by
incremental improvements within the one true theory. The result
is a *cumulative* rather than a revolutionary model of the growth of
knowledge. (Justificationist scepticism, however, results in a *stagna-
tion* model because it denies at the outset the possibility of growth.)
According to inductive justificationism, all genuine progress must
take place in Kuhnian normal science. No revolutions can occur
within the justificationist conception of the growth of knowledge,
because science never overturns facts which have already been
established as true.

2.2 POPPER'S NON-JUSTIFICATIONIST
PHILOSOPHY

Justificationist conceptions of the nature of science, its growth and
methodology have been critically examined in recent years and have
largely been repudiated. New theories of the growth of knowledge
have emerged.

Many philosophers in the growth-of-knowledge tradition started
with Popper's views, and in applying some ideas from the philosophy
of science to the treatment of knowledge and learning in economic
theories, I too begin with Popper's philosophy. For Popper, the

most exciting and central problems of epistemology (the theory of knowledge) are those connected with the growth of knowledge (Popper 1959: 21, 15). By the growth of knowledge, Popper means the growth of systems of conjectures, some of which are well-criticised and severely tested.

According to the justificationist theory of knowledge, science and common-sense decision-making are inherently different. In contrast, for Popper and other philosophers in the growth-of-knowledge tradition, the difference between science and practical decision-making is one of degree and not kind.

> My interest is not merely in the theory of scientific knowledge, but rather in the theory of knowledge in general. Yet the study of the growth of scientific knowledge is, I believe, the most fruitful way of studying the growth of knowledge in general. For the growth of scientific knowledge may be said to be the growth of ordinary human knowledge *writ large*. . . .
> (Popper 1963: 216)

Scientific knowledge is merely a development of ordinary knowledge. Its very problems are enlargements of the problems of common-sense knowledge. Both ordinary and scientific knowledge grow by fundamentally the same procedure: the method of learning by trial and error-elimination, the method of learning from mistakes (Popper 1959: 18, 22; 1960: 85–87; 1963: 216; 1972: 259, 261). The main difference is that in the case of scientific knowledge we consciously and systematically search for errors and contradictions (Popper 1976c: 115).

Popper's philosophy of science represents one of the most important developments in Western philosophy during the twentieth century. The originality of Popper's contribution lies in the fact that it is historically the first fully-fledged *non-justificationist* philosophy. According to Popper, conjectures can never be positively justified. They can neither be established as certainly true nor as probable. Rather scientific theories are:

> *genuine conjectures* – highly informative guesses about the world which although not verifiable (i.e. capable of being shown to be true) can be submitted to severe critical tests. They are serious attempts to discover the truth.
> (Popper 1963: 115; original emphasis)

According to Popper's philosophy, all knowledge is tentative and uncertain. There can be no ultimate and absolute knowledge (not even knowledge which is objective can be absolute). All statements in science can be tested at any time and, in principle, all are capable of being refuted. Popper's fallibilistic epistemology denies the existence of any royal road to truth. The foundations of all knowledge and hence of all criticism remain forever conjectural:

> The empirical basis of objective science has thus nothing 'absolute' about it. Science does not rest upon rock-bottom. The bold structure of its theories rises, as it were, above a swamp. It is like a building erected on piles. The piles are driven down from above into the swamp, but not down to any natural or 'given' base; and when we cease our attempts to drive our piles into a deeper layer, it is not because we have reached firm ground. We simply stop when we are satisfied that they are firm enough to carry the structure, at least for the time being.
>
> (Popper 1959: 111)

Justification plays no integral part in Popper's epistemology, theory of method or critical rationalism (see, for example: Popper 1972: chs 1–3; 1974: section 15). Popper showed that even neojustificationism, with its retreat from proof to probability, was inadequate: under very general conditions the mathematical probability of any universal statement or theory is zero, whatever the amount of observational evidence in its favour (Popper 1959: appendix *vii). Thus, according to Popper all theories are not only equally unprovable, they are also equally improbable (Lakatos 1970: 95; 1978: 3). Popper elaborated new, non-justificationist criteria for critically and rationally evaluating scientific theories which arise naturally from his solution to the problem of induction. Popper's theory of (scientific) rationality constitutes a major step forward in relation to its justificationist predecessors, especially inductivism.

2.2.1 Popper's (dis)solution of the problem of induction

In order to solve the problem of induction, Popper generalised and restated the original problem: [12]

> Can the claim that an explanatory universal theory is true or that it is false be justified by 'empirical reasons'; that is, can the assumption of the truth of test statements justify either the claim that a universal theory is true or the claim that it is false?

To this problem, my answer is positive: Yes, *the assumption of*

the truth of test statements sometimes allows us to justify the claim
that an explanatory theory is false.
(Popper 1972: 7; original emphasis)

Having dissolved the problem of induction, Popper develops a purely deductivist methodology which shows how *rational* choices between competing hypotheses are possible *without* inductive justification or the computation of relative degrees of confirmation. His deductivist methodology relies upon the asymmetry between verification and falsification by experience (see Popper 1959: 41; 1972: 12; 1983b: section 22). The asymmetry arises from the logical form of universal statements. A universal statement (e.g. all swans are white) cannot be verified by singular observation statements (e.g. observations of white swans), no matter how many there are. But a universal statement may be falsified with the aid of deductive logic by only one singular statement (e.g. the observation of a black swan). No inductive inferences are required in the falsification of a universal theory through the falsification of its deductive consequences (i.e. predictions).

Whereas justificationists located the rationality of science in verification, Popper attempts to ascertain the nature of scientific rationality if it is located in falsification and the elimination of error. Seen in this light, scientific method is not a way of justifying results. Scientific theories cannot be rationally justified, but they can be rationally criticised and tested:

> science is one of the very few human activities – perhaps the only one – in which errors are systematically criticized and fairly often, in time, corrected. This is why we can say that, in science, we often learn from our mistakes, and why we can speak clearly and sensibly about making progress there.
>
> (Popper 1963: 216)

2.2.2 Popper's elimination of psychologism

Reichenbach (1938: ch.1, section 1) coined the terms 'context of discovery' and 'context of justification' to distinguish between the manner in which a scientific result is discovered and the manner in which that result is submitted to and evaluated by the scientific community, respectively. Almost all adherents to logical positivism upheld this distinction. Popper follows the received view in confining his attention to the logical 'context of justification' rather than the psychological 'context of discovery'. According to Popper (1959: section 2), the philosophical analysis of theories can ignore how discoveries are made (i.e. the context of discovery) and should restrict its inquiry to theories as finished products of human intellectual activity (i.e. the context of justification).[13] Problems related to the act of inventing a theory are considered to be the concern of psychology, not epistemology and the philosophy of science. The logical analysis of knowledge can ignore the psychological process by which that knowledge is created, because in the absence of an inductive logic of discovery and of justification, knowledge of the psychological process of forming theories cannot give theories logical validity if they are otherwise logically inconsistent. Consequently, Popper focuses upon the analysis and appraisal of scientific theories after they have been conceived, and he emphasises that the logical analysis of finished discoveries cannot supply a logical method of discovering new ideas.

Unlike the justificationists, however, Popper combats the psychologistic notion that statements can be justified by perceptual experience. Statements can only be justified by other statements. This rejection of a psychologistic empirical basis is reinforced by his denial that there is any natural (i.e. psychological) demarcation between observational and theoretical terms. According to Popper, discoveries and observations are stimulated and guided by theory, rather than theories being discoveries due to observation (see Popper 1959: section 25, appendix *x; 1963: 41–48; 1972: 342–347; and also Musgrave 1974b: 566–573). Popper's thesis is that theory, or at least some crude expectation or hunch, precedes observation in all cases. Thus, all facts are theory-laden; all observation statements are theoretical to some degree. The latter all transcend immediate experience because they use universal terms which in turn presuppose universal theories.

Furthermore, the justificationist conception of knowledge as justified true belief conflates the content of some belief with the particular psychological attitudes that people may have towards that content. It thus confuses the objective dimension of knowledge with its subjective dimension. The objective dimension of knowledge is explained away in subjective, psychological terms (i.e. psychologism). Popper's logical analysis of knowledge, however, seeks to explore the non-psychological, objective or inter-subjective aspects of scientific knowledge, with the result that the content of knowledge becomes the focus, rather than psychological attitudes (Musgrave 1974b: 566–570). Science is a rational enterprise concerned with obtaining objective knowledge of the real world. According to Popper, the growth of scientific knowledge takes place essentially in 'world 3', the world of objective knowledge, which is independent of 'knowing subjects'.[14] Indeed, Popper (1972: 73) goes so far as to say that purely subjective knowledge does not exist.

Popper's logic of knowledge is also concerned with the formulation of objective standards (such as testability) which can be applied in the critical appraisal of (scientific) theories. These objective standards are independent of any psychological facts about the people who produce or evaluate theories (Musgrave 1974b: 570).

The objective concept of truth also plays a crucial role in Popper's elimination of psychologism from his theory of knowledge. Justificationist philosophies rely upon psychological theories of truth which conceive truth as a property of our state of mind. Truth (i.e. true knowledge) is regarded as a very special kind of belief, one that can be shown to be justified. The theory of objective truth, on the other hand, asserts that although we search for truth, it may well be impossible for us to recognise truth even when we hit upon it. There is no infallible means of detecting objective truth. It is only the idea of an absolute or objective truth – in Tarski's formulation as correspondence to the facts – which makes rational criticism and rational theory-choice possible (see Popper 1963: 223–233; 1972: ch.9). In the absence of objective truth, it would not make sense and would not be possible for us to adopt critical policies with the express aim of finding our mistakes and learning from them. 'Thus the very idea of error – and of fallibility – involves the idea of an objective truth as the standard of which we may fall short. (It is in this sense that the idea of truth is a *regulative* idea.)' (Popper 1963: 229; original emphasis).

2.2.3 Popper's theory of the growth of scientific knowledge

As discussed earlier, inductive justificationists maintained that scientific progress arises from intertheoretic reduction, that is, from the succession of more universal theories which include earlier theories as special cases:

> The only aspects of the growth of scientific knowledge relevant to philosophy were the inductive justification or confirmation of knowledge claims and the incorporation of older theories into more comprehensive theories via intertheoretic reduction.

The resulting view of scientific knowledge was a static one which, ignoring the dynamics of scientific progress and being tied to an untenable observational/theoretical distinction and associated epistemology, led to a highly distorted portrait of science and the knowledge it provided, which had little to do with the epistemic activities science was actually engaged in.

(Suppe 1977a: 704)

Popper flatly rejects the thesis of scientific development by inter-theoretic reduction. According to Popper, a new theory of a higher level of universality is not just a mere conjunction of previous lower-level theories. It may actually contradict and correct them. For instance, Newton's theory of dynamics not only achieved a unification of Galileo's terrestrial and Kepler's celestial physics, but it also explained them by correcting them (Popper 1972: ch. 5). Popper claims that it is not even necessary that the 'new theory should contain the old one approximately, for appropriate values of the parameters of the new theory' (1972: 202). Thus, successor theories can be *fact-correcting* and can deny the validity of their predecessors.

The justificationist conception of the continuous accumulation of eternal truths is antithetical to Popper's image of the growth of scientific knowledge. According to Popper, science does not advance by repeated attempts at confirmation of hypotheses. Rather it involves endless testing, the constant overthrow of existing scientific theories and their replacement by wholly new and better kinds of knowledge, that is, new systems of theories of ever greater content (Popper 1976c: 79). 'Revolutions in permanence!' is a more appropriate characterisation of the growth of knowledge. Popper regards the growth of knowledge as unidirectional and irreversible, and as fundamentally discontinuous in nature.

Popper's *revolutionary* model of the growth of knowledge depicts learning to be the result of a process of natural selection between hypotheses:

our knowledge consists, at every moment, of those hypotheses which have shown their (comparative) fitness by surviving so far in their struggle for existence; a competitive struggle which eliminates those hypotheses which are unfit.

(Popper 1972: 261)[15]

The natural selection conception of the growth of knowledge is intended to describe how knowledge actually grows, it is not meant as a metaphor. Popper cautions against interpreting too narrowly the method of conjecture and refutation and the survival of the fittest hypothesis. The fittest hypothesis is the one which best solves the problem that it was intended to solve and which stands up to severe testing better than its competitors.

The process of natural selection between hypotheses may appear to give rise to results similar to those of induction. In this connection, it is worth pointing out the differences between Lamarckism and Darwinism. Lamarck conceived adaptation of organisms to be the result of direct instruction conveyed repetitively by the environment to aim-seeking organisms. In contrast, Darwin explained such adaptation to be the result of selection, and he showed that the outcome of a selection process may resemble the outcome of instruction (Popper 1972: 149, 266–272; 1974: 1023). Just as Darwinian biological evolution by natural selection may *simulate* Lamarckian evolution by instruction, so too may the fundamental procedure of the growth of knowledge (i.e. the method of conjecture and refutation) simulate induction. In his earlier work (1959: 276–281), Popper describes scientific knowledge as evolving in what is sometimes termed the 'inductive direction' – i.e. the direction from theories of lower universality to theories of higher universality. However, he rejects the doctrine that an advance in the 'inductive direction' can only be explained in terms of a succession of inductive inferences. Popper prefers, therefore, to characterise progress towards theories of increasing generality as the '*quasi*-inductive' evolution of knowledge, a process which does not contain any inductive elements. Thus, it might appear on the surface that individuals learn inductively – i.e. that they start from observations and proceed by induction to generate their theories – whereas in fact they learn by trial and selective error-elimination.

The actual pattern of the growth of knowledge depends upon whether knowledge is subjective or objective:

> knowledge in the subjective sense grows or achieves better adjustments by the Darwinian method of mutation and elimination of the organism. As opposed to this, objective knowledge can change and grow by the elimination (killing) of the linguistically formulated conjecture: the 'carrier' can survive – he can, if he is a self-critical person, even eliminate his own conjecture.
>
> (Popper 1972: 66)

Subjective knowledge grows mainly through the elimination of the carrier of the false subjective expectations. Thus, in the case of subjective knowledge, we ourselves are likely to perish along with our unfit beliefs, whereas with objective knowledge we can eliminate our mistaken theories before such theories lead to our own elimination (Popper 1972: 148, 261).

It should also be noted that Popper asserts that revolutionary growth is crucial for the rational and empirical character of objective scientific knowledge:

> if science ceases to grow it must lose that character. It is the way of its growth which makes science rational and empirical; the way, that is, in which scientists discriminate between available theories and choose the better one or (in the absence of a satisfactory theory) the way they give reasons for rejecting all the available theories, thereby suggesting some of the conditions with which a satisfactory theory should comply.
>
> (Popper 1963: 215)

Popper's revolutionary framework leads to *theoretical pluralism*, sometimes referred to fervidly as the 'philosophy of proliferation'. Since theories can only be refuted and not verified, the development of a wide variety of rival theories is essential for the growth of knowledge. Monolithic theoretical structures can only hamper growth. Theories are conjectures, and we should create as many bold new ideas as possible, exposing them to critical tests and possible refutation. Unlike Kuhn, Popper (1970: 54–55) argues that rarely does one single ruling theory (or a paradigm) ever dominate to the exclusion of all others. Typically, there are competing dominant theories in any one scientific domain.

Before I embark upon a discussion of Popper's criteria of scientific progress, a few comments should be made about the origin of scientific theories. Although factors in the genesis of theories (i.e. the context of discovery) are not the concern of a logical analysis of knowledge, Popper nevertheless argues insistently that whatever is the origin of scientific generalisations, it is not induction from a series of observations. Popper rejects any doctrine which asserts that knowledge *starts* from observation, perception or sensation. Knowledge does not start from observations but always from problems, whether practical or theoretical. The generation of hypotheses is therefore not purely random but is *problemistic*. Theories are stimulated by a particular problem which they attempt to solve. 'It is the problem which challenges us to learn; to advance our knowledge; to experiment; and to observe' (Popper 1963: 222). The problem often determines the range within which creative innovations are proposed and may exert a plastic control over them. Problems arise when expectations are disappointed, or when contradictions are discovered either within a theory, between theories or between a theory and observations. Thus, the growth of knowledge can be visualised as a process in which we progress – by the method of conjectures and refutations – from old problems to newer problems of increasing depth.[16]

2.2.4 Popper's requirements for the growth of knowledge

Which brings us to Popper's theory of method. 'Logical analysis of scientific knowledge must, if it is to give an adequate theory of science, be supplemented by *methodology*' (Musgrave 1974b: 575; original emphasis). Both are required to provide an adequate characterisation and explanation of the growth of (scientific) knowledge. In particular, Popper's methodology is intended to assist the achievement of the scientific aims specified by his logic of knowledge. Given that the aim of science is conjectured to be the search for truth (i.e for true explanatory theories), his methodology addresses the frankly normative problem of providing criteria of progress towards the truth. This system of methodological rules can therefore be regarded as a proposal to encourage the growth of knowledge. It specifies the criteria according to which a new theory should be judged in order to determine whether it represents an important advance upon its rivals and predecessors. The following discussion examines three requirements for the continual growth of knowledge: testability, empirical success and successful refutations.

Three further points should be noted with respect to Popper's theory of method. First, the following methodological rules are regarded as conventions which are to be accepted only tentatively. They are the rules of the game of science (Johansson 1975: 15; Popper 1959: 53–56). Second, Popper (1959: 52) explicitly rejects the idea that his methodology studies the actual behaviour of scientists at work. He does not presume to have supplied us with a rationale of actual scientific practice. Third, Popper's theory of method amounts to *sophisticated* falsificationism, and it must not be confused with *dogmatic* or *naive* falsificationism (the implications of this will be made clearer shortly).

Testability

The first requirement of a good theory is that it is independently testable.[17] A theory is testable if it implies that events of a certain kind cannot happen – that is, conceivable events which could refute the theory. Apart from explaining all the states of affairs which it was designed to explain, a new theory must offer new and bold predictions (especially of new kinds of events) by prohibiting certain things to happen.[18] The new theory must predict things which have never been observed before. The requirement of independent testability is needed to eliminate uninteresting, *ad hoc* theories from our choice set; for provided we have sufficient ingenuity, we can always invent a theory to account for any given set of *explicanda* (i.e. states of affairs to be explained) (Popper 1963: 241).

An example of an unsatisfactory explanation which is *ad hoc* and circular is as follows: Q. Why is product *x* not being sold in market *a*? A. Because there is insufficient market demand. Q. But what evidence supports the claim that there is insufficient market demand for product *x* in market *a*? A. Isn't it obvious? If there were sufficient demand for product *x* in market *a*, it would be sold in market *a*.

Such circular explanations are unsatisfactory because the only evidence for the explanatory statements (i.e. the *explanans*) is the state of affairs to be explained (i.e. the *explanandum*) itself. To be a non-circular explanation, the *explicans* must possess some testable consequences which differ from the *explicandum* (Popper 1972: 191–192).

The testability criterion measures the degree to which the new theory's explanatory power exceeds that of the best theory previously offered as a possible solution to the problem. 'It characterizes as preferable the theory which tells us more; that is to say, the theory which contains the greater amount of empirical information or *content*, ... which has the greater explanatory and predictive power; and which can therefore be *more severely tested* by comparing predicted facts with observations' (Popper 1963: 217; original emphasis). In this respect the novelty of Popper's critical approach has been recognised: 'He was the first philosopher of science ... to recognise that science aims, above all, to say a lot; he analysed what "saying a lot" involves, and based an entire philosophy of science upon it' (Musgrave 1974b: 566).

It can be shown that the testability of a theory is *inversely* related to its logical probability (in the sense of the calculus of probability).

Thus, according to this criterion, the growth of knowledge means progress towards *less* probable or plausible knowledge, that is, towards theories which are more severely testable and which have a lower probability of resisting falsification. This is of course the complete opposite of inductive neojustificationism which assumes that we should aim at a high degree of probability for our theories if we want to promote the growth of knowledge (Popper 1963: 218–220, 236).

From his analysis of testability as a crucial logical property of a scientific theory, Popper derives the first rule in his theory of method, *the rule of demarcation*, which separates the statements of science from non-scientific statements. According to the demarcation rule, only theories which are intersubjectively testable are to be admitted into science. All other theories are to be rejected as pseudo-scientific or unscientific (though not necessarily as meaningless). Closely related to the demarcation rule is the *preference rule* or the *rule demanding a high degree of testability*: theories with high information content (and hence a high degree of falsifiability) should be given preference to theories with a lesser amount of information. These rules are supplemented by Popper's *supreme meta-rule* which says that 'the other rules of scientific procedure must be designed in such a way that they do not protect any statement in science against falsification' (Popper 1959: 54).

Methodological rules are thus to be formulated so as to ensure the applicability of the demarcation criterion and the testability of scientific theories. The implication is that testability is not only a logical but also a methodological matter. According to the logical definition (i.e. the demarcation criterion), theories are testable if they make predictions which can be checked by independent experiments. However, even if theories possess the logico-epistemological property of being testable, they will cease to be testable (and hence scientific) if the *critical* method of dealing with theories is no longer applied to them (Nola 1987: 443; Popper 1959: 54). (However, a theory must be testable in the logical sense if Popper's methodological rules are to be applied to it.) As a methodological supplement to the logical definition of testability, the critical method requires that one specify in advance a potential observation or state of affairs which, if observed, would refute the theory. In this sense, scientific theories are not so much demarcated from pseudo-scientific theories, as scientific method is demarcated from non-scientific method (Lakatos 1978: 3).

To ensure testability, methodological rules are needed which prohibit the adoption of dogmatic ways of immunising theories against refutation. These *rules against immunising stratagems* tell us not to modify a theoretical system in order to avoid falsification if so doing reduces the testability of the system as a whole (e.g. by adding an *ad hoc* auxiliary hypothesis).[19] We are urged not to reject outright observations or experiments which conflict with our firmly held theories. That is to say, we are not to refuse to acknowledge falsifying observations or experiments (Popper 1959: 82–84).

In addition, a *no stopping rule* requires that scientists must keep testing their theories indefinitely and that they must never regard their theories as conclusively verified. Scientists must not lapse into dogmatism (Popper 1959: 53; Nola 1987: 453).

Empirical success

The next requirement for progress is empirical success, which means that a good theory should make at least some successful bold, new predictions and that it should resist refutation for a time. The successful new predictions a new theory must make are identical with the severe tests which it must withstand in order to be counted as superior to its competitors. In a purely logical sense, these predictions are highly improbable in the light of previous theories and hence they are easily refutable (Popper 1963: 247).[20]

The requirement of empirical success is translated into a methodological directive via Popper's *corroboration rules* for theories. These rules state that a theory which in fact survives severe attempts at refutation is to be accorded a positive degree of corroboration. (A theory which is falsified by an intersubjectively testable experiment is given a negative degree of corroboration.) It should be noted that a theory which is well corroborated by a severe test is not justified or established as true: indeed, it may be refuted at a later date by different tests or by repetitions of the same test which may or may not be more rigorous (Musgrave 1974b: 569). The degree of corroboration of a theory is backward-looking, and it does not involve any prediction about the theory's continued success in the future: it is merely an evaluative report of a theory's *past* performance, not an index of its future performance (Agassi 1959; Popper 1959: section 82; 1972: 17–21; Watkins 1968b: 63).

Popper denies the existence of formal algorithms for corroboration. Although he proposes formulae for defining the degree of corroboration (1959: appendix *ix), a major purpose of the formulae is to demonstrate that no algorithm of a probabilistic theory of induction can be adopted as an algorithm for corroboration. 'In fact, our choosing one of a set of competing theories, far from being an application of an algorism, is an act of preference; and any preference of a theory over another is in its turn a conjecture (of a higher order)' (Popper 1974: 995).

Because scientists are always operating with theories, they need to be able to make choices between theories. The aim of the formulae for corroboration is to show that the more *improbable* hypothesis is preferable, so that a probabilistic theory of preference cannot be employed in theory choices. However, scientists can rationally use the degrees of corroboration of competing theories to help them choose the hypothesis which warrants further development, application, critical examination and empirical testing. Such choices are risky and fallible. Consequently, the idea of degree of corroboration should *not* be interpreted as a *criterion* for the *acceptance* of scientific hypotheses (Musgrave 1974b: 584; Popper 1963: 218; 1972: 18–19).

The requirement of empirical success is radically different from the first requirement of testability. Finding out the extent to which a new theory meets the first requirement depends upon logical analysis, whereas determining the degree to which it fulfils the second requirement relies upon empirical tests of the new theory. A sequential screening procedure is implied: at the first stage, testability is applied as a criterion of *potential* satisfactoriness; at the second, empirical success is used as a criterion of *actual* satisfactoriness. The first requirement of testability is needed in order to screen the multitude of possible solutions – many of them trivial and *ad hoc* – to any particular problem. It is necessary for deciding *ex ante* whether the new theory is worth testing empirically: does it constitute a potential advance upon previous theories, regardless of the outcome of testing? Is it worth making experiments for this theory? The requirement of empirical success then investigates whether the theory can withstand new and severe tests, especially crucial ones: are its new and bold predictions corroborated by experimental evidence? (Popper 1963: 219–220, 242).

The growth of knowledge would cease if we were only able to generate theories that satisfied the first requirement but never the second. The testability requirement stipulates that a new theory must entail new predictions of new kinds of events. This is not sufficient to ensure the growth of knowledge, however. Theories must also fairly frequently be successful in some of their new predictions if scientific progress is to continue (Popper 1963: 243).

The independent testability of a theory (i.e. the first requirement) does not guarantee that the theory is not *ad hoc*. A highly unsatisfactory explanatory theory can always be produced which is totally *ad hoc* despite the fact that it makes independently testable predictions. It is always possible to make an *ad hoc* theory independently testable, if that theory is not also required to withstand the newly-formulated independent tests: the theory simply has to be connected conjunctively with any testable but as yet untested fanciful *ad hoc* prediction (e.g. 'All Bavarians eat black pudding'). The second requirement, like the first, is needed in order to further screen out uninteresting theories.

Furthermore, empirical corroboration of some theories is required in order to interpret the results of successful refutations:

> It seems to me quite clear that it is only through these temporary successes of our theories that we can be reasonably successful in attributing our refutations to definite portions of the theoretical maze. (For we *are* reasonably successful in this – a fact which must remain inexplicable for one who adopts Duhem's and Quine's views on the matter.)
>
> (Popper 1963: 243)

A never-ending sequence of refutations would make it impossible for us to identify tentatively the source of a falsification of our theoretical system (Popper 1963: 243–4; 1972: 193).

This discussion of the requirement of empirical success should also make it clear that Popper's theory of method is not an entirely negative methodology, as construed by some commentators. Scientists aim for the truth (or at least for theories which are a better approximation to the truth than existing ones), not for refutations. If scientists were only able to succeed in refuting their theories and were never able to corroborate some of them by severe and crucial tests, they might retire from the game of science in the belief that the structure of the world is too complex, and scientific problems too difficult, in relation to the limits of their rationality (Popper 1963: 245).

Successful refutations

As well as emphasising the importance of empirical successes to the growth and rationality of science, Popper also stresses that science would stagnate and would fail to keep its empirical and rational character if theories were never refuted. If over time a theory consistently resisted attempts to find a refutation, the epistemic returns from further empirical tests would diminish along with the severity of these tests. The empirical character of such a strikingly successful theory would thus become less and less. The theory might come to be regarded as just a set of conventions, until it is eventually refuted, thereby establishing its empirical character once more (Popper 1963: 240).

At this juncture, it is appropriate to emphasise that *sophisticated* falsificationism does not conflate the refutation of a theory with its rejection. The fact that a theory has been refuted does not mean that it is necessary to abandon the theory. False consequences are necessary for the rejection of a theory, but they are not sufficient. A theory possessing false consequences is *eliminated as a contender for the truth*, i.e. it is *refuted*, but it need not be abandoned. Even if we admit its falsity (i.e. accept that it is refuted), we may carry on with our attempts to make it better – as Einstein did with his theory of general relativity (Nola 1987: 454; Popper 1974: 1009). (By sometimes referring to refutation as 'elimination' or 'rejection', therefore, Popper only means that a theory is eliminated or rejected as a serious candidate for the truth.) If we cannot produce a satisfactory replacement for the refuted theory, then the refuted theory should continue to be used until a new and better theory is available. However, when operating with the refuted theory (e.g. in practical action and technology), we must not forget that there is something wrong with it and that it may therefore lead us badly astray in at least some circumstances (Magee 1971: 72).

It can be seen that the refutation of a theory is a logical affair, whereas rejection is a matter of methodology and depends, among other things, on what competing theories are currently available. Hence, refutation or falsification only involves a relation between the theory in question and the set of observations, whereas rejection involves a multiple relation between the particular theory, rival theories and the body of evidence. (Lakatos (1970, 1974) repeatedly misrepresents Popper's position in this connection.) It is accepted that in practice scientific theories can be displaced only by an alternative theory (or 'falsifying hypothesis') and not by experiments and observations in isolation:

In most cases we have, before falsifying a hypothesis, another

one up our sleeves; for the falsifying experiment is usually a *crucial experiment* designed to decide between the two.
(Popper 1959: 87; original emphasis)

The foregoing insights are embodied in Popper's *rules for the rejection of theories*: once a theory has been positively corroborated it should not be abandoned unless it is replaced by another theory which is better testable. Another formulation of this rule is that if a theory is contradicted by accepted empirical evidence, then the theory should be rejected only if the evidence corroborates a new and better theory at the same time.[21]

As to falsification, Popper is very well aware that empirical observation can never provide conclusive falsification of a theory any more than it can provide conclusive verification:

In point of fact, *no conclusive disproof of a theory can ever be produced*; for it is always possible to say that the experimental results are not reliable, or that the discrepancies which are asserted to exist between the experimental results and the theory are only apparent and that they will disappear with the advance of our understanding.
(Popper 1959: 50; emphasis added)

Perhaps on this subject more than any other, Popper's remarks have either been ignored or misunderstood to the extent that he is constantly misinterpreted as advocating dogmatic falsificationism, and particularly the doctrine that false theories can be conclusively disproved by hard facts. All this, in spite of the fact that he has often emphasised that any refutation is fallible and that identifying the source of a refutation is a conjectural exercise (Popper 1959: section 18; 1963: 112, 238–239; 1974: 1009–1010).

Although science is essentially critical and revolutionary, consisting of bold conjectures controlled by empirical testing, it is nevertheless upheld that the *critical* defence of theories can play a significant methodological role (Musgrave 1974b: 580–581). There is something akin to a type of infant industry argument in the context of budding new hypotheses:

The dogmatic attitude of sticking to a theory as long as possible is of considerable significance. Without it we could never find out what is in a theory – we should give the theory up before we had a real opportunity of finding out its strength; and in consequence no theory would ever be able to play its role of bringing order into the world, of preparing us for future events, of drawing our attention to events we should otherwise never observe.

(Popper 1963: 312)

Lakatos (1970) extends the Popperian analysis of the critical defence of hypotheses to form the central part of his methodology of scientific research programmes (see below).

2.3 SUBSEQUENT NON-JUSTIFICATIONIST PHILOSOPHIES

Popper's distinctive programme was the progenitor of the growth-of-knowledge tradition. However, even though the non-justificationist philosophies in this tradition may have originally been inspired by Popper's philosophy, or may at least share some important Popperian assumptions on the acquisition of new knowledge, these positions have in some cases been transformed to such an extent that they are flatly incompatible with Popper's philosophy of science (Freeman and Skolimowski 1974; Newton-Smith 1981). It is perhaps ironic that one of the unintended consequences of Popper's programme was to open the door to a trend in the philosophy of science which abandoned his conception of rationality.

Most prominent among such 'renegade' philosophies are the *Weltanschauungen* analyses of Feyerabend (1963, 1970, 1975a, 1978), Hanson (1958), Kuhn (1970c, 1977a, 1977b), Polanyi (1958, 1966) and Toulmin (1953, 1961). (With the exception of Polanyi, these philosophical opponents are either students of Popper or have at least acknowledged that they have been influenced by him (Popper 1974: 1068).) They all reject the dichotomy of the context of discovery and the context of justification and, in stark contrast to Popper, they regard genetical problems to be an essential concern of epistemology. What follows is intended to indicate the diversity of directions in which non-justificationist philosophies have evolved. It is not a detailed analysis.

Both Toulmin and Hanson revived topics which had previously been rejected as psychological and therefore outside the domain of the philosophical analysis of theories.[22] For instance, Hanson's analysis of 'retroductive reasoning' attempts to account for the logic by which theories are discovered. He claimed that theories are arrived at by 'retroductive inferences' from conceptually organised and hence theory-laden data rather than by inductive generalisations from hard facts.

Polanyi and Kuhn, subsequently joined by an ex-Popperian, Feyerabend, try to explain scientific change in terms of social psychology. Kuhn's 'blockbuster',[23] *The Structure of Scientific Revolutions*, has given the most significant impetus to work in the sociology of science. Kuhn maintains that in order to explain scientific development, it is necessary to go beyond the logic of discovery and to investigate the sociology and psychology of scientific communities:

> the explanation [of the growth-of-knowledge process] must, in the final analysis, be psychological or sociological. It must, that is, be a description of a value system, an ideology, together with an analysis of the institutions through which that system is transmitted and enforced.
>
> (Kuhn 1970a: 21)

In seeking to explain scientific progress and the behaviour of scientific groups, Kuhn examines the value systems which scientists use in making choices in the course of research and also the set of institutions which organise research.

A fundamental idea in Kuhn's original elaboration of his new image of science is the *paradigm*. In one of its most important senses, Kuhn's paradigm is a sociological concept (Masterman 1970: 65–68). A sociological paradigm is a set of institutions or mutually agreed conventions (whether verbal, behavioural, intellectual, technological, political, methodological and so on) which facilitates systematic problem-solving and the process of scientific discovery.[24] Sociological paradigms exist even at the early stages of an actual science; they are much wider than, and prior to, scientific theories (Kuhn 1970c: 11).

Following criticism of the multiplicity of meanings implicitly given to the term 'paradigm', Kuhn then restated his model of science in terms of the twin notions, *disciplinary matrixes* and *exemplars*.[25] The original notion of a paradigm, he admitted, conflated these two more recent concepts in spite of the fact that they are very different from each other (1970b: 271–272; 1970c: 175, 181–191; 1977b). A disciplinary matrix comprises all the shared commitments of a scientific group: 'the entire constellation of beliefs, values, techniques, and so on shared by the members of a given community' (Kuhn 1970c: 175). This more global concept corresponds to the sociological notion of a paradigm; it is a kind of scientific

Weltanschauung (or world view). A common disciplinary matrix binds together a scientific community which carries out *normal* science – a habit-governed, puzzle-solving activity within a definite theoretical framework.[26]

Exemplars, on the other hand, are the 'concrete puzzle-solutions which, employed as models or examples, can replace explicit rules as a basis for the solution of the remaining puzzles of normal science' (Kuhn 1970c: 175). Shared exemplars are an important sort of commitment, one element in the disciplinary matrix. Kuhn's socio-psychological conception of learning by exemplars is a development of Polanyi's (1958, 1966) tacit knowing.

In summary, the *Weltanschauungen* analyses focus on the psychological, sociological and historical factors which affect the emergence, acceptance and rejection of scientific world views. These analyses characterise scientific knowledge as a sociological phenomenon and science as a social enterprise which is more or less a subjective and non-rational process.[27] The approaches attack Popper's logical analysis of knowledge, and they emphasise (some would say, over-emphasise) the non-logical, 'external' aspects of theory-choice. In his masterly surveys, Suppe finds the *Weltanschauungen* analyses to be generally unsatisfactory, and in his *Afterword* he maintains that they are no longer serious candidates for a viable philosophy of science: 'The *Weltanschauungen* views, in a word, today are passé . . .' (Suppe 1977a: 634). In particular, he repudiates the sociological basis of knowledge inherent in such analyses, doubting very much whether a *Weltanschauung* can be the joint possession of members of a scientific community – as required specifically by Kuhn's analysis of scientific change:

> I conclude, then, that there is no reason to suppose that there is anything like a *Weltanschauungen* having the status of a single entity possessed by working scientists; and even if there were good reason to postulate such an entity, doing so would contribute little to our understanding of the scientific enterprise.
> (Suppe 1977b: 219)

Lakatos's (1970) methodology is an attempt to steer midway between the Scylla of justificationism and the Charybdis of *Weltanschauungen* analyses. He attempts to 'de-psychologise' Polanyi and Kuhn and to depict scientific revolutions as constituting rational growth in our objective knowledge of the real world (Lakatos 1970: 93). Lakatos revises and develops Popper's theory of science: his methodology can even be viewed as the product of a creative shift within Popper's philosophical research programme (see, for example, Worrall 1978: 65).[28] Indeed, Bartley (1976: 38) observed that Lakatos's concept of a scientific research programme is an idea 'that he took over completely developed from the accounts by Popper, Agassi, and Watkins of "metaphysical research programmemes"'. (On this point, see too Wartofsky 1976: 731.) A scientific research programme is an extension of Popper's insight that the growth of knowledge requires a set of conventions which imposes a framework for enquiry (Loasby 1989: 164). For this reason, Lakatos's methodology is sometimes referred to as *generalised conventionalism* or *conventional fallibilism* (as distinct from Popper's *critical fallibilism*).

Lakatos's methodology of scientific research programmes also provides a sophisticated falsificationist analysis of the critical defence of hypotheses, a subject largely neglected by Popper. In other words, Lakatos (1970: 179) provides a Popperian account of Kuhnian normal science, and his concept of a scientific research programme is accordingly a Popperian reformulation of Kuhn's sociopsychological concept of a paradigm. Unlike Kuhn, however, Lakatos (1970: 121–122) advocates theoretical pluralism. Following Popper and Feyerabend, Lakatos insists that the contemporaneous proliferation of competing research programmes is potentially more profitable in terms of gains in knowledge than is a succession of periods of normal science. He claims that 'what he [Kuhn] calls "normal science" is nothing but a research programmeme that has achieved monopoly' (Lakatos 1970: 155).

Whatever the similarities, however, we must not overlook some significant differences between Popper and Lakatos. In spite of being in the Popperian tradition, Lakatos's model of science is designed to obscure the Popperian demarcation between science and metaphysics. Consequently, a Popperian *metaphysical* research programme is irrefutable (i.e. non-testable) by virtue of its syntactical form, whereas the hard core of a Lakatosian *scientific* research programme is irrefutable because of the methodological decision of that programme's proponents and not necessarily because of any syntactical reasons (Lakatos 1970: 183–184). In addition, Popper sees metaphysics as an external influence, whereas for Lakatos (1971a: 103) it is a vital part of the rational reconstruction of science.

Furthermore, Lakatos takes Kuhn's challenge to (naive) falsificationism much more seriously than Popper. Following Kuhn, he emphasises that refutations are not important to the direction of the growth of knowledge. The heuristic power of scientific research programmes is expected to preserve the relative autonomy of theoretical science from the verdict of experiment.[29] Thus, in some sense Lakatos's methodology is actually *non*-empiricist because research programmes are argued to develop without any regard for empirical refutation (see Lakatos 1970: 121–123, 151–152, 175).

2.4 CONCLUSIONS

Popper's non-justificationist philosophy equates the rationality of science with its critical procedures and the ability to learn from mistakes. The scientific process is one which involves rationally evaluating new contributions to science without trying to justify them. A choice of theory is rational if the new theory can be more severely tested than its predecessors, and if it has also been corroborated by some of these new tests, so that it may therefore be a better approximation to the truth than its competitors. Such choices show that we have learnt from our mistakes and that we have added to our knowledge. Popper's programme also emphasises that the growth of knowledge – both its rational and empirical aspects – relies upon empirical successes as well as successful refutations. In the chapters which follow, I apply Popper's (and to a lesser extent, Lakatos's) conception of rationality to entrepreneurship. Among other things, I attempt to explain how entrepreneurs – in spite of being fallible – can make rational choices under uncertainty and how they can eliminate their own errors.

NOTES

1 An exposition of Popper's philosophy is made difficult because Popper's views evolved over time. Lakatos (1970: 181) even distinguishes between four Poppers: Popper$_0$, Popper$_1$, Popper$_2$ and Popper$_3$. The classic work is Popper (1959), which is further elaborated in Popper (1963, 1972, 1982, 1983b). For a convenient account of Popper's views on the growth of knowledge, see Popper (1963: chs 3, 10; 1972, chs 1, 5, 7).

For accessible and thorough critiques of Popper's philosophy of science, see Ackermann (1976), Bartley (1982), Burke (1983), Caldwell (1991), Magee (1973), Musgrave (1971a) and O'Hear (1980). Important collections of scholarly essays which explain, criticise and defend Popper's philosophy include Bunge (1964a), Levinson (1982) and Schlipp (1974). Miller (1983) contains a useful selection of readings. For an assessment of the significance of Popper's philosophy for economics, see Blaug (1980), Caldwell (1991) and de Marchi (1988c).

2 That is, a hypothesis h is scientific, given relevant evidence e, only if the probability of that hypothesis being true is equal to 1 or certainty: $P(h, e) = 1$. For a discussion of justificationism, see: Agassi (1971b); Bartley (1964, 1984); Boland (1982: 14, 177); Lakatos (1968a; 1970: 91–103, 123–124; 1971a; 1978: 193–201); Popper (1963: 3–30, 228ff.; 1972: 25–30, 35–37, 122, 127–128); Rutherford (1984: 377–378); Settle (1974: 702–713); Watkins (1978b: 23–27); and Weimer (1974a: 254–255; 1979: ix–xii, 8–38, 95–139).

3 For a more detailed comparison of classical intellectualism with classical empiricism, see: Bartley (1964: 12); Lakatos (1968a: 317–321; 1970: 93–94); Musgrave (1974b: 562); Popper (1963: 324ff.); and Weimer (1979: 102–103).

4 For an excellent survey of eight major classes of attempts to justify induction, see Salmon (1967) which is also summarised in Weimer (1979: 123ff.).

5 For a detailed examination of psychologism, see Nottorno and Wettersten (1989). See too Popper (1972: esp. chs 1, 2) and Agassi (1975).

6 That is, $P(h, e) = C$ (the degree of confirmation), where $0 < C < 1$, and $P(h, e) = C$ can be proved. On neojustificationism, see Lakatos (1968a: 321–330; 1970, 91–95; 1971a: 108).

7 For excellent critiques of these empiricist philosophies, see: Blaug (1980); Caldwell (1982); Lakatos (1968a); Popper (1959) and Suppe (1977b).

8 A statement of the probabilistic problem of induction can easily be obtained by reformulating Hume's logical problem of the justification of induction, which was discussed earlier: namely, are we justified in reasoning from repeated instances of which we have experience to the *probability* of instances (*probable* conclusions) of which we have no experience? (Popper 1972: 4). Hume demonstrated that, even when it was restated in probabilistic terms, the logical problem situation did not change.

9 Many contemporary philosophers of science reject instrumentalism (Caldwell 1980b, 1982). Suppe maintains that 'despite occasional flirtations with instrumentalism, science generally is concerned to obtain knowledge or truths about the real, physical, psychological, or social world. . . . In short, science overwhelmingly is committed to a metaphysical and epistemological realism . . .' (Suppe 1977a: 716).

For Popper's critique of instrumentalism, see Popper (1959: 59; 1963: ch.3, esp. 107–114, ch.6; 1983b: part I, sections 12–14). For a re-examination of previous critical assessments of instrumentalism (including Popper's), see Giedymin (1976). See too: Caldwell (1982: 51–53); and Suppe (1977b: 29–36, 167–170; 1977a: 716ff.).

10 Boland (1979a; 1982: 152) claims that Lakatos is mistaken since instrumentalism on its own terms does not suffer from the alleged logical errors. For a conventionalist critique of instrumentalism, see Caldwell (1980a). For an instrumentalist defence of instrumentalism against conventionalist critiques, see Boland (1979a; 1980; 1982: ch.9).

11 Justificationists had a very convenient way of rationalising scientific changes which resulted from previous errors: 'if one abandons a theory, then the very fact of the abandonment shows that the refuted theory was not really a result of scientific communion with truth, and that the psychotherapy [that must precede the start of cumulative scientific growth] had failed' (Lakatos 1978: 197). That is, the discoverer of the abandoned theory had led us astray because he or she was originally not in the right (scientific) state of mind for perceiving the truth, so that the theory was not proven in the first place. For further analysis of the justificationist conception of the growth of knowledge, see Lakatos (1968a: esp. 320–322; 1971a: 95; 1978: 193–197) and Weimer (1974b: 369; 1979: chs 2, 5).

12 Following his earlier contributions (now published as 1959 and 1979b), Popper (1963: 54) first claims that 'the problem of induction is only an instance or facet of the problem of demarcation' of science from non-science, and then he applies his demarcation criterion to solve the problem of induction. For a summary and restatement of Popper's claims to have developed a solution to the problem of induction, see Popper (1972: ch. 1; 1974: section 13). Like most solutions, Popper's involves a reformulation of the problem: 'Popper has not so much solved the problem of induction . . . as dissolved it' (Blaug 1980: 15). Lakatos (1974) is a criticism (from within the Popperian research programme) of Popper's position on induction. In particular, Lakatos claims that the problem of induction is definitely more than merely a facet of the problem of demarcation. He also argues that Popper has not drawn out the full implications of his own achievement. For Popper's rather condemning reply to Lakatos, see Popper (1974: sections 12, 13).

13 Amsterdamski (1975: ch.3) examines the question of whether Popper is justified in restricting the philosophy of science to the context of justification, and he spells out the essential difficulties which arise from Popper's delimitation.

14 On Popper's theory of objective knowledge, see Popper (1972: esp. chs 3, 4) and Popper and Eccles (1977: ch. P2). See Bloor (1974) and Musgrave (1974b) for contrasting critiques of this objective epistemology.

15 The best account of Popper's evolutionary epistemology is contained in Popper (1972: esp. ch. 7, and chs 2–6). See too Popper (1959: 108, 131, 276–281; 1960: 133; 1974: 1059–1065, 1083). Ackermann (1976: 4) regards Popper's evolutionary conception of the growth of knowledge to be perhaps his outstanding contribution to the philosophy of science. For a detailed analysis of Popper's evolutionary theory of knowledge, see Campbell (1974).

16 For more Popperian insights into the genesis of knowledge and creativity, see: Popper (1959: 31–33; 1960: section 28, 121ff.; 1963: 222, chs 1, 16; 1972: 258–259, 263; 1974: 1031–1037, 1061–1062; 1976c, 46–47; 1983b: 191); and Koertge (1975; 1978: 277); and Medawar (1967).

17 Simplicity is actually the first requirement that Popper (1963: ch. 10)

says a new theory must meet if it is to qualify as an advancement upon its predecessors. But since he equates (though somewhat controversially) simplicity with testability (Popper 1959: ch. 7), I can omit his discussion of simplicity without any loss of content. Furthermore, I discuss Popper's theory of scientific method without recourse to his notion of the verisimilitude of theories.

I do not suggest that the explicit introduction of the idea of verisimilitude will lead to any changes in the theory of method. On the contrary, I think that my theory of testability or corroboration by empirical tests is the proper methodological counterpart to this new metalogical idea.

(Popper 1963: 235)

For Popper's theory of verisimilitude, see: Popper (1963: ch. 10, esp. 228–237, Appendices 3, 4, 6, 7; 1972: 47–60). For his reply to critical objections advanced against his analysis of verisimilitude, see Popper (1974: 1100–1103, 1192; 1979a: section 5).
18 For his original discussion of testability, see Popper (1959: ch. 6). On the idea of independent tests, see Popper (1972: ch. 5, the appendix). For a definition of a measure of the severity of tests, see Popper (1959: appendix *ix; 1963: appendix 2).
19 On immunising stratagems in general, see: Popper (1959: 82–83; 1972: 15–16, 30; 1976c: 42–44); and Albert (1967: 149, 227, 309, 341). Popper's *no ad-hoc hypotheses rule* has been criticised vigorously by Grünbaum (1976) as a logical impossibility.
20 Agassi (1961: 90) finds the requirement of empirical success unacceptable because he considers it to be a remnant of verificationism. Popper (1963: 248) replies that he would prefer a hint of verificationism to 'a whiff of some form of instrumentalism', which would be the result of not including the requirement of empirical success.
21 See, for example: Johansson (1975: 19–20); Nola (1987: 453–454) and Popper (1959: 53–54, 86–87; 1974: 1035; 1983a: xxiv).
22 Inspiration for the philosophies of Toulmin and Hanson can be traced to the later work of Wittgenstein (1953) on language and philosophical psychology (Suppe 1977b: 126; Wartofsky 1976: 729). Wittgenstein's investigations into language learning and language games had in turn been influenced by Bühler, a cognitive and developmental psychologist, who was also a teacher of Popper. It must also be noted that although Toulmin's earlier work embraced a moderate version of *Weltanschauungen* analysis, his later work (1972) withdrew from this approach.
23 The term is Wartofsky's (1976: 729).
24 Popper also emphasises that conventions have an essential role to play in scientific method and in scientific development (1959: 13, 37, 104; 1963: 27, 122; 1970: 56).
25 Masterman (1970) and Shapere (1964) in particular have attacked the extreme breadth and ambiguity of the paradigm concept in Kuhn's earlier work. Masterman (1970: 61–65) counts at least twenty-one different usages of the term 'paradigm', many of which are incompatible with each other. Masterman suggests that the term 'paradigm' be

restricted to three main uses: metaphysical, sociological, and artefact or construct. For devastating criticisms of Kuhn's subsequent notions of disciplinary matrixes and exemplars, see Shapere (1971).

26 From a *methodological* point of view, Popperians have been rightly critical of Kuhn's idea of normal science. Watkins (1970: 27) refers to it pejoratively as 'hack science'. Equally scathing, Popper remarks that:

> in my view the 'normal' scientist, as Kuhn describes him, is a person one ought to be sorry for. ... The 'normal' scientist ... has been badly taught. He has been taught in a dogmatic spirit: he is a victim of indoctrination ... I believe, however, that Kuhn is mistaken when he suggests that what he calls 'normal' science is 'normal'.
>
> Popper (1970: 53)

27 For detailed critiques of the *Weltanschauungen* analyses, see Suppe (1977b: 191–219) and Scheffler (1967). On the specific issue of subjectivity and irrationality, see: Lakatos (1970); Popper (1970); Scheffler (1967: 18–19, 74–89); Shapere (1964; 1966; 1971); Suppe (1977a: 705) and Toulmin (1970).

For Kuhn's defence against the charge of subjectivity and irrationality, see Kuhn (1970a; 1970b: sections 5–6; 1970c: 191–204). Kuhn claims that he does not exclude logic from theory-choice; nor does he deny that scientists employ logic in their arguments. He accepts that there may be *good reasons* for theory-choice (1970b: 234, 261–262). Kuhn's thesis is that logic is not compelling: scientists must often resort to persuasion in matters of theory-choice.

28 However, there is no universal agreement that Lakatos's model of science keeps within the Popperian camp. For instance, Koertge (1978: 269ff.) in fact regards Lakatos's methodology as an inversion of Popper's programme. Moreover, Bloor reaches other dubious conclusions:

> We are ostensibly given a creative development of the Popperian research programme, plus an attack on the Kuhnian approach for its irrationality. What we are in fact presented with is a massive act of revisionism, amounting to a betrayal of the essentials of the Popperian approach, and a wholesale absorption of some of the most characteristic Kuhnian positions.
>
> (Bloor 1971: 104)

For a similar characterisation of Lakatos's work, see Weimer (1974a: 240).

29 Lakatos (1970: 155) defines heuristic power as the 'power of a research programme to anticipate theoretically novel facts in its growth'. It also refers to the capacity of a research programme to predict and to assimilate its empirical refutations in the course of its growth (Lakatos 1970: 135–137). However, Musgrave (1976: 467–473; 1978: 188–190) argues that no matter how powerful it is, a positive heuristic cannot predict refutations of any specific variant of a research programme, a view which Worrall (1978: 69) and Urbach (1978: 110) later came to share. See too Radnitzky and Andersson (1978a: 6–7).

3

THE DIMENSIONS OF
THE ENTREPRENEUR'S
PROBLEM SITUATION

In this chapter I attempt to identify and to describe the major dimensions of the entrepreneur's problem situation. By means of these dimensions I distinguish entrepreneurship from neoclassical economising. The stage is then set to discuss in more detail the *structural uncertainty* characterising the entrepreneur's environment and the fact that problem-solving is a process that takes place in *real time*.

3.1 THE DEFINITION OF
ENTREPRENEURSHIP AS PART
OF A CONTINUUM OF HUMAN ACTION

A number of authors have suggested that entrepreneurship is part of a continuum of human action, at one end of which is the act of innovation and at the other the purely routine. Schumpeter purposefully chooses to define entrepreneurship in a way which does not draw a sharp line between entrepreneurial and non-entrepreneurial activities:

> For actual life knows no such divisions, though it shows up the type well enough. It should be observed at once that the 'new thing' need not be spectacular or of historic importance. ... To see the phenomena [sic] even in its humblest levels in the business world is quite essential.
>
> (Schumpeter 1947: 151)[1]

Similarly, in his examination of entrepreneurship, Ronen concludes that:

> What is suggested ... is a *continuum* of entrepreneurship. The managerial, least entrepreneurial, individuals operate within

the well-defined and prescribed domain of business activity: existing products, existing markets, existing processes. At the other extreme lies the constant and dynamic innovator, who incessantly seeks new endeavours that involve research and development, market testing, and other uncertainty-reducing activities.

(Ronen 1983b: 148; original emphasis)

The main idea underlying these remarks, therefore, is that of a spectrum ranging from mechanical and routine reactions at one pole, to imaginative entrepreneurial activity at the other. In line with these suggestions, I portray entrepreneurship as the creative and critical segment of the continuum of human action or as the apex of the hierarchy of human cognitive processes. The continuum of human action is defined by several dimensions that characterise the problem situations facing economic actors within economic theories: namely, the nature of uncertainty and of time, the degree of novelty and of complexity, and the extent of indeterminacy (see Table 3.1).

These dimensions can be used as a framework for defining entrepreneurship. Entrepreneurship is defined as a real-time problem-solving activity which involves the exercise of imagination and critical faculties in the context of structurally uncertain and complex problem situations that are conjectured to present profit opportunities. Entrepreneurship can be distinguished from other categories of human action, and it is useful to discuss each class before investigating in detail the dimensions of the entrepreneur's problem situation.

As we move from the left pole of the continuum to the right, we are progressively widening the system boundaries employed by the economic agent for making a decision. We are relaxing the assumptions of what are taken as given in the agent's problem situation, so that we (as economic theorists) are progressively increasing the scope of choice for the decision-maker. Three broad categories of human action can be identified: neoclassical constrained maximisation (or Robbinsian economising), satisficing and entrepreneurial choice. Robbinsian economising involves the economic agent facing a perfectly specified problem; satisficing depicts the agent as facing a well-structured problem; and entrepreneurial choice entails the identification and formulation of ill-structured problems by the agent. However, it should be appreciated that the boundary between categories is not always well-defined. Rather the divisions of the continuum merge into one another to some extent.

Table 3.1 Dimensions of the continuum of human action

No structural uncertainty (parametric uncertainty)	*Un*bounded structural uncertainty
Perfect or probable knowledge (justificationism)	Total ignorance (scepticism)
Newtonian time	Real time
No novelty/zero surprise	Absolute maximum surprise
Simplicity	Extreme complexity
Perfectly determinate	Pure chance
Equilibrium (no change in the underlying data)	Inherent disequilibrium (extreme volatility in 'the news')
Closed system	Open system
Unequivocalness	High ambiguity
Objects of choice are objective	Complete subjectivity

↑ MECHANICAL *Neoclassical economising*	↑ HEURISTIC *Satisficing*	↑ CREATIVE *Entrepreneurial problem-solving*
Solution dictated by the problem	Solving given problems by heuristic procedures	Conceiving new problems (new ends-means frameworks)
Perfectly specified problem situation	Well-specified problems	Ill-specified problems
Reflexes	Not snap-decisions	Process of deliberation
Parametric uncertainty	Parametric uncertainty	Structural uncertainty
Perfect or probable knowledge	Reliable knowledge	Fallible knowledge
Static conception of knowledge	Knowledge largely static	Dynamic conception of knowledge
Newtonian time	Newtonian time	Real time
No novelty	Limited novelty	Novelty
Subjective utility	Subjective utility	Subjective utility
Subjective interpretation	Subjective interpretation	Subjective interpretation Subjective expectation
Determinate	Determinate	Indeterminate
No urgency: very long-run	Moderate urgency implied	Urgency
Substantive rationality	Procedural rationality	Non-justificationist rationality
Inductive learning method	Inductive learning method (Simon's approach)	Non-inductive learning method
Perfectly reliable learning method (supposedly)	Learning method fallible	All learning methods fallible
Learning process exogenously given (Robbins, Walras, Arrow–Debreu)	Learning process exogenously given (Simon)	Learning process becomes endogenous (Shackle, Schumpeter, Penrose)
Neoclassical research programme	**Behavioural research programme**	**Austrian research programme. Growth-of-knowledge (GK) programme**

3.1.1 Neoclassical economising

Within the hard core of the neoclassical (or more precisely, neo-Walrasian) research programme is the assumption that economic agents possess true and perfect knowledge of the relevant features of their problem situations – that is, they do not encounter structural uncertainty (Latsis 1972, 1976a, 1976c; Weintraub 1979).[2] This hard core assumption means that the problem situation is automatically known by or given to the agent, so that the problem does not even need to be discovered, structured or defined by the agent. The ends between which the agent can select and the criteria of selection are given, and the means to achieve each end are also known. 'Choice in such a theory is empty' (Shackle 1969: 273). Economic agents are limited to economising in the allocation of given means to achieve a set of given ends.

Furthermore, in keeping with the positive heuristic (the normative part of the hard core) of the neoclassical research programme, the problem situations that neoclassical maximisers face are set up by the economic theorist as 'single-exit' situations: problem situations where the optimal solution is determined uniquely by objective situational characteristics (costs, prices, consumer preferences, technology) (Kirzner 1973: 35–38, 46); Latsis 1972: 211; 1976c: 16–17). The solution is implicit in the definition of the problem. 'Any other decision would have been unthinkable' (Kirzner 1982c: 143). In such cases, genuine problem-solving is not involved – only highly constrained and passive reactions. 'Problem-solving' within neoclassical economic theory is thus a strict determinate process.

Neoclassical maximisers do not face genuine problems, because the situations that they encounter exclude all elements of surprise and novelty. Even in game theory, a decision is specified for every imaginable situation: genuine surprises in the course of the game are excluded (Littlechild 1979a; Rapoport 1968; Shackle 1972). Economic actors in neoclassical theory do not face problems in deciding what to do (i.e. the choice of ends) and how to do it (i.e. the choice of means) (Knight 1964: 267). They are able to react to their situations instantaneously, and their responses are in general immune from the hazards of error:

> If a stimulus situation arises, to which the organism reacts without hesitation, because it is fully prepared, *there is no problem.*
>
> (Guilford 1967: 435; emphasis added)

The rationality postulate (in the narrow sense of consistency of the agent's behaviour with the relevant given ranking of ends) is sufficient to explain pure economising activity (Kirzner 1982c: 143). Neither entrepreneurial alertness nor imagination is required.

Modern neoclassical models typically treat (parametric) uncertainty by introducing known probability distributions of possible future events.[3] Such distributions merely substitute the traditional assumption of perfect knowledge with a more sophisticated version of the same assumption (Baird 1987: 191). Rational expectations models, in particular, generally assume that economic agents predict future economic outcomes using a model of the economy which is known *a priori* to be true (Boland and Newman 1979: 76).

Even though modern versions of neoclassical economics (such as rational expectations models) do not assume perfect knowledge, there is still the presumption that every economic agent is guided by a perfect method of learning, albeit a slow method (Boland 1986b: 120–121). The neoclassical tradition presumes that inductive learning by economic actors is the one and only method of learning, and that it is perfectly reliable. '[I]nductive learning is considered to be an objectively "rational process" that is so reliable that any rational individuals who collect the same information will reach the same conclusion. Learning in the usual neoclassical analysis is a universal process that is exogenously given and thus unexplained' (Boland 1986b: 157).

Thus, the assumption of inductive learning in the context of limited or imperfect information still gives rise to the kind of situational determinism described above: 'By viewing all individuals as inductive learners, theorists have been able to rely on observations of the individual's objective situation to ensure unique and consistent choices' (Boland 1986b: 89).

3.1.2 Satisficing

The next category of human action is satisficing, which involves the agent being presented with well-structured problems that can be solved routinely with the help of algorithms or heuristic procedures. (Algorithms are methods guaranteed to provide a solution to a problem, whereas heuristics are 'rules of thumb' that tend to lead to, but do not guarantee, a successful solution.) Subjectivity is limited to the agent's perceptions of the problem presented. Satisficing implies 'procedural' rationality rather than the 'substantive' rationality of neoclassical economics (Simon 1976). The agent is armed with a battery of decision rules, information-gathering rules and learning procedures. The set of tentative solutions is given and objective; they can be learnt, determined and discovered by heuristic strategies which take into account the bounded rationality of the agent. Problem-solving thus becomes a somewhat mechanical operation taking place in a closed system which excludes real time. Solutions are ultimately determined by situational variables, because the environment determines which alternatives are taken into consideration and which of the heuristic strategies stored in the agent's memory will be activated (March and Simon 1958: 139; Newell *et al.* 1958: 163).

3.1.3 Entrepreneurial problem-solving

Further to the right of the continuum (but stopping just short of the right-hand pole) is the highest form of human activity and rationality in the economic sphere: entrepreneurial problem-solving. Entrepreneurial decision-making involves the discovery of a new market problem (and a potential profit opportunity), the generation of possible solutions (e.g. new product ideas), the selection of one or more preferred solutions, the trial implementation of chosen solutions, and the critical evaluation of these attempts at solving the problem. Entrepreneurial decision-making thus entails the germination of novelty in the pursuit of economic gain. The details of the problem, the elements of the choice set, and the criteria for selection are formulated by the entrepreneur:

> Economic choice does not consist in comparing the items in a list, known to be complete, of given fully specified rival and certainly attainable results. It consists in first creating, by *conjecture and reasoned imagination* on the basis of mere suggestions offered by visible or recorded circumstance, the things on which hope can be fixed.
>
> (Shackle 1972: 96; emphasis added)

The problem situation is not closed, fixed or given to the entrepreneur. A problem must first be identified, structured and defined by the entrepreneur (in this sense it is *created* or constructed by the entrepreneur), and the entrepreneur can change the problem situation that he or she faces at any time.

According to the growth-of-knowledge (GK) theory of entrepreneurship, entrepreneurs encounter 'multiple-exit' situations: that is, their choices of a course of action are not tightly delimited by objective situational conditions (Latsis 1976c: 16). Accordingly, entrepreneurial decisions are neither reflexes nor snap-decisions: rather they are reached by a process of deliberation involving trial and error (cf. Popper 1972: 228, 233–234). Consequently, a deterministic theory of entrepreneurial action is ruled out. However, the products of entrepreneurial imagination are partly *evoked* (though by no means are they strictly determined) by situational variables, especially objective problem situations and entrepreneurs' previous experiences. In addition, entrepreneurs' solutions to problems are *plastically controlled* by their aims and methodologies (i.e. their systems of evaluation) (cf. Popper 1972: ch. 6).[4]

Furthermore, there are always external conditions – physical, social, cultural, economic and so on – which impose limits on what individual entrepreneurs can achieve (though they are free to try their best at surpassing such limitations).

Thus, the domain of entrepreneurial action falls within the two polar extremes of perfect determinism and total disorder (or pure randomness), combining as it does both the elements of creative freedom and selective control with feedback. This accords with Popper's characterisation of rational decision-making: 'what we need for understanding rational human behaviour . . . is something *intermediate* in character between perfect chance and perfect determinism' (1972: 228; original emphasis). With reference to Table 3.1, therefore, it should be noted that entrepreneurial choice is located just to the west of the right pole of the continuum. This is because entrepreneurial imagination must operate within bounds. Entrepreneurial decision-making would be powerless in an extreme environment characterised by unbounded structural uncertainty, total ignorance, complete randomness and unpredictability, and an absolute maximum degree of novelty. In reality, of course, entrepreneurs are not entirely without knowledge; their decisions are not made in the face of complete ignorance. And they do have some degree of control in shaping market events.

The most important dimensions of the entrepreneur's problem situation are structural uncertainty and real time (see sections 3.2.1 and 3.2.2). The implications of this characterisation are that the entrepreneur's knowledge is always fragile and that it is often false. Because entrepreneurs may base their actions on false knowledge, they are liable to make mistakes, both singly and collectively. Furthermore, entrepreneurs can never know that they have found the truth (even if they have found the truth or even if they are making profits). There is no method of verification by which entrepreneurs can attain justified, proven true knowledge of their problem situations. All the methods by which entrepreneurs can make decisions and acquire knowledge are themselves fallible.

In comparison with other categories of human action, entrepreneurial choice implies the highest degree of proactiveness in problem-solving on the part of the decision-maker. Neither calculative reason nor alertness is by itself (or in conjunction with the other) sufficient to account for entrepreneurial activity. Entrepreneurial *critical imagination* is also required: the entrepreneur must employ active, spontaneous, intuitive and prelogical cognitive processes in the discovery and formulation of new problems (i.e. new ends–means frameworks) and in the generation of solution concepts (i.e. conjectures); and the entrepreneur must then apply a second-order critical method (or learning methodology) to these first-order conjectures in order to carry out ongoing tests of their adequacy and to choose between them. The resultant replacement of old hypotheses by new and better ones is what constitutes entrepreneurial learning. Through its dependence on a particular critical method, the entrepreneur's process of acquiring knowledge thus becomes endogenous, and the conception of the entrepreneur's knowledge also becomes dynamic (cf. Boland 1978: 250; 1982: 185).

The GK approach treats the entrepreneur's learning methodology as a choice variable, rather than as a natural or psychological datum. Moreover, there is no reason to suppose *a priori* that all entrepreneurs will employ the same methodology. Unlike neoclassical economics, the GK theory therefore does away with any presumption that all economic actors possessing the same knowledge will make the same decision. The interpretation of experience is acknowledged to be a very individualistic exercise. As a consequence, two entrepreneurs who differ only with respect to their learning methodologies may well respond in diverse ways to the simultaneous discovery of market intelligence that contradicts their shared assumptions (cf. Boland 1978: 255; 1982: 183–185).

It should be noted that different types of entrepreneurial activity also extend over a continuum, ranging from the less creative, such as arbitrage, to the more imaginative, such as innovation (with speculative activity emerging somewhere in between). Arbitrage involves the discovery and exploitation of interlocal price differences in a pre-existent market for a single good within a single period. It is a relatively non-complex problem-solving activity which entails limited forms of reallocation. Pure arbitrage excludes real time and structural uncertainty. It is limited to situations of pure exchange in which the exploitation of present profit opportunities is instantaneous and does not require time-consuming investment in capital and productive processes. In contrast, innovation is an economic process taking place in real time. Indeed, the time-span can be significant, typically requiring the investment of capital for at least a few years. Innovative entrepreneurs seek to make profits from intertemporal revenue–cost differences which are to be brought about by their own actions. However, the innovative entrepreneur recognises that perceived opportunities are at best only *possible* profit opportunities. In a world of structural uncertainty and real time, there is no assurance that an opportunity does exist or that it will last long enough for the entrepreneur to be able to secure its successful exploitation.

This discussion of various types of entrepreneurial activity suggests that different theories of entrepreneurship can also be classified along a continuum according to their treatment of the dimensions of the entrepreneur's problem situation (see Table 3.2). Kirzner's theory of entrepreneurship is essentially an arbitrage theory (indeed, Kirzner rarely, if ever, distinguishes between arbitrage and entrepreneurship): the entrepreneur is an arbitrageur who discovers imperfect coordination between transactions in different parts of the market. Thus, at least in its original formulation, Kirzner's approach spatialises the function of entrepreneurship and squeezes out real time and uncertainty. Casson's analysis of the entrepreneur as one who specialises in taking judgmental decisions about the allocation of scarce resources is largely neoclassical: he integrates an Austrian view of entrepreneurship into what is fundamentally neoclassical microeconomic theory (Vaughn 1983: 991).[5]

Both Casson's and Kirzner's theories are concerned with *adaptive* responses to exogenous changes in the data. In contrast, Shackle's radical subjectivist approach depicts entrepreneurship as injecting essential novelty into the sequence of market events. Entrepreneurial decisions are creative acts of origination which are totally unpredictable (see Littlechild 1979a). For Shackle, the future is truly indeterminate: decisions are 'inspired from without the bounds of pre-existing thoughts and experiences' (1958: 104).

Table 3.2 The characterisation of the entrepreneur's problem situation in alternative theories of entrepreneurship

Dimensions of the entrepreneur's problem situation	Alternative theories of entrepreneurship (narrow < —— relative range of action open to entrepreneurs ——> wide)		
	Kirzner's and Casson's theories	*Growth-of-knowledge (GK) theory*	*Shackle's theory*
Uncertainty	Kirzner 1973, 1979b: no uncertainty at all; 1982c: introduces uncertainty but leaves function of entrepreneurship unchanged. Casson 1982: parametric uncertainty.	Structural uncertainty.	Structural uncertainty.
Time	Real time excluded (but Kirzner 1982c introduces time).	Real time.	Subjectivist conception of time.
	Instantaneous exploitation of perceived profit opportunities. *Ex post* view of entrepreneurship.	Non-instantaneous exploitation of opportunities, long lags possible. *Ex ante* and *ex post* view.	Non-instantaneous exploitation of imagined opportunities. *Ex ante* view of choice.
Conception of entrepreneurial knowledge	Subjective 'hunches' and 'syntheses', private, inexpressible, non-deployable, spontaneously discovered, non-conjectural.	Potentially objective 'conjectures', can be exposed to interpersonal criticism, both spontaneously and deliberately acquired, theoretical.	Purely subjective 'thoughts' and 'figments', private, inexpressible.
	Static; exogenous acquisition process.	Dynamic; endogenous.	Dynamic.
Entrepreneur's learning methodology and learning process	Implicit: justificationism.	Explicit: non-justificationism.	Implicit: justificationist scepticism.
	Psychological, exogenous.	Cognitive-logical, endogenous.	Psychological, exogenous.

Entrepreneurial fallibility (possibility of errors)	Entrepreneurs tend to be successful (by definition).	Entrepreneurs make mistakes and their conjectures are often false.	Recognition of errors is very problematic (1958: 18–19).
Entrepreneurial problems and opportunities	Objective existence, often unnoticed. Produced by exogenous changes in the data (tastes, resources, technology). Inevitably destined to be perceived and exploited.	Objective existence. Produced both endogenously by the (often unintended) results of human action and by exogenous changes. May never be discovered, exploited or solved.	Purely subjective status. Produced endogenously by the active exercise of entrepreneurial imagination. Their origination is not preordained in any way.
Determinism	Relaxed form of determinism.	Plastic control: intermediate between determinism and pure chance.	Indeterminism: choice is essentially uncaused and wholly undetermined by external market conditions.
Entrepreneurial qualities emphasised	Alertness, judgment, timing.	Imagination, a consciously critical attitude towards his/her own ideas, experience of target market.	Imagination, originality.

The GK theory has several points of contact with Shackle's approach (see Table 3.2). Like Shackle, the GK theory portrays entrepreneurial decision as a choice between alternative mental constructs or conjectures, that is, entrepreneurial imagination is required to assemble the elements between which choice is to be made. Thus, in both theories, the objects of choice are individualistic images or hypotheses about the future. Furthermore, both approaches emphasise the structural uncertainty which characterises the entrepreneur's decision-making environment, and both are extremely sceptical about the strictly equilibrating effects which Kirzner and Casson attribute to entrepreneurial activity.

However, there is an important respect in which the GK theory diverges from Shackle's approach and aligns itself more closely with Kirzner's and Casson's theories: namely, it rejects the radical subjectivist notion that the only existence that market problems, opportunities and constraints can have is simply what people think of them. Like the theories of Kirzner and Casson, the GK theory argues that new market problems and opportunities have an objective existence independent of their discoverer: they exist in the world outside the mind and are not just the figment of the entrepreneur's imagination. (Though only in the case of the GK theory is it expressly admitted that the entrepreneur's assumptions may not necessarily correspond with the facts of market reality.) Although these three approaches argue that entrepreneurial activity is related to external market conditions (i.e. objective reality), in no sense do they imply that entrepreneurs respond deterministically or frictionlessly to given market circumstances. The GK theory, however, does not share Casson's and Kirzner's optimism that opportunities will be discovered and exploited sooner or later; it predicts that some market problems may never be discovered or solved.

If the theories of Schultz and Knight had been presented in Table 3.2, they would be to the left of Kirzner's and Casson's theories, nearer the neoclassical end of the spectrum of human action. Schumpeter's theory, with its emphasis on the role of the entrepreneur as a source of creative change, would be somewhere to the right, in the vicinity of the GK and Shacklean approaches.

Thus, the continuum is useful for describing the range of human decision-making, for defining entrepreneurship, for specifying the minimum requirements of a theory of the entrepreneur (in terms of how the entrepreneur's decision environment must be characterised), and for categorising and comparing rival economic theories of entrepreneurship. The GK treatment of the entrepreneur's problem situation will now be developed further.

3.2 THE MAJOR DIMENSIONS OF THE ENTREPRENEUR'S PROBLEM SITUATION

In this section, the major dimensions of the entrepreneur's problem situation – structural uncertainty and real time – are examined in some detail. It should be recognised that the dimensions for characterising the entrepreneur's problem situation are interconnected. Real time, structural uncertainty and novelty are correlative concepts, since each of these phenomena simultaneously implies the emergence of the others (cf. Blaseio 1986: 137, 183; Shackle 1958: 93). They are complementary ways of conceptualising crucial aspects of the entrepreneur's decision environment. It should also be noted that complexity is not discussed separately in this section because extensive treatments of it already exist in the economics literature (see, for example, Hayek 1967: 22–42; 1978: 23–34; and Simon 1957b, 1962a, 1969, 1972, 1982). In any case, the implications of complexity are similar to those of structural uncertainty when the complexity of the problem situation exceeds the cognitive boundaries of the decision-maker.

3.2.1 Uncertainty

The entrepreneur as used by catallactic theory means: acting man exclusively seen from the aspect of uncertainty inherent in every action. In using this term one must never forget that every action is embedded in the flux of time and therefore involves a speculation. . . . There's many a slip 'twixt cup and lip.

(Mises 1949: 254)

Uncertainty is germane to the entrepreneurial function. Mises, for instance, as the above quote suggests, even defines the entrepreneur in terms of uncertainty. The following discussion of uncertainty adopts Langlois's (1984a: 27–30) useful distinction between parametric and structural uncertainty. Structural uncertainty is the most important dimension for characterising the entrepreneur's problem situation. However, a better appreciation of structural uncertainty is derived by first distinguishing it from the very restricted and narrowly construed concept of parametric uncertainty.

Parametric uncertainty

In a world of parametric uncertainty, decision-makers do not know the outcome of every available action. But they do have a full listing of all possible courses of action, together with an exhaustive listing of the set of all possible outcomes. They also know the chance of each outcome occurring.[6] More formally, in conditions of parametric uncertainty, economic agents look upon the future as being in one or another of a range of states of the world. Each decision-maker possesses a complete listing of the set of all possible states of the world relevant to each choice and a probability distribution which is fully defined over these states. The decision-maker is unsure about which of the given states of the world will arise in the future, but not about which future states of the world are possible.

Parametric uncertainty is the conception of uncertainty which is depicted as facing economic agents in neoclassical economic theory. The decision-maker is able to use the probability distribution of outcomes to calculate the expected value (i.e. the probability weighted-average) of each choice and, in combination with his or her known objective function (utility), the decision-maker is able to optimise *as if* in a world of perfect certainty (i.e. the decision-maker is able to maximise the expected utility of his or her actions) (Langlois 1984a: 28; 1984b: 3; Loasby 1976: 7).

It can be seen that the major characteristic of parametric uncertainty is that the structure of the future is known to the decision-maker in advance:

> 'Tomorrow' can be characterised as a vector of random variables, where the range the variables can take is known today and, more important, so is the set of variables itself. ... [The agent] is unsure what the price of honey will be tomorrow, but he knows that honey will be traded. Conversely, he never finds honey in shops if he had not previously expected it to be there.
>
> (Littlechild 1986: 28)

In such an environment, decision-makers have certain knowledge of the structure of the problem that they are facing. They have *perfect structural knowledge* – perfect knowledge of the adequacy of means to ends. Such knowledge is regarded as justified or proven true. As a consequence, economic agents are able to exactly and exhaustively describe their environment in probabilistic terms. Each agent perceives the world as generating 'all the necessary (and quite *unambiguous*) frequency distributions from *a stable population of events*' (Loasby 1976: 8; emphasis added). Thus, the paradox is that parametric uncertainty implies certain or epistemic structural knowledge more than it does conjectural knowledge or genuine uncertainty:

> A cosmos in which outcomes have calculable probabilities which men seek to discover and upon which they act is *a cosmos where in effect certainty and not uncertainty prevails*; where the outcomes of any available act can be listed and where the list can be known to be complete; and where therefore there is no room for decision which is both non-arbitrary and non-predictable.
>
> (Shackle 1969: 10; emphasis added)

However, this assertion must be qualified by noting that the agent may have only imperfect knowledge of the specific parameters of the problem, that is, *imperfect parametric knowledge* (Langlois 1984a: 29). The upshot is that learning in a parametrically uncertain world is restricted to updating beliefs about the values of coefficients in a correctly specified model – that is, improving parameter estimates. The agent never acquires new structural knowledge. Littlechild has captured the situation vividly:

> The agents are equipped with forecasting functions and decision functions to enable them to cope with uncertainty. Indeed, the agents *are* these functions. But though their specific forecasts and decisions may change over time in response to changes in economic conditions, *the functions themselves remain the same*. Nothing will ever occur for which they are not prepared, nor can they ever initiate anything which is not pre-ordained. They are clockwork Bayesians, wound up with prior distributions and sent on their way, to attain eventually, if circumstances permit, that everlasting peace in which they never need to move their posteriors.
>
> (Littlechild 1977: 7–8)

Structural uncertainty

For at that point of time when the decision is taken to commit some resources to a particular line of production, it is the nature of things impossible for anyone to know precisely and for certain what will be the market exchange value of the end-product at that future date when it will be ready. This situation is part of the essence of things. . . . In all production, because it takes time, there is ineradicable uncertainty.

(Shackle 1955: 81)

Parametric uncertainty is clearly untenable as a description of the open-ended environment in which entrepreneurs operate. In an environment characterised by parametric uncertainty, there is no scope for entrepreneurship: people are not able to discover new market problems or to generate novel approaches for dealing with familiar problems. Nor is it possible for economic actors to shape the structure of the future, since the future is precast. In reality, of course, entrepreneurs very definitely do not possess perfect structural knowledge, and ends–means frameworks are not given to them ready-made. Consequently, the GK theory portrays the entrepreneur's problem situation as exhibiting structural uncertainty.[7] The two main features of structural uncertainty are: imperfect knowledge as to the structure of future events; and the endogeneity of uncertainty. Each of these distinctive elements is discussed in more detail below.

The first feature of structural uncertainty is that, as the term implies, the structure that the future can take is not known beforehand. In other words, it is impossible for the entrepreneur to derive a complete list of all possible courses of action and of all possible sequels resulting from a given action. The problem situation facing the entrepreneur is thus not well-specified. The entrepreneur not only does not know the probabilities of various outcomes; the entrepreneur does not know the outcomes and actions that are possible (Loasby 1976: 9). There is no upper limit to the number of alternative possible actions that can conceivably be imagined by the entrepreneur. Each alternative possible action in turn has an endless range of rival possible outcomes. In Shackle's (1979b: 24) terms, the possibilities envisaged by the entrepreneur must be treated as 'incomplete and uncompleteable'. Entrepreneurial actions involve outcomes which entail uniqueness, novelty and surprise. The imagined outcomes of any entrepreneurial action cannot therefore be exhaustively categorised into a finite set of pre-established classes, as is needed for the derivation of a probability distribution. Thus, in making choices, the entrepreneur is not able even in principle to calculate probabilities or to average outcomes according to some probability distribution. 'The data for such exercises are not available' (Loasby 1984a: 80).

The implication of this feature of structural uncertainty is that the entrepreneur's environment exhibits qualitative and categorical uncertainty as well as quantitative uncertainty (Langlois 1984a: 29–33; Littlechild 1986: 29). With respect to economic contracting, structural uncertainty implies that it is impossible for individual entrepreneurs to know in detail the structure of transactions that will be available to them in future periods, let alone the terms that will be achievable for any conceivable transaction. The entrepreneur cannot foresee all the relevant contingencies and is therefore unable to specify explicitly all possible contingencies in a long-term market contract. Hence, contracts must often be short-term, implicit, loosely specified and incomplete. Contractual gaps will be large, and sequential adaptations will be necessary at some future date. The entrepreneur is likely to expect future conflicts at the time of contract renewal, especially if resources are irreversibly committed by one or both parties to a contract. If some economic agents are opportunistic and cannot be easily distinguished from non-opportunistic types, and if transaction-specific investments are involved, the entrepreneur may regard market contracts to be infeasible, in terms of prohibitively high transaction costs. Entrepreneurs concerned with the possibilities of effective sequential adaptation may therefore choose to organise recurrent transactions of this type within a firm, rather than to conduct these activities by decentralised market contracting. Thus, 'the leading efficiency explanation for internal organisation – the danger of opportunism in contracting situations – can be reduced to and understood in terms of imperfection in *structural* knowledge' (Langlois 1984a: 31; emphasis added).

The second important feature of structural uncertainty is that it is endogenously created: '[u]ncertainty comes full circle and engenders its own source' (Shackle 1972: 165). This uncertainty is dependent on real time and is generated within the processes of operation of the economic system (i.e. it is caused by the actions of the agents themselves).[8] Consequently, beyond a certain level, structural uncertainty is ineradicable, in the sense that entrepreneurs cannot eliminate it by acquiring further knowledge (cf. Dahrendorf 1968: 238; Frydman 1982).[9] Indeed, because entrepreneurs always act in real time, the very actions which they may undertake in an attempt to overcome uncertainty (i.e. knowledge-acquiring activity) may merely transform rather than eliminate that uncertainty (O'Driscoll and Rizzo 1985: 66–67, 74). For example, the entrepreneur cannot undertake extensive market research to find out consumers' opinions about an existing product without changing those opinions (though the effect may sometimes be negligible). Because of competitive interaction within and between markets, however, such activity may trigger other changes in the system if rivals monitor the entrepreneur's ongoing programme of market research and launch their own counterstrategies to distort the results (for example, by a policy of misinformation or by persuasive comparative advertising designed to confound consumers of competing brands).

An important factor which accounts in part for the endogeneity of uncertainty is the fact that in their decision-making, entrepreneurs must often make predictions of other individuals' predictions rather than just simply predictions of future changes in consumer preferences, of future natural events or of future technology (O'Driscoll and Rizzo 1985: 74).[10] Many entrepreneurial actions are based on expectations of expectations – this applies especially to speculators in stock markets and entrepreneurs in oligopolistic industries.[11] The reason is that entrepreneurs interact with each other through markets; they are not isolated individuals making decisions in perfectly decomposable systems. The argument will be stated briefly.

The outcomes of entrepreneurs' actions will depend upon the particular nature of the environment in which their actions are attempted. This environment consists partly of the *simultaneous* decisions being taken by other entrepreneurs. These decisions are indeterminate, and their character and effects cannot *in principle* be known by entrepreneurs at the moment when they are planning their own actions: 'any imagined sequel of present choice will include choices to be made in time-to-come by others, unforeknowable as to their occurrence or their own sequels' (Shackle 1979b: 24). Hence, entrepreneurs cannot know for certain what will be the consequences of their own choices of action because they cannot be certain of what other entrepreneurs will do. There is thus no escaping the uncertainty of decision, even in the unlikely hypothetical case when entrepreneurs do not make strategic plans in relation to each other.[12] Entrepreneurs must base their plans for the future on their own guesses about the concurrent and future actions of other entrepreneurs.

However, this is not the whole story. For in trying to predict the actions of other entrepreneurs, each entrepreneur must also make his or her own best guess about the predictions upon which rival entrepreneurs will base their individual plans of action. For example, '[i]f an oligopolist . . . decides to change his price, this decision will in part depend on his expectation of the prices to be charged by competitive firms. But the prices that they will charge depend on their expectations of the price he will charge' (O'Driscoll and Rizzo 1985: 61). The entrepreneur must therefore determine their expectations about his expectations of their expectations, and so on. On an *a priori* basis, there is no need to assume that economic decision-makers must share the same expectations about the future.

Indeed, in disequilibrium, different entrepreneurs will necessarily hold different theories and will therefore make different forecasts of future market events (including different forecasts of economic variables relevant to their decisions). At the level of the market, the pattern of these forecasts will influence the future itself (i.e. actual market outcomes).[13] If the future is indeterminate, individual entrepreneurs cannot know *ex ante* the distribution of forecasts (or even summary measures of that distribution, such as the 'average opinion'). In effect then, these forecasts must themselves become an object of conjecture: in order to decide on their own production and investment plans, individual entrepreneurs will have to form expectations about the expectations of other entrepreneurs.[14]

O'Driscoll (1979: 162) points out that an implication of agents' forming expectations about others' expectations is the logical possibility of self-fulfilling expectations which are perhaps unrelated to the underlying objective data. To this can be added the possibility of self-denying forecasts:

A prediction is a social happening which may interact with other social happenings, and among them with the one which it predicts. . . . It may, in an extreme case, even *cause* the happening it predicts: the happening might not have occurred at all if it had not been predicted. At the other extreme the prediction of an impending event may lead to its *prevention*.

(Popper 1960: 15)[15]

These considerations highlight the lack of realism of rational expectations models, such as Lucas (1975), in which agents' forecasts are pooled and the average is made common knowledge. (Furthermore, even if an institution external to the market were to disseminate to individual agents survey data on business expectations and investment plans, the existence of that institutional device would not necessarily reduce structural uncertainty but would merely shift it to a higher level, so that agents would still not be able to forecast optimally (Frydman 1982: 661–664; O'Driscoll and Rizzo 1985: 73–74).) The existence of structural uncertainty and its endogeneity also bring into question the validity of many attempts by outside observers (i.e. economic analysts) at modelling individual agents' learning to form rational expectations. In particular, it casts doubt on that part of the literature concerned with 'rational learning' in which agents' are assumed to learn using *correctly specified* models (i.e. perfect knowledge of the structure of their problems). Models in this class include Townsend (1983) and Bray and Kreps (1987).

As an aside, it should be noted that the endogeneity of structural uncertainty asserts itself even if it is assumed that every entrepreneur has perfect knowledge of the existence of a particular profit opportunity and perfect knowledge of the plans of other entrepreneurs (i.e. perfect foresight). Morgenstern and others have shown that the assumption of perfect foresight may result in a failure to attain an overall stable pattern of coordinated plans and that it may therefore yield an endless process of conjectural responses.[16] In such cases, perfect foresight does not resolve uncertainty but transforms it to ever higher levels of conjecture and of counterguessing. 'Perfect knowledge of what [others] intend to do . . . paralyzes the ability of each to make any decisions at all' (O'Driscoll and Rizzo 1985: 91).

On a methodological note, it should be recognised that the endogeneity of uncertainty (including the existence of the 'Oedipus effect') is not limited to economic or social systems. It cannot serve to demarcate practical rationality from scientific rationality. For even in the natural sciences (e.g. biology), expectations can play a role in precipitating the events that are expected (Popper 1976c: 121–122). The ineradicable nature of the structural uncertainty facing entrepreneurs also finds its analogy in physics: namely, as Heisenberg's principle of indeterminacy in quantum mechanics.

Expressed simplistically, the Heisenberg principle states that it is impossible to find both the position and the momentum of a single subatomic particle with complete accuracy (see Popper 1950, 1982). The implication is that the 'state' of the particle (as defined by classical mechanics) can never be completely determined. The principle can be illustrated by means of the following thought experiment which involves trying to measure the position of an electron by shining light on it. Every observation in the physical world requires an exchange of energy between the observer and the observed object.

For the scientist to be able to 'see' where the electron is will require radiation of very high frequency and, hence, of very high momentum. As soon as a photon of this momentum strikes the electron, it will produce a non-negligible disturbance in the electron which will make it impossible to determine its momentum directly after it has been illuminated.[17] Indeed, if it were possible to eliminate the indeterminacy in position completely, then it follows from the Heisenberg principle that the indeterminacy in momentum would become infinite, and vice versa (Lindsay 1968: 100–102).

For my purposes, the Heisenberg principle can now be generalised as showing that, where knowledge (including predictions and expectations) is a parameter of a dynamic system, any attempt to acquire knowledge about the system will cause a disturbance which changes the system: 'Any attempt to improve the measurement of a parameter which characterizes a system will have the inevitable result of disturbing the value of another parameter of the system' (Suppe 1977b: 182). The generalised Heisenberg principle specifies an absolute and irreducible barrier to discovering more about the dynamics of a system, whether it be physical, biological or social. In the context of economic processes, the entrepreneur's situation is not unlike that of the professional economist, which has been aptly described by Boulding (1966a: 9) in these terms: 'we are not simply acquiring knowledge about a static system which stays put, but acquiring knowledge about a whole dynamic process in which the acquisition of the knowledge itself is a part of the process'.

Bounded uncertainty

The above characterisation of the uncertainty inherent in the entrepreneur's problem situation is still not quite complete, however. It should be noted that the uncertainty which the entrepreneur faces must be bounded: if it were not, and market events were purely random, all entrepreneurial choice would be purposeless and ineffectual. Entrepreneurs would be unable to alter the randomness in economic processes and would thus be incapable of influencing and bringing about future market events. *Bounded* uncertainty is thus a logical prerequisite to purposeful entrepreneurial action.[18] Only under conditions of bounded uncertainty is the entrepreneur able to act creatively and able to make meaningful choices. Bounded uncertainty is enclosed between the extremes of pure arbitrariness and deterministic order (see Table 3.1):[19]

101

In a predestinate world, decision would be illusory; in a world of perfect foreknowledge, empty; in a world without natural order, powerless. Our intuitive attitude to life implies non-illusory, non-empty, non-powerless decision. . . . Since decision in this sense excludes both perfect foresight and anarchy in nature, it must be defined as choice *in face of bounded uncertainty.*

(Shackle 1969: 43; emphasis added)

To be genuine, choice must be neither random nor pre-determined. There must be some grounds for choosing, but they must be inadequate; there must be some possibility of predicting the consequences of choice, but none of perfect prediction.

(Loasby 1976: 5)

Uncertainty is bounded, if only because the entrepreneur expects constraints upon the range and variety of events that can take place. More specifically, the entrepreneur considers that particular conceivable events are *impossible* as sequels to some action which he or she is contemplating. (In Shacklean terms, such outcomes have an absolute maximum degree of potential surprise.) 'It is natural . . . for the decision-maker (and ourselves, as outside, detached observer) to look upon *possible* and *impossible* as the two fundamental categories, in relation to some given present action, into which statements about future history should be distributed' (Shackle 1966: 86; original emphasis). (Indeed, in section 6.3.1, I show that an entrepreneurial conjecture, if it is to be testable and falsifiable, must partition the universal set of possible market events into two mutually exclusive subsets: those events with which the theory is compatible and those events which are inconsistent with the theory and ruled out by it.)

These bounds on what can happen are not objective, given facts but a matter of individual judgement. These judgements will depend upon entrepreneurs' metaphysical assumptions about the category of causality and about the existence of regularities in the world, and more specifically, they will depend upon their metaphysical speculations about the order and consistency of sequences of market situations. Different entrepreneurs will hold different ideas about the constraints that limit the ways in which market events can follow each other. Furthermore, individual entrepreneurs may revise or replace their original ideas, thereby loosening or tightening the bounds of uncertainty that they conceive to be inherent in their environment.

A variety of institutional factors sets bounds to the degree of uncertainty that entrepreneurs face (Hayek 1973; Loasby 1976, 1989; Marshall 1961; Richardson 1960, 1972). First, every society possesses some sort of order which gives rise to uniformities and regularities in social phenomena. Informal custom and social norms (especially moral commitments, business practices, rules, social values and norms of reciprocity) impose restrictions on individual actions and hence on the kinds of behaviour the entrepreneur can expect from others. Second, the institutional framework, the system of property rights (including patents), contracts, money and other institutions of the market (such as networks of relationships, conventions of collaboration, goodwill and reputation) have also evolved spontaneously to mitigate the arbitrariness of future outcomes in a structurally uncertain environment.

Furthermore, a range of governance structures can be devised by the entrepreneur for organising novel transactions exposed to high uncertainty. Internal hierarchies reduce structural uncertainty by eliminating ownership boundaries and by creating a common organisational language and channels of communication which promote the transfer of knowledge regarding the decisions being taken by others (Teece 1982a: 6–22). Within the firm, managerial fiat, organisational routines and a sense of group mission may also facilitate the development of an entrepreneurial venture by promoting the coordination of plans with respect to quality assurance, the scheduling of complementary investments, and even with respect to the identification of customer requirements.

3.2.2 Real time

Time is a real world device which prevents everything from happening at once.

(Davidson 1980b: 158)

The individual is an arrow pointed through time in one way.

(Wiener 1948: 46–47)

Newtonian time

With the exception of instantaneous arbitrage, attempts by entrepreneurs to solve market problems take place in *real time*. Consequently, the economic analysis of entrepreneurship, including the characterisation of the entrepreneur's problem situation, must acknowledge the fact that real time matters.[20] Real time must be distinguished from the Newtonian conception of time described by Wiener (1948: 40–56) and O'Driscoll and Rizzo (1985: 53–59).[21] The Newtonian treatment of time in neoclassical economics is inadequate for the specific problems addressed by this book, namely, providing a dynamic theory of entrepreneurial learning and explaining processes of economic change (see section 1.1.1).[22]

Repeated games (including supergames) in neoclassical theories of oligopolistic behaviour provide a good opportunity for illustrating the essential nature of Newtonian time and its inadequacy for modelling entrepreneurial activity. These games go beyond static, one-shot games by permitting economic agents to make repeated decisions as well as allowing them to react to the corresponding actions of their rivals. However, a fundamental limitation of repeated games is that they only pertain to stationary environments: they are merely identical repetitions of static games, so that the set of feasible actions and the payoffs per period remain exactly the same (Shapiro 1989: 356–357). In this stationary world, one moment or interval of time is just like another. Nothing new ever happens. A repeated game describes a market subsystem which is analogous to a stationary physical system, such as the solar system. Both systems are repetitive: they do not evolve or grow; nor do they exhibit any structural changes. This failure to take time seriously means that the agent is never confronted with genuine novelty or unpredictable change. There is no scope for tactical surprise, for 'the outflanking of imagination by superior imagination' (Shackle 1972: 422).

Second, and very much related to the first point, players do not increase their knowledge of opportunities over time. Truly novel discoveries cannot be made by economic agents. They can neither bring new structural knowledge into the game nor can they change the economic problem that they face. The nature of strategic choices in repeated games thus remains inherently static.

Third, there is no direct linkage between intervals of time, so that (action in) one period does not have any influence upon (events in) any other. Thus, players cannot make lasting commitments or accumulate resources from one period to the next in order to make possible later market events. Repeated games are thus limited because 'history has no tangible effect on prospective competition' (Shapiro 1989: 381). Furthermore, there is no malinvestment or clustering of entrepreneurial error. The equilibrium of a stationary, Newtonian-time game is thus an unsatisfactory theoretical apparatus for analysing entrepreneur-driven market processes which take place in real time.

Exclusive reliance on equilibrium outcomes in neoclassical economics has the effect of reducing time to a space, which is an extended, homogeneous continuum:

> The Newtonian conception of time is spatialized; that is, its passage is represented or symbolized by 'movements' along a line. Different dates are then portrayed as a succession of line segments (discrete time) or points (continuous time). In either case, time is fully analogized to space, and what is true of the latter becomes true of the former.
>
> (O'Driscoll and Rizzo 1985: 53)

According to the Newtonian conception of time in neoclassical economics, just as an individual decision-maker is able to allocate portions of space (i.e. land) among particular ends, so too can the individual allocate specific periods of time (e.g. hours in the day) to certain purposes, such as leisure and production (O'Driscoll and Rizzo 1985: 3).[23] The Newtonian conception of time emphasises the scarcity of time and the need for decision-makers to economise time as they do other scarce factors. Examples of models which treat time as an exogenously scarce resource that can be optimally allocated are Becker's (1971) theory of time allocation and Böhm-Bawerk's (1959) 'period of production' in his theory of capital. In these approaches, the stock of time available to a decision-maker is viewed as a static given. There are no features of time which differentiate it from space.

The asymmetry and irreversibility of real time

In a Newtonian system, time and processes are eminently reversible. If we were to take a movie-picture of any process describable by means of the laws of that system, and if we were then to run the film backward, it would still depict a possible process adhering to these laws (Wiener 1948: 42–43). Thus, the analogy which reduces time to a spatial dimension appears to break down:[24]

> The subject's position in space can be elected, but his position in time cannot be elected. This should warn us that, in human

experience and perception as distinct from human intellectual construction, time is of a different nature from a space whether we mean by that word the space of the senses or the mathematician's purest abstraction.

(Shackle 1969: 42)

More specifically, the spatial representation of time excludes an essential aspect of real time: its irreversibility. It is part of the structure of economic reality that time is asymmetric and that it is unidirectional (cf. Popper 1974: 1141). Economic processes, such as developing innovations and learning about the market, are all processes where time has an arrow. These processes always run asymmetrically because they entail novelty. The irreversible nature of innovation and economic development was emphasised by Schumpeter (1947: 150): '[c]reative response changes social and economic situations for good, or, to put it differently, it creates situations from which there is no bridge to those situations that might have emerged in its absence. This is why creative response is an essential element in the historical process'.

The asymmetry of real time is not without connection to other aspects of the structure of reality. In particular, it is related to the asymmetry of causation:

If we want to justify an asymmetry between past and future, it helps if we can base it on something we believe independently to be asymmetrical in this respect. Why not use the fact (if it is one) that causality is asymmetric? What we do now can only affect later events, not earlier ones. In general, an event cannot affect an event outside its forward light cone.

(Simons 1983: 23–24)

The cause–effect relation entails a succession of events in time and thereby involves a definite temporal order. The category of causality thus implies the category of real time: 'the categories of cause and effect ... imply the notions before and after. At this point, time has already entered the picture' (Rizzo 1979a: 1). In the absence of backwards causation – according to which the entrepreneur could perform an action in the present so as to bring about an earlier market event – the irreversibility of real time implies that it is impossible for entrepreneurs' (or any other economic agents for that matter) to change the past. It constitutes a metaphysical limitation on the scope of entrepreneurial action because after market events have occurred, the entrepreneur can do nothing to prevent them or modify them (cf. Simons 1983: 8). Events that have already occurred are no longer open to action. In their theories, therefore, entrepreneurs take it for granted that the past is immutable. This assumption is so fundamental that it is rarely, if ever, made explicit. It is accepted implicitly as a deep-lying cosmological fact. Consequently, human action is always forward-looking: only within the context of an indeterminate future can entrepreneurial activity influence market events.[25] 'In short, we are directed in time, and our relation to the future is different from our relation to the past' (Wiener 1948: 44).

Several prominent philosophers, among them Reichenbach (1956) and Grünbaum (1962a, 1962b, 1963), argue that there is also a connection between the asymmetry of time and the statistical concept of entropy, a measure of the degree of disorder in a system. Indeed, they seek the basis for the idea of the direction of time in the entropy concept. The second law of thermodynamics, the entropy principle, states that in any closed system there is a constant tendency for entropy to increase with time, so that ordered arrangements tend to degenerate into disordered ones.

To highlight its relevance to economic problems, such as entrepreneurship, the entropy law can be generalised into Boulding's law of diminishing potential (or negative entropy).[26] This states that 'if anything happens, it is because there was a potential for it to happen, and that after it has happened, that potential has been used up' (Boulding 1978: 34–35).[27] Any entropic process is irreversible and so would appear to provide an objective asymmetry giving directionality to time.[28] Indeed, entropy is 'one of time's arrows' (Boulding 1978: 35).

In Kirzner's single-period model of alertness, for example, if an entrepreneur exploits an arbitrage profit opportunity, there must be an economic potential for it happening in the form of existing interlocal price differences for the same good. The price discrepancy arises from incomplete mutual adjustment between transactions in different parts of the market, which in turn arises from market ignorance. Once the arbitrage opportunity has been exploited, that part of the potential has been used up. The act of capturing a profit opportunity reduces these price differences: it gradually communicates increasingly accurate information to more and more market participants (Kirzner 1973: 228–229). Assuming no further exogenous changes, as the entrepreneurial process proceeded and market ignorance were constantly corrected, the potential for a market process would be gradually eroded until the market economy would eventually reach an equilibrium state and stay there. 'The full realization of potential is equilibrium' (Boulding 1978: 35). (Of course, this does not exclude the possibility in Kirzner's theory that new potential for entrepreneurship may be recreated by *continual exogenous changes* in preferences, resources and technologies.)

Entrepreneurs cannot predict their own future knowledge

In a general equilibrium world, the future is logically predictable, at least in an actuarial sense. All future contingencies are specified in advance (Davidson 1980b; Hahn 1980: 130; Koopmans 1957: 161–162). In Arrow's model of general competitive equilibrium, the contingencies encompass future *discoveries* of the characteristics of nature as well as all future natural events, and in Debreu's version, future changes in consumer tastes are included too. The result of assuming that all Arrow–Debreu markets exist is to collapse the future into the present: all economic exchange is reduced to a 'single gigantic once-for-all forward "higgle-haggle" in which all contingent goods and services . . . are bought and sold once and for all now for money payments made now' (Meade 1971: 166).

In contrast, the asymmetry and unique directionality of real time imply that the future cannot be logically derived from the present. Consequently, the fact that entrepreneurs act in a world of real time means that it is logically impossible for entrepreneurs to predict the knowledge that they will acquire in the future: 'if there is such a thing as growing human knowledge, then we cannot anticipate today what we shall know tomorrow' (Popper 1963: vi).[29] The growth of their knowledge, if it is genuine growth, must be unpredictable in principle:

> The hypothetico-deductive interpretation of science . . . teaches us that science cannot predict the content of future scientific discoveries. . . . [A] path-breaking hypothesis could never be derived from *existing* observation-statements. Nor could a path-breaking hypothesis . . . be derived from existing lower-order hypotheses . . . since it says more than they do and will usually show them to be false unless they are saved by special assumptions. ∴ . . . There is thus no possibility of deducing, and so no possibility of rationally predicting, new scientific hypotheses from existing information. And if, without a

108

rational procedure but with luck and genius, you hit upon a new hypothesis you will be too late to predict its discovery.

(Watkins 1955: 75)

[T]o claim that the world is predictable seems to be to deny that life consists of a sequence of experiences temporally separable. Complete prediction would require the predictor to know in complete detail at the moment of making his prediction, first, all 'future' advances of knowledge and inventions, and secondly, all 'future' decisions. To know in advance what an invention will consist of is evidently to make that invention in advance. But this is of course to destroy the possibility of the invention being made at its 'own' date, unless the predictor keeps secret his prior knowledge of what someone else is going to invent. . . . To suppose that invention and scientific discovery can be predicted is to suppose that all experience throughout all time can be compressed into a single moment.

(Shackle 1958: 103–104)

As in science, the emergence of new ideas in business – new products, new technologies, new methods of organisation and of marketing, and new ventures – can never be anticipated precisely in advance. Indeed, Popper (1972: 298) regards 'unpredictability in principle' to be *the* salient element accounting for the *emergent* character of new ideas. Similarly, Schumpeter considered the unpredictability of innovative ideas to be an essential characteristic of entrepreneurship: creative response in business 'can practically never be understood *ex ante*; that is to say, it cannot be predicted by applying the ordinary rules of inference from the pre-existing facts' (Schumpeter 1947: 150). If entrepreneurs could predict their future discoveries, they would become present discoveries, and the growth of their knowledge would thus come to an end.

The unpredictability of future knowledge in turn implies that there are features of economic decisions, actions and patterns of behaviour, both individual and social, which are also fundamentally beyond the reach of complete prediction. For if entrepreneurs base their actions on their stocks of knowledge, and if they cannot predict their own future knowledge, it follows that they cannot predict their own future behaviour either (O'Driscoll and Rizzo 1985: 25). At time t_1, entrepreneurs cannot know their state of knowledge at t_{1+n} until t_{1+n}, and they cannot know exactly what contingent choice sets will appear at t_{1+n} until t_{1+n}, nor what particular course of

109

action they themselves will choose at that future date. For similar reasons, it is impossible for entrepreneurs to foretell in any detail the future actions of other agents since these too will be based on conjectures as yet unthought of. As O'Driscoll and Rizzo (1985: 83) have emphasised, this implies that economic agents can never make plans which are perfectly dovetailed (in respect to their unique features) with the plans of other agents.

The impossibility of complete prediction is not just a symptom of the immense complexity of the economic process, of deficiencies in the entrepreneur's knowledge of present circumstances or of some computational incompetence on the part of the entrepreneur. The argument applies even if predictors have access to all relevant theories together with complete information about their initial states and even if they experience no cognitive limits in processing that information (Ackermann 1976: 135). It also applies to complex teams of interacting entrepreneurs who are engaged in prediction (cf. Popper 1960: vii).

It has been argued that since economic change is a function of the growth of knowledge, and that the growth of knowledge is unpredictable by rational means, it follows that the process of economic change is itself also unpredictable (Lachmann 1959: 71; Popper 1959: 279). However, this argument does not refute the possibility of all types of prediction on the part of entrepreneurs. It is completely consistent with testing entrepreneurial theories by way of predicting that particular market developments will occur under particular circumstances (Popper 1960: vi). Furthermore, it does not preclude the possibility that entrepreneurs may be able to generate what Hayek (1967: ch. 2; 1978) has called pattern predictions: 'predictions of some of the general attributes of the structures that will form themselves' (1978: 27). Entrepreneurs may have the capacity to speculate usefully about the types of things that can happen, but not the precise thing that will happen (cf. Shackle 1966: 74). Their predictive ability is necessarily limited to the common characteristics (or typical features) of market events but does not extend to predicting the unique details of specific events. They may sometimes be able to forecast possible kinds of discoveries but not their precise content.

Time is not a flow of events

A further issue remains to be discussed briefly. This point challenges a subjectivist conception of time as a flow of events. According to that conception, *passage* is the essence of time. This confused idea of time results implicitly from conceiving time as if it were in some ways a dimension of space, even though it is often advanced in the same breath as an alternative to the spatialised concept of time.

According to O'Driscoll and Rizzo (1985: 3, 59–62), time is subjectively perceived by each individual to be a *flow* of events.[30] The 'dynamic conception of time' or 'real time', they tell us, consists of 'a dynamically continuous flow of novel experiences. This flow is not *in* time . . . ; rather, it *is* or constitutes time. We cannot experience the passage of time except as a flow' (O'Driscoll and Rizzo 1985: 60; original emphasis). They make it clear that their treatment of time is deeply influenced by the writings of the French philosopher of evolution, Henri Bergson. Bergson (1910) distinguished between the mathematical conception of time, which neither 'flows' nor 'acts', and the time that we directly experience, which is said to be a flowing, indivisible succession of conscious states. Bergson referred to the latter concept as 'pure time' or 'real duration' (*la durée réelle*).[31]

It is ironic that although O'Driscoll and Rizzo, following Bergson, argue strongly against spatialised time, their description of 'real time' relies crucially upon spatial images. They do not acknowledge that the ideas of a *flow* of events and of the *passage* or *elapse* of time are as much spatial metaphors as is representing time by movements along a line or calendar-axis. The problem involves more than just an inappropriate and misleading metaphor, however. Their notion of 'real time' is riddled with an underlying malaise which Williams (1951) dubs pejoratively 'the myth of passage'. This illusion of time flow has been aptly described by Simons (1983) and Smart (1949, 1955, 1967):

> Time is the very last thing that could flow, since something flows when it moves in more or less even fashion past a given point. But movement presupposes time, so time cannot flow, unless we suppose a *hypertime* in which it flows, an assumption we can well do without. . . . Nor, it should be added, do events flow or pass. Only something that is all or partly in one place and then later all or partly in another can flow or pass, and events are not like that, since an event which is not instantaneous is not all in one place and then all in another: rather some of its earlier parts are in one place and some of its later parts in another. . . . [W]hat is sometimes called a change in an event

consists in later parts of the event having different properties from earlier parts. . . . .

(Simons 1983: 11–12; emphasis added)

The idea of time as passing is connected with the idea of events changing from future to past. We think of events as approaching us from the future, whereupon they are momentarily caught in the spotlight of the present and then recede into the past. Yet in normal contexts it does not make sense to talk of events changing or staying the same. Roughly speaking, events are happenings to continuants – that is, to things that change or stay the same.

(Smart 1967: 126)

A major source of the myth of passage is the idea that our private stock of memories is constantly increasing.[32] O'Driscoll and Rizzo (1985: 3, 61, 64) presume that as time goes by, the individual's memory is 'continuously enriched', so that each individual's perspective for viewing the future is also supposed to change constantly. That is, they take it for granted that the passage of time ('the past flow of events') adds to the stock of an individual's experiences and that it thereby improves his or her state of knowledge. Here they are echoing a Shacklean idea that '[t]ime is what *brings* new knowledge' (Shackle 1972: 151; emphasis added).

The time-flow conception has unfortunate implications for the nature of learning. It suggests that the acquisition of knowledge is a passive, cumulative process of osmosis or absorption. It fails to recognise that individuals must actively *decide* to reject their existing ideas in favour of new ideas. Identifying the source of a refutation is not an instantaneous process but always takes time (see section 8.2). Furthermore, this way of thinking does not take account of the fact that individuals can also forget things as well as acquire new memories. In some circumstances, their net stock of memories might even be diminishing, though they still will not experience time as returning in the opposite direction (Smart 1967: 127).[33]

The illusion of time flow can also lead to the confounding of time with the experience of time. Like Bergson's notion of duration, O'Driscoll and Rizzo's concept of 'real time' implies that the present is connected to other periods via the experiences and perceptions of the individual. In particular, the individual's memory is the structural component of 'real time' which links the past to the present (Capek 1971: 127; O'Driscoll and Rizzo 1985: 60–61). Bergson even went so far as to contend that 'pure' memory *retains* our past in the present. This approach fails to distinguish the recollection of the past event from the past event itself or the thought from the object of thought (Russell 1961: 763–764). '[C]onsciousness of time is not the same as time' (Simons 1983: 13). In spite of his radical subjectivism, Shackle (1958: 16, 18–19) avoids these difficulties by recognising that the present moment (the 'moment-in-being') always remains solitary and self-contained:

> Expectation and memory do not provide a means of comparing the *actuality* of the moment-in-being at one of its stations with that at another, they do not enable *two moments*, distinct in location on the calendar-axis, to be *in being together*, for the nature of 'the present', the essence of the moment-in-being, is an impregnable self-contained isolation.
>
> (Shackle 1958: 16; emphasis added)

Falsificationist entrepreneurs – who are described in detail in later chapters – do not deny the reality of the arrow of time. They admit the objectivity of time, that is, its independence of what they and others think about time (cf. Popper 1974: 1141). They recognise the distinction between their own subjective experience of time (and the concepts they apply to it) and time itself.

Closely connected to the idea of time as a flow of events is the notion that time is '*causally* potent and creative' (O'Driscoll and Rizzo 1985: 62). It is argued that the passing of time itself can produce or cause change and that it is a source of novelty and true surprise (see too Shackle 1972: 25–26, 279; 1973: 126). Expressed in its most extreme form, the argument goes that the mere elapse of time *necessarily* and continuously changes the expectations, and hence the tentative plans and actions, of economic actors. O'Driscoll and Rizzo refer to this feature of 'real time' as causal efficacy.

If one disposes of the myth of passage, one can simultaneously do away with the idea that time itself is a causative agent that has effects. Simons rejects the view that time is causally efficacious, 'since time is neither an event, which could cause another, nor a continuant, which could possess the power to change something else' (1983: 17). It is a mistake to hypostatise time by describing it as if it were a material object or a process which could exert an influence in its own right on the physical and social world. It is what entrepreneurs and other economic actors learn and do *in* time, not time itself, that affects economic transactions. Only people themselves, not time, can

113

change their expectations, plans and actions. And the change of their expectations is a result of their own interpretations and decisions. Because time is causally inert, it is not appropriate to treat it as an independent mathematical variable in functional relationships as is customarily done, say, with the price of a commodity in a demand function (Baird 1987: 191, 197). 'Time is neither a continuant, nor a state, nor an event or process. Its importance lies in its being the *medium* of all actions, changes, events, processes' (Simons 1983: 30; original emphasis). Time is simply the non-spatial *order* in which things change, events happen, actions are carried out, contracts are entered into and in which knowledge is acquired.

NOTES

1 However, Schumpeter's (1947: 150) discussion of creative and adaptive responses to economic change does give the impression of a sharper dichotomy. Adaptive response arises whenever the economy, an industry or particular firms in an industry, adapt to a change in their data by doing something within the range of existing practice (such as increasing the supply of some input which does not require a change in production methods). On the other hand, creative response occurs whenever the reaction to change involves something outside the scope of existing practice.

2 The perfect competition model does not need to assume complete and perfect knowledge of every conceivable datum, but complete knowledge in the sense that market participants know all that is relevant for their decisions (Casson 1982: 367; Hayek 1937: 45, 49, 53; White 1976: 13–14). It should be noted that Latsis (1972: 208–219) maintains that the theory of imperfect competition (monopoly, monopolistic competition and oligopoly) is also a variant of the same neoclassical research programme as perfect competition, because it has the same hard core.

3 A more complex version takes account of the fact that the form of the probability function may not be perfectly known. Economic agents are portrayed as having *a priori* probability distributions of the probability distributions themselves. But this approach gives rise to an infinite regress, because the agent could hold beliefs of the probability distribution of the probability distribution of the probability distribution, and so on.

4 Popper has this to say about the idea of a plastic control in the context of the growth of knowledge:

For the control of ourselves and of our actions by our theories and purposes is a *plastic* control. We are not *forced* to submit ourselves to the control of our theories, for we can discuss them critically, and we can reject them freely if we think that they fall short of our regulative standards. So the control is far from one-sided. Not only do our theories control us, but we can control our theories (and even our standards): there is a kind of *feed-back* here. And if we submit to our theories, then we do so freely, after deliberation; that is, after the critical discussion of alternatives, and after freely choosing between the competing theories, in the light of that critical discussion.

(Popper 1972: 240–241; original emphasis)

5 Kirzner (1985: 11) too claims that entrepreneurship can be incorporated into economic analysis 'without surrendering the heart of [received] microeconomic theory' and argues further that such integration is indeed necessary to rescue neoclassical theory.

6 Parametric uncertainty is prefigured in the economics literature by Knightian statistical or measurable uncertainty, which Knight (1964) defined as risk, and Misesian class probability (Mises 1949: 107–110).

7 Structural uncertainty is of course akin to previous definitions of uncertainty in the economics literature: Knightian (1964) true or unmeasurable uncertainty; Misesian (1949) case probability; Shacklean (1972) radical uncertainty; Loasby's (1976) partial ignorance; and O'Driscoll and Rizzo's (1985) genuine uncertainty. Structural uncertainty also appears in post-Keynesian economics in the form of 'non-ergodic' uncertainty. This concept implies that individuals recognise that they are facing a not statistically predictable future (i.e. the future is not predictable in any probabilistic sense) and that they are ignorant of the outcomes of their current actions (Davidson 1991; Davidson and Davidson 1984: 52, 59). In the context of mainstream economics, Cohen and Axelrod's (1984) treatment of agents' misspecification of their problems corresponds to structural uncertainty.

8 Much of this section owes an obvious intellectual debt to O'Driscoll and Rizzo (1985: ch. 5).

9 In contrast to this characterisation of uncertainty, the neoclassical literature on the economics of information and Casson's (1982: 119) theory of the entrepreneur both implicitly assume that (parametric) uncertainty can at least in principle be reduced and eradicated by the search for information.

10 The endogeneity of uncertainty discussed in this section bears obvious similarity to the *secondary* uncertainty described by Koopmans (1957). Secondary uncertainty arises from a lack of communication between decision-makers, that is, 'from one decision maker having no way of finding out the concurrent decisions and plans made by others' (1957: 163). Koopmans regards this secondary uncertainty as 'quantitatively at least as important as the primary uncertainty arising from random acts of nature and unpredictable changes in consumers' preferences' (1957: 163). For a critique of Koopmans's view of uncertainty, see Williamson (1984a: 204).

11 This notion is encapsulated in the first proposition of Boland's theory of social institutions which asserts that '[a]ll sociological acts are based on expectations of expectations. Specifically, all interactive decision making involves the actor's knowledge of the other individuals' knowledge' (Boland 1979b: 964). For a criticism of the view that agents in

typical market settings make predictions of predictions, see Baird (1987: 199–200).

12 Opportunism compounds the endogeneity of *ex ante* uncertainty and vastly complicates the entrepreneur's problem situation. Opportunistic non-disclosure and distortion of information gives rise to a strategic kind of uncertainty, which Williamson (1984a) refers to as 'behavioural uncertainty'.

13 Note that past forecasts will influence but not determine the future: '[t]he future course of events is in general certainly not constrained by past forecasts; nor, unfortunately, are forecasts constrained by the actual future events these forecasts seek to foretell' (Kirzner 1982c: 148).

14 Structural uncertainty also implies that individual entrepreneurs' forecasts of the forecasts of others cannot be known by other people. Furthermore, this deficit of knowledge applies at any higher level of guessing and counterguessing.

15 Popper (1960) referred to this impact of a prediction upon the event predicted as the 'Oedipus effect' (not complex!) because the oracle in the legend of Oedipus Rex in Sophocles's play contributed crucially to the chain of events which resulted in the future realisation of the oracle's own prophecy. (The legendary King Oedipus unknowingly killed his father whom he had never seen before. This event was the direct result of the oracle's prophecy which had led to Oedipus being abandoned in the first place.) On the Oedipus effect, see: Ackermann (1976: 138); Popper (1960: 13–16; 1976c: 122); Shackle (1958: 104–105); and Watkins (1955: 76).

The sociologist, Robert Merton (1948), also focused on the manner and the conditions in which emergent social phenomena are shaped by prior expectations. He concentrated, in particular, on the extent to which forecasts could be self-denying or self-fulfilling.

16 See: Morgenstern (1935) on the Holmes–Moriarty story; O'Driscoll and Rizzo (1985: 84–85, 90–91); Richardson (1960: 57–58); and Shackle (1958: 95–96). Apart from the assumption of perfect foresight, however, the applicability of these examples to the competitive market process in general is limited by their zero-sum nature, unlike most market interactions which, being based on voluntary exchange, are positive-sum games (Baird 1987: 199, 202).

17 In fact, Heisenberg's disturbance theory of measurement (the account sketched above) is only one of several treatments of the Heisenberg indeterminacy principle. Other interpretations and derivations make no reference to the indeterminacy resulting from the disturbing effect of measurement.

18 Other treatments of bounded uncertainty, which represent varying degrees of subjectivism, include: Hayek (1967: ch. 2; 1978: ch. 2); Kirzner (1982c: 148–149); Knight (1964: 199); Loasby (1976: 4–5); Mises (1949: 22); O'Driscoll and Rizzo (1985: 76–79); Shackle (1966: 74, 86, 133, 301; 1969: 3–7, 43, 271; 1979a: 20); and Simon (1965: 97–98). Shackle represents the most radical subjectivist position with respect to decision-making under bounded uncertainty. Kirzner's (1982c: 148–150) stance is distinctive in that entrepreneurial alertness

is argued to be the only force responsible for some degree of correspondence between the future as it is envisaged and the realised future.

19 Some philosophers, following Hume and Schlick, reject the idea of a middle ground between perfect determinism and pure chance (Popper 1972: 227–228, 248). Their ontological thesis is that the only alternative to determinism is perfect chance. Consequently, they would deny the existence of bounded uncertainty or of any similar concept, such as Popper's idea of a plastic control which was mentioned in section 3.1.3.

20 References to real time in this book should not be confused with the same term used by O'Driscoll and Rizzo (1985: ch. 4). They present an extremely subjectivist view of time, based on Bergson's idea of the subjective experience of the passage of time. To avoid confusion, references to their temporal concept will be distinguished by quotation marks (i.e. as 'real time').

21 It should be noted that to some extent I am hereby setting up an imaginary construct as an object of criticism. The main features of Newtonian time (as described here) are not necessarily part of a modern scientific concept of time (see Simons 1983: 16–17).

22 For a recent review of the ways in which several eminent economists have taken time into account and of the problems inherent in incorporating time into economic analysis, see Currie and Steedman (1990). In particular, Shackle's and Lachmann's subjectivist views of time are examined extensively in this work. Other useful discussions of the role of time in economic theory are: Bausor (1982: 163–167); Boland (1978); Georgescu-Roegen (1971: 130, 198–210); Hicks (1976); Lachmann (1959, 1986); Mises (1949: 99–104); O'Driscoll and Rizzo (1985: 52–70); Rizzo (1979a, 1979b); Robinson (1980); Rosenstein-Rodan (1934); Shackle (1958; 1972: 155, 231, 263–332); and Simons (1983).

23 Most modern Austrian economists, following Mises, would also agree with the neoclassicists that people allocate time in this manner (Baird 1987: 192; Simons 1983: 29). However, Mises (1949: 101) notes that '[t]he economization of time has a peculiar character because of the uniqueness and irreversibility of the temporal order. . . . The economization of time is independent of the economization of economic goods and services' .

24 A further breakdown of the analogy is that, in a decentralised market system, entrepreneurs can buy and sell space. They can transfer and exchange the rights to control, to benefit from, and to dispose of, space. However, there are no property rights over time, neither private nor communal. The entrepreneur cannot possess time or buy and sell it. Nor can the entrepreneur claim the right to use a period of time in production or marketing to the exclusion of other entrepreneurs (cf. Simons 1983: 29–30).

25 The future-directedness of action is emphasised by subjectivists in the Austrian and LSE traditions, particularly Mises (1949: esp. 100–101), Buchanan and Thirlby (1973) and Shackle (1972). Mises regarded the irreversibility of the temporal order as an essential concept in the theory of action: 'That which can no longer be done or consumed because the

opportunity for it has passed away, contrasts the past with the present. That which cannot yet be done or consumed, because the conditions for undertaking it or the time for its ripening have not yet come, contrasts the future with the past' (Mises 1949: 101). However, Simons (1983: 15) criticises Mises' proposition that 'action can influence only the future, never the present' (1949: 100) by commenting that an action may influence the present pertaining to another action and that it may even affect its own present.

26 Georgescu-Roegen (1971, 1987) is the most energetic champion of the entropy concept in its application to economics. See too Boulding (1978: 34–35; 1981: 10, 147–151, 154–155) and Rifkin (1980). In his thorough investigation of the conceptual links between economics and physics, Mirowski (1989) contends that neoclassical economics has failed to incorporate the implications of the second law of thermodynamics (especially with respect to irreversibility and path dependency in modelling).

27 More precisely, Boulding's generalisation relates only to the classical-thermodynamic definition of entropy (i.e. a measure of the unavailability of a system's energy for doing mechanical work) rather than to the statistical-mechanical definition of entropy (i.e. a measure of a system's disorder). Indeed, the former definition can be interpreted as a special case of the latter.

28 For a criticism of attempts to base temporal directionality on entropy, see Popper (1974: 1140–1144) and the references therein.

29 Popper (1950) gives a complicated logical proof of the impossibility of predicting the future growth of knowledge. He uses three arguments to demonstrate that human and non-human predictors may fail to predict scientifically their own future states of knowledge: the Tristram Shandy paradox, Gödelian sentences and the 'Oedipus Effect'. See: Ackermann (1976: 129–140); Magee (1973: 100); O'Driscoll and Rizzo (1985: 9, 25–26, 61, 83); O'Hear (1980: 137–146); Popper (1950; 1959: 279; 1960: v–vii; 1972: 298; 1982); and Watkins (1955: 75). O'Driscoll and Rizzo (1985: 25) apply the Tristram Shandy paradox to the case of economic decision-makers.

30 In economics, the idea of the flow or passage of time is not unique to O'Driscoll and Rizzo. It is also shared by: Georgescu-Roegen (1971: 130–137); Hicks (1976: 135); Lachmann (1959: 73; 1977: 36; 1986: 74–75, 95); Mises (1949: 99–101), who also draws on Bergson; and Shackle (1958: 15; 1979a: 46–47). According to Baird (1987: 197), Hayek's view of time and his equilibrium notion of plan coordination are also based on treating time as a subjectively experienced flow of events.

31 Bergson's account of time is of central importance in his philosophy. He regarded it as the key to solving major philosophical problems, such as those related to human freedom of action and determinism. See Capek (1971), Pilkington (1976) and Russell (1961: Book 3, ch. 28; 1977) for interesting, and often highly critical, critiques of Bergson's philosophy.

32 Another source of the illusion of time flow is the failure to recognise that tenses and words, such as 'past', 'present' and 'future', are 'token-

reflexive' or indexical expressions (i.e. they are utterances which implicitly refer to themselves). See Smart (1967: 127) and Reichenbach (1947: sections 50–51).

33 The confused notion of the flow of time also results in the mistaken idea that the present is real in a sense in which the past and the future are not: the past has ceased to exist, and the future does not yet exist (Smart 1967: 126). But it only makes sense to describe continuants (e.g. firms, market institutions) as ceasing to exist or coming into existence, and neither the past nor the future is a continuant. This mistaken idea is espoused to some extent by Baird (1987: 191), Shackle (1979a: 47) and White (1976: 6).

4

THE RATIONALITY
AND AIM STRUCTURE OF
THE ENTREPRENEUR

Rationality is a multidimensional concept. In section 1.5, it was mentioned that the growth-of-knowledge (GK) theory of entrepreneurship is limited to the cognitive-logical dimension of inquiry and that it does not include other important dimensions within its ambit. It aims to explore the hidden structure of rationality which underlies entrepreneurial activity. It must be emphasised that the entire entrepreneurial learning methodology that is developed in the following chapters (i.e. the methodological rules of the falsificationist entrepreneur) constitutes the GK conception of entrepreneurial rationality. This chapter is restricted to only a few general comments on the rationality of the entrepreneur. GK (or non-justificationist) rationality can be succinctly described as consisting in the disposition to learn from mistakes. The GK theory of entrepreneurship assumes that entrepreneurs are rational in this sense: at least some entrepreneurs are presumed to proceed by the critical method of trial and the elimination of error. It is predicted that entrepreneurs who adopt GK rationality are more successful than entrepreneurs who do not (see sections 6.1 and 10.1). But the new theory does *not* claim that (successful) entrepreneurs always adopt critical and rational policies with respect to their own ideas.

This chapter is organised as follows. Section 4.1 outlines the aim structure of the entrepreneur as assumed by GK rationality. The discussion then digresses to examine the correspondence between the postulated aim structure and the economic and psychological literatures on the entrepreneur (sections 4.1.1 and 4.1.2). Section 4.2 examines the use of deductive logic by economic agents in their reasoning. Finally, section 4.3 investigates the extent to which entrepreneurs are supposed to be conscious of the methodological rules which they apply.

4.1 THE AIM STRUCTURE OF THE ENTREPRENEUR

The GK theory assumes that entrepreneurs behave as incipient scientists in their economic decision-making.[1] Like scientists, entrepreneurs are constantly engaged in solving problems which tend to involve much novelty and which are ill-specified. Problems are not avoided, but actively sought as a challenge.

If characterising economic agents as scientists appears to be a fanciful construction to some neoclassical readers, then consider the attributions made to economic agents by rational expectations theorists, who portray economic decision-makers as economists – or rather as *monetarist economists* (Gomes 1982). Work on the convergence to rational expectations equilibrium even goes so far as to portray individual decision-makers in the economy as 'inside econometricians' who under certain assumptions can learn to form rational expectations (see, for example: Bray and Savin 1986; Marcet and Sargent 1989a, 1989b; and Townsend 1978).

Because entrepreneurship is characterised as a rational, problem-solving activity, and given that a rational activity must have one or more aims, so too must entrepreneurship. It is assumed that, in the face of structural uncertainty, the ultimate aims of entrepreneurs are *to predict*, *to explain* and *to control* aspects of their experience in the pursuit of economic gain. 'As a scientist, man seeks to predict, and thus to control, the course of events' (Kelly 1963: 12).[2] Entrepreneurs attempt to gain better knowledge about their environment, which in turn presupposes that they have a drive or motive for active exploration, for inquiring into new situations, and for making discoveries about their world.

However, the GK approach does not investigate the entrepreneur's unconscious motives or innate dispositions. Similarly, it does not explain the entrepreneur's behaviour as the result of many complex motivating factors. Instead, the GK theory simply assumes that entrepreneurs are problem-solvers who pursue particular goals in unique decision situations. These goals or aims need not be psychologically motivated or psychologically given; they are not identified with, or reduced to, the entrepreneur's psychological states. Different entrepreneurs may choose to have different aims, and entrepreneurs can change their aims, although at any point in time they may decide to treat their aims as given – as the unchangeable result of their own past decisions (cf. Boland 1982: 36–37).

This approach is part of the method of situational analysis, and it is consistent with Popper's version of methodological individualism (termed institutional individualism by Agassi (1975)). Entrepreneurs' problem situations are defined to include their aim structures and any relevant theories that they hold as well as their learning methodologies. Psychological elements, such as agents' motives, are replaced with the corresponding objective situational elements, such as the agents' goals. Entrepreneurs with particular motives are thus transformed into entrepreneurs whose situations may be distinguished by the fact that they seek to attain specific objective aims (Popper 1976a: 102–103; 1983c).

Prediction, explanation and control have been identified as the aims of the entrepreneur. For the time being these aims will be defined somewhat loosely. (More precise and detailed descriptions are given in section 4.2.) Prediction refers to specifying unknown economic and market events beforehand. In making predictions, entrepreneurs try to forecast the future behaviour of the environment: in particular the decisions of competitors, suppliers, resource owners and customers. 'To use a hypothesis in practical applications is, fundamentally, to use it to predict future events' (Musgrave 1974b: 584). Entrepreneurs aim to predict not only impending market problem(s) but also the future results of their attempts to solve those problems.

Entrepreneurs are not only interested in generating predictions of unknown events, however. Like scientists, they are also concerned with explaining particular economic and market phenomena which they have observed and which interest them. But what does a causal explanation consist of? 'In the widest sense of the word, to explain is to answer a Why? question' (Blaug 1980: 6). In the context of entrepreneurship, examples of such 'Why? questions' include: why did one of our competitors choose that particular marketing strategy (including pricing policy)? Why has our major rival overinvested in physical capacity? Why have potential customers not bought our new product? Why did venture capitalists reject our latest application for further funding? Why have our own competitive actions had certain unexpected consequences? In seeking to explain, the entrepreneur also aims to answer 'How? questions' connected with the market: How did our competitors achieve superior financial performance? How did they overcome the marketing, production and transaction-cost problems that we encountered?

In everyday parlance, to explain something is to make it

intelligible. Explanation is thus a way for entrepreneurs to cope with their environment and to make sense of the world. More precisely, entrepreneurs seek theories (of latent demand, of governance, of production, etc.) that are explanatory and possibly true, even though they can never prove that any particular theory is true. Falsificationist entrepreneurs thus reject instrumentalism because they want their theories to be true as well as predictively adequate. They are realists who prefer causal explanation to (statistical) correlation.

In contrast to the previous two aims, control implies that rather than merely treat the environment detachedly as something to be explained and predicted, entrepreneurs seek to make it controllable. Entrepreneurs are not simply concerned with foreseeing the unravelling of a predetermined pattern of economic events but rather with creating a state of affairs which is geared to their advantage: '[F]uture is not there to be discovered, but must be created' (Shackle 1969: 16). More specifically, the inclusion of control in the set of entrepreneurial aims implies that, in the pursuit of profits, entrepreneurs must attempt to shape the kinds of, and terms of, transactions that will be entered into during future market periods.

The entrepreneur's aims extend deeper into the realm of practical action than do those of the theoretical scientist. From a new scientific theory, a novel prediction is deduced which is typically independent of the actions of the theoretical scientist who proposes that theory. For example, Einstein's prediction that light could be bent by a strong gravitational field was a prediction, the fate of which did not depend upon any actions that Einstein himself may have taken (although it did indirectly depend upon the practical ingenuity of the experimenter to control and exclude possible interfering factors).

In contrast, entrepreneurs' predictions of the existence of profit opportunities are deduced directly, among other things, from assumptions about their own actions. Intuitively, one would expect that an important component of entrepreneurs' conjectures about the potential success or failure of commercial ventures is their personal evaluation of their own ability to influence results, which in turn implies an intention to control market events. Action-oriented entrepreneurs who propose business plans intend to play a major role in bringing about the very phenomena predicted in their own plans. Entrepreneurs choose situations in which they can have a personal impact on problems and outcomes. Prediction *and* control are thus crucial for the ultimate decision to undertake a particular entrepreneurial venture.

4.1.1 Consistency with the economics literature of entrepreneurship

The economics literature of the entrepreneur is consistent with the aim structure that has been proposed above. Marshall and Knight both emphasised the predictive aims of entrepreneurs. Competing entrepreneurs 'must have the power of forecasting the broad movements of production and consumption, of seeing where there is an opportunity of supplying a new commodity that will meet a real want or improving the plan of producing an old commodity' (Marshall 1961: 297). Knight maintained that in a world of structural uncertainty, the distinguishing characteristic of entrepreneurship is foresight in anticipating the future constellation of market demand and supply. He argued that individuals differ in the degree of foresight that they possess and that competition exerts a tendency to select individuals with the greatest degree of foresight to specialise in making entrepreneurial decisions.

Although expressed in somewhat different terms, the works of Mises, Kirzner and Casson are also compatible with an emphasis upon prediction and control as essential components of the entrepreneur's aim structure. Mises argued that successful entrepreneurs are those who are able to 'anticipate better than other people the future demand of the consumers' (1949: 288). Hence, Mises is identifying successful entrepreneurs *ex post* on the basis of their superior predictive ability. Similarly, Kirzner's later work on multiperiod alertness is consistent with the GK approach:

> [A]cting man really does try to construct his picture of the future to correspond to the truth as it will be realized. . . . He is thus motivated *to bring about* correspondence between the envisaged and the realized futures.
>
> (Kirzner 1982c: 149; original emphasis)

In fact, Kirzner actually defines alertness as the motivated propensity of human beings to form an as accurate as possible image of the future – which is tantamount to what I describe in objective terms as the entrepreneur's aim to predict the future. Furthermore, Kirzner argues that the function of entrepreneurship (at the level of the individual) is to limit the divergence between an entrepreneur's own anticipated future concerning market transactions and the future as it will actually develop (1982c: 149–153). He refers to alertness as the entrepreneurial element in human action 'which provides the only pressure to constrain man's envisaged future toward some correspondence with the future to be realized' (1982c: 150). At a later juncture, he adds: 'the entrepreneur may, by his own creative actions, in fact construct the future as he wishes it to be' (1982c: 155). Kirzner's interpretation of the function of entrepreneurship at the level of the individual thus revolves around each entrepreneur's aiming to predict and to control market events.

Like Kirzner, Casson (1982: 124) regards prediction and control as key elements in entrepreneurial success. Indeed, Casson (1982: 49) argues that there are two main ways that entrepreneurs can coordinate decisions: either by contract or by conjecture. Coordination by conjecture is of particular interest because it involves one or more entrepreneurs aiming to predict or to control the decisions of other agents without their agreement.

The discussion now shifts away from economic theories of entrepreneurship towards psychological studies of the entrepreneur, in order to see whether there is any tentative correspondence between the aim structure that I have assumed and this literature.

4.1.2 A psychological digression

Unfortunately, many empirical studies into the psychology of the entrepreneur have not been distinguished by conceptual clarity: definitions of the entrepreneur have often been vague and do not correspond directly to the precise notions of entrepreneurship in economic theory (Kets de Vries 1977: 38). The entrepreneur is often defined loosely as an individual who sets up a business venture, usually a firm. The distinction between entrepreneur and manager is also often unclear. In spite of these methodological and definitional problems, however, there is some consistency between the GK conception of the entrepreneur's aim structure and the psychological literature of the entrepreneur, especially that applying Rotter's (1966) theory of locus of control.[3]

According to the theory of *locus of control*, individuals believe that the outcomes of events are either within or beyond their personal control. An individual with a belief in internal control perceives that an event is 'contingent upon his own behavior or his own relatively permanent characteristics' (Rotter 1966: 1). 'Internal' people thus believe that they have some control over events in their life and that they are, therefore, responsible for their own destiny. They expect that the environment can be manipulated by their own actions. In contrast, an individual with a belief in external control perceives an event 'as following some action of his own but not . . . entirely contingent upon his action' (Rotter 1966: 1). 'External' people interpret events as the result of outside factors which they cannot influence, such as luck, chance and fate, or they see events as under the control of 'powerful others' (see Levenson 1974) or as 'unpredictable because of the great complexity of the forces' surrounding them (Rotter 1966: 1).

The entrepreneur in the GK theory has been characterised as a scientist in the general sense of one who tries to predict, to explain and to control events. The proposition that entrepreneurs can be treated as if they are scientists can now be restated in terms of the theory of locus of control: namely, it is hypothesised that entrepreneurs are internal people.

Indeed, there is some support within the empirical psychological literature for characterising an entrepreneur as an internal person. Shapero (1975) and Brockhaus and Nord (1979) found that entrepreneurs in their samples tended to hold more internal locus of control beliefs than those reported by Rotter (1966) for all groups in the general population except Peace Corps volunteers. In addition, there is some suggestion that the concept of internal locus of control may be a better predictor of entrepreneurial intentions to start a business venture than McClelland's concept of need for achievement, or *n Ach* (Borland 1974; Brockhaus 1975, 1982). Hence, internal locus of control may be a useful concept for identifying entrepreneurs.[4] Furthermore, the locus of control concept may also hold some promise for distinguishing between successful and unsuccessful entrepreneurs (Brockhaus 1980).[5]

Psychological studies have suggested that certain characteristics, abilities and behaviour patterns are correlated with internal locus of control. For my purposes, it is quite significant that various studies have discovered that a belief in internal locus of control is associated with a more active role by individuals in shaping events and with striving to control their environment (Brockhaus 1975; McClelland 1961; Shapero 1975). It has also been found that internals are more likely to have a high *n Ach* than individuals with external locus of control beliefs. Furthermore, internal persons have been found to more actively search for strategic information and knowledge relevant to their situation, to be more likely to attain such knowledge, and to be more efficient at processing information (Seeman and Evans 1962; Wolk and DuCette 1974). Thus, if it is accepted that entrepreneurs are internal people, then entrepreneurs may also exhibit these other characteristics – characteristics which are not unrelated to the GK conception of entrepreneurship.

Related to the concept of locus of control is attribution theory. Attribution theory is a psychological approach which also bears some similarity to the GK portrayal of the entrepreneur's aim structure for it too is concerned with how people try to make causal explanations of events and actions (see, for example: Heider 1944; Jones and Davis 1965; Kelley 1967).[6]

However, the causal explanations of economic actions and events that are acceptable within attribution theory are typically incomplete from the point of view of the GK theory of entrepreneurship. According to attribution theory, people's causal explanations usually only provide information on the initial conditions (i.e. the conditions pertaining to the individual event or action in question). As I shall explain in the next section, however, these conditions by themselves never suffice as satisfactory explanations for economic agents within the GK theory (cf. Popper 1959: 60; 1972: 350–352). The initial conditions describe what the attribution theorist would call the 'cause' of the event in question. The explanations that people find acceptable according to attribution theory usually do not include universal laws or even loose generalisations, even though from a logical point of view at least one general law is needed for any complete explanation. People in attribution theory by and large omit general laws from their causal explanations supposedly because they regard them as being redundant.

For example, according to attribution theory, an entrepreneur's success in concluding a profitable transaction may be attributed by a venture capitalist to an *internal* cause, such as the entrepreneur's high level of leadership ability (which is a *stable* personal characteristic). But from the initial condition alone ('This particular entrepreneur has a high level of leadership ability'), the venture capitalist is not able to validly deduce the state of affairs to be explained (namely, this entrepreneur's commercial success). Hence, the venture capitalist's explanation of entrepreneurial success is incomplete. A more complete causal explanation requires that the venture capitalist add a general law regarding the effects of entrepreneurial leadership ability, such as, 'If any individual entrepreneur has a high level of leadership ability, he or she will successfully conclude a profitable transaction'. Clearly, if the venture capitalist had held the general hypothesis that, 'Any entrepreneur's leadership ability is irrelevant to his or her success in concluding profitable transactions', then the original initial condition ('This particular entrepreneur has a high level of leadership ability') obviously could not be an acceptable explanation of the entrepreneur's success.

Furthermore, in contrast to the GK theory, the explanations made by agents in attribution theory are not necessarily independently testable: it is not required that the premises of their explanations have testable consequences which are quite independent of the state of affairs they are trying to explain. Finally, agents in attribution theory are likely to commit the fallacy of *post hoc, ergo propter hoc*, that is, of inferring causation from coincidental conjunction. The application of Kelley's (1967) covariation principle, for example, is likely to lead people to mistakenly assume that if one event is observed on several occasions to happen after another event, then the later event is necessarily caused by the earlier one. So-called 'valid causal attributions' are thus prone to being fallacious. Unlike the attributional approach, the GK theory claims that there are no inductive inferences involved in economic agents' predictions and explanations.

4.2 ECONOMIC AGENTS' USE OF DEDUCTIVE LOGIC IN THEIR REASONING

As the embodiment of canons of rationality, truths of logic, supplemented with appropriate methodological rules, are constitutive of the critical approach or attitude which Popper takes to be the proper one for the scientist.

(Krige 1978: 314)

In line with its hard-core assumptions HC6 and HC7 described in section 1.4.1, the GK approach portrays entrepreneurs and other actors as using deductive logic in their reasoning and decision-making. These hard-core assumptions are not intended to imply that economic agents usually conduct their reasoning in terms of precisely formulated syllogisms. Both in science and in economic life, the mental act of deductive reasoning may in practice be silent or expressed, unconscious or deliberate; some premises may be so obvious or well known that they are applied quite intuitively, rather than stated explicitly (Jarvie 1976: 331; cf. Popper 1972: 350–354; Stewart 1979: 15). The hard core of the GK programme merely claims that, in so far as they embody rational decision-making, entrepreneurs reason correctly when reaching conclusions by connected thought.[7] For the rules of deductive logic are simply the rules of correct (syllogistic) reasoning. (In the present context, it is not necessary to justify the principles of deductive logic. Their rationality is assumed to be beyond question.) Thus, as part of developing a line of analysis, the GK theory assumes that entrepreneurs do not make gross errors of propositional inference, such as passing truth backwards (reverse *modus ponens*) and passing falsity forwards (reverse *modus tollens*). Similarly, I assume that entrepreneurs do not purposefully violate the law of contradiction whenever they adjust their sets of conjectures in the light of results from their market experiments. It must also be noted that nothing here implies that entrepreneurial rationality is unlimited with respect to its powers of prediction, explanation and control.

The GK programme assumes that deduction is central to the pattern of reasoning in all sciences and in practical decision-making (HC6). Consequently, entrepreneurs are assumed to use deductive logic whenever they: (i) attempt to predict the economic future; (ii) provide a causal explanation of an observed market event; or (iii) test their conjectures against market reality. Each of these uses of deductive logic will now be discussed in turn.

From their premises, entrepreneurs are assumed to logically deduce predictions about market events which they have not yet observed. Their premises are of two different kinds. The major premise comprises one or more general hypotheses about the market or economy (e.g. 'Whenever market events of type X occur, market events of type Y also occur'). The minor premise consists of a set of specific initial conditions that describe the state of the market at particular times and places (e.g. 'A market event of type X occurred in New York on 29 September 1994').[8] From the conjunction of these two premises (i.e. the general hypothesis about the market and the relevant initial conditions), each entrepreneur proceeds to deduce a specific prediction about the practical market situation which is of interest. An example of such a specific prediction is the claim: 'A market event of type Y will also occur in New York on 29 September 1994'.

Similarly, an entrepreneur explains a market phenomenon by a logical deduction, the conclusion of which is a description of the market state to be explained, and the premises of which include one or more general hypotheses about the market and a set of initial conditions.

Prediction and explanation are two different sides of the same activity, the only difference being that prediction is before the event and explanation is after. The derivation of predictions is simply an inversion of the logical scheme of explanation.[9] Explanation involves accounting for the known by the unknown, whereas prediction entails deducing statements of the unknown from the known. In a causal explanation, the entrepreneur takes the conclusion of the logical deduction as given (i.e. the market event to be explained is assumed to be known from observation) and the entrepreneur searches for suitable premises of the deduction (at least one general hypothesis plus a set of initial conditions). Any premises created by the entrepreneur to form the heart of the explanation are hypothetical or conjectural. The derivation of predictions proceeds in the opposite direction to that of explanations. In making a prediction, the entrepreneur takes the premises as given (i.e. both the general hypotheses about the market and the description of particular market conditions are assumed to be true), and from them the entrepreneur deduces logical conclusions (i.e. predictions) about particular unknown market events (Popper 1972: 191–192, 349–353).

Entrepreneurs are also presumed to draw on logic as an instrument for evaluating their own conjectures. 'Logic is there to help us unpack the consequences of statements [e.g. predictions] we are considering, with a view to discovering inconsistencies between those statements and others, and then transmitting the falsity thus disclosed back through the system' (Jarvie 1976: 331). In order to learn from the testing of plans in the market, economic agents need logical rules for rationally rejecting the particular theories, conjectures or expectations on which their disappointed plans were based. The testing of plans in the market involves comparing the market events they predict with the actual market events they observe. If any one of their predictions about the market does not conform with the observed market situation, then by means of an important part of deductive logic – namely, the principle of *modus tollens*[10] – entrepreneurs are able to conclude that not all their supposed knowledge (i.e. the basis for their practical actions) can be true. In other words, provided their argument is logically consistent, they will reach the conclusion that there must be a false premise: either their general hypotheses about the behaviour of the market are false and/ or the initial conditions are false (i.e. the initial conditions describe a state of market affairs which does not actually correspond with real market conditions). Prior to further testing and investigation, the entrepreneur cannot know what is to blame for the falsity of the market prediction, for indeed both kinds of premise may be false. This point is elaborated in section 8.4.

A highly simplified neoclassical example can serve to illustrate how learning from the experience of error requires the use of deductive logic. For the sake of convenience, let us start by assuming that all prices observed in the real world are market-clearing prices and that each agent is a price-taker. Suppose that an 'entrepreneur' holds speculative stocks of laser video players, which she intends to sell whenever the price rises above the current level quoted in the market. The entrepreneur holds a general theory about the market which asserts that 'If there is an increase in demand for laser video players, its price will rise'. Suppose too that, having commissioned market research immediately prior to the opening of the next period's trading, the entrepreneur discovers that the demand for laser video players has in fact risen as a result of a change in consumer tastes in favour of this product. From these two premises (i.e. the general hypothesis about the market and the initial conditions), the entrepreneur validly deduces the prediction that the market-clearing price for laser video players will rise. Thus, the entrepreneur plans to sell her speculative stocks because she expects to be able to sell them at the higher price.

Now suppose that the real world disappoints the entrepreneur by not conforming to expectation. The entrepreneur observes that the price of laser video players does not actually rise. From a logical perspective, the entrepreneur thus discovers an *apparent* contradiction between her *supposed* knowledge and the *putative* empirical evidence generated by market participation (cf. Popper 1976a: 88). Say that the entrepreneur decides to accept the evidence that the price of laser video players has not actually risen[11] and that, therefore, her prediction is false. The entrepreneur now needs deductive logic in order to recognise that at any time any one of her predictions is false at least one of her premises must also be false. By *modus tollens* she can argue from the falsity of her predictions against the truth of her premises. In terms of the example, she therefore deduces the conclusion that at least one of her two premises is false: either her general theory about the market is false or the demand for laser video players did not actually rise, or both premises are wrong. The entrepreneur cannot at first know which premise caused the false prediction. The entrepreneur may finally decide to reject her general theory about the market and resolve to replace it with a new theory (still fallible) which contains more than one condition in its antecedent clause: 'If there is an increase in demand for laser video players (and if the demand curve is downward-sloping and if there are no compensating shifts in the supply schedule and if the supply curve is neither perfectly elastic nor perverse), then the price of laser video players will rise'.[12]

Hayek (1945; 1949: 92–106; 1978: 179–190), Kirzner (1973, 1979b, 1992) and O'Driscoll and Rizzo (1985: 103) do not emphasise that learning from market experiences, and especially the experience of error, involves deductive reasoning. For example, Kirzner writes that 'if they (decision-makers) find that their plans cannot be carried out, this *teaches them* that their anticipations concerning the decisions of others were overly optimistic' (Kirzner 1973: 10; emphasis added). But economic agents must *deduce* this conclusion for themselves from their market experience. In order for 'newly acquired information of the plans of others' to generate a 'revised set of decisions' for the succeeding time period, decision-makers require deductive logic to recognise the need for a change in their expectations. Adjusting one's hypotheses and expectations by a logical process of examining their deductive consequences is simply another instance of what in cybernetics is called negative feedback. Furthermore, Kirzner (e.g. 1979b: 6) tends to imply that the inability to execute plans is always caused by false initial conditions (i.e. false market information upon which plans are based), whereas plans can also be frustrated if economic agents' general hypotheses about the behaviour of the market are false (i.e. even if the initial conditions are true).

4.3 FALSIFICATIONIST ENTREPRENEURS' AWARENESS OF THEIR RATIONALITY

The depiction of entrepreneurs as sophisticated falsificationists could be argued to overstate the degree to which entrepreneurs are conscious of their rationality. But just as real-world entrepreneurs do not have to know that they are using the rules of deductive logic whenever they are responding rationally to the disappointment of their plans (i.e. refuting market evidence), so too entrepreneurs do not always have to be consciously aware that they are applying falsificationist methodological rules in their attempts to learn from their market experiences. They are not expected to be experts in scientific method or to be conversant in philosophical lingo. The GK theory merely says that at least some entrepreneurs will behave within a specific framework (set of rules) which is not particularly complex. Thus, in some situations, falsificationist entrepreneurs may follow Popperian rules tacitly: it is conceivable that entrepreneurs know how to learn in a Popperian fashion without being aware of it or being able to articulate that knowledge. (In the same way, a thirteen-year-old newspaper-seller on a busy street corner does not need to know that she is a Kirznerian alert entrepreneur in order to exploit perceived opportunities for personal gain.)

These considerations notwithstanding, there *is* a prominent entrepreneur in the financial markets who consciously thinks of himself as a kind of Popperian – that person is George Soros, a phenomenally successful fund manager. In a recent paper, he explicitly acknowledges that Popperian ideas have assisted him in business:

> Karl Popper's philosophy has had a formative influence on my entire outlook on life. It has affected not only my thinking but also my actions. Strange as it may seem, *it has made a tangible contribution to my business success.*
>
> (Soros 1992: 1; emphasis added)

> I have formulated a theory about the way financial markets function, which bears a curious resemblance to Popper's model of scientific method. It is generally recognized that financial markets try to anticipate the future. The way they do it, I contend, is by adopting a hypothesis which yields a prediction about the future. The actual course of events then serves as a test of the hypothesis. If the test is successful, the hypothesis is reinforced; if it fails, the hypothesis is undermined.
>
> (Soros 1992: 4)

The theory to which Soros is referring is developed and applied in his book, *The Alchemy of Finance: Reading the Mind of the Market*. It views financial markets as a laboratory for testing hypotheses. 'Making an investment decision is like formulating a scientific hypothesis and submitting it to a practical test' (Soros 1987: 14). The more severe the test a hypothesis withstands, the greater the profit afterwards.[13] Similar issues are discussed in Part II of this book.

NOTES

1 Not coincidentally, this assumption is similar to that made in Kelly's (1955, 1963) theory of personality which argues that it may be useful to treat individuals as if they were scientists. Kelly's theory applies to

all people – not just to a particular class of individuals, and it makes no specific mention of entrepreneurs at all (Kelly 1963: 5). The application of Kelly's theory to economics has already been undertaken by Loasby (1983, 1986b, 1991) and by Earl (1983a, 1983b, 1984, 1986a, 1986b).

2 Similarly, Frank (1932: 31) regards science as 'an instrument' whose purpose is 'to predict from immediate or given experiences later experiences, and even as far as possible to control them'. Similarly, Dennis writes of Dewey (1903):

Dewey himself certainly did stress the role of prediction, not only in scientific inquiry, but for the whole sphere of rational human conducts. By choosing from among various possible courses of action the best one, according to what we predict about them, we seek to control or influence the course of events in pursuit of our goals.

(Dennis 1986: 634)

3 For extensive surveys of research into the psychology of the entrepreneur, see: Begley and Boyd (1987); Brockhaus (1982); Brockhaus and Horwitz (1986); Gilad (1982, 1984, 1986); Gilad, Kaish and Ronen (1988); and Maital (1988: vol. II, part 9).

4 However, Hull, Bosley and Udell's (1980) study of business school alumni did not find a relationship between people's locus of control beliefs and the decision to set up a business.

5 In addition to these studies, at least two established 'profiles' of entrepreneurial characteristics appear to follow locus of control theory in emphasising the entrepreneur's basic aim to control events:

Entrepreneurs demonstrate to themselves that they are in control. . . . They see the future in their life as within their control and they strive to exert their influence over future events to prove to themselves, and others, that they are in control.

(Welsh and White 1981: 506)

Entrepreneur's do not believe that success or failure depends mostly on luck, fate or external factors beyond their control. Rather they believe that personal accomplishments as well as setbacks lie within one's personal control and influence.

Entrepreneurs . . . believe that events in their lives are mainly self-determined, and that they have a major influence on their personal destinies.

(Timmons, Smollen and Dingee 1977: 77ff.)

6 See Harvey and Smith (1977) for a comprehensive introduction to attribution theory and Van Raaij (1985: section II) for a brief summary. Weiner's (1974) attributional approach to achievement motivation (which includes an analysis of how people attribute causality to other people's successes and failures) may be especially pertinent to entrepreneurship. Following Weiner, Van Raaij (1985) examines people's attributions of causality to success and failure in economic tasks.

7 This does not mean that the conclusions that an entrepreneur deduces

are materially true (i.e. true of the real world). The correctness of deductive reasoning does not depend upon the material truth of the premises from which the conclusion is derived.

8 It is important to note that the initial conditions identified by the entrepreneur are still hypothetical in character. They are hypothetical in the sense that the entrepreneur may derive testable consequences from them (in conjunction with his or her empirical theories and other initial conditions) such that the falsification of these consequences may entail the falsification of the initial conditions under test (cf. Popper 1959: 75–76). Initial conditions are thus fallible and theory-laden, and the entrepreneur cannot prove them to be true.

9 This notion that prediction and explanation are formally equivalent is often called the symmetry thesis. 'It constitutes the heart of the hypothetico-deductive . . . model of scientific explanation' (Blaug 1980: 4).

10 *Modus tollens* is a logically valid mode of inference which passes falsity backward from the conclusions to one or more of the premises:

Premise: If P, then Q;
Observation: not Q;
Conclusion: therefore not P.

Boland (1979a: esp. 504–505, 512) provides a useful and concise statement on deductive logic.

11 More technically, the actual truth-value of the singular market-test statement is decided by the entrepreneur (cf. Lakatos 1970: 106–107).

12 As I shall show later in my discussion of immunising stratagems, such a response by the entrepreneur is not entirely satisfactory since it reduces the informative content and hence testability of the entrepreneur's claims about the market. However, it may constitute progress towards the truth, in that it involves replacing a stronger falsehood by a weaker truth.

13 Soros accepts most of Popper's ideas on scientific method, with one major exception. He rejects Popper's doctrine of the unity of method and takes the opposite position – that is, Soros maintains that the methods that apply to the study of social events differ fundamentally from those that apply to the study of natural phenomena (Soros 1987: 11–14, 34–40; 1992: 4–9). This is because the phenomena the social sciences deal with have 'thinking participants' whereas natural phenomena do not. He uses this perspective in developing his 'theory of reflexivity'. 'Reflexivity' refers to the two-way connection between market participants' perceptions, which are inherently flawed, and the actual course of events.

I am grateful to an anonymous referee for bringing Soros's views to my attention.

5

THE ENTREPRENEUR'S SYSTEM OF THEORIES

The business man who forms an expectation is doing precisely what a scientist does when he formulates a working hypothesis. Both business expectation and scientific hypothesis serve the same purpose; both reflect an attempt at cognition and orientation in an imperfectly known world, both embody imperfect knowledge to be tested and improved by later experience.

(Lachmann 1959: 65)

Theories are nets cast to catch what we call 'the world': to rationalize, to explain, and to master it. We endeavour to make the mesh ever finer and finer.

(Popper 1959: 59)

5.1 WHY DO ENTREPRENEURS NEED THEORIES?

In this chapter, I try to be more explicit about what an entrepreneurial theory is and about the cardinal features that it has. I emphasise the hierarchical structure of the entrepreneur's theoretical system and discuss both the metaphysical and empirical aspects of the entrepreneur's stock of knowledge. Throughout this book, the terms 'theories', 'hypotheses' and 'conjectures' are used more or less interchangeably. They do not necessarily indicate conceptual units of different sizes or of different degrees of generality.

The aim structure of the entrepreneur and the rationality assumptions described in the previous chapter imply that the entrepreneur needs to construct theories.[1] Entrepreneurs need to devise theories so as to fulfil their basic aims of explaining, predicting and controlling market events in the pursuit of economic gain. Theoretical systems serve as a basis for interpreting, understanding, and imposing order upon, aspects of their experience. They provide entrepreneurs with a framework for action and control. The formation of theories and abstract concepts is an essential means by which entrepreneurs adapt to, and cope with, the structural uncertainty and complexity inherent in their environment:

> Abstractness will here be regarded, therefore, not only as a property possessed to a greater or lesser degree by all (conscious or unconscious) mental processes, but as the basis of man's capacity to move successfully in a world very imperfectly known to him – an *adaptation to his ignorance* of most of the particular facts of his surroundings.
>
> (Hayek 1973: 30; emphasis added)

Entrepreneurs must formulate theories in order to create and to discover potential market opportunities for improved coordination. Prior theoretical frameworks are required for the selection and interpretation of market data. Abstract relations – which are equivalent to theories – 'enable us to discriminate between different things and to respond to them differentially' (Hayek 1978: 37). Entrepreneurs are only able to recognise something as new and different (e.g. changes in consumer tastes, technology or resources) if they are equipped with expectations of what is ordinary. In addition, their perceptions of similarity in two or more market events presuppose the adoption of a point of view, that is, the adoption of a theory (Popper 1959: 420–421). If entrepreneurs did not have any system of theories, market events would seem to them to be of such an indistinguishable homogeneity that they would not be able to make sense of what is happening in the market. (Of course, this is itself a theoretical proposition.) Entrepreneurial action would be purposeless.

If entrepreneurs are to have any possibility of understanding the world and of effecting changes within it, they will be forced to abstract and to simplify. Entrepreneurs must select those aspects of a situation which are related to their specific purposes and to the particular problems in which they are interested. Their theories and models assist them in focusing their attention on specific segments of the dense complexity which characterises their concrete existence. 'We never act, and could never act, in full consideration of all the facts of a particular situation, but always by singling out as relevant only some aspects of it' (Hayek 1973: 30). For example, an entrepreneur marketing computer software does not typically consider the colour of customers' hair in the development of marketing strategy, although hair colour is indeed one of countless variables to which the entrepreneur could conceivably attend in this empirical situation. One potential reason for such selectivity is that the entrepreneur assumes that the colour of customers' hair is not relevant to his or her problem: it is hypothesised that this factor has no effect or no detectable effect upon the phenomenon of interest. More specifically, the entrepreneur implicitly makes the *negligibility assumption* that the colour of customers' hair does not affect the success of policies to market computer software (cf. Musgrave 1981). However, for a completely different problem, such as the marketing of cosmetics, spectacles, clothing, or jewellery etc., hair colour may be considered especially pertinent and worthy of the entrepreneur's attention.

5.2 GENERAL CHARACTERISTICS OF ENTREPRENEURS' THEORETICAL SYSTEMS

The theoretical systems that entrepreneurs construct (and the entrepreneurial action programmes they derive from them) possess several important properties:

- a hierarchical structure and near-decomposability;
- openness to change, revision and replacement (i.e. theories are not static);
- limitations of scope;
- a conjectural (non-verifiable) and potentially objective character;
- individuality (i.e. theories are specific to individual entrepreneurs, of whose imaginations they are a product).

The following discussion will concentrate upon the first of these – the hierarchical structure of the entrepreneur's system of knowledge – because it contributes most to explaining aspects of entrepreneurial behaviour, such as why an entrepreneur may act as if his or her conjectures in one domain are not interlinked with those in another.

The entrepreneur's theoretical system, like that of the scientist, is a hierarchically organised structure. Among other things, an entrepreneur's theoretical system comprises individual theories at different epistemological levels of abstraction: theories about interactions at one level (e.g. within a particular market or industry) and theories at higher levels (e.g. a set of markets) or lower levels (e.g. specific market segments). Those of the entrepreneur's theories on higher levels of abstraction describe *deeper* layers of reality, even though the states of affairs these theories describe are more hypothetical or conjectural (cf. Popper 1963: 115–116). Thus, the more *general* the entrepreneur's empirical theories about the world, the greater the *depth* in the entrepreneur's claims about reality (see section 6.3.1 on the falsifiability principle).

Each entrepreneurial theory is in turn a hierarchical system of deductively linked hypotheses which incorporate different degrees of generality (though by no means does the entrepreneur make all deductive linkages explicit).[2] At the apex of the scale of generality are the highest-level postulates and hypotheses which the entrepreneur builds into a particular theory. They are the propositions from which the entrepreneur derives all others in elaborating that theory. In a sense these assumptions determine and entail all the lower-level claims made by the entrepreneur about reality. However, like real-life scientists, entrepreneurs often have some difficulty in assessing whether one hypothesis is really of a higher or lower level than another.

Each entrepreneurial theory comprises a number of individual elements conjoined together into a more or less coherent whole. Entrepreneurs try to minimise the mutual contradictions and irrelevancies between these elements. However, because the environment is in a state of flux and entrepreneurs are continually changing their conjectures, it is very rare for an entrepreneur's theoretical system to exhibit perfect unity and total consonance at any point of time.

At the risk of oversimplification, it may be fair to say that the criticism, plastic control and correction of the entrepreneur's hypotheses proceed upwards from lower to higher levels of the hierarchy of knowledge, whereas prediction goes in the opposite direction:

> 'Reasoning downwards in generality' means deducing consequences – making predictions – from hypotheses; while reasoning upwards [to higher-level statements] corresponds to the hypothetico-deductive 'testing' process, where a hypothesis that is not directly testable is checked by reference to a directly testable consequence (or where a more general hypothesis is assessed by reference to one that is less general).
>
> (Stewart 1979: 72)

More specifically, the entrepreneur's theoretical system is a multilevel hierarchy which consists of the following major structural components: metaphysical principles, empirical theories, and specific predictions.[3] Each of these is discussed separately in the remainder of this chapter. I also have some comments to make about the entrepreneur's action programmes.

5.3 THE ENTREPRENEUR'S METAPHYSICAL PRINCIPLES

The entrepreneur's metaphysical ideas are purely speculative and can often be quite vague and fuzzy. They are articles of faith which the entrepreneur holds firmly. The configuration of these ideas is thus likely to be highly stable over quite a long period of time. Included in this category are the following sorts of assumptions:

- the cluster of hard-core assumptions that the entrepreneur makes about the world, its regularity, and his or her location in space, time, society and nature;
- the entrepreneur's basic beliefs about people, their openness to change, their needs (including their needs for self-esteem and social regard), the driving forces that motivate them, their honesty and trustworthiness (including the extent to which they act in good faith when unanticipated events occur), their altruism, asceticism and obedience, and the entrepreneur's beliefs about the attributes of human nature which are important to contracting processes. Two divergent sets of assumptions about human nature are neatly exemplified by McGregor's (1960) *Theory X* and *Theory Y*. The particular pattern of these assumptions will in turn shape the entrepreneur's theory of leadership;
- the entrepreneur's beliefs about wealth, material gain and economic security;
- the entrepreneur's beliefs about the forces or constraints, if any, which delimit market events, and his or her beliefs about the control of fate in business (and especially about his or her influence over the outcomes of ventures) (Gasse 1986: 52);
- the entrepreneur's assumptions about the sovereignty of consumers and the autonomy of consumer preferences (including assumptions about the extent to which marketing strategies can alter, reveal or create consumer tastes and thereby change consumers' behaviour to suit the entrepreneur's own ends);
- the proverbs about 'the economy' that the entrepreneur accepts, the entrepreneur's preconceptions about the economic process as a whole and about what is causally or teleologically significant

within it, and his or her common-sense ideas about economic theory. Also included here are the entrepreneur's convictions about the extent to which market prices reveal the private information of other agents (Bacharach 1986: 175–176, 181).

These fundamental presumptions correspond to what Kelly in his theory of personality (1955, 1963) refers to as an individual's 'core constructs' and to what Converse (1964) calls 'central idea-elements' in a person's political 'belief-system'. Taken together, they also resemble Boulding's (1956) notion of 'the Image' and Gasse's (1986) concept of an ideology of business. It should be noted that it is not so much the effect of one particular metaphysical idea taken in isolation that is important in explaining entrepreneurial behaviour, but rather the effect of the metaphysical programme as a whole (cf. Rokeach 1960). Another point is that entrepreneurs are often not aware of their own metaphysical speculations and rationalisations.

Metaphysical theories are not testable, either because of their logical form or because of dogmatic decisions made by the entrepreneur to allow them to go unquestioned for the time being. Entrepreneurs may develop them into testable empirical theories at later stages of the venture process or of their careers. Although metaphysical ideas may at times slow down the entrepreneur's learning, it must be remembered that they are a prerequisite to entrepreneurial discovery: they are an important source of entrepreneurial inspiration and perform a useful heuristic role in guiding the entrepreneur's search for information. New entrepreneurial ventures would be impossible without them.

5.4 THE ENTREPRENEUR'S THEORY OF LATENT DEMAND

An entrepreneur's theoretical system (T) is a superordinate construct which encompasses at least three subordinate empirical theories:

- a theory of latent demand (t^d);
- a theory of production (t^p);
- a theory of governance or, of the organisation of, transactions (t^g).

The entrepreneur's theory of latent demand is discussed in detail in this section. The other two components are examined in the following sections.

The entrepreneur's theory of latent demand involves conjectures about the most urgent of the as yet unsolved problems of consumers and hypotheses about the new bundles of product characteristics that will satisfy these latent demands. It also includes conjectures about the price–quantity–quality configurations by which target consumers will be willing to buy the entrepreneur's new product over a period of time. More specifically, the entrepreneur forms a complex set of conjectures about:

- the factors which determine the demand for the new product; the rate of growth and variability over time of demand, including the significance of seasonality in demand;
- total market demand for alternative forms of the entrepreneur's new product, that is, the total quantity that will be bought by the target customer group in a selected geographical area during a specified time period under a given marketing programme (especially product and pricing strategies) and assuming given environmental conditions; the maximum price that the entrepreneur thinks possible without inducing production by potential or actual rivals; the sales profile of the entrepreneur's venture as consumer learning from experience with the product takes place; minimum and maximum possible first-time sales, replacement sales and repeat sales of the new product in each period (these conjectures in turn will depend upon the entrepreneur's assumptions about the factors which affect the actual timing of replacement and repeat sales, such as the survival-age distribution of the product and possible competitive offerings available at the replacement date etc.);
- the characteristics of potential end-use customers (i.e. the structure and composition of market demand): who will buy, where they will buy, when they will buy, how often they will buy, why they will buy; the degree of heterogeneity of potential customers in terms of their goals, resource endowments, knowledge and problem situations; the possible dimensions for segmenting markets (e.g. geographic, demographic, psychographic/life-style, benefit, volume, situation-specific and person–situation segmentation); the characteristics which a resulting market segment must exhibit for it to be profitable to develop a separate marketing programme tailored to it (e.g. measurability, accessibility, responsiveness and substantiality); taxonomic principles for classifying the problem situations of groups of consumers; the knowledge that potential consumers have about the products in existence, the terms on which they are available, their qualitative characteristics and their

power to cater to consumers' requirements; how to take consumers' transaction costs of exchange into account when designing alternative marketing strategies and pricing schemes; the purchasing methods employed by buyers (e.g. haggling, acceptance of list prices, solicitation of quotes);

- the elasticities of demand with respect to changes in relative prices or product characteristics; how elasticities of demand can depend upon complementarities – linkages between consumers' activities – and the associated costs of disrupting consumers' existing patterns of choice; how demand elasticities vary across groups of potential customers; how the price-elasticity of demand facing the entrepreneur will change over the product life cycle, especially with increased product standardisation and consumer experience with the product;

- the extent, if any, to which the entrepreneur can engineer people's individual demand functions by marketing strategies and by particular tools in the marketing communications mix (especially advertising, sales promotion, personal selling and publicity); whether the demands of individual consumers are independent of one another or whether there are interaction effects;

- the events and situations which cause problems for consumers (e.g. the failure of existing products); how entrepreneurs can stimulate potential consumers into recognising the urgency of hitherto overlooked problems;

- how consumers create a choice agenda of possible activities: that is, how they identify a relevant set of options that could conceivably be solutions to their problems;

- the methods consumers use to evaluate and choose between rival possible schemes of action; the sets of decision rules and evaluative criteria used by consumers to choose between competing products (conceived as bundles of characteristics); the relative importance different segments of consumers assign to these criteria in particular use-contexts; whether consumers evaluate product characteristics simultaneously or sequentially and the number of characteristics that they consider; in particular, whether target customers for the entrepreneur's new product employ neoclassical, compensatory or non-compensatory decision procedures, and if the latter, then whether they use disjunctive, lexicographic or conjunctive choice models (or some hybrid form).

Following Cantillon (1931), the growth-of-knowledge (GK) theory rejects the notion that demand functions are in any way given to the entrepreneur. Rather it is assumed that the *constellation of demand* must be discovered (however tentatively) by the entrepreneur through a process of trial and error-elimination. This process of learning is not confined to the discovery of the demand function for a pre-specified new product which possesses a given set of physical attributes. The reason for this is that the entrepreneur must also try to discover the combinations of product characteristics that are valued by particular groups of potential consumers in particular situations. (More on this shortly.) In order to test hypotheses about which combinations consumers value most, the entrepreneur must typically experiment in a piecemeal fashion with the elements of the marketing mix. Not surprisingly, the entrepreneur is considered unlikely to subscribe to formal neoclassical theories of demand, for reasons that Richardson has elaborated:

> Formal demand theory assumes that consumers are able to determine an order of preference between different combinations from a fixed list of distinct commodities; it represents no more than a simple application of the logic of choice. If we wish to consider, as does an entrepreneur, which *kinds* and *qualities* of goods to produce, then this model of consumers' behaviour needs to be replaced.
>
> (Richardson 1960: 102; emphasis added)

Even Lancaster's (1966) modified neoclassical theory of demand, which to its credit portrays consumers as wanting goods for the characteristics they expect them to contain, is not satisfactory because it fails to emphasise the *situations* of decision-makers sufficiently.[4] Consequently, his theory cannot account for the immense variability in consumer behaviour that the entrepreneur must somehow attempt to explain and harness. Furthermore, it retains much of the neoclassical apparatus, such as utility maximisation and convex preference orderings, and thus leads to deterministic models of consumer behaviour.

According to the GK theory, the entrepreneur applies the *method of situational analysis* in order to explain and to predict consumer behaviour and to segment market demand. Consequently, the entrepreneur analyses the *situations* of groups of consumers because demand is conjectured to be a function of the interaction of individuals with their situations.[5] The entrepreneur subdivides market demand into distinct groups of consumers who are conjectured to have different demand schedules and to require substantially different product characteristics in different usage situations. The entrepreneur seeks explanatory theories of consumer behaviour which appeal not to psychological elements (such as consumer preferences, tastes, wants and motives, etc.) but rather to objective elements of the situations in which consumers find themselves (such as consumers' goals and knowledge, and the physical, social and temporal dimensions of purchase situations). For any particular case, the entrepreneur reconstructs two distinct problem situations: the usage situation as it is, and the situation as it appears to consumers (i.e. consumers' subjective perceptions of the situation). Both reconstructions are of course conjectural but may be corroborated by independent evidence.

This method of explanation has even found favour with some marketing specialists: 'buyers can be just as naturally described and categorised in terms of the situations they will primarily use the product in, as describing them in terms of demographics, personality-traits or their attitudes' (Dickson undated: 5). Indeed, in the marketing literature there is a growing recognition that individual consumer characteristics are by themselves severely limited in their ability to explain variation in buyers' behaviour. This has prompted marketers to investigate explicitly the role of objective situations (and consumers' perceptions of usage situations) in determining consumer choices (Belk 1974, 1975a, 1975b; Fennell 1978; Lutz and Kakkar 1975). Consequently, both the 'product-use situation' and the 'person within situation' can be regarded as potentially useful bases for explaining and segmenting market demand and for targeting marketing strategy.

From the perspective of person–situation demand analysis, the entrepreneur views each consumer as a problem-solver and thus interprets consumers' actions in any specific situation as attempts to solve problems: '[The ultimate objectives of consumers' activity] can scarcely be described as the satisfaction of individual "tastes"' (Richardson 1960: 103). In particular, most problems arise for consumers in their (disappointed) attempts to predict, explain and control events in their lives. It is the entrepreneur's contention that goods and services are demanded not so much for themselves but rather as possible *means* for obtaining the *ends* of prediction, explanation and control (Alderson 1971: 143; Earl 1986b: 94; 1990a: 732; Gutman 1982). The entrepreneur therefore treats a new product as a novel bundle of situation-specific problem-solving services. (Conversely, any novel bundle of such characteristics may be thought of as a joint product in that it may be able to solve several problems in various situations.)

As part of the method of situational analysis, the entrepreneur may form conjectures about the *net* implications to individual users of utilising his or her new product in particular problem situations. From the subjective standpoint of consumer i in product-use situation j, the key issue is whether or not the *positive* implications appear to exceed the *negative* implications of making the switch to the entrepreneur's new product (see Figure 5.1).[6] In the case of markets for durable capital goods, the *positive* implications for potential industrial buyers (as construed by the entrepreneur) may comprise expected reductions in production costs and/or in transaction costs as a result of using the entrepreneur's new capital item, and/or possible increases in sales revenues. By way of example, a new machine may be expected to lead to lower direct operating costs for the user if it automates some stage of the manufacturing process. If the new capital good is designed to reduce the uncertainty of physical output quality, it may also be anticipated to reduce the user's transaction costs (especially, control, monitoring and measurement costs). The entrepreneur's new good may also be expected to increase the user's sales revenues if demand-enhancement effects are generated by using it in the production process – for example, if the new machine makes possible improvements in product performance and design which are valued by consumers.

On the other hand, the *conjectured negative implications* of starting to use a new good may consist of the amount the consumer must pay for the entrepreneur's new product as well as the consumer's expected transaction costs of organising this exchange. (Indeed, the common distinction made in the marketing literature between convenience goods, shopping goods and specialty goods is based upon the price of the consumer product and the level of transaction costs the consumer bears in evaluating, selecting and obtaining the appropriate item.) Because consumers do not have proven true knowledge of the merits of every product or characteristics-bundle compared to another, they will often make experimental purchases as part of their continual quest to discover new and better ways of solving their problems and achieving their specific goals. In this way, their patterns of choice can be expected to change over time.

Entrepreneurs' theories of consumer behaviour will have a major impact upon their theories of production, and especially upon their product differentiation strategies. For example, if an entrepreneur

THE ENTREPRENEUR'S THEORIES

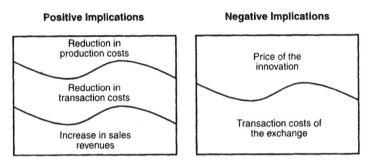

Figure 5.1 The conjectured implications of using a new industrial product

holds the theory that most target customers will use a disjunctive model of choice in the relevant class of purchase situations, the entrepreneur will seek to design the new product so that it performs better than rivals with regard to the single evaluative attribute which is conjectured to dominate consumer choice. (See Earl (1983b: 108–112) for further implications of non-compensatory choice models for product design.)

The entrepreneur's theory of consumer demand, and especially the market segmentation strategy the entrepreneur derives from it, may be a source of competitive advantage. If the entrepreneur's rivals interpret market demand in terms of traditional categories of consumers (e.g. geographic and demographic segments), they may not be alert to the existence of hitherto uncatered for market segments. Suppose then that on the basis of his or her novel segmentation theory, the entrepreneur develops a new product (or characteristics-bundle) specifically tailored to the situation-dependent problems of users in that segment and that the entrepreneur subsequently dominates the target market at a profit. If competitors do not share the same theory of market segmentation, they may be unable to discover the reasons for the entrepreneur's success. And since they cannot explain the source of the entrepreneur's success, the types of people purchasing the new product and the specific problems they are seeking to solve by consuming it, then rivals will experience some difficulty in encroaching upon the entrepreneur's dominant market position, unless they can construct new and better theories of market

147

segmentation. Consequently, the entrepreneur's profits may continue for some time (Haley 1968: 34; O'Driscoll and Rizzo 1985: 105).

5.5 THE ENTREPRENEUR'S THEORY OF PRODUCTION

The entrepreneur's theory of production contains conjectures about the technological possibilities of combining given inputs into novel products or of obtaining given product concepts from novel combinations of inputs. More specifically, the entrepreneur forms hypotheses about:

- how to characterise the productive transformations of which the entrepreneur's venture may be capable; the nature of the relation between inputs and outputs (e.g. many-to-many relation between sets of inputs and outputs because labour services may be of a variable specification and yield a variable performance);
- alternative possibilities of plant size and production capacity; for a given plant, the level of capacity utilisation that can be achieved during specified periods under normal working conditions and the plant's maximum technical capacity; the appropriate scale of initial entry and the effect of scale of entry on the entrepreneur's relative cost position; the appropriate length of production runs and how it may change over the product life cycle; the length of production runs necessary if the entrepreneur is to be able to experiment with new product designs so as to test the reactions and needs of consumers; the conditions under which it is appropriate to employ batch mode production rather than continuous process manufacturing, or vice versa; possible adjustments to plant capacity as production and product-mix change during the life of the venture;
- the sequencing of, and the activities involved in, different stages of the production process; the specific input requirements for various production stages; the time schedule of production (e.g. start-up, initial plant tests, full capacity production); the time pattern of production (i.e. whether the new product is to be produced to order or delivered from inventory); possible procedures for quality control, production control and inventory control within a multistage production process;
- possible techniques of production; the elasticity of input substitution; the extent to which the production process will tend to be

labour or capital-intensive; the extent to which relatively skilled workers are required who can participate in the problem-solving process and in the modification of product designs;

- the specificity of inputs used in the production process (e.g. the mix of general purpose machinery and specialised machinery); how production costs change as asset specificity increases; the divisibility of inputs (especially of the manufacturing plant and of major machines); the degree of integration of the production process; the flexibility of alternative technologies and the rate of technological change in the entrepreneur's industry;

- the categorisation of production costs, that is, what to include under the rubric of production costs and how to classify them. Entrepreneurs form conjectures about the amounts they will have to 'pay out' to all factors to produce the planned level of output, including payments to shareholders and any imputed costs (e.g. depreciation and a sufficient rate of return on the money capital invested);

- the relevant dimensions for distinguishing between different kinds of production costs: the components into which total production costs can be divided (e.g. total fixed costs and total variable costs, both of which can in turn be further divided into sunk and salvageable parts);

- the structure of production costs, and the complex set of supply-side mechanisms which continually alters it; the structure of relative factor prices and its determinants; the quantity and quality of factors of production to which the entrepreneur has access at particular factor prices; the effects of organisational slack and X-inefficiency on production costs;

- how production costs vary in the short-run as the level of output changes, together with which costs are constant over a specified range of output; the potential for reducing average production cost over time through the exploitation of possible economies of scale and of scope and also through learning by doing (the 'experience-curve effect'); the lowest level of output which can be expected to yield the envisaged minimum average cost (i.e. the conjectured minimum efficient scale); the determinants of economies of scale and of scope in production; the sacrifices in economies of scale necessitated by alternative market segmentation strategies;

- the production costs of rivals, existing or potential, who could produce near-perfect substitutes for the entrepreneur's product; the likely volume of both competitive and complementary output;

- the ranking of, and the interaction between, the various factors which are critical to the selection of an industrial location (e.g. the location and ownership of essential inputs, the proximity of principal product markets, the existence of infrastructural investment, the socioeconomic environment, public policies, etc.); possible locations and specific sites suitable for the particular venture (especially for the erection and operation of any manufacturing plant);
- the array of possibilities for qualitative variation in output (i.e. for product differentiation).

The GK theory excludes the possibility that entrepreneurs characterise their firms as well-defined, fully specified production sets. It denies that entrepreneurs choose points on a unique production frontier which exists independently of economic agents and the firms which they create. By referring to the entrepreneur's *theory* of production, the GK approach emphasises the experimental elements involved in the production process – the circumstance that the outcome of any particular input decision is not known with certainty. In this connection, Leibenstein (1968: 73) deserves special mention as having identified two subtle assumptions of the neoclassical theory of the production function which he considers to be a major impediment to a satisfactory theory of entrepreneurship: namely, that 'the complete set of inputs are specified and known to all actual or potential firms in the industry, and that there is a fixed relation between inputs and outputs'. He objects to economists treating the production function as a datum. Implicitly pursuing a subjectivist Hayekian argument (Hayek 1937: 39), Leibenstein takes issue with observing economists assuming that actors know facts they do not and cannot actually know: 'Where and to whom in the firm this knowledge is supposed to be available is never stated. In fact, there are great gaps of knowledge about the production function' (1968: 73).[7]

It is clear that the entrepreneur's theory of production is intimately connected to the entrepreneur's other theories. For example, the entrepreneur chooses a capital equipment rig and a target level of capacity utilisation in the light of conjectures about strategic aspects of pricing, such as those related to possible competitive reactions and latent market demand. Economies of scale can be realised only if the output is more or less continually sold, though inventory buffers can be used to some extent to absorb variations in demand. In addition, the envisaged pros and cons of producing to order and of producing to stock will depend, among other things, upon the entrepreneur's conjectures about the importance of being able to satisfy customers quickly (which favours producing to stock) and his or her conjectures about the significance of being able to custom design products which precisely match the buyer's specifications (which favours producing to order).

5.6 THE ENTREPRENEUR'S THEORY OF GOVERNANCE

Different entrepreneurs will hold different theories about the critical dimensions with respect to which economic transactions differ, and they will form different hypotheses about the most efficient and flexible ways of organising certain types of transactions. Different entrepreneurs will have different ideas about the circumstances under which market transaction costs will tend to be relatively high, and they will therefore have different conjectures about the circumstances under which internal organisation is appropriate. As outside observers, we see no *a priori* reason why the governance theories to which entrepreneurs subscribe must necessarily coincide with or conform to Williamson's transaction cost approach, especially since the entrepreneur is entirely absent in Williamson's framework.[8] (In other words, there is no need to invoke some Muth-like rational expectations hypothesis, according to which the forecasts of economic agents are assumed to correspond to the predictions of the 'relevant' economic theory.) As a result, two entrepreneurs, who are otherwise identical except for their theories of governance and who are exposed to the same objective situation, are likely to choose different ways of arranging production and marketing, and their ventures will probably exhibit different patterns of growth.

The entrepreneur's theory of governance comprises conjectures on at least some of the following factors:

- the sets of environmental and human factors, and combinations thereof, that generate obstacles to trade and hence transaction costs;
- the definition of transaction costs (e.g. 'resource losses due to lack of information' (Dahlman 1979: 148)) and the boundaries of the concept of transaction costs;
- the classification of transaction costs into functional categories (e.g. search and information costs, bargaining and decision costs, and policing and enforcement costs);

- the specificity of the inputs which are required in the production and marketing of the entrepreneur's new product (that is, the degree to which assets are fixed in terms of location, function or user). In addition to conjectures on how governance costs vary with asset specificity, level of output and governance structure, the entrepreneur also makes hypotheses about the demand-enhancement effects (e.g. design or performance benefits) and the production-cost consequences (e.g. savings in transportation and inventory costs) that may be yielded by greater asset specificity. Thus, entrepreneurs' theories of governance are linked inextricably to their theories of latent demand and of production;
- the frequency with which transactions recur in bringing the new product to market (i.e. one-time, episodic, highly recurrent);
- the uncertainty in economic transactions, and the sources of such uncertainty (e.g. whether it is exogenously or endogenously created);
- the extent and variety of appropriability, measurement and divisibility problems that can be expected during the development of the venture; in particular, the extent of externality problems which can be expected to arise when independent distributors do not appropriate all the benefits of their efforts to enhance the quality of the entrepreneur's new product or when they do not bear all the costs of quality debasement;
- the cognitive competence of decision-makers with whom the entrepreneur will be engaged in contracting (i.e. the limits to their rationality), and the sophistication of their judgmental decision-making;
- the different types of self-interest seeking to which other parties are prone, including the extent to which the propensity to act opportunistically varies among members of the contracting population, and the difficulties of distinguishing opportunistic from non-opportunistic actors. These conjectures of course are derived from the entrepreneur's metaphysical beliefs about human nature, which were discussed earlier;
- the importance placed on human dignity by parties to different kinds of transactions, and the types of transactions for which dignity is most crucial (especially transactions in internal and external labour markets);
- the potential conflicts which can emerge in contracting processes, the sources of such conflict, and the major transactional milestones which are most critical to the success of the entrepreneur's venture.

Included here are the entrepreneur's conjectures on how competitive (large-numbers) exchange relations can be transformed into small-numbers bargaining conditions, with the associated possibility of 'hold-up' problems at recontracting stages;

- the existence of first-mover advantages which arise when the winner of the original contract acquires a cost advantage (e.g. by virtue of the acquisition of a unique location) (Williamson 1971: 116);
- the comparative merits of alternative governance structures (e.g. firms and markets) as institutions for acquiring knowledge and for coordinating diverse transactions across space and time;
- the kinds of governance structures (and alternative forms of hierarchy) which will: promote a culture of creativity and of critical inquiry into highly complex market problems; safeguard the venture's transaction-specific assets; permit the entrepreneur to appropriate the economic gains from innovation, speculation and arbitrage; help the entrepreneur to cope with the structural uncertainty inherent in competitive market processes; and permit adjustment (at the appropriate speed) to changes in technology, consumer requirements and resource availabilities;
- the possible trade-off between economic efficiency in a static sense (i.e. the minimisation of the sum of production and transaction costs at any particular conjuncture) and flexibility (i.e. the potential for effective adaptation to unanticipated environmental changes); how the nature of what is transaction-cost efficient depends upon whether the entrepreneur perceives the environment to be in equilibrium or disequilibrium; the relative efficiency and the relative flexibility of alternative governance structures under specified circumstances (e.g. under disequilibrium conditions when markets and technologies are constantly changing); and the path-dependency of transaction costs;
- the potential transaction-cost savings that can be realised by switching from one governance structure to another, and the conditions under which such economic gains can be expected to arise;
- the determinants of different forms of divestment and disintegration (i.e. the splitting up of integrated structures into different parts);
- the potential trade-offs between production-cost economies of scale and scope on the one hand and governance-cost economies on the other;
- the interdependence between organisational forms and techniques of production.

153

At the hub of the entrepreneur's theory of governance are his or her ideas about the spectrum of governance structures that can be devised to effect different kinds of entrepreneurial transactions (including arbitrage, speculation and innovation). For any particular economic activity, the entrepreneur's choice of governance structure is not limited to the polar cases of pure markets or hierarchical organisation. There are complex hybrid modes of governance located between both ends of the continuum, and entrepreneurial activity in this intermediate range is widespread (see Best (1990); Joskow (1985); MacMillan and Farmer (1979); Richardson (1972); Williamson (1983a, 1984c, 1985a). Belonging to this middle group of hybrid transactions are venture capital contracts, venture nurturing (including corporate new venture divisions and R & D partnerships), venture spin-offs, joint ventures, franchising, reciprocal trading (including product exchange agreements), share contracts, quasi-vertical integration and other forms of non-standard contractual arrangements. These sorts of transactions can sometimes involve the use of 'hostages' to support the exchange relationship.

From this standpoint, the entrepreneur regards the firm as only a nexus of interrelated contracts, so that the line between the firm and the market becomes blurred. In particular, both the outer boundaries of the new firm, which the entrepreneur sets up as a vehicle for product innovation, and the internal structure of the firm itself are not given but are open to entrepreneurial initiative and imagination. Upon deciding to internalise some sets of related transactions, the entrepreneur must then apply his or her theory of governance in order to design the internal organisational structure of the venture, and especially its degree and form of hierarchy. In addition, the entrepreneur's theory of governance is used to design the external organisation of the venture firm, that is, the linkages and relationships of cooperation between the entrepreneur's venture and other firms which are completely separate in ownership and control. (As omniscient economists, however, we may observe *ex post* that the *actual* structure of the venture is not the sole result of conscious design on the part of the entrepreneur: although of pragmatic origin, much of the structure – such as connections of goodwill and other institutions of inter-firm cooperation – will evolve at least in part spontaneously over time. Because of structural uncertainty, the development of an innovating firm will depend upon many actual circumstances and economic changes which the entrepreneur could not have predicted.)

The transaction cost literature identifies the condition of asset specificity as the most important attribute of transactions and thus as the major determinant of the most efficient governance structure for organising transactions.[9] (Indeed, because the transaction cost approach is mainly presented as a descriptive rather than prescriptive analysis, it implicitly assumes that entrepreneurs and corporate strategists also consider asset specificity to be the critical transactional dimension (cf. Earl 1984: 21).) Asset specificity is defined as the condition which arises when inputs cannot be 'redeployed to alternative uses or by alternative users without the sacrifice of productive value' (Williamson 1986d: 15). For the growth-of-knowledge theorist, this definition should make it clear that the degree of specificity of durable inputs is not, as is typically assumed in transaction cost economics, an exogenous given known with certainty by the economic agent.[10] Rather it is matter of conjecture on the part of the decision-maker. The conjectured degree of asset specificity depends on the entrepreneur's expectations at time t_1 (the moment of the decision to acquire the asset or to set up the governance structure) of the second-best use of the asset at some future date, $t_1 + n'$ when the entrepreneur may foreseeably wish to dispose of that very asset.[11] (At time $t_1 + n'$ of course, the entrepreneur's expectations of the asset's second-best use may differ from those held at time t_1.) Because of structural uncertainty regarding the nature of transactions, both present and future, the entrepreneur may hold false hypotheses about the opportunities for redeploying malinvested assets to other uses or users, and hence the entrepreneur may also hold false conjectures about the specificity of the assets employed in any particular production technique. Such conjectures are most severely tested whenever the entrepreneur actually goes about turning capital goods to their perceived second-best purposes or whenever the entrepreneur tries to sell or lease out the assets to other potential users.

The entrepreneur's theory of governance is predicted to be one of the most important sets of conjectures crucial to entrepreneurial success. Many entrepreneurs fail to consider transaction costs explicitly, or they consistently underestimate the relevance of transaction costs (Picot 1986: 4; Picot and Schneider 1988: 27–31). Transaction costs are conjectured to be the hardest category of costs for entrepreneurs to measure and to predict. In particular, this class of costs is expected to be much less predictable than production costs (cf. Walker and Weber 1984: 378). Consequently, it is conceivable that some entrepreneurs may not even possess a theory of governance, with the result that they will omit transaction costs entirely from their evaluations of the profitability of competing innovative activities. Such entrepreneurs are likely to view their firms as mere production functions (however crude or ill-defined), rather than as governance structures. The assessment of potential transaction costs, and the importance assigned to them, can be expected to depend in part upon the previous functional specialisation of the entrepreneur. More specifically, entrepreneurs with a technical background in engineering are predicted to emphasise production costs and to downplay or ignore governance costs to a greater extent than entrepreneurs with extensive experience in purchasing.

The failure of entrepreneurs to include transaction-cost factors in their formation of business strategies may result in entrepreneurs making incorrect and ill-fated decisions about where to draw the boundaries of their firms.[12] Indeed, false theories of governance are predicted to be a frequent cause of entrepreneurial error and losses.[13] 'Manufacturers sometimes operate on the mistaken premise that more integration is always preferred to less' (Williamson 1983c: 116). Williamson (1983c: 112–116) reports on the losses suffered by manufacturing firms which had made mistaken decisions to integrate forwards into distribution or backwards into the supply of raw materials. Among other things, substantial penalties from full vertical integration are conjectured to have arisen when the integration strategy involved a large sacrifice in economies of scope (and to a lesser extent, when it led to the failure to exhaust scale economies fully).

The emphasis placed upon the entrepreneur's theory of governance is also consistent with the results of an empirical study by Picot, Laub and Schneider (1988, 1989) into innovative business start-ups in Germany. They found the organisation of transactions to be a decisive determinant of the performance of newly founded ventures in their sample. Compared with less successful innovators, the very successful entrepreneurs appeared to adapt their governance structures much more sensitively (and in the direction predicted by Williamson's transaction cost theory) to changing economic conditions. Whereas very successful innovative start-ups tended to shift to external procurement in factor markets as soon as conditions were favourable, less successful new firms tended to do the reverse and brought the production of components in-house. Furthermore, very successful firms utilised more sophisticated and specialised modes of contracting for externally procured resources than did the less successful enterprises. (Less successful firms were also more rigid in their procurement policies and tended to manufacture standardised inputs themselves to a greater degree than very successful firms.) Very successful innovative entrepreneurs made more extensive use of long-term supply contracts, cooperation agreements, written contracts, and complex contracts involving intensive negotiations. In this way, the very successful ventures were able to focus their limited pools of resources upon their hard-core innovative activities which could not be delegated to the external market, and at the same time they were able to govern their contractual relations with external suppliers more efficiently and flexibly. On the basis of their results, Picot *et al.* concluded that the 'design and development of transaction-cost efficient coordination modes seem to be a very important property of innovative entrepreneurs in a dynamic environment' (1988: 28).[14]

5.7 THE ENTREPRENEUR'S SPECIFIC PREDICTIONS

So far I have described the three main types of empirical theories which each entrepreneur puts together in developing an entrepreneurial idea for a new business venture: namely, the entrepreneur's theories of latent demand (t^d), of production (t^p) and of governance (t^g). Entrepreneurs combine their insights into latent demand with their theories of production and of governance in order to make their discoveries and to derive their specific predictions about the existence of profit opportunities. I will now discuss this point in more detail.

From the conjunction (T) of these three empirical theories (together with any auxiliary hypotheses he or she makes), the entrepreneur derives the prediction (P) that a new product embodying a particular bundle of characteristics can be marketed to a target set of potential consumers in a definite spatial region over a specified future time period to yield revenue which will more than cover the sum of production costs and governance costs.[15] More formally and succinctly, the entrepreneur predicts:

$T \cdot A \rightarrow P$ or
$T \cdot A \rightarrow \pi, \pi = R - (PC + GC)$ such that $\pi > 0,$

where:

T = some conjunction of the entrepreneur's theories of

latent demand, of production, and of governance, that is, $T \equiv t^{\mathrm{d}} \cdot t^{\mathrm{p}} \cdot t^{\mathrm{g}}$;

$\quad$ = the conjunction (simultaneous assertion) of hypotheses;

A $\quad$ = the entrepreneur's set of auxiliary hypotheses, especially his or her account of the initial conditions of a market situation (i.e. the entrepreneur's 'knowledge of the particular circumstances of time and place' (Hayek 1945: 521));

$\rightarrow$ $\quad$ = the relation of deducibility or analytical implication;

P $\quad$ = the entrepreneur's set of specific predictions;

π $\quad$ = anticipated profit;

R $\quad$ = total expected revenue from selling the new bundle of product characteristics;

PC = total expected production costs;

GC = total expected governance costs.

The entrepreneur's predictions that opportunities for profit exist are low-level elements in his or her theoretical system which are in closer empirical contact with reality than higher-level elements. The entrepreneur specifies these predictions in such a way that they apply only to finite 'regions' of space and time. The entrepreneur's prediction (P) is thus that 'There is an opportunity for profit in the space–time region k'. The entrepreneur's prediction (P) has the logical form of a singular existential statement or a singular 'there-is' statement: it belongs to that class of propositions that asserts that 'There is an x in the space–time region k' or that 'An (market) event of type x is occurring in the region k'.

It should be made clear that in the present context the term 'predictions' does not just comprise the entrepreneur's forecasts of unknown future events. As used here, the term also includes assertions about past market history (i.e. retrodictions) as well as descriptions of known economic events which the entrepreneur wants to explain (i.e. *explicanda*) (cf. Popper 1959: 60; 1960: 133).

5.8 THE ENTREPRENEUR'S ACTION PROGRAMMES

The entrepreneur also possesses an incompletely specified hierarchy of *action programmes* which are applied in particular *types* of situations. These programmes organise the entrepreneur's actions into *patterns* of various levels of complexity, generality and abstraction: 'configuration is just as important a property of behavior as it is of perception [and I might add, of conjecture]' (Miller, Galanter and Pribram 1960: 12–13).[16] Entrepreneurs' action programmes are punctuated by long-range goals and short-run objectives. In addition, entrepreneurs develop policy recipes to guide their actions towards the attainment of prescribed goals. An entrepreneur may consider major policies, procedures and rules to be the hard core of one action programme which is itself part of the protective belt of another, higher-level action programme, thereby giving rise to a kind of core/demicore map of entrepreneurial action programmes (see Remenyi 1979).

Langlois provides a novel matrix approach which is useful for depicting the hierarchical structure of economic agents' plans:

> We can . . . think of the agent's actions as organized in hierarchical fashion, with the set of actions A divided into subsets A_i composed of subactions a_{ij}, which are, in turn, composed of sub-subactions a_{ijk}, etc. . . . An action or plan at the highest level of the hierarchy is abstract in the sense that it is oriented toward a typical situation and consists in a general pattern of response. As we examine the plan at lower levels of the hierarchy, we see that more details have been filled in. The plan is increasingly more concrete in its orientation and more specific in the response it embodies.
>
> (Langlois 1986a: 183–185)

The common distinction between business strategy (e.g. A_i) and tactics (a_{ij}) reflects the hierarchical nature of the entrepreneur's planning process.

The end of this chapter concludes the introduction to the basic concepts of the GK theory of entrepreneurship. The next three chapters apply these concepts to the question of how entrepreneurs operate within the market system. In particular, they elaborate the notion of the 'sophisticated falsificationist' entrepreneur.

NOTES

1   The notion that it may be fruitful to treat economic agents as possessing theories was first enunciated by Schutz. See, for example, Schutz (1943, 1967). More recently, Denzau and North (1994) advocate

depicting individuals as possessing 'mental models' which they use to interpret and structure their environment and to guide their choices.

2 The hierarchical nature of theories and mental constructs is emphasised by a number of writers, including Earl (1984: 49–51, 55–56), Kelly (1955; 1963: 56–59), Margenau (1966), and Simon (1962a). For systems-theoretic arguments in favour of hierarchical structures, see Milsum (1972: 155–158).

3 Not included in this discussion are the entrepreneur's empirical generalisations about the world. These are on a slightly higher level of generality than that of his or her specific predictions. Furthermore, this chapter does not examine other low-level elements, such as the initial conditions identified by the entrepreneur. Initial conditions are spatio-temporally singular: they relate only to individual market events at particular times and places and have already been discussed in Chapter 4.

4 Lancaster was not the first to provide a demand theory based upon the characteristics of a good rather than on the good itself. See Ekelund and Hébert's (1991) discussion of the pioneering characteristics-based theory of consumer behaviour that was provided in the nineteenth century by the transport economist, Jules Dupuit. His theory is superior to Lancaster's model in several important respects, including the extent to which it facilitates integrating consumer demand theory with theories of entrepreneurship (1991: 28). With regard to the foregoing discussion of demand discovery, I acknowledge some intellectual indebtedness to Dupuit's analysis as presented by Ekelund and Hébert.

5 More formally, the entrepreneur conjectures that the demand function is of the form: $Q_{ij} = F_{ij}(x_1, x_2, x_3 \ldots x_n)$ where Q is the market demand for the entrepreneur's new product, i is the ith group of consumers, j is the jth product-use situation, and where $(x_1, x_2, x_3 \ldots x_n)$ represents the characteristics of the entrepreneur's augmented product (which includes quality, packaging, and after-sales service, as well as the core product).

6 Cf. Earl's (1986a: esp. 32) behavioural analysis of demand elasticities. The accompanying figure is an adaptation of a diagram in Picot, Schneider and Laub (1989: 365), though its content and perspective are quite different.

7 See too Leibenstein (1979: esp. 133–134). These points were taken up by Nelson and Winter (1982: 59–65) in their behavioural theory of the firm. In particular, they raise three questions as damning criticisms of the neoclassical theory of the production set:

If 'technological knowledge' is what defines a firm's capabilities, where in the firm does that knowledge reside? What rationale can be given for the presumption that there is a sharp boundary line between what a firm can and cannot do? How does the knowledge possessed by one firm relate to that possessed by others, and to the 'state of knowledge' in the society generally?

(Nelson and Winter 1982: 62)

8 Cf. Kirzner's comments:

Unfortunately, it [Williamsons' transaction cost framework of organisational change] throws little light on the nature or consequences of entrepreneurial endeavor as such. The entrepreneur is not merely an elusive figure . . . ; he is absent entirely. Instead, there is an *impersonal* process of organizational change that tends to somehow conform to requirements dictated by transaction-cost efficiencies.

(Kirzner 1983a: 288; emphasis added)

However, the entrepreneur does receive explicit attention in some of the literature on transaction costs and related issues. See, for example: Anderson and Hill (undated); Buchanan and Faith (1981); Casson (1990a, 1991); Dietrich (1994); Harper (1989); Michaelis (1985); Picot and Schneider (1988); Picot *et al.* (1989); Ricketts (1987a, 1987b); Dieter Schneider (1985); Dietram Schneider (1988); and Wegenhenkel (1980b, 1981, 1983).

9 See, for example: Alchian (1984: 38–39); Klein, Crawford and Alchian (1978); Riordan and Williamson (1985: 366–367) and Williamson (1971; 1975; 1979; 1981a: 562–567; 1983a; 1984a: 202–207; 1985a: 52–56).

10 In a more formal presentation of transaction cost theory, asset specificity has been assumed unrealistically to be a *decision variable* that is available at a *constant per unit cost* (Riordan and Williamson 1985: 370). See too Williamson (1981a: 558).

11 More specifically, the entrepreneur's conjectures about the specificity of an asset associated with a particular production technique are related to his or her hypotheses about the future demand for that asset: expectations of steadily growing (declining) demand being in general associated with anticipated decreases (increases) in asset specificity. As Williamson says: 'As generic demand grows and the number of supply sources increases, exchange that was once transaction-specific loses this characteristic and greater reliance on market-mediated governance is feasible' (1979: 260). The entrepreneur's conjectures about asset specificity also depend upon hypotheses about: market structure (the number of potential buyers and sellers of the asset), thinness of the market being positively correlated with the conjectured degree of asset specificity; the market demand and market supply for the final products manufactured with the asset (and the determinants thereof); changes in the institutions for exchange (the creation and destruction of markets for the sale or lease of the asset in question); and changes in technology which will determine the availability of substitutes.

12 For transaction cost approaches to corporate strategy, see: Casson (1987b); Dietrich 1994; Earl (1984: ch. 2); Kay (1982, 1983, 1984); Jones and Hill (1988); Teece (1980, 1982a, 1982b, 1986); and Williamson (1975, 1985a, 1986a).

13 See section 8.1 on the causes of refutation.

14 The empirical investigation involved personal interviews with fifty-two high-tech entrepreneurs based in the Federal Republic of Germany and West Berlin. (The study was conducted in 1987 prior to reunification.) All the ventures in the sample were still operating in the market. The

sample was divided into a group of less successful new firms (n = 18) and a group of very successful new firms (n = 16). Unfortunately, from the perspective of the efficient use of information in statistical testing, the remaining middle group of businesses (i.e. those between the less successful and very successful firms) was excluded from all statistical tests which sought to determine whether transaction-cost factors could explain the degree of economic success of innovative business start-ups within their sample.

15 Process innovations can also be included within this framework. In such a case, the entrepreneur predicts that a new process will bring the sum of production costs (e.g. by automation of manufacturing) and governance costs (e.g. by new forms of organisation, new ways of communicating with the market) to a level below that of the revenue which is expected to be generated from selling the end-product.

16 In their conception of psychological agents, Miller *et al.* define a 'plan' as a hierarchy of instructions which guides behaviour:

A Plan is any hierarchical process in the organism that can control the order in which a sequence of operations is to be performed. A Plan is, for an organism, essentially the same as a programme for a computer, especially if the program has the sort of hierarchical character described above.

(Miller *et al.* 1960: 16; original emphasis)

Impressed by Newell, Shaw and Simon's computer simulations of human cognitive processes, Miller *et al.* concur with the hypothesis that 'a hierarchical structure is the basic form of organization in human problem-solving' (1960: 16).

Part II

THE METHODOLOGY OF THE FALSIFICATIONIST ENTREPRENEUR

6

INTRODUCING THE FALSIFICATIONIST ENTREPRENEUR

A good scientist tries to bring his constructs up for test as soon as possible. But he tries them out initially in test-tube proportions. . . . This straightforward testing of constructs is one of the features of the experimental method in modern science. It also characterizes any *alert* person.

(Kelly 1963: 13; emphasis added)

6.1 INTRODUCTION

I portray entrepreneurs as Popperian falsificationists who learn from the discovery of refuting evidence which falsifies (though never conclusively) their theories, rather than model them as inductivists who acquire knowledge by gathering data. In other words, entrepreneurs are depicted as learning from their mistakes rather than from their successes.[1] It is through refutation that falsificationist entrepreneurs learn from their mistakes, and as they correct their mistakes their knowledge grows (cf. Popper 1963: vii, ix).

Falsificationist entrepreneurs are expected to be more successful than innovative entrepreneurs who adhere to the principles of other methodological schools. The entrepreneur's adoption of falsificationist methodology yields relatively more efficient procedures for screening conjectures than do other methodologies. This is because it is relatively more efficient to eliminate the many false entrepreneurial ideas than it is to identify the very few 'potentially true' ideas which may be corroborated by the market. Expressed in somewhat different terms and in another context, Block suggests that:

> Successful corporate venturing depends on keeping the cost of inevitable failures down rather than achieving a high

165

percentage of profitable ventures. Damage control of the losers is more important for total programme effectiveness than is frequency of successes.

(Block 1989: 22)

Falsificationist entrepreneurs act in a way which assists the efficient progress of their own knowledge. They test their conjectures in a systematic manner: they do not proceed to undertake advanced critical tests until their theories have resisted refutation during earlier stages of testing. I shall have more to say on the efficiency of such screening procedures later.

Poor performance or even failure of new business ventures may (though not necessarily) arise from not following falsificationist methodological rules:

Poor management performance is characterized by the failure to articulate and test critical assumptions, failure to interpret results, failure to alter plans according to the interpretation of the test results.

(Block 1989: 28)

Maidique and Zirger (1985) provide interesting case studies of entrepreneurs in high-growth companies who allegedly inferred general theories about the market from past experience of success in individual markets – sometimes with devastating results.[2] They recount the tale of a startup venture to manufacture computer systems. The firm had developed a new product idea for a computerised system of inventory control for jobbers (small distributors) in a particular industry (1985: 308–309). Based on many years of spectacular success, the company took what seemed an inductively logical step of developing an inventory system for a higher-level but closely-related market in the same industry: large wholesale (warehousing) distributors. The ensuing débâcle meant that the new product did not even achieve its first-year revenue target during the three years after its initial launch. The failure of the new product could be construed as the result of the venture team's reliance upon inductive assumptions that new markets would be like old markets (in terms of competitive intensity and customer sophistication) and that repeating past practices would reproduce past successes.

Another alleged example of inductive fantasising is Apple Computer's launch of the Apple III. This personal computer was targeted to the small business and professional market following the huge success of the Apple II in the home computer market. Plagued with technical flaws and distribution problems, however, the Apple III resulted in the company losing its lead in the personal computer market and in its conceding a large share of the market to IBM (Hartley 1985: ch. 17; Maidique and Zirger 1985: 305, 309). Here again, it could be argued, entrepreneurs saw the future through the inductivist prism of present successes; their overly optimistic expectations of future market events were engendered by their past experience. (However, it should be noted that learning from the Apple III fiasco did contribute to the company's subsequent dramatic success with the Apple II-plus.)

These unflattering remarks about inductivism are not meant to imply that sophisticated falsificationism is a panacea. No method, be it justificationist or non-justificationist, scientific or non-scientific, is a guaranteed means to achieving specific ends. 'It [the "scientific method"] is not a method in the sense that, if you practise it, you will succeed; or if you don't succeed, you haven't practised it; that is to say, it is not a definite way to results: a method in this sense does not exist' (Popper 1963: 313; parenthesis added). Hence, some falsificationist entrepreneurs may fail and other entrepreneurs who do not subscribe to falsificationism may succeed.

However, it is predicted that falsificationist entrepreneurs are more likely to be successful than other types of entrepreneurs. This claim is also consistent with Popper (1960: 58). Popper regards entrepreneurs, who set up businesses and introduce new products or new forms of business organisation, to be conducting piecemeal social experiments. He presents *piecemeal* social engineering as the most appropriate and successful method for obtaining knowledge for practical problems:

> The piecemeal engineer knows, like Socrates, how little he knows. He knows that we can learn only from our mistakes. Accordingly, he makes his way, step by step, carefully comparing the results expected with the results achieved, and always on the look-out for the unavoidable unwanted consequences of any reform; and he will avoid undertaking reforms of a complexity and scope which make it impossible for him to disentangle causes from effects, and to know what he is really doing.
>
> (Popper 1960: 67)

To avoid confusion, *piecemeal* social engineering must be distinguished from *holistic* or *utopian* social engineering, which aims at reconstructing the whole of society on the basis of a definite blueprint and which seeks to control further social developments (methods often attributed to collectivist or centralised planning). Both Popper and the Austrian school of economists regard utopian engineering with suspicion and consider its execution to be logically and practically impossible. 'Holism, whether philosophical or sociological, is the culprit that will lead us into errors' (Sklair 1973: 146).

It is no coincidence that the description of the piecemeal social engineer bears a considerable likeness to the growth-of-knowledge (GK) conception of the falsificationist entrepreneur. Piecemeal social engineering is merely the sociological parallel to Popper's philosophy of piecemeal criticism. The common theme is that complex structures – whether scientific, economic or social – are only to be created and changed by means of a negative feedback process of sequential adjustments (Magee 1973: 67). Piecemealism thus applies to the entrepreneur's market-making activities.

Piecemeal *product* engineering is a case in point. Minor product innovations directed towards existing markets have a substantially higher likelihood of success than new generic product categories which depend upon markets which do not yet exist and which require a significant shift in customers' normal patterns of usage behaviour.

> [T]he more distinctive the newness [of the product], the greater the risk of failure resulting either from insufficient working capital to sustain a long and frustrating period of creating enough solvent customers to make the proposition pay, or from the inability to convince investors and bankers that they should put up more money.
>
> (Levitt 1986: 180)

Revamping and repositioning existing products, product differentiation (i.e. variations in quality, style, or image), product line extensions, product improvements (i.e. minor changes in product attributes, package redesign, new after-sales services etc.) and other product revivification strategies pose a lower chance of failure than holistic strategies because they reduce the scope for errors arising from product complexity and novelty. Minor product innovations are also cheaper to evaluate prior to launching because they can be readily tested in existing markets.

Market segmentation strategies can also be interpreted as the piecemeal engineering of existing markets rather than the creation of new markets. The application of this marketing tool represents an attempt by firms to discover how their markets are divided into groups of people with different problem-situations, different views (i.e. theories) of their products and even different world-views.

6.2 GENERAL CHARACTERISTICS OF THE FALSIFICATIONIST ENTREPRENEUR

Before examining the technical aspects of the falsificationist methodology as applied to entrepreneurship, I discuss the essential characteristics which distinguish the falsificationist entrepreneur from other entrepreneurs.

6.2.1 Active disposition, problem-sensitivity and customer-orientation

The first point to be made is that falsificationist entrepreneurs are active explorers who make their experiences, rather than passive observers who receive information osmotically from their environment. It is entrepreneurs who actively formulate trial solutions (i.e. conjectures) to specific market problems, and it is entrepreneurs who of their own accord design new experiments in order to test the implications of their ideas in new situations.

In addition, the falsificationist entrepreneur possesses a sensitivity to problems.[3] Indeed, it can be said that entrepreneurial activity begins and ends with problems (see section 7.9 on the evolution of entrepreneurial knowledge). Because entrepreneurial problems are ill-structured, the entrepreneur's task does not begin with the attempt to solve a problem, but rather the attempt to define the problem and to account for why it is a problem (Pounds 1969). Entrepreneurs focus on the formulation of problems before shifting their efforts to the generation of tentative solutions: their degree of success in the former often determines their degree of success in the latter.

Given that customers and the satisfaction of their needs are considered to be a vital part of the entrepreneurial problem, it follows that entrepreneurs also have a heightened sensitivity to product usage situations, customers and market segments. They ask questions, such as: What particular sets of problems are customers trying to solve in their purchase of a particular good in a particular situation?[4] What is the frequency and intensity of these problems? To what extent do current products solve these problems? What new product characteristics could solve those problems better than existing products? Consequently, falsificationist entrepreneurs exhibit an external orientation towards urgent and impending market problems that are conjectured to exist in reality rather than an internal focus on the venture firm, its product portfolio, technology and personnel. '[L]acking resources, successful small entrepreneurs soon find that it pays to approach potential customers early, test their solutions in users' hands, learn from these interactions, and adapt designs rapidly' (Quinn 1985: 74). In the terminology of marketing management, falsificationist entrepreneurs are customer-oriented rather than product-oriented. They organise their production and exchange relations in accordance with the logic of the marketing concept. The entrepreneur selects from among the innumerable market problems which emerge those which seem soluble, and from among this subset, the entrepreneur chooses those problems whose solutions are imagined to yield the most profit. Entrepreneurship, like science, is the 'art of the soluble' (cf. Medawar 1967), though of course problems which appear tractable may well turn out to be unmanageable.

6.2.2 Fallibilism, theoretical pluralism and pre-emptive product cannibalism

The falsificationist entrepreneur acknowledges the tentative and conjectural nature of all knowledge and recognises that many entrepreneurial forays into the unknown turn out to be mistakes in their original form. Such fallibilism has been well articulated by Soros:

> My partner and I took a malicious pleasure in making money by selling short stocks that were institutional favorites. But we differed in our attitudes to our own activities. He regarded only the other participants' views as flawed, while I thought that we had as good a chance of being wrong as anyone else. *The assumption of inherently flawed perceptions suited my self-critical attitude.*
> (Soros 1987: 15; emphasis added)

> [Entrepreneurial ideas and new products] are just as conjectural as new theories about the causes of cancer or the number of fundamental particles – not least in that any of them may be misconceived and that even those which are not refuted by the tests currently available are liable to fail at some later date in different circumstances, and therefore to call for replacement by new conjectures.
> (Loasby 1984a: 76)

Consequently, falsificationist entrepreneurs develop criteria for identifying weak products, and they design product strategies which specify the conditions under which products in their portfolios should be considered for elimination. The consistent application of Popperian methodology also requires that product-elimination strategies, such as simply dropping the product or selling it to another firm, be tested before implementation (cf. Sevin 1965).

The falsificationist entrepreneur's emphasis upon the tentativeness of knowledge expresses itself in the entrepreneur's commitment to theoretical pluralism (also referred to as 'parallel development' by Quinn (1979; 1985) or as 'the method of multiple hypotheses'). Theoretical pluralism involves producing at least two explanations of, or tentative solutions to, the same problem, in contrast to theoretical monism which involves the explicit development of only one approach to a problem. Falsificationist entrepreneurs encourage competing approaches at all levels of the innovative process. 'The need for producing alternatives is not something that one eventually outgrows' (Mitroff 1974: 240). Falsificationist entrepreneurs try to programme differing approaches to market and technical problems into the decision-making process and avoid confining themselves to just one theoretical base. Just as scientists hedge their bets, so too entrepreneurial teams may pursue several diverse options concurrently (e.g. by developing competing prototype alternatives) when this is practicable in terms of cost and time. For example, Sony Corporation pursued ten major options in developing its technology for videotape recorders, and each option in turn had two to three alternative subsystems (Quinn 1985: 78).

The advantage of theoretical pluralism is that it prevents dogmatic commitment to any single approach (Quinn 1979: 24). In making different approaches to a problem compete intensively and for as long as possible, falsificationist entrepreneurs try to prevent an idea gaining a monopoly in its hold on their problem-solving endeavours. The model of dynamic competition is thus applied to the internal markets for resources within the firm as well as to the external factor and goods markets. As a consequence of their theoretical pluralism, falsificationist entrepreneurs come to regard the innovative process as a non-linear, parallel process rather than a partitioned sequence of activities.[5] Theoretical pluralism gives entrepreneurs the opportunity to see how their decision problems change when they are modelled differently (cf. Mitroff 1974: 229). It is appropriate for dealing with problems which are wickedly ill-structured, that is, for handling

171

novel situations which require considerable time and resources for defining the problem. Entrepreneurial problems – especially innovative problems – are generally of this nature (see Chapter 3).

Using a single hypothesis to guide one's practical actions (i.e. theoretical monism) has opportunity costs. Theoretical monism may promote the efficient development of one potential solution to a specific market problem as it is currently defined. If the entrepreneur were to have perfect foresight, a single-hypothesis approach would be optimal. However, with structural uncertainty the entrepreneur can never identify a course of action which is certain to succeed. Thus, reliance upon a single hypothesis runs the danger of directing, from the very commencement of the venture, the entrepreneur's investigation and resources along a narrowly-defined path which leads to a dead-end. By steering the entrepreneur's attention in one direction, theoretical monism may distract the entrepreneur from focusing in other directions which may be more profitable avenues for market-making.

The development of more than one potential solution to a problem may be conjectured to increase costs (relative to theoretical monism). However, there are likely to be economies of scale in the generation and testing of competing approaches. Furthermore, the entrepreneur may expect the additional benefits from investing in a certain number of rival options to outweigh the additional costs.[6] This may be the case if a particular degree of theoretical pluralism is anticipated to reduce development time, to increase the speed of market impact and to thereby reduce the likelihood of refutation or to improve the overall chance of corroboration by severe market testing (i.e. by increasing the chance that the entrepreneur's portfolio of solution concepts contains at least one satisfactory alternative). The entrepreneur may conjecture that a pluralist approach will reduce development time because competition between rival teams or individuals instils a sense of urgency to the generation of solutions and limits agency problems (Quinn 1979: 24).

Potential benefits are also associated with the possibility of choosing better solutions under the pluralist approach. Entrepreneurs are not able to make rational choices if they do not have access to a minimum of objective knowledge. The proliferation of rival entrepreneurial ideas improves the objectivity of the knowledge available to the entrepreneur and consequently speeds up the entrepreneur's rate of learning. From the interplay and contest between ideas the entrepreneur is better able to learn where each may be deficient (cf. Popper 1963: 246). Parallel development of several programmes provides more objective knowledge for making decisions which are better attuned to market requirements for adequate problem solutions (Quinn 1985: 79).

The magnitude of benefits from theoretical pluralism will depend directly upon the seriousness for the entrepreneur of being mistaken. It is best suited to situations in which there are heavy penalties for poor performance – as is often the case with product innovations. The more novel a product, the more crucial it is that the first experience of opinion leaders in using the product is not unfavourable in some fundamental way. Their negative experiences may have repercussions – through discouraging their local peers who are less venturesome – which are far out of proportion to their level of dissatisfaction with the innovation (Levitt 1986: 181).

Pre-emptive product cannibalism is also consistent with the provisional nature of entrepreneurial knowledge. Product cannibalism arises when a firm's new product or brand gains sales by diverting them from the company's existing product(s) or brand(s) (Heskett 1976; Kerin, Harvey and Rothe 1978). Whereas product cannibalism is generally unplanned, *pre-emptive* product cannibalism is planned and expected: it is an intended consequence of the new product development process.

Pre-emptive product cannibalism reflects the view that entrepreneurs should never regard their own products or ideas as unchallengeable, no matter how dominant and successful those products or ideas have been. Accordingly, entrepreneurs should never stop treating their products, ventures or R & D activities as anything other than mere experiments with which to test and to gain knowledge. The implication is that entrepreneurs must recognise that they will at some stage have to destroy their own once-profitable assets, that is, that they will have to engage in some form of self-imposed creative destruction (cf. Levitt 1986: 160). Consequently, falsificationist entrepreneurs attempt to refute their own theories by developing new and better solution concepts which supersede them.

The methods and organisational practices of 3M (the Minnesota Mining and Manufacturing Company) are paradigmatic of such a philosophy (see Roberts 1980: 139–141). To a greater degree than the majority of other large corporations, 3M has organised itself to promote and sustain the development of internal corporate ventures (that is, separate entities established within the company itself for the purpose of developing new markets or radically different products), and it has had a long-term record of success in developing these new businesses. The company is organised on the basis of individual product lines, each of which has its own product development department. According to its rather unconventional charter, each product development department can develop new ventures outside its division's present business area, even if the new product competes with the existing output of other product divisions.

Pre-emptive product cannibalism is a strategy which can enable a firm to reduce the gaps in its existing portfolio of customer-oriented products, gaps that might otherwise be filled by competitors. The strategy is based on the assumption that it is better to have the firm's existing buyers substituting between items in its own portfolio of solution concepts than it is to have them switching to competitors' products. Roberts's (1980: 139) paraphrasing of 3M's philosophy is apt: 'We would rather have one of our own new products competing with an existing product line of 3M than have a competitor's new product competing'.

The experience of the Gillette Company in the early 1960s is an interesting case study of how dominance in an industry can be eroded by a dogmatic reluctance to introduce a new product – in this case, its own stainless steel razor blade (see Hartley 1986: ch. 7). In particular, its conservative management held the theory that a likely consequence of embracing this upstart innovation would be to cannibalise the major product in its existing line – the highly profitable, carbon-steel 'Super Blue' blade. In addition, management disliked the disruptive consequences of installing new production lines and retraining technicians for the new process. The result of management's procrastination was that Gillette left itself vulnerable to competitive inroads, brought a stainless steel blade to market months after its competitors and lost considerable market share (15 percentage points in eighteen months) which need not have been surrendered.

Pre-emption is a matter of degree, however. An example of pre-emptive cannibalism carried to the extreme is Osborne Computer. The management of this venture prematurely announced the planned introduction of 'the Executive', a more sophisticated and powerful model of its existing personal computer, before the new product was even marketable. The result was to practically kill the sales for its existing model, the Osborne 1 (Hartley 1986: ch. 16).

Cannibalism effects must be anticipated and planned for on the basis of the entrepreneur's theories of market dynamics and of competition. Moreover, conjectures on the market impact of cannibalisation should be tested throughout the new product development process. At the concept testing stage, market research techniques can be applied to detect the potential for end-use substitution between product concepts which can be applied by customers in particular situations (Kerin *et al.* 1978: 30). The business analysis and test marketing stages should also try to assess the source of potential sales volume for the new product to test whether it will arise from the company's existing products, competitors' products or an expansion of the market.

6.2.3 Extensive application of the critical method

Falsificationist entrepreneurs artificially make the growth of their knowledge more intensive by consciously setting their problem-solving endeavours in an overtly critical framework. They adopt a scientifically minded 'technology' for defining customer problems (and potential markets) and for creating and delivering possible solution concepts. They embrace a systematic approach to market-making which is based on critical thinking as well as piecemeal, practical experimentation. Falsificationist entrepreneurs attempt to expose their theories to deliberate critical tests of differing degrees of severity (see Chapter 7). They undertake an extensive range of screening and testing procedures even at very early stages of new product development and critically examine their ideas throughout all phases prior to, during, and after, full-scale commercialisation.

Falsificationist entrepreneurs emphasise that since they can learn from their mistakes, it is desirable to make their mistakes as fast as possible (cf. Popper 1963: vii). As with new scientific ideas, a novel entrepreneurial idea cannot be fully developed into a workable hypothesis and exposed to some empirical (market) tests without a large expenditure of time and research resources, both physical and human. The exponential rise in product development costs during the development process increases the importance of the early rejection of ideas which are not promising to be technically or commercially viable. By speeding up the growth of the entrepreneur's knowledge, theoretical pluralism at the prototype stage aids the early detection of projects with poor profit potential.

Similarly, falsificationist entrepreneurs appreciate that it is very difficult to learn from a very big mistake because it is hard to distinguish causes from effects. They thus attempt to break down a major problem into a number of subproblems – each of manageable scope and intricacy. Consequently, they are geared towards piecemeal rather than holistic experiments, as we have already observed.

Falsificationist entrepreneurs are critically vigilant and are alert to evidence that their actions are not having the desired effects. The falsificationist entrepreneur recognises that there are no piecemeal economic experiments (such as business startups, new product intro-ductions, and price changes) which do not have unintended and unwelcome consequences (e.g. unintended product cannibalism). The falsificationist entrepreneur looks out for these mistakes and attempts to identify them, to analyse them and to learn from them, and to apply this knowledge so that they can be avoided in the future (cf. Popper 1960: 88). By the adoption of the critical method, entrepreneurs seek to avoid making many mistakes in a more expensive form, and discovering them later, than need be.

The falsificationist entrepreneur extends the critical method as far as possible beyond product R & D, engineering and production. The falsificationist entrepreneur thus contrasts with the engineer-managers and scientist-managers of high-technology firms who limit their critical policies to the 'hard, practical realities' of the laboratory in which they can concentrate on 'controllable variables'. In a classic article on marketing myopia, Levitt aptly characterises these scientists who have turned managers:

> The irony of some industries oriented toward technical research and development is that the scientists who occupy the high executive positions are totally unscientific when it comes to defining their companies' overall needs and purposes. They violate the first two rules of the scientific method – being aware of and defining their companies' problems, and then developing testable hypotheses about solving them. They are scientific only about the convenient things, such as laboratory and product experiments.
>
> (Levitt 1986: 164)

6.2.4 Sophisticated falsificationist entrepreneurs aim for partial corroboration not refutation

The portrayal of entrepreneurs as falsificationists could be (wrongly) criticised on the grounds that real-life entrepreneurs aim for corroborations and profits, whereas falsificationist scientists aim for refutations. Because such a misconception may impede understanding of the argument developed in this and later chapters, it is convenient to deal with it here at a preliminary stage before delving into finer detail. The supposed criticism that is advanced rests upon a rather naive interpretation of Popper's theory of method (Lakatos 1970: 119–121). Falsificationists do not simply produce theories so that they can be superseded but rather search for theories that are nearer to the truth than those of their competitors (Popper 1963: 15, 245). They try to discover new facts. The corroboration of bold conjectures plays a vital role in the sophisticated falsificationist's account of the growth of knowledge.[7] Indeed, even the leading falsificationist, Popper, makes it an explicit requirement of a good theory that it *pass* some new and severe tests (see section 2.2.4). On this matter, the Popperian position of sophisticated falsificationism has been well summarised by Chalmers:

> [W]hile the fact that it does lead to the possibility of new tests makes a hypothesis worthy of investigation, it will not rank as an improvement on the problematic theory it is designed to replace until it has survived at least some of those tests. This is tantamount to saying that before it can be regarded as an adequate replacement for a falsified theory, a newly and boldly proposed theory must make some novel predictions that are confirmed.
>
> (Chalmers 1982: 55)[8]

Like scientists, entrepreneurs want theories which are well-corroborated because they aim to find non-*ad hoc* explanations of the phenomena that interest them. An explanatory theory is the more satisfactory, the more severe are the tests that it has survived – that is, the greater is its degree of corroboration (Popper 1972: 192–193). Both scientists and entrepreneurs want theories which are successful in their unexpected or improbable predictions. (In the case of entrepreneurship, the extent of profits that are forthcoming may even increase with the improbability of the corroborating cases.) Indeed, the progress of their knowledge requires empirical successes as well as successful refutations.

Consequently, scientists and entrepreneurs alike may adopt critical methods towards their own hypotheses without necessarily hoping or expecting to refute their hypotheses. In conducting severe empirical tests, scientists and entrepreneurs may in fact attempt to corroborate their theories in a spectacular manner by demonstrating that their particular theories successfully predict events of a new kind (cf. Musgrave 1974b: 578–579). In adopting critical methods, therefore, scientists and entrepreneurs do not aim to develop falsifications of their theories at any price (as with dogmatic and naive brands of falsificationism) but can aim to obtain partial corroborations of their theories (sophisticated falsificationism).

Sophisticated falsificationism thus does not share the purely negative character of dogmatic and naive falsificationism (Lakatos 1970: 119–121). As a corollary, sophisticated falsificationist entrepreneurs do not just learn from their mistakes: they can also learn from the corroboration of the novel predictions derived from their bold, risky conjectures. If a conjecture resists refutation by a severe test, an entrepreneur can learn much about the problem and his or her conjecture, its adequacy and its consequences (cf. Popper 1972: 261). Hence, sophisticated falsificationism is not necessarily a negative way for entrepreneurs to orient themselves towards the world.

6.3 TECHNICAL ASPECTS OF THE FALSIFICATIONIST METHODOLOGY AS APPLIED TO ENTREPRENEURSHIP

Having identified the general characteristics that distinguish falsificationist entrepreneurship, I will now move on to elucidate its technical aspects. At the formal level, the falsificationist entrepreneur adopts the falsifiability principle, which offers broad policy direction for the selection of hypotheses, *and* the (negative) methodological rules which should be used in testing procedures. The falsifiability principle can also be expressed in terms of a methodological or preference rule for choosing between theories. I discuss each of these elements of the falsificationist methodology in turn below.

6.3.1 The basic rule: the falsifiability principle

An entrepreneurial theory is an attempt to solve a specific (market) problem. For any given problem situation, the falsificationist entrepreneur prefers tentative solutions which can be tested to theories which are not amenable to testing. As a consequence, the entrepreneur favours theories which are potentially objectifiable, that is, theories which can be represented in a linguistic or symbolic form (e.g. a business plan) so that it can be criticised (see the discussion of objective surrogates in section 7.4). Of those theories which can be tested, the entrepreneur prefers those theories which can be more severely tested (for the moment I ignore cost considerations). Falsificationist entrepreneurs attempt to formulate theories which are falsifiable, and the more falsifiable their theories are, the better from their point of view.

An entrepreneurial conjecture is falsifiable *in principle* if there exists some imaginable (but observable) market event, or set of events, which is inconsistent with the theory, that is, which, if it were in fact to occur, would falsify the conjecture.[9] The degree of falsifiability is a measure of the empirical information conveyed by a theory (Nola 1987: 449). Falsifiability can best be illustrated by means of an analogy (cf. Popper 1959: 90, 112). Let the set of all possible market events be represented by a circular area, and let each member of that set be represented by a radius of the circle. For a theory to be falsifiable, at least one radius must be incompatible with the theory and ruled out by it. In addition, consider the case in which the entrepreneur is thinking over two competing theories, T_1 and T_2 , as tentative solutions to a given market problem. Each theory is assumed to be internally consistent and thus to divide the set of all possible market events into two groups: those which it contradicts and those with which it is compatible. It is assumed that the sector of market events ruled out by the first theory, T_1, is greater than that prohibited by the second, T_2 (see Figure 6.1).

For example, suppose that the entrepreneur is considering the following two conjectures:

T_1 = all male consumers will respond favourably (in terms of attention, interest and arousal) to the advertising copy for our innovative superannuation package;

T_2 = all male consumers with an internal locus of control will respond favourably (in terms of attention, interest and arousal) to the advertising copy for our innovative superannuation package.

A priori , there are more opportunities for the first theory, T_1 , to clash with conceivable market events than for T_2, that is, there is a greater chance for T_1 to be refuted by experience. There are tests of T_1 which are not tests of T_2 ; but there are no tests of T_2 which are not simultaneously tests of T_1. Consequently, T_1 is more falsifiable than T_2 : it asserts more about the market because it rules out more market events which could conceivably happen. Its informative

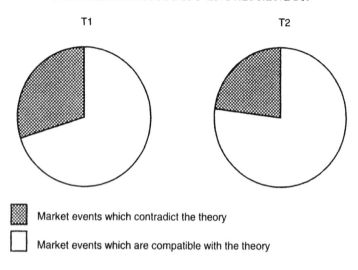

Figure 6.1 Comparison of the falsifiability of two theories

content is greater. The fact that a theory is highly falsifiable also makes it highly testable: 'informative content, which is in inverse proportion to probability, is in direct proportion to testability' (Magee 1973: 36).

The discussion so far has assumed that the entrepreneur's theory is internally consistent. The falsificationist entrepreneur makes consistency a compulsory requirement of any theory; it is the most general condition that every theory must satisfy (Popper 1959: 91–92). To be internally consistent, a theory must be compatible with one or more potential market events (in terms of Figure 6.1, at least a narrow *un*shaded sector of permitted events must exist). On purely logical grounds, a falsificationist entrepreneur will always reject a self-contradictory theory as false.[10] The reason is that from an inconsistent set of premises, the entrepreneur can use valid rules of inference to deduce any conclusion (or prediction) at all about the world of experience (cf. Popper 1959: 91–92; 1963: 317, 319). An entrepreneurial theory which is internally inconsistent thus logically entails *all* conceivable states of the world, including all possible conditions of latent demand, governance costs and production costs. For example, it might imply the following assertions *and* their negations: 'the price of good X will rise' and 'the price of good X will not rise'; 'governance costs will depend on asset specificity' and 'governance costs will not depend on asset specificity'; and 'the average cost curve is U-shaped' and 'the average cost curve is not U-shaped'. As a consequence, a self-contradictory theory also *forbids* all possible market events, so that it is falsified by any market event whatsoever (Popper 1959: 91).

Prior to testing, therefore, falsificationist entrepreneurs submit their theories to definite standards, such as the standard of internal consistency. Besides internal consistency, they appraise competing theories on the basis of their informative content – which is identical with their degree of falsifiability. They prefer the theory with the highest degree of falsifiability: 'the "better" or "preferable" hypothesis will, more often than not, be the more *improbable one* ' (Popper 1972: 17).

Furthermore, if two or more tentative solutions to a particular problem have the same informative content – i.e. the same degree of falsifiability, and if the entrepreneur must decide between them because of economic constraints in testing theories, the entrepreneur will choose that theory which can be severely tested at the lowest cost. Conversely, among a class of equally costly tests of trial solutions to a problem, the entrepreneur will choose the most severe test. (See section 7.8 for a more detailed discussion of the economic costs of testing.)

The question arises as to why entrepreneurs should prefer a higher degree of falsifiability. The crucial step in answering this question is to recognise that the critical analysis of conjectures, whether in science or in economic activity, is merely one context for the much more general strategy of negative feedback (cf. Medawar 1969: 54; 1967).[11] Seen in this light, the falsifiability principle is simply a way of enhancing the quality of negative feedback in the cybernetic process of regulating and controlling conjectures. It increases the speed and efficiency of learning from experience. How much entrepreneurs learn from experience is determined to a large extent by the nature of the questions that they themselves ask of the situations and competitive environments which they face.[12] The falsifiability principle implies that entrepreneurs should be prepared to risk a trial: they should pose provocative questions and put forth daring answers: 'Nothing ventured, nothing gained'.

More formally, entrepreneurs require a high degree of falsifiability because they aim for a high degree of corroboration of their theories, and ultimately, for a high degree of explanatory power. The more falsifiable an idea (i.e. the greater its informative content), the more severe are the possible tests that can be conducted (i.e. the more

THE FALSIFICATIONIST ENTREPRENEUR

testable is the idea). Should the idea survive those severe tests, it will then be better corroborated by these tests. Thus, the opportunities for corroborating an idea increase with its falsifiability (i.e. testability) and informative content: 'Thus . . . corroborability . . . must increase with testability' (Popper 1963: 256).

The basic thrust behind the falsifiability principle is that entrepreneurs must attempt to specify in advance under what conditions they will regard their theories as refuted.[13] (Block and MacMillan (1985: 184–185) make a similar recommendation in their normative model of venture planning.) The entrepreneur should specify those falsifying conditions as exactly as possible in order to avoid *ad hoc* post-experimental adjustments. The setting of fairly precise performance targets at the *ex ante* stage is necessary if entrepreneurs are to be able to judge whether their ventures are failing or succeeding.[14] Williams and Scott's (1965) study of investment decisions highlights the role of precise standards in facilitating learning. In their investigation, a number of projects yielded outcomes which were judged to be less than satisfactory. But whereas the failure to reach a well-specified target prompted successful remedial measures, a disparity between actual achievement and imprecise expectations demonstrated itself to be a low-powered incentive for correcting mistakes.

Entrepreneurs who apply the techniques of market segmentation (e.g. life-style segmentation, usage situation segmentation, person–situation segmentation) and market targeting can be interpreted as attempting to increase the testability of their theories of latent demand. Customer-oriented entrepreneurs who specify discrete target markets prior to a full-scale launching of their ventures are spelling out in detail the potentially observable situations (e.g. a situation in which target customers do not buy the product) which, if they were actually observed, would mean that their theories of latent demand are refuted.

In contrast, product-oriented entrepreneurs do not stipulate beforehand the potential market conditions which could refute their theories. They do not specify at which customer problems, markets or market segments their ventures are aimed. They fail to make explicit conjectures about the parts of the market (i.e. the subsets of customers) that they can serve most effectively, and they neglect constructing hypotheses about the buying requirements and buying practices of different market segments. Customers are regarded uncritically as a batch of homogeneous buyers who respond favourably to complex, technically superior products. Their entrepreneurial theories focus on technology and production and exclude a marketing dimension. Consequently, their theories of latent demand are either so implicit or so vague that they rule out few market events that could conceivably occur (in terms of Figure 6.1, the shaded segment is extremely narrow). There is thus little possibility of their theories clashing with market experience and being refuted by market tests. The consequences of such behaviour can be grave. The failure of top management to define their purposes, their policies, their industries and their 'cluster of know-how' in testable, customer-oriented terms has been identified by Levitt (1986: 141–172) as the major reason for the decline of companies in what were formerly major growth industries.

The specification of precise targets also applies to entrepreneurs' theories of production. Tight product descriptions must be developed prior to committing resources to full-scale production, and it is preferable that they be specified in writing. Detailed objectives must be set with respect to particular product attributes, production costs, service requirements, quality control, development time and so on.[15] For example, the prediction that 'product development will be completed within nine months' is not as precise as the prediction that 'in nine months a prototype motion analyser can be completed which will cost no more than $300, 000, which can be manufactured for a direct cost of $25, 000, which can store images on chips electronically instead of on magnetic tape, which will shut itself off automatically once sensors have detected a failure in the operation of a particular high-speed factory line, which can replay the event in stop-action or as slowly as 1/1000 of actual speed, and which qualified engineers can learn how to operate with less than seven hours' training'.

In concluding my discussion of the falsifiability principle, I must emphasise that entrepreneurial theories which do not meet the standard of practical testability need not be rejected as meaningless. Some entrepreneurial conjectures may not be falsifiable because there are no experimental or measurement techniques yet available for testing them or because the necessary market tests are currently impracticable within the existing social and economic environment. 'The "material requirement" for a proposition to be a potential falsifier depends on the experimental techniques of the time' (Latsis 1972: 239). Consequently, an entrepreneurial conjecture might be untestable at some given time t but testable at some later stage $t + 1$, $t + 2$, $t + n$, etc. as a result of the development of new market-research methods (such as new techniques for measuring consumers' beliefs and attitudes, preferences and purchasing behaviour) or as a result of changes in the economic and social landscape (e.g. changes in business ethics).

Other ideas may still be at a metaphysical stage of their development,[16] awaiting to be developed into empirical and refutable hypotheses which can be tested by current techniques. In line with their ambition to extend the critical method as far as possible, falsificationist entrepreneurs can subject such metaphysical theories to criticism and rational argument, even though these theories are not capable of being tested empirically. Because an entrepreneurial theory (including a metaphysical idea) is an attempted solution of a problem, it can be criticised and rationally evaluated in terms of whether it successfully solves the problem that it was intended to solve, and whether it solves the problem better than other theories (cf. Popper 1963: 199; 1976c: 150). The falsificationist entrepreneur can thus generalise the criterion of falsifiability (i.e. intersubjective *testability*) into the broader concept of intersubjective *criticism* (cf. Popper 1976c: 115–116; 1966b: ch. 24; Freeman and Skolimowski 1974: 488).

6.3.2 Methodological rules prohibiting immunising stratagems

Falsificationist entrepreneurs adopt methodological rules which ensure the falsifiability of their theories. In the previous section, we have already seen that the falsifiability principle requires that entrepreneurs formulate strategies which can be tested and that entrepreneurs also choose those theories which can be most severely tested. These methodological rules are conventions; entrepreneurs make the *decision* to adopt them in order to promote the growth of their knowledge.

However, the falsifiability principle has to be supplemented by other methodological rules if learning is to be encouraged: if the entrepreneur decides not to submit a particular theory to any further tests or to protect the theory against falsification, the theory would no longer be falsifiable (in the methodological sense of the term), even if it exhibits the logico-epistemological property of being falsifiable in principle. In other words, what makes a theory falsifiable is the set of methodological rules that the entrepreneur applies to it, and not just its degree of falsifiability in the purely logical sense (but a first-order entrepreneurial theory will have to meet the requirements of the falsifiability principle if these second-order rules are to be applicable).

Apart from the rules for acceptance and rejection of hypotheses (which are discussed in sections 7.5 and 7.6), the most important group of rules are those which prohibit safeguarding theories against refutation. The basic tenet of these negative methodological rules is that entrepreneurs should not systematically evade refutation by continually reformulating either their theories or their evidence in order to avoid a conflict between them[17] Consequently, falsificationist entrepreneurs impose methodological limits on the strategies that they themselves adopt to defend their own theories against refutation. In general, if his or her theory T clashes with observation, then the entrepreneur will tentatively accept a modification of T to T' only if the degree of falsifiability of T' is greater than that of T.

Popper refers to dogmatic tactics to evade refutation as immunising stratagems. These stratagems must be avoided because they serve to reduce informative content and so diminish the scope of what the entrepreneur can say about the world. (In Lakatos's version of sophisticated falsificationism, these manoeuvres are in fact referred to pejoratively as *content-decreasing* stratagems or as *degenerating* problem shifts (Lakatos 1968a: 378; 1970: 118).) If entrepreneurs were to adopt these stratagems, they would lapse into an uncritical, conservative kind of conventionalism. Immunising stratagems are a barrier to experience because they are conducive to complacency, and they therefore impede the growth of the entrepreneur's knowledge. They result from a poverty of entrepreneurial imagination, an inability to generate bold conjectures which predict novel facts about the market or economic environment. Whereas the falsificationist entrepreneur is a piecemeal evaluator, the immunising entrepreneur is thus a piecemeal improviser who resorts to cognitive fudging whenever this is permitted by situational ambiguities.

Before I can describe how falsificationist entrepreneurs counter immunising stratagems, it is necessary to specify the various forms that these stratagems may take. The main types of immunising stratagems that falsificationist entrepreneurs attempt to avoid are as follows:[18]

IS1 Introducing *ad hoc* hypotheses. It arises, for example, when entrepreneurs explain away refuting evidence, such as poor sales, by saying that personal disposable incomes have not yet grown sufficiently to induce the demand for their new innovative product; or when they dismiss evidence of a substantial decline in market growth as a normal seasonal fluctuation in consumption; or when they explain poor performance away as the result of transient environmental pressures, such as a recession in the local economy or competitors' foolhardy strategies. *Ad hoc* explanations are not independently testable: independently, that is, of the effect to be explained (Popper 1972: 16).

IS2 Always adopting a sceptical attitude to the reliability of experiments (e.g. test marketing) and/or the competence of experimenters (e.g. market research firms) whose observations (e.g. market research results) threaten entrepreneurs' firmly held theories. Entrepreneurs reject the results on the grounds that they are fabricated, fudged, corrupted, insufficiently supported, not systematically acquired or not objective. The only evidence which they can produce in support of their claims that market research results are unreliable is that the results contradict the predictions of their theories of latent demand. Another example is entrepreneurs' dogmatic insistence that parts of the theoretical apparatus used to test their theories – such as business accounting and reporting systems – are not functioning properly or are not reliable for the tests in question.

This immunising method also manifests itself in propaganda campaigns to discredit dissenters who uphold inconvenient evidence and in public relations efforts to deny the existence of any serious difficulties whose resolution would require a major strategic reorientation. These campaigns can be directed at shareholders, employees, customers and the general public. (Indeed, Starbuck, Greve and Hedberg (1980) explain how the top managers of Facit, a manufacturer of business machines and office furnishings, pursued this sort of propaganda campaign in the face of organisational crisis.) Such propaganda drives to evade criticism of losing courses of action invariably involve opportunism – fraud in the extreme case – in the choice of financial reporting alternatives (e.g. lengthening accounting periods, altering or suspending depreciation charges, and including gains from sales or re-evaluations of assets within operating profits etc. (Starbuck *et al.* 1980: 118–119; Verrechia 1986)).

IS3 Simply ignoring or purposefully overlooking the results of market tests which conflict with one's theories (i.e turning a blind eye to counterevidence), thereby rendering an entrepreneurial theory totally immune from criticism. (Indeed, Steinbruner (1974: ch. 4) surveys a number of experiments which demonstrate clearly that people may preserve their theories by ignoring inconsistencies between their theories and the evidence.)

IS4 Succumbing to the 'not invented here' syndrome – a methodological pathology, sometimes prevalent at various levels within innovative organisations, which can impede the acquisition of knowledge. It is 'a myopic disease that causes engineers and others to assume that anything that owes its parentage to others is inferior – is "foreign" or suspect in some way' (Edwardes 1983: 282). Its major symptom is a denial of, or lack of interest in, the corroboration of new and better ideas (e.g. new product concepts) which have originated outside the organisation. This amounts to dogmatic commitment to one's own provincial viewpoint when new ideas are being put forward progressively in such a rapid succession (as was the case in the computer software industry) that the refutation of one theory appears only as the corroboration of its successor (cf. Lakatos 1970: 121). Thus, the failure to acknowledge the corroboration of competitors' hypotheses may be equivalent to the failure to recognise the refutation of one's own hypothesis (i.e. the failure to accept that one's theory has been superseded). This immunising stratagem is a special case of IS2 and IS3. It too involves blinkering with respect to counter-evidence.

IS5 Upholding the truth of one's theories in the face of recalcitrant experience by amending one's system of logic or theory of deduction (that is, one's theory about the transmission of truth and the retransmission of falsity (Popper 1972: 304)). Typically, entrepreneurs might retreat into the use of some weakened form of traditional logic (e.g. by revising the logical 'law of the excluded middle' (Quine 1980: 43)) or they might adopt a new, dialectical logic which does away with the 'law of contradiction'. If entrepreneurs adopt a dialectical logic, for example, they may no longer search for contradictions with the aim of eliminating them. Indeed, they may conclude that contradictions are better than non-contradictory theoretical systems because they are extremely fruitful and because they propel the growth of knowledge (cf. Popper 1963: 316; 1972: 126). Hence, entrepreneurs may simply tolerate or accept any contradictions that they discover between their particular theories and the evidence.

IS6 Staving off counter-examples to an entrepreneurial conjecture by suitable *ad hoc* redefinitions of its terms (e.g. 'By such and such I only meant . . . and not . . . '). Whenever new counter-examples are discovered, entrepreneurs restate their positions by redefining key concepts (e.g. the target market) more narrowly – because, in hindsight, they had unintentionally been defined too widely.[19]

IS7 Rejecting refuted conjectures as false but then restating them for a restricted domain of applicability that bars exceptions (i.e. the alleged counter-examples). Exceptions are thus excluded in an *ad hoc* and piecemeal fashion. Indeed, this 'exception-barring' stratagem is a special case of IS1.

IS8 Consistently turning alleged counter-examples, in the light of some contrived theory, into humdrum examples or 'corroborations'. (Lakatos calls this stratagem 'monster-adjustment'.) These entrepreneurs claim that interpretations of particular market situations cannot possibly be true if they would conflict with their conjectures. They are smugly confident that if exceptions are analysed more closely they will turn out to be only apparent and will in fact 'corroborate' their conjectures.

The falsificationist entrepreneur responds to each of the potential immunising stratagems with the appropriate counter-measure (cf. Popper 1959: 82–83, 273). The full battery of the entrepreneur's counter-moves comprises the following rules for guarding against immunising stratagems:

• the 'no *ad hoc* solutions or hypotheses' rule;
• the rule against always attacking inconvenient observations or experimental results;
• the rule against ignoring counter-examples;
• the rule against refusing to acknowledge the corroboration of theories which supersede one's own;
• the rule against using some weaker logic;
• the 'no *ad hoc* definitions' rule;
• the 'no exception-barring' rule;
• the 'no monster-adjustment' rule.

I discuss the most important of these in this section.

To avoid the first of the immunising stratagems described above (IS1), the falsificationist entrepreneur tries to be wary of using auxiliary assumptions and only introduces auxiliary assumptions which do not reduce the testability, and hence falsifiability, of his or her cluster of conjectures as a whole. (More generally, the entrepreneur stipulates that all explanations of why an apparent refutation is in error must be independently testable and non-*ad hoc* (cf. Musgrave 1971a: 12).) Thus, the falsificationist entrepreneur does not exclude all defences of a theory, not even all those which introduce auxiliary assumptions. But the entrepreneur will only introduce *testable* auxiliary assumptions which strengthen a theory by making it rule out more events than it did previously, so that its informative content increases. The introduction of a testable auxiliary hypothesis may thus be regarded as contributing to the growth in the entrepreneur's knowledge (cf. Popper 1976c: 42–44).

In order to avoid the second immunising stratagem (IS2), the entrepreneur could arrange either for market experiments (e.g. test markets) to be undertaken in parallel or for an external referee to evaluate the quality of research design and analysis (i.e. trilateral governance of the market research contract). In addition, the entrepreneur could devise, where possible, a specialised contract which better aligns the incentives of the agent and reduces the scope of the market research firm to act opportunistically (i.e. bilateral governance).

Sophisticated falsificationist entrepreneurs are well-equipped to counter the last three immunising stratagems (IS6, IS7, IS8). Their arsenal of counter-moves includes three rules specifically designed to neutralise each of these defensive tactics. These methodological rules are more concrete instances of the general principle that falsificationist entrepreneurs must impose particular well-defined conditions on the theoretical adjustments by which they may safeguard their theories against refutation. Immunising stratagems IS6–IS8 result in *ad hoc* theories which in general do not offer any novel, excess empirical content over their predecessors: that is, these tactics do not increase, and usually reduce, the amount of information in a theory. For example, exception-barring (IS7) replaces a bolder or more falsifiable theory with a weaker or less falsifiable one. These stratagems are therefore *ad hoc*, irrational changes of theory, and in accordance with falsificationist methodological rules, they must in general be rejected.

However, qualifications need to be made. In some limited circumstances, monster-adjustment (IS8) may be empirically progressive: it may predict a novel fact (Lakatos 1970: 149). It then satisfies the standards for a rational theoretical adjustment. In addition, it may be that exception-barring involves progress towards the truth if it replaces a stronger falsehood by a weaker truth (which, however, can never be conclusively established): '[W]e cannot unreservedly condemn such modifications: we value strength but we also value truth, and the weaker theory might be true where its stronger ancestor was false' (Musgrave 1981: 381). Furthermore, changing the meaning of concepts in an entrepreneur's theory is not necessarily monster-barring (IS6): changes in explicit definitions are permissible provided the new theoretical system has a higher degree of falsifiability than that of the system before such modification (Nola 1987: 452).

A further point to be made is that falsificationist maxims do not prohibit the *critical* defence of a theory; they only prohibit the universal and dogmatic use of immunising stratagems – which save theories without being critical with respect to other parts of the test situation (Musgrave 1974b: 580). Thus, it is quite legitimate for an entrepreneur to try to defend a particular hypothesis against a refutation by criticising any of the situational elements involved in that refutation, such as the arrangements for the market experiment, the system of assumptions underlying the apparent refutation, or the description of the particular experimental conditions. Similarly, the falsificationist rules against immunising stratagems do not imply that the entrepreneur can *never* explain away apparent refutations by blaming the experimenter (e.g. a market research firm which conducts test marketing). As Musgrave remarks:

> The rule against *ad hocness* does not mean that we should never impute a refutation to the idiosyncrasies, or the unreliability, or the dishonesty of an experimenter. What the rule does mean is that when this is done, it must be done in an independently testable fashion: it must be possible to obtain other evidence for the experimenter's idiosyncrasy, or unreliability, or dishonesty apart from the fact that he has reached unwelcome results.
>
> (Musgrave 1971a: 13)

Finally, when the exploitation of perceived profit opportunities involves setting up new firms, falsificationist entrepreneurs design their organisational structures (widely defined) so as to reduce the scope for immunising stratagems aimed at protecting losing courses of action. (The design of such falsificationist learning mechanisms is described in Harper 1992: 238–248).

6.3.3 Psychological and sociopsychological counterparts to immunising stratagems

A combination of psychological and sociopsychological factors increases the tendency of economic agents to immunise their theories against criticism.[20] Even though psychological and sociological elements do not form part of the GK research programme, it is worth providing a brief sketch of the major types of these factors which bear upon immunising tactics. They will be discussed in the context of safeguarding business ventures from elimination, but the discussion can be generalised to cover all uncritical attempts by entrepreneurs to preserve their conceptual frameworks.

One psychological mechanism which can inhibit termination of failing ventures is cognitive dissonance and the perceptual biases to which it gives rise.[21] The argument is that people have a general tendency to filter evidence in the light of their own preconceptions: 'It is easier to understand and accept information congruent with previous beliefs than to overcome cognitive dissonance' (Arrow 1974: 75). Cognitive dissonance is defined by Festinger as the presence of 'non-fitting' relations among *relevant* cognitions. Dissonance theory asserts that, whenever two relevant cognitions do not fit, this leads to psychological inconsistency within the individual. Such a psychologically uncomfortable state is expected to motivate the individual to attempt to reduce or to eliminate the dissonance.[22] Individuals can achieve dissonance reduction by changing existing cognitions in an *ad hoc* fashion or by adding new ones which bring seemingly contradictory ideas into congruence. They can also actively avoid situations and information which are likely to increase dissonance and may also choose activities oriented towards consonance (Festinger 1957: 3). Opportunities to fudge things in this way are most prevalent in situations of structural uncertainty and of high ambiguity.

The effect of cognitive dissonance on a person's belief system, like that of immunising stratagems, may well be long-lasting: once chosen, beliefs tend to persist over time (Akerlof and Dickens 1982: 307, 310, 316). By implication, entrepreneurs who justify to themselves starting up a business venture are likely to have a strong and persistent belief that the venture is going to be successful. They may tend to ignore or reject new information that could imply that crucial decisions they have made are mistaken, because the cognition that a particular decision might be in error conflicts with their image of themselves as smart, inquiring people. Such entrepreneurial cognitive dissonance has been explored by Comegys (1976). He contends that when entrepreneurs quit a job and invest a substantial proportion of their own wealth in a venture, they can become 'supercommitted' to the belief that their venture will succeed. (In this respect, of course, entrepreneurs are not only pure entrepreneurs but are simultaneously capitalists who lend capital to themselves.) Commitment of this kind causes entrepreneurs to lose objectivity and to subconsciously select sources of information which are likely to reinforce already established beliefs and past decisions.[23]

In this connection, one is reminded of Lakatos's description of the methodological decisions taken by conservative conventionalists:

> [A]fter a considerable period of initial empirical success scientists may decide not to allow the theory to be refuted. Once they have taken this decision, they solve (or dissolve) the apparent anomalies by auxiliary hypotheses or other 'conventionalist [i.e. immunising] stratagems'. This *conservative conventionalism* has, however, the disadvantage of making us unable to get out of our self-imposed prisons, once the first period of trial-and-error is over and the great decision taken.
>
> (Lakatos 1970: 105; original emphasis)

For both conservative conventionalists and dissonance reducers, the power of empirical evidence to overthrow ideas diminishes once they have made up their minds to commit themselves to particular ways of thinking.[24]

Cognitive dissonance theory is also compatible with Shackle's radical sujectivist approach to economics. Like cognitive dissonance theory, Shackle's approach implies that people's beliefs depend upon their individual preferences. Economic agents (and economists!) thus choose the beliefs that appeal to them: 'Theories by their nature and purpose, their role of administering to "a good state of mind", are things to be held and cherished' (Shackle 1967: 289). Furthermore, they may choose to ignore evidence which threatens their state of mind: 'I decide by choosing that imaginative vision which I prefer. To give me "more information" might spoil it' (Shackle 1965: 308).

Another psychological counterpart to immunising stratagems is Kuhn's account of the tenacious commitment of scientists to established paradigms or disciplinary matrices. According to Kuhn, anomalies are often identified as normal at first; they are immediately fitted into the conceptual framework prepared by prior experience.

Only after further exposure does the observational and conceptual recognition of anomalies emerge (Kuhn 1970c: 62–63). Furthermore, some decision-makers may never be able to make the necessary adjustments to their paradigm categories: 'novelty emerges only with difficulty, manifested by resistance, against a background provided by expectation' (Kuhn 1970c: 64). The propensity to engage in defensive strategies is likely to be greater for Kuhnian decision-makers than for Popperian ones because the former *must* be committed to the truth of their theories before they will use them as a basis for action, whereas Popperians realise they are proposing only tentative conjectures which can be refuted at any time.[25] Expressed in Bayesian terms, Kuhnian entrepreneurs are so confident about their theories that they attach an extremely high prior probability (say, 0.9995) to the proposition that a particular profit opportunity exists. Consequently, they may be prepared to introduce whatever *ad hoc* auxiliary hypotheses (IS1) are required to protect their theories against refutation.

The result, Kuhn claims, of the commitment to the prevailing world view is that the persons who first adopt a new paradigm are mainly newcomers into the field: revolutions are predominantly brought about by either young scientists or by scientists who have changed fields (1970c: 66–76). This pattern applies not only to the history of science, however. New technological paradigms and large-scale innovations too tend to come from outside the industry – a point which has not gone unnoticed in economic theories of entrepreneurship.[26] In his pure model, for example, Schumpeter (1934) emphasised that new products and new processes are usually pioneered by entrepreneurs who establish new firms: 'new combinations are, as a rule, embodied as it were, in new firms which generally do not arise out of the old ones, but start producing beside them' (1934: 66).[27] In so doing, entrepreneurs bypass the limited capacity of established organisations to change: 'It is to avoid the commitment of existing organisations to established patterns of behaviour that Schumpeter's (1934: 80) entrepreneurs create new organisations, and it is their subversions of these well-corroborated frameworks that destroys them' (Loasby 1986b: 56). In a classic empirical study of the sources of innovation, Jewkes, Sawers and Stillerman (1959) found that in some cases major discoveries came from newly established firms and in other cases from firms in other industries. Path-breaking advances seldom, if ever, came from dominant firms in the industry. Similarly, Hamberg (1963) reported that large industrial research laboratories are minor sources of radically new, commercially significant, inventions (see too Klein 1977: 17, 143–144).

Sharing many points of connection with Kuhn's approach, Kelly's (1955, 1963) theory of personal constructs also predicts that individuals tend to avoid making adjustments to their core constructs when they encounter anomalies and inconsistencies.[28] According to Kelly's theory, constructs are organised into hierarchical systems: superordinate constructs determine subordinate constructs (1963: 12, 78). Individuals may be unwilling or unable to adjust their construct systems in the light of new experience because so much is at stake:

> In general man seeks to improve his constructs. . . . In seeking improvement, he is repeatedly halted by the damage to the system that apparently will result from the alteration of a subordinate construct. Frequently his personal investment in the larger system, or his personal dependence upon it, is so great that he will forgo the adoption of a more precise construct in the substructure.
>
> (Kelly 1963: 9)

Such a superordinate construct is, to use Kelly's terminology, relatively *impermeable* : it has a limited capacity to accommodate new events or new variations in subordinate constructs (1963: 79–81).[29] Adjusting to new circumstances may also entail disrupting the compatibility and interrelationships between local subordinate constructs, thereby intensifying the difficulties of, and resistance to, any revision. In interpersonal relationships, a challenge to an individual's world view can be met by hostile reactions of various intensity. Defined in terms reminiscent of immunising stratagems, hostility involves 'the continued effort to extort validational evidence in favour of a type of social prediction which has already proved itself a failure' (Kelly 1955: 510). This perspective is particularly relevant in the context of resistance to change in large organisations.

The need for self-justification is another psychological factor which can lead economic agents to try to immunise a difficult undertaking. The termination of a venture may be perceived as personal failure. In order to protect their self-esteem or self-image, economic agents may commit further resources to a venture to make it a success. The decision to proceed is converted into a commitment to succeed at all costs.

An individual's need for external justification also plays a role.

Economic actors may be induced into continuing their ventures because they do not wish to expose their mistakes to others. Economic decisions are made in a social setting, that is, in the presence of several social groups. If entrepreneurs publicly declare their commitment to their ventures, they have an incentive for remaining committed to that course of action, in spite of burgeoning expected losses and doubts about its feasibility, so as to justify their past behaviour and to preserve their credibility as a decision-maker to others (Earl 1983a; 1983b: 171–174).

The impact of a decision-maker's need for self-justification and external justification has been illustrated by Wolf (1970, 1973). Wolf (1970) develops a formal model which indicates how prior actions can influence current choices. The model assumes that an economic agent's utility function includes an argument representing the present value of some set of prior events. Applied to entrepreneurship, the approach underlying the model suggests that entrepreneurs' investment in the past is of great concern to them in the present. Their needs for self-justification and external justification are often intimately bound up with investment in past time, so that present choices are affected by whether and how a current decision makes their investment in past time appear sound or imprudent. Thus, entrepreneurs might persist in the development of a venture as a result of, rather than in spite of, sunk costs.[30] If sunk costs need to be justified to themselves and to others, entrepreneurs can be expected to behave as if prior actions have a present value (cf. Earl 1983a: 185–186; 1983b: 175).

This discussion of entrepreneurial choice in a social setting brings us naturally to the consideration of organisational factors which are likely to promote Procrustean methods for dealing with unexpected changes in the environment.

6.3.4 Intraorganisational factors conducive to immunising stratagems

From a comparative institutional standpoint, internal markets can be expected to be more conducive than external markets to immunising stratagems. The immunisation of losing corporate ventures is particularly common within large corporations: 'If the . . . administrative system has committed itself in advance to the correctness and efficacy of its reforms, it cannot tolerate learning of failure' (Campbell 1969: 410).

195

The incentives to pursue immunising stratagems are legion in large organisations. Traditional systems for performance evaluation and control create pressures for protecting the commitment of funds to failing ventures (Block 1982, 1989; MacMillan *et al.* 1986). In particular, conventional accounting systems have been identified as partly responsible for organisations not devoting sufficient resources to tracking and interpreting unexpected problems and events (Starbuck *et al.* 1980: 116–117). Accounting reports focus upon formalised, numerical measures of readily 'observable' phenomena,[31] whereas anomalies may involve poorly 'observed' variables which are communicated spontaneously, orally and informally. Established policies (e.g. regarding transfer pricing, internal cross-subsidisation, corporate layoffs), rigid procedures (e.g. seniority and hiring procedures), the structure of social relations within the firm (especially norms of reciprocity), internal politics, organisational routines and an entrenched corporate culture, all intensify the incentives to safeguard theories again refutation, and all promote administrative inertia.

Furthermore, the traditional methodology of planning within large corporations is a convention-making activity which is conducive to immunising stratagems. For example, the failure of a new corporate venture to conform to plan, especially its quantitative projections, may result in an intense spending drive to obtain unachievable planned results, compounding the magnitude of financial losses (MacMillan *et al.* 1986: 178). Thus, one immunising stratagem that is likely to be employed in corporate venturing – especially between the fourth and sixth years – is to sink money into a venture in the light of evidence (typically declining returns on investment and on sales) that the rate of its growth is slowing down, which commonly occurs after the fourth year (Weiss 1981: 42–43, 49). The venture is rescued from eliminative criticism by the dogmatic introduction of an *ad hoc* auxiliary hypothesis (IS1). Without any contemplation of potential weaknesses in the venture itself, it is hypothesised that the corporate venture is showing poor financial performance because of insufficient resources.

Drucker (1973: 52) considers that most organisations are better at starting up ventures than they are at ending them and contends that although '[n]o institution likes to abandon anything', budget-based (or means-oriented) institutions are more susceptible to immunising failing or outmoded ventures than are revenue-based (or ends-oriented) institutions, because the market will eliminate support for unsuccessful ventures of revenue-based firms. The traditional methodology of corporate planning promotes the means-orientation of the bureaucratic enterprise. Because corporate ventures enjoy greater budget-based support than do ventures backed by independent venture capitalists, they are also more likely to be rescued by immunising stratagems.

6.3.5 Examples of immunisation in operation

It is easiest to give an idea of what falsificationist methodology is by showing what it is not. To this end, in this section I provide three stylised case studies of firms which have explained away refutations by immunising stratagems, the total negation of falsificationist methodological rules. The three firms are Tandberg, Ford and General Dynamics.

Starbuck *et al.* (1980: 117–118) provide an interesting case study of Tandberg, which was at the time a Norwegian manufacturer of consumer electronics products (televisions, radios etc.). At the first sign of an apparent refutation, top managers invented the *ad hoc* explanatory theory that rising labour costs were to blame for the company's poor financial performance (profits were half that of the previous year). They also put forward the hypothesis that this problem would be redressed by new automated production facilities (including two new factories) which were still under construction.

Contrary to expectation, financial performance in the following year did not improve. The growth in sales was far below planned levels, costs continued to rise rapidly, and accounting losses were incurred. Public statements made by top management explained away the deceleration of sales growth as the result of economic recession in foreign markets. This was an *ad hoc* auxiliary hypothesis, given that Tandberg's domestic and foreign sales were behaving identically (Starbuck *et al.* 1980: 118). It is the result of decision-makers pursuing immunising stratagems of the IS1 type (see Section 6.3.2). Inadequate budget control and long-range planning, and the need for yet more new equipment to substitute for labour were also cited as causal factors. Management predicted that performance would improve in the next year as a result of planning, budgeting and rationalisation measures.

However, Tandberg's financial performance in the ensuing year in fact worsened drastically. The rate of sales growth declined still further, and there was a large loss. Top management responded art-fully with a plethora of stopgap ancillary hypotheses as a result of its dogmatic commitment to its world view and its ongoing investment programme. In particular, the large loss was attributed to increased competition, devaluation of sterling, high research costs, high labour costs, and last but not least, delays in bringing the new automatic equipment into operation. They also resorted to the second of the immunising stratagems described above (IS2) when they insisted that 'The figures for [this year and last year] cannot be compared to the preceding years because of changes in accounting procedures' (Starbuck *et al.* 1980: 118). Losses in the following year were so dramatic that a loan from the Norwegian government was obtained in order to stave off the company's imminent collapse.

Henry Ford's Model T is a classic example of how a brilliant theory – which continually resists falsification over many years – can grow stale and become ossified into an immutable system of conven-tions which is no longer capable of being refuted because the entrepreneur has stopped applying critical methods to it (cf. Popper 1963: 240).[32] This case history also serves to remind us that even theories which have been spectacularly corroborated are still at best only tentative, being liable at any time to be supplanted in a dramatic way by better theories, that is, better solutions to new and existing problems.

On the basis of his insights into the car market, Henry Ford predicted that he could make a profit if he could bring the motor car within the price range of the average American. Ford and his employ-ees created a production system that was designed to solve this market problem. The idea was a car manufactured by an innovative mass-production process involving moving assembly lines (so that the work moved to the workers).[33] Ford is sometimes criticised for having held a production-oriented theory which focused totally on cost reduction, to the exclusion of significant marketing dimensions (Earl 1984: 48). However, according to Ford's way of thinking, mass production was the byproduct of his market orientation. In other words, mass production techniques were not the cause of his low prices, but the result:

> Our policy is to reduce the price, extend the operations, and improve the article. You will notice that the reduction of price comes first. We have never considered any costs as fixed. Therefore, we first reduce the price to the point where we

believe more sales will result. Then we go ahead and try to make the prices. We do not bother about the costs. The new price forces the costs down.

(Ford 1923: 146–147)

Ford's theory was corroborated by the market for many years and brought rich rewards. Klein (1977: 98–99) reports one estimate which claimed that from 1908 to 1920 the Ford Company's profits on net worth never fell below 20 per cent per annum and that they sometimes reached as high as 300 per cent per year. Furthermore, the Ford Motor Company sold half the new cars manufactured in the United States up to 1926. It had more than twice the production level of its immediate competitor, General Motors (Hartley 1986: 190). The very success of the Model T resulted in a dogmatic refusal by Ford to give customers anything other than a basic, black car. Seventeen years after its initial introduction in 1909, the Model T was still only available in its original colour; neither model changes nor substantial improvements had been made to the car. The only thing to change had been its selling price which had been reduced dramatically over the years (Hartley 1986: 190).

However, by the middle of the 1920s, the problem situations of American consumers had become more differentiated. General Motors introduced the Chevrolet which featured colour, comfort, styling, safety, modernity, and more importantly, an ostentatious appearance (Hartley 1986: 190). This innovation was a progressive programme which enjoyed immediate empirical corroboration by the market.

In the face of a competitive onslaught and burgeoning counter-evidence (namely a sales crisis), Ford employed *ad hoc* immunising stratagems to try to safeguard his theory against refutation. For example, Ford advertised the car for the first time in 1926 (Selznick 1957: 109–110). Makeshift and minor product modifications were also introduced in desperation: the Model T was painted in appealing colours, the bumpers were curved, the body was extended and lowered, and the windscreen was sloped at an angle (Hartley 1986: 189–190). However, sales continued to decline in spite of these last ditch attempts to rescue the idea. Ford was forced to accept somewhat belatedly that his theory of the car market had been falsified, and in 1927 the company completely discontinued production for almost a year while a new car, the Model A, was being developed.

Another classic example is General Dynamics's project to develop

199

the Convair 880/990 jet airliner. Here too managers adopted *ad hoc* measures to immunise their venture against refutation – with conspicuously unsuccessful results.[34] The corporation had based the development of the Convair 880 and 990 on false assumptions about the problem situations faced by their customers. Management had assumed that airlines would be prepared to trade off payload for extra speed in order to have the fastest passenger airliner at that time in the world (Hanan 1976: 174). Accordingly, the 880 was built with a slim body which contained less seating per row over the entire length of the cabin. This meant an 18 per cent reduction in the plane's earning capacity. The Convair venture resulted in General Dynamics writing off $US425m as losses on the project during 1960–1962 (Earl 1984: 95).

Earl's analysis highlights several features which are particularly relevant in the context of immunising stratagems. In particular, what is most extraordinary is the extent and frequency of the *ad hoc* post-experimental adjustments that the Convair managers made to their conjectures on market size, break even and minimum acceptable order levels in order to preserve their theories in the face of mounting anomalies (namely, poor orders and rising costs of design and production). The originally projected break-even level of sales was sixty-eight aircraft, and it was intended that the project would proceed only if orders were at 60 per cent of this level. Two years' later the break-even figure had risen to seventy-four planes (because of rising costs), but the minimum acceptable level of orders was reduced to 50 per cent of the new break-even level, in order to accommodate the fact that forty solid orders had been obtained (and even then most of these had only been achieved on terms which restricted future sales) (Earl 1984: 96). Dogmatic commitment to the project was such that it still received approval on this fudged basis.

These cases should suffice to illustrate the kinds of behaviour that falsificationist entrepreneurs try to guard against. It is now necessary to examine in more detail how falsificationist entrepreneurs go about testing their conjectures, a task which I take up in the next chapter. Among other things, I provide an account of the methodological rules which falsificationist entrepreneurs apply for tentatively accepting and rejecting their hypotheses.

NOTES

1 In the light of sophisticated falsificationism, this statement may appear somewhat oversimplified. See section 6.2.4 for a discussion of the qualifications which need to be made.

2 This passage is intended for those readers who are accustomed to thinking along inductivist lines. It must be remembered that induction remains the conception of learning held by many people (including some philosophers), even though it has been argued convincingly that it is impossible to draw inductive inferences from past experience to the prediction of future events. See section 2.1.1.

3 The identification of problems as the focus of entrepreneurial activity is consistent with psychological profiles of successful entrepreneurs. These profiles point out that problem-solving is an important aspect of entrepreneurship. For example, Welsh and White (1977; 1978; 1981: 508–511) attribute three characteristics (superior conceptual ability, perspective of a generalist, realism) to entrepreneurs which they claim are associated with problem-solving. Similarly, Timmons, Smollen and Dingee (1977) list four traits which can contribute to entrepreneurial success in problem-solving (goal setting, use of feedback, use of resources and dealing with failure).

4 Customer problems can be defined by differences: the difference between the customer's situation prior to purchase and some desired situation (cf. Pounds 1969: 5). Of course, entrepreneurs are not only responsive to customer problems. The arbitrage-type entrepreneur, for example, is alert to market problems arising from the failure of the attainments of buyers and/or sellers to match their respective expectations.

5 Quinn (1985) and Ansoff (1984: part 6) attempt to develop models of the management of innovation and of strategic change, respectively, which reflect the parallel rather than the sequential nature of the growth-of-knowledge process during innovation and strategic activity.

6 This argument implicitly assumes that the development of one tentative solution has greater positive net benefits than developing no solutions at all.

7 For example, in line with sophisticated falsificationism, Chalmers (1982: 54–55) argues more specifically that important contributions to the growth of scientific knowledge include both (i) the *corroboration* of bold and highly falsifiable conjectures and (ii) the *falsification* of cautious conjectures. The former case indicates the discovery of something previously unimagined or considered improbable (or even impossible) in the light of previous knowledge, whereas the latter shows the falsity of what had been taken as unproblematically true.

8 Chalmer's usage of the term 'confirmed' is not to be confused with justificationist confirmation which claims that a theory or prediction has been proven true (see section 2.1).

9 Falsifiability is a purely logico-epistemological property of a theory. From the point of view of the sophisticated falsificationist, the logical concept of falsifiability does *not* imply that a theory which is falsifiable

in principle can ever be *definitively* falsified: such conclusive practical empirical proof of falsity is always impossible (Popper 1983a: xxii–xxiii). See section 2.2.4.

10 The so-called 'law of contradiction' in traditional logic asserts that two contradictory statements p and $\sim p$ (i.e. not p) cannot be true together: $\sim p$ is true if, and only if, p is false, and vice versa (Popper 1963: 316). In a formal sense, 'two propositions are inconsistent if . . . there is no interpretation of their descriptive terms in which [their] conjunction is true' (Lakatos 1970: 143; parenthesis added).

11 Radnitzky (1976: 525–540) provides a diagrammatic exposition of Popper's model of the growth of scientific knowledge which highlights its cybernetic properties.

12 Interestingly, it is also a central point in Kelly's analysis of 'the person as a scientist' that how much people discover depends upon 'how *brittle* they dare to make their hypotheses' (Earl 1990a: 733; emphasis added). This corresponds to Popper's methodological recommendation that scientists should formulate their theories in as clear-cut (i.e. as falsifiable) a way as they can.

13 The present formulation of this basic rule may seem too naive for adherent's of Lakatos's variant of sophisticated falsificationism (Lakatos 1970: 96, 118–122, 181; 1971a, 111–114). A quick re-read of section 6.2.4 may serve to placate Lakatosians somewhat. Lakatos (1970: 181) claims that Popper is still largely a naive falsificationist because of his (naive) rules for eliminating theories (particularly, the basic rule just described in the text). However, Lakatos is here mistaking Popper's pronouncements at the level of logic for Popper's methodological recommendations. At the level of logic, Popper is a naive falsificationist, but at the level of methodology, he is a sophisticated falsificationist (Magee 1973: 23–24). This is demonstrated quite clearly by the following remarks:

> Although one accepted observational proposition may refute a theory (this is just a logical fact), we should not, as a rule, regard a good theory as refuted [i.e. rejected] merely because it appears to be in conflict with a few observations which (we may even know) can be explained in other ways.
>
> (Popper 1974: 1035)

14 Even then, the entrepreneur may have difficulty in deciding whether or not the venture has failed or succeeded, especially if the venture is complex and involves a long period of gestation. See section 8.2 for a discussion of the difficulties in determining whether a conjecture has been effectively refuted.

15 For an example of how fuzzy design specifications can lead to a final product with lacklustre attributes, see Turner's (1971) and Earl's (1984: 64–65) discussion of British Leyland's Marina.

16 Metaphysical statements in Popper's methodology are non-testable because of their logical structure (e.g. isolated purely existential assertions and all–some statements).

17 Ackermann adds a qualification to these falsificationist methodological rules:

One cannot satisfactorily always forbid a change of mind as a result of experiment. Data may be so unexpected as to not have been foreseen clearly, or the data may cluster around the decision surface provided by the methodological rules. In such cases a postexperimental readjustment may be rational. . . . In spite of these possible objections, therefore, Popper's rule seems a good rule of thumb if not a true methodological generalization.

(Ackermann 1976: 20)

18 Cf. Popper (1959: 80–84) and Lakatos (1963/64: 15–25, 120–130; 1970: 117; 1971a: 125). This list of immunising stratagems does not claim to be complete. Although for simplicity the following discussion may tend to imply that an immunising entrepreneur uses one method consistently, it should be noted that this type of entrepreneur may use one immunising tactic against some counter-examples but another tactic against others.

19 Lakatos (1963–64) discussed immunising tactics IS6, IS7 and IS8 in detail in the context of informal, quasi-empirical mathematics. He referred to these tactics as monster-barring, exception-barring and monster-adjustment, respectively. For a discussion of monster-barring, see Lakatos (1963–64: 15–25, 138, 315) and Popper (1959: 83–84). On exception-barring, see Lakatos (1963–64: 120–127). On monster-adjustment, see Lakatos (1963–64: 127–130, 135–136 and 1970: 149). It is important to recognise that monster-barring (IS6) is not a concept-narrowing defence of a theory. It leaves the original concept unchanged. It only narrows unintendedly wide definitions of intended concepts (Lakatos 1963–1964: 316).

20 For more complete reviews of psychological and sociopsychological foundations of immunising stratagems, see Brockner and Rubin (1985) and Staw and Ross (1987a, 1987b). For literature on psychological experiments investigating the escalation of resource commitment to losing ventures (e.g. as a result of the need for self-justification), see Bazerman, Beekun and Schoorman (1982), Staw (1976) and Tegar (1980).

21 The theory of cognitive dissonance was first proposed by Festinger (1957) in an attempt to explain the dynamic cognitive processes within individuals after they have made decisions. It is one of three major formulations of the so-called cognitive consistency theories, the other two being Heider's (1958) structural balance theory and Osgood and Tannenbaum's (1955) congruity principle. For a review and critical evaluation of cognitive dissonance theory, see Aronson (1968, 1979). For a brief discussion of the relevance of cognitive dissonance theory to economics, see Earl (1990a: 735–736) and van Raaij (1985: 8–10).

22 Festinger's definition of a non-fitting or dissonant relation among two cognitions is perfectly reconcilable with the definition of internal *in*consistency in an entrepreneurial theory given in section 6.3.1: 'These two elements (*cognition*) are in a dissonant relation if, considering these two alone, the obverse (*opposite*) of one element would follow from the other. To state it a bit more formally, x and y are dissonant

if *not-x follows from y*' (Festinger 1957: 13; emphasis added). However, according to Festinger, logical inconsistency is one of only several situations giving rise to dissonance.

23 Similarly, Brockhaus (1980) considers that cognitive dissonance may possibly have affected the results of his study on the effect of previous job dissatisfaction on the entrepreneur's decision to start a business. In contrast to the general population, entrepreneurs were found to be significantly less satisfied with all aspects of their previous job except pay. However, Brockhaus (1980: 43) suggests that entrepreneurs may not have been as dissatisfied at the time they decided to leave their previous organisation as the data indicate: 'If they continued to view the prior place of employment as satisfactory, it would be more difficult for them to believe that they had made the correct decision [to quit their previous job and to start a business venture]'. In this context, insights can be drawn from Akerlof and Dickens's (1982) attempt to represent cognitive dissonance theory in a formal economic model. In economic terms, entrepreneurs who consider that their previous job was more unsatisfactory than it really was do not have to pay the cost of the belief that they made an incorrect decision to quit their previous job. They also enjoy the benefit of being more satisfied with their present position.

24 See too Earl's (1992) characterisation of the economic consequences of dissonance reduction strategies that may be employed by both scientists and ordinary decision-makers.

25 'According to [Polanyi and Kuhn], most if not all scientific research needs not only to be guided by an *awareness* of a prior theory, but must, if it is to be "adequately motivated", be based upon a semi-religious irrational *commitment* to that theory' (Musgrave 1974b: 583; original emphasis). See, for example, Kuhn (1970c: 18, 25, 163) and Popper (1983a: xxxii).

26 On a somewhat smaller scale, consider too Shapero's (1975) discussion of displaced entrepreneurs, who launch new businesses because they have been dislodged from a familiar situation (e.g. political refugees, persons who have been fired or made redundant, people who lose a promotion to an outsider, etc.).

27 In his later work, Schumpeter relaxed the requirement that only some-one who sets up a new firm to produce a new product (or an existing product by a new process) is to be called an entrepreneur. He accepted that entrepreneurs could also choose to operate in existing corporations so as to exploit the existing corporate infrastructure (Schumpeter 1947: 151). On Schumpeter, see too Loasby (1982b: 240–242; 1984a: 79–82).

28 For a short summary of Kelly's theory, see Earl (1983b: ch. 5). For extensive reviews, see Adams-Webber (1979), Bannister and Fransella (1980) and Bannister and Mair (1968). For a review from the perspective of economic psychology, see Earl (1990a: 732–735; 1992). The latter provides an illuminating discussion of the theoretical compatibility of cognitive dissonance theory and personal construct psychology in economic applications.

29 Entrepreneurs who are *extreme* internals (according to Rotter's instrument for measuring locus-of-control) may well possess impermeable thought-systems and schemes of action. They may defensively disregard recalcitrant evidence of forces beyond their control in order to preserve their radical internal locus-of-control beliefs, and they may also black out experience of failure. For these reasons, they can be expected to continue to make the same mistakes as a result of constantly over-estimating their ability to control their environment (Gasse 1982: 60). A major adjustment to their thought system may pose too great a threat to their self-image.

30 Incidentally, this sunk cost effect is also recognised in Thaler's (1980) theory of (consumer) choice.

31 That is, phenomena which can be observed with the relevant, generally accepted, measurement techniques that are available at the time. In fact, Popper (1959: 103) prudently declines the opportunity to define the terms 'observable' or 'observable event', although he does his best to rid these concepts of any psychologistic connotations.

32 For more detail on the vicissitudes of the Model-T Ford and the Ford Motor Company, see: Ford (1923); Hartley (1986: 189–190); Hughes (1966: 274–358); Klein (1977: 87–109); Levitt (1986: 155–156); Nevins and Hill (1954, 1957); Rae (1965); and Selznick (1957: 109-110).

33 The concept of moving production lines was not in fact solely Ford's brainchild. 'It is clear that the impression given in Ford's *My Life and Work* that the key ideas of mass production percolated from the top of the factory downward is erroneous; rather, seminal ideas moved from the bottom upwards' (Nevins and Hill 1954: 474). In fact, they credit Clarence Avery, a recent university graduate, as having played the largest single role in introducing the new production technique into Ford.

34 The *ad hoc* stratagems that the managers at General Dynamics employed to safeguard their jet air transport programme are described by Earl (1984: 95–97) and discussed in more detail by Austin Smith (1966).

7

THE TESTING OF
ENTREPRENEURIAL
CONJECTURES

As mentioned in the previous chapter, to give a critical test maximum learning value, entrepreneurs must avoid dogmatism and immunising strategies by specifying in advance the significant events that would falsify their theories. In particular, entrepreneurs must identify the conjectures which are crucial to their own venture's success (these are often articulated in a business plan – see section 7.4) and then they must ask if each conjecture will be tested. Falsificationist entrepreneurs test their conjectures by testing the predictions deduced from them. They adjust and reformulate their conjectures by examining the deductive consequences of their conjectures in the light of actual events. If they decide that their predictions are false (i.e. that they clash with reality), then by means of deductive logic (especially *modus tollens*) entrepreneurs come to recognise that there must be at least one false premise in their stock of knowledge (see section 4.2).

In this chapter I identify the main types of critical tests to which falsificationist entrepreneurs expose their ideas, and I examine the nature of the testing environments in which they can conduct these tests (sections 7.1–7.3). Falsificationist entrepreneurs set about subjecting their theories to severe tests, which may be defined generally as tests which, according to their *a priori* expectations, might easily have falsified their theories.[1] I explain the outcomes of testing (refutation and corroboration) and their implications, the speed with which entrepreneurs respond to those outcomes and the economic costs of testing (sections 7.5–7.8). This sequence of conjecture and exposure to refutation is extended to result in an evolutionary conception of the entrepreneur's learning process (section 7.9).

7.1 TESTING ENVIRONMENTS

At various stages, entrepreneurs have a number of 'testing environments' in which to conduct particular critical tests of their conjectures. At least eight testing environments can be identified, and these are illustrated in Table 7.1. These testing environments refer to various types of product and factor markets, which involve different participants and different screening criteria.

By 'internal market', I mean a hierarchical governance structure or firm. For example, an internal capital market involves redeploying surplus capital from one unit of an enterprise into another business activity within the firm.

Depending upon their particular circumstances, entrepreneurs can often exercise some freedom in choosing among alternative environments. The individual entrepreneur's choice of testing environment at any one time has an effect on the evolutionary course of the growth of his or her knowledge, and it influences the relation between the entrepreneur's venture and its ecological niche. This is so because in the choice of target market and testing environment, the entrepreneur partly chooses the set of selection pressures which will act upon the venture and its development (cf. Popper 1972: 149; 1976c: 180; Röpke 1977: 69). For example, if Alistair Pilkington, who championed float glass, had limited his attempts for funding this project to external venture capital markets, the venture is likely to have been weeded out because of the degree of uncertainty involved and the level of resources required (more on this project shortly). It should also be noted that organisational slack and buffering may allow a firm to loosen its connections to its environment and to reduce its selection pressures by choosing less 'severe' testing environments (e.g. internal privately-held capital

Table 7.1 Testing environments

	External market	Internal market	Formal	Informal
Product market	Sale to independent distributor	Internal transfer to downstream user	Test marketing	Sale to family, relatives friends
Factor market	Venture capital market	Corporate venture division	Startup financing test	Seed money test

markets instead of external capital markets) and by attempting to manipulate environmental characteristics (Cyert and March 1963; Starbuck *et al.* 1980: 115; Thompson 1967).

Each testing environment implies different selection pressures for the entrepreneurial ideas which are tested within it. Some rather tentative generalisations can be put forward. Other things being equal:

- testing in product markets is more 'severe' than testing in factor markets;[2]
- testing in external markets is more objective and 'severe' than testing in most internal markets[3] (subject to the qualification that testing in the internal capital markets of multidivisional, conglomerate firms can be more 'severe' than testing in atomistic, widely-dispersed external capital markets);
- testing in formal markets is more objective and 'severe' than testing in informal markets;
- testing in multidivisional (M-form) internal markets is more objective and 'severe' than testing in large functionally-organised (U-form) structures.[4]

An entrepreneurial conjecture which is tested in a product market is appraised by distributors and potential consumers. In contrast, an entrepreneurial conjecture which is tested in a factor market is examined by resource suppliers who hold private property rights over inputs, such as raw materials, tools and equipment, physical space, technical information, venture capital, and labour and managerial services. In deciding whether or not to commit funds to a new venture, capitalists usually have at least some conjectures of their own regarding the likely market acceptance of the new idea, conjectures which may well be false. Thus, tests involving capitalists are once-removed from the end-users, i.e. the consumers. Critical appraisal by targeted consumers is more 'severe' and direct because individual consumers are more likely to be the best judge of their own preferences and the best to assess whether an entrepreneur's new idea solves their most urgent problems, given their income and wealth constraints. Furthermore, a resource-owner, such as a capitalist, may reject an entrepreneurial theory for reasons unrelated to the extent to which it fails to satisfy consumers' needs – for example, because its investment policy precludes it investing in particular markets or industries or because the new idea conflicts with existing investments in its portfolio.[5]

For these reasons, falsificationist entrepreneurs open up the boundaries of the firm in order to include target consumers in the problem-solving process during new product development. They aim to subject their ideas to 'severe' testing by consumers as early as possible. This is in line with the recommendations of Barnard (1968) who long ago recognised that customers should be regarded as part of the social organisation of the firm. More recently, the schematic model of the new product development process advanced by Maidique and Zirger (1984: 202; 1985) also emphasises a firm's degree of connectedness to its customers. Open, frequent, and in-depth interaction with customers is required throughout all phases of the new product development process in order to test hypotheses regarding consumers' most pressing unsolved problems. An important method by which entrepreneurs can solicit customer reactions is beta testing (or product-use testing). Beta testing involves a sample of potential consumers evaluating a prototype or product in a typical field situation (such as in a factory or home).[6] The objective of such testing is to screen out lacklustre products at an early stage in the development process. Focus groups, consumer interviews and consumer surveys are other means by which potential users can be encouraged to articulate their needs, even when the product idea lacks physical form (Sommers 1982: 54). Section 7.3 discusses in more detail the methods by which entrepreneurs can involve customers in the testing of conjectures.

The falsificationist entrepreneur's approach is to be contrasted with the pattern of new product development that was typical in previous decades (Sommers 1982: 54–55). In the early 1970s, the development process for new consumer products usually involved six stages: exploration of new product concepts, screening, business analysis, development into prototypes, testing and commercialisation. New product concepts were formulated, screened, analysed for their profit potential and redefined – all in isolation from consumers or parties external to the firm. Only once a prototype had passed the development stage was it tested on a trial basis by consumers in the market place – that is, just prior to commercialisation. Thus, according to this sequence of tests, entrepreneurial theories were primarily evaluated within a hierarchy during the new product development process.

It is claimed that criticism within a hierarchy does not kill projects as fast as that within independent venture capital markets. However, within the context of new high-tech ventures, a smaller elasticity of response to prima-facie refutations is not necessarily an impediment to the progress of knowledge. The 'incubating' advantages of internal capital markets for radical innovations must be recognised. Indeed, it may be that some potentially path-breaking new ideas can only be realised within existing firms on the basis of 'internally generated funds, over whose allocation the external capital market has little control' (Earl 1984: 169).

The development of the float-glass process at Pilkington Brothers, the British glass manufacturer, is a classic example of how a highly successful innovation can emerge from a protracted period of gestation within the boundaries of a hierarchy. The float-glass process involved a radically novel technology for manufacturing plate glass. The company was privately owned and was thus not exposed to outside capital market pressures arising from short-term share-price movements. The company was prepared to absorb a significant drain of internal funds month after month in order to meet the development needs of the scheme. (Indeed, the venture received top-level support: the chairman of the board assumed the role of sponsor by channelling resources to the programme.) The company experienced negative cash flows for eleven years in its introduction of float glass (Quinn 1979: 25). The external venture capital market (and indeed, the strict M-form conglomerate too) would most probably not have tolerated the magnitude of losses for the length of time involved in pioneering the new process. The venture might have been eliminated prematurely before it had been given an opportunity to prove its mettle. In the event, the programme was a resounding success: the company later reaped $US250m in royalties from its competitors and controlled access to important world markets (Maidique 1980: 68–69; Quinn 1979: 24).

As an aside, it is important to note that although the venture was given breathing space to survive, the development of the float-glass process still involved piecemeal, critical methods: the fundamentals of the process were tested and corroborated in the laboratory, and a pilot plant was constructed to test the process (Maidique 1980: 68). Consequently, the project was continued as a result of a *critical,* rather than a dogmatic, defence of its potential.

210

7.2 THE RELATIONSHIP BETWEEN TESTING ENVIRONMENTS

Factor markets and product markets are vertically related to each other.[7] A vertical relationship exists between two testing environments when the screeners (e.g. venture capitalists) in one market supply resources or goods to entrepreneurs, who in turn sell them (either alone or in combination with other inputs) to screeners (e.g. consumers) in a downstream market. Testing in one environment is thus linked to that in the other environment (see Figure 7.1). Entrepreneurial theories are simultaneously appraised by those the entrepreneur intends to buy from and by those the entrepreneur intends to sell to.

The appraisal of an entrepreneur's theory is not only conditioned by the new ideas presented by competing entrepreneurs actually or potentially selling within the same product market, but also in part by the competing theories offered in horizontally related product markets. For example, the market for new telecommunications products is related horizontally to the product market for computer peripherals, because the entrepreneurs in either of these markets will be bidding against one another in the same resource market – that for venture capital. Hence, both product market-testing environments are horizontally related.

7.3 TYPES OF CRITICAL TESTS

At least ten types of critical tests of theories may be undertaken by falsificationist entrepreneurs at various stages of a new business venture:[8]

- concept test;
- prototype test;
- start-up financing test;
- initial plant test;
- small-scale testing in the product market (i.e. test marketing);
- production start-up test;
- larger-scale testing in the external product market (including appraisal by distributors and large industrial customers);
- competitive reaction test;
- first redesign test;
- first price-change test.

At each stage, entrepreneurs expose their theories to the possibility of refutation and determine whether, how and when to proceed to

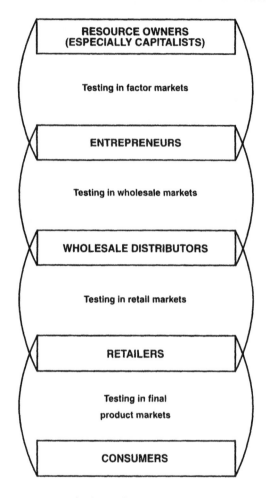

Figure 7.1 Vertical relationship between testing environments

the next critical test. The decision on whether to move to each new critical test is based on the knowledge learned from the test conducted in the previous stage. Entrepreneurs use the results of their tests to make go, no-go or redirection decisions.

The characteristics of each of these critical tests are given in Table 7.2. The table outlines briefly the testing environment involved in each test (which has implications for the types of economic agents involved in appraising a theory and the criteria that they apply). The particular theory and specific conjectures tested are also identified. It must be remembered that the testing of entrepreneurial theories is in itself a creative process. There is much scope for entrepreneurs to apply their imaginations to the development of new methods for eliminating errors (i.e. new types of critical tests). The entrepreneur requires conceptual and practical ingenuity to produce severe tests and to formulate experiments which exclude potential interfering factors as much as possible. The following sections elaborate on some of the more important methods for testing new entrepreneurial ideas prior to commercialisation.

Before I proceed, it is important to emphasise that the tests described here generally fall into what von Hippel (1978, 1982a, 1982b) calls the 'manufacturer-active paradigm' for consumer products. This paradigm, it is argued, is not universally applicable because the buyers of consumer and industrial products are quite different, and the appropriate methods of market testing thus differ markedly. In particular, von Hippel claims that consumer-need research and product-idea generation methods are not extensively applied to industrial buying situations. Rather the 'customer-active paradigm' is more appropriate for the industrial-product sector (see too section 9.2.1).

7.3.1 Concept testing

Concept testing occurs at an early stage in the process of new product development or in the planning of a new venture.[9] Concept testing involves presenting objective surrogates of the entrepreneur's trial solution concept (i.e. a depiction of the product in symbolic, pictorial, oral, written or physical form) to a group of target consumers and then obtaining their reactions. Potential customers are requested to evaluate the objective surrogate which describes the new product or venture rather than the actual product or venture. In the course of an interview, respondents are asked to use their imaginations to form hypotheses of themselves using the product and to make predictions of the extent to which the product's specific attributes would solve their particular problems. On the basis of this conception, potential users are then requested to indicate the like-lihood that they will purchase this product. Concept testing is most appropriate for single-product ventures which involve continuous but not discontinuous innovations. It is also most applicable to ventures which are dominated by product-strategy considerations,

Table 7.2 Types of critical tests for new entrepreneurial ventures

Type of test	Major testing environment	Entrepreneurial theory tested	Specific conjectures tested
Concept testing and product model testing	Product market	Theory of latent demand	Conjectures about the most urgent of the as yet unsolved problems of consumers, desired product characteristics, the size, growth and share of target markets, pricing range, future competitive offerings to meet presently unsatisfied needs of consumers.
Prototype testing	Hierarchy and external factor market	Theory of production Theory of governance	Conjectures about development time, development costs (labour, material and equipment), the availability of inputs, important suppliers and service distributors, resource utilisation, ability to produce a good with the characteristics to meet the original product concept.
Startup financing test	Factor market (esp. capital market)	Theory of governance Theory of latent demand Theory of production	Conjectures about investors and debt-holders; in particular, conjectures about what investors and lenders regard as acceptable financial and expense structures, cash flow projections, break-even requirements, gross and net margins.
Initial plant tests (trial production runs)	Hierarchy and external factor market	Theory of production Theory of governance	Conjectures on material suitability and material costs, processing costs and skills, investment prerequisites, needs for production personnel, rejection rates, quality control, material uniformity from suppliers, processing specifications, physical robustness of the product and packaging, ability to produce at the required scale, ability to coordinate production with marketing.

Test market	Product market	Theory of latent demand	Conjectures on customers' demand for the product, their reasons for buying or not buying it, its differentiation from competitive offerings, pricing (given increased knowledge about costs from previous tests), product performance in different field applications, achievable market share, target markets, servicing requirements.
Production startup test (first production run test)	Hierarchy	Theory of production Theory of governance	Conjectures on the costs of producing a steady flow of the product and of meeting quality requirements; conjectures about scale-up problems and the impact of production delays on marketing and financing plans; conjectures about product quality, rejection rates, resource utilisation and inventory accumulation.
First significant sale (sale to a major targeted distributor or large industrial customer)	Product market	Theory of latent demand Theory of production	Conjectures on how the product compares with competitive offerings in an authentic environment rather than in a limited test area; conjectures on whether the product is functional; conjectures about marketing methods, service requirements, quality control and specifications.
Competitive reaction test	Product market	Theory of latent demand	Conjectures on existing and potential competitors and their responses to the new product in terms of price and marketing strategy; conjectures on the duration of competitive advantage.
First redesign test	Product market	Theory of latent demand Theory of governance	All the basic conjectures about market size, market segments, investment requirements, pricing and financing (both requirements and availability).
First price-change test	Product market	Theory of latent demand	Conjectures on the price elasticity of demand, the reactions of particular market segments to the price change, potential price resistance, opportunities for product bundling and unbundling.

though it can be moderately or even highly appropriate for ventures that place significant importance on distribution and promotion (Hills 1981: 29–32).

7.3.2 Prototype development and testing

Prototype development involves the construction of one or more alternative physical models that attempt to realise the key features specified in the entrepreneur's trial product concept. One method for developing a new product idea into a prototype is the 'skunkworks'. The skunkworks procedure brings together a small team of engineers, technicians, designers and model-makers so that they can work unencumbered by the rigid bureaucratic structures associated with larger organisational units. A workable definition of the skunkworks has been provided by Klein:

> [A]n organization in which the leaders operate on the basis of rough drawings (instead of detailed designs) and interact freely with general machinists (rather than production departments). The general theory of a skunkworks is that new hardware is not developed as it was originally designed, but rather it is developed on the basis of the *knowledge gained from testing it.*
> (Klein 1977: 168–169; emphasis added)

Thus, the skunkworks is an extremely organic way of organising R & D; it is an approach which epitomises piecemeal methods of practical experimentation. It is based on the assumption that major innovations cannot be successfully planned by way of detailed blueprints but must be developed by the general method of practical trial and error-elimination. The economic rationale for this type of organisation is that a great expenditure of resources at the design stage is likely to lead to a very complex system which is difficult to develop and which is costly to produce: hence, the objective is to construct and to test a physical prototype as soon as possible. The skunkworks fosters a highly interactive learning environment which orients the innovative team towards its problem; it allows fast communication between its members, even if they are of different ranks. The result is that the approach reduces the turnaround time for practical experiments, and thus it increases the number of experiments that can be conducted within any given period (Quinn 1985: 79).

The skunkworks approach has been used by numerous large

innovative enterprises (e.g. the Pilkington float-glass development team and Seymour Cray at Control Data) in order to emulate small entrepreneurial ventures (Quinn 1979: 28). The approach in its modern form originated at the Advanced Development Projects Division of the Lockheed Aircraft Corporation. (In fact, the term 'skunkworks' was coined by Kelly Johnson, an aeronautical engineer at Lockheed.)

The Convair venture discussed in section 6.3.5 also serves as a lesson of how holistic experiments based on blueprints can lead to bigger mistakes than are necessary. In an attempt to sell a radical modification of the 880 to American Airlines (made necessary because of Convair's highly restrictive sales contracts with TWA regarding the 880), Convair promised to supply a new and faster plane (dubbed the 990). The production of the 990 was to be achieved within a short period by skipping the prototype stage, even though it was in effect a new aircraft with a revolutionary engine. In the event, the 990 did not meet American Airline's speed specifications, and the contract had to be renegotiated at a tremendous cost to Convair. Bypassing the prototype stage also meant that technical problems (specifically, wing-flutter problems) were only discovered in the first production models, at which stage the costs of rectifying these design mistakes were extremely high (Earl 1984: 97). Had the aircraft been developed by piecemeal methods, these problems may well have been averted.[10]

During the prototype testing stage, it may be necessary to organise so-called 'developmental shoot-outs' in order to assess competing prototype options (Quinn 1985: 79).[11] This procedure is consistent with a *generalised* Popperian conception of objectivity: namely, the idea of mutual rational control by critical evaluation (Popper 1966a, 1966b).[12] The shoot-out is a method for formalising the critical evaluation of rival projects. It is a forum which injects intersubjective criticism into the new product development process.

At the shoot-out, participants consciously adopt critical methods: they attempt to find flaws in each other's ideas and to hunt for contradictions either within an idea itself, between the idea and other provisionally accepted ideas, or between the idea and particular market facts (cf. Popper 1963: 316; 1972: 260–261). The discovery of contradictions, and the demand for their elimination, results in the emergence of new problems or subproblems, the solution of which may require participants to generate other ideas (including new prototype models) that resolve earlier contradictions (Popper

217

1972: 126). By means of developmental shoot-outs, entrepreneurs and their subordinates may learn much about the intrinsic difficulties of the market problems that they are attempting to solve, about the fundamental assumptions that they have been making with regard to these problems, and about the adequacy and ranking of competing prototypes which have so far been submitted as tentative solutions.

The shoot-out process has been applied at the prototype stage in successful large-scale innovative companies, such as Sony Corporation. A similar procedure is 3M's monthly Technical Forum, at which technical staff members within the firm exchange views on their respective projects (Maidique and Hayes 1984: 22). The shoot-out approach can also be extended to cover smaller entrepreneurial firms and other phases of the new product development process.

A number of preconditions must be met if developmental shoot-outs and other organisational procedures for instituting interpersonal criticism are to be effective. The first is that there must be a tolerance of failure – an acknowledgement that failure is a necessary part of the growth of knowledge. 'In the simplest terms, failure is the ultimate teacher. From its lessons the persistent build their successes' (Maidique and Zirger 1985: 309). The organisational implication is that those members of the firm who fail to turn an innovative project into a commercial success, or those whose prototypes are rejected in favour of superior options, must not be penalised. They must be reinvolved in their particular specialities and reintegrated quickly into other programmes (Maidique and Hayes 1984: 24; Quinn 1985: 79). Second, organisational cohesion is required for collaboration and cooperation in problem-solving. Formal and informal linking mechanisms (cf. Likert's linking pins) are needed which build relationships between members in the firm and which facilitate intraorganisational communication and interaction. Finally, an effective procedure for interpersonal criticism, such as the shoot-out process, calls for a multidisciplinary group of individuals who can bring a plurality of perspectives to bear both upon problems and the evaluation of proposed solutions (e.g. alternative prototypes). Consequently, the entrepreneur's decisions on whom to hire and the resulting mix of skills and expertise available have important ramifications which go beyond usual operational considerations.

7.3.3 Initial plant tests

The process for manufacturing a new product is typically developed concurrently with the new product itself. The product and the manufacturing process are interrelated: neither the product design nor the production technique can be determined independently of one another. 'Their choice must evolve through a closely coupled, interactive process' (Sommers 1982: 56). As in new product development, the exploration, planning, development and operation of new types of manufacturing processes are carried out by means of a step-by-step method. In the chemical industry, for instance, process development does not shift directly from the laboratory to full-scale production without the construction of small-scale experimental plants and the testing of critical phases beforehand.

Although restricted in scope, a pilot plant serves a number of purposes:

- it allows the testing of specific elements in the operation to see how they work;
- it permits the discovery and ironing out of unanticipated pitfalls, such as may occur from a particular juxtaposition of two operations;
- it provides a test of whether members of the operational team can work together;
- it provides a test of the entrepreneur's theory of production and governance.

It is usually *not* the function of a pilot plant to provide a precise prediction of what will happen in the large-scale plant. It is assumed that the final plant will be different from the pilot operation, since size almost always has an independent effect on outcomes. Consequently, experimental plants are not 'infallible predictions, as is shown by the cost and difficulty of commissioning full-scale plant, and the occasional failure to make a plant work at all' (Loasby 1976: 39).

7.3.4 Test marketing

Test marketing represents one of the more severe critical tests undertaken by the entrepreneur.[13] Test marketing is experimentation conducted in a confined but carefully selected part of the product-market. 'It is essentially the use of the marketplace as a laboratory . . . which differentiates this test from other types of market research' (Achenbaum 1974: 4-32). Test marketing is the first stage at which the final product is tested in a limited, but nonetheless authentic, product market. The purpose of test marketing is to determine how consumers and distributors react to both the new product and other elements of the full marketing pro-gramme (including pricing, advertising and distribution strategies).

The scientific character of test marketing extends over a contin-uum, representing different degrees of systematic experimentation and conscious application of critical methods. At the one extreme, test marketing involves an individual entrepreneur pragmatically trying out a hypothesis in a very small area of the target market to see whether the idea works. In such cases, the entrepreneur pays little, if any, attention to the design of the experiment and does not question whether the test market is representative in any way. The emphasis is upon obtaining test results as speedily and as cheaply as possible.

At the other extreme, some test markets (especially, those to evaluate alternative marketing strategies, such as in-store promotions) can involve complex experimental designs originally developed by biological and physical scientists to equalise and measure the effect of extraneous sources of variation on test variables.[14] As in biological investigations of many kinds, the entrepreneur – though unable to set up fully controlled experiments – may be able to overcome this to some extent by using sophisticated experimental designs, such as randomised blocks, the Latin square and the double changeover design, as well as factorial experiments which investigate the effects of two or more factors simultaneously. Statistical procedures can then be applied to attach cause to effect. Thus, statistical analysis rather than direct physical control of experimental conditions is used to eliminate the effects of undesired variation from test data.

Test marketing is especially appropriate for manufacturing ven-tures which seek widespread geographic distribution of a single new product, whether it be a continuous or a discontinuous innovation. Because test marketing is costly, the target market must be sufficiently large for it to be worthwhile to pretest consumer acceptance in a small portion of the market. Test marketing is most applicable to new ventures which place emphasis on the product itself for successful market penetration. In the case of new product introductions, the entrepreneur treats the entire marketing mix as a single variable which is to be tested as a whole. Because test marketing attends to all the major elements of the marketing mix, entrepreneurs can also apply it to new ventures which stress distribution and/or promotion strategies as well (Hills 1981: 30–32). In addition, test marketing gives the entrepreneur the opportunity to experiment with various elements of the marketing mix. The entrepreneur can use it to try to evaluate alternative marketing variables or strategies: that is, different executions in price, packaging, positioning, distribution, advertising and promotion (Achenbaum 1974: 4–37; Scanlon 1978).

One problem with test marketing is that it can usually only test a very limited number of alternatives and even then only for a relatively short duration. It is often simply physically impossible for the entrepreneur to try out a large number of variations, so the number of observations is likely to be unsatisfactorily small. In addition, there may be instances in which a real test cannot practically be set up: for example, when it is not possible to translate a national advertising or promotion programme into the test-market area. Furthermore, as I shall show later in my discussion of the Duhem–Quine thesis (section 8.4), it may be extremely difficult for the entrepreneur to measure the effect of a single variable in the total marketing mix because the variable to be tested cannot be isolated in the test design:

> Market experiments are almost never *controlled* experiments, so that the observations which they yield are likely to be colored by all sorts of fortuitous occurrences – coincidental changes in consumer incomes or in competitive advertising programmes, peculiarities of the weather during the period of the experiment, etc.
>
> (Baumol 1965: 213)

Whatever the level of sophistication, market testing attempts to approximate the actual market situation on a small scale. It can thus fulfil the very same function as an experimental manufacturing plant by serving as a miniature pilot operation for the large-scale activity, especially if it involves the marketing of a new product. 'Its purpose is to help improve the *mechanics* of the marketing operation, to find out if unanticipated problems in fact exist, to constantly improve one's approach while doing the job on a limited scale.' (Achenbaum 1974: 4-35). Through a pilot introduction of a new product, the entrepreneur may discover physical problems (related to its functional performance, robustness, delivery, handling, shelf-life, stocking, and storage) that were not recognised at earlier stages of development. The entrepreneur may also identify marketing difficulties (such as potential problems of distribution, advertising and promotion), which can be very costly mistakes if committed on a large-scale.

Even if an entrepreneurial theory survives test marketing (or any other test prior to commercialisation, for that matter), there is no guarantee that it will resist refutation when the new product is launched commercially in the marketplace. A large number of new products fail in spite of favourable test-market results. Factors which may lead to this outcome are:

- The market is not sufficiently decomposable into test-market subsystems which are representative of the market as a whole. The heterogeneity of markets may be such that the so-called market for a new product is not a smooth canvas but an uneven mosaic comprising numerous local markets of many different shapes and colours. Consequently, corroboration (or refutation) within a specific test-market subsystem does not entail corroboration (or falsification) in the whole complex system.
- The market is not stable over the relevant time period (i.e. structural change impinges on the particular innovation): given that the market process takes place in real time and that novelty is continuously generated, there is no necessity that the character of the competitive environment must remain constant during the period between test marketing and commercialisation, even if the system is geographically decomposable.
- Competitive response to the firm's test-marketing activities may be more intensive at the market-wide level than at the local level. Even if an entrepreneur is the first to test market a new product, competitors may monitor the results of the test and may be first to launch the product on a full-scale, perhaps even improving on the entrepreneur's own marketing programme.

Such limitations have led Achenbaum (1964, 1974) to question the utility of test marketing as an instrument for forecasting future sales. Consequently, he asserts that the main function of test marketing is to facilitate learning about unexpected problems and the opportunities associated with new products or alternative marketing plans. In other words, the predictive or *instrumentalist* value of test marketing is questioned, but its explanatory value is upheld – which corresponds to the *realist* aims of the sophisticated falsificationist entrepreneur.

7.4 THE OBJECTIFICATION OF ENTREPRENEURIAL THEORIES

The process of testing entrepreneurial conjectures in both factor and product markets increases the degree of objectivity (more precisely, intersubjectivity) of an entrepreneur's theory. Entrepreneurial theories typically start life as bold, unsubstantiated conjectures which can best be described as hunches. Initially, entrepreneurial theories have a purely tacit, private and subjective quality, which implies that they cannot be successfully articulated or explained to other parties. They are not explicit blueprints which can be laid on the table for all to see. At the seed financing stage, for instance, neither a functioning prototype nor a business plan has been developed (Ruhnka and Young 1987: 170–171). Objective surrogates of the entrepreneur's idea do not exist.

The process of testing and realising entrepreneurial ideas in markets requires that entrepreneurs communicate their ideas to resource owners and consumers, in order to convince them of the originality and excellence of their new ideas. Testing requires that entrepreneurs at least partially present their theories in some tangible form, whether they be stated orally, in writing (as in business plans), by means of visual images (advertising, diagrams) or by means of physical constructs (such as prototypes). Objectifying an entrepreneurial theory is not costless. An entrepreneur faces costs in converting an idea from a purely subjective concept into a form which can be comprehended and criticised by other market participants. In this context, costs are to be understood as opportunity costs, not just as the out-of-pocket monetary costs that may, for example, be incurred by the entrepreneur in having outsiders prepare a business plan.

Of all objective surrogates, business plans are perhaps the most important means by which entrepreneurs attempt to articulate their theories in an explicit form so that they can be evaluated intersubjectively.[15] A business plan is devoted to elaborating the entrepreneur's theories of latent demand, of production and of governance (Figure 7.2):

> For the entrepreneur, the careful preparation of a plan is an important opportunity to think carefully through all of the facets of a business expansion or startup, to examine the consequences of different marketing, operations, and financing strategies, and to determine what human, physical and financial resources are required. Much of this *can* be done effec-

223

tively on paper without the often crippling expense of trial-and-error operation.

In one venture that we helped develop, the discipline of writing his business plan caused the entrepreneur to realize that the major market for his biomedical product was in nursing homes, not in hospital emergency rooms as he had previously supposed. He changed the focus of his marketing effort accordingly.

(Haslett and Smollen 1985: 23; original emphasis)

The entrepreneur is not the only person to find the business plan invaluable. The business plan is examined by venture capitalists as a surrogate for the entrepreneur's theory.[16] On the basis of the business plan, the venture capitalist tests the internal consistency of an entrepreneurial theory by determining the compatibility of predictions deduced from the theory and its subordinate constructs (cf. Popper 1959: 32–33). Comparisons are then made between the entrepreneur's theory and other theories, in order to assess whether it produces any novel predictions. (What does the business plan predict are the most urgent unsolved problems of consumers? How plausible is this prediction? How plausible are the assumptions?) Business plans outlining extensions to existing product lines and so-called me-too items are likely to be turned down.

Thus, by submitting their theories to a certain degree of inter-subjective criticism, entrepreneurs are able to test – albeit to a limited extent – whether their initially subjective concepts are the symptom of unbridled optimism or even of self-delusion. Interpersonal criticism enables entrepreneurs to check that they are looking out of the window at the customers' problem situations (and market reality), and not into a mirror clouded by their own product-oriented biases (Levitt 1986: 170).

An interesting case study of the role of objective surrogates is Akio Morita's (1986: 79–83) discussion of how he tried to convince his once-sceptical project team about the potential of the Walkman portable-stereo concept, which was his very own idea. The idea began to take shape when Masaru Ibuka, the founder of Sony Corporation, complained to Morita about the weight of his portable stereo tape recorder. The first stage of objectification started when Morita ordered Sony engineers to construct an experimental unit based upon the firm's existing Pressman cassette tape recorder by replacing the recording circuit and speaker with a stereo amplifier.

Factor market

Business plan
Feasibility study
Crude demonstration
  device
Prototype
Product functional
  specifications
Detailed product designs
Prospectus
Strategic plan
Advertising
Trade show exhibit
Oral presentation to
  investors
Historical financial
  statements
Accountants' report
Documentation of market
  research and analysis
Organisation chart
Mission statement

Product market

Prototype
Written description
  of product concept
Copy statement prepared
  for concept testing
Oral presentation to
  customers
Advertising
Sales presentations
Free samples
Visual demonstration
Trade show exhibit
Promotional film
Final product
Letters of support from
  trial users
Brand name, trademark

Figure 7.2 Objective surrogates of the entrepreneur's theory

He also sketched the functional specifications for new miniature, lightweight headphones. On the basis of trying out early prototype models, Morita perceived potential problems with the idea and set about designing solutions, such as the provision of sockets for two sets of headphones and the addition of a button-activated microphone which enabled two people to talk to each other over the music (as a result of market testing, these features were eventually omitted in most later models).[17] In spite of an initial lack of enthusiasm from Sony's marketing division, the idea took hold and was a tremendous success right from the very beginning. Heavy advertising was used to help create a market for the product and to educate the public about the idea. In Tokyo, young couples were even hired to stroll through the Ginza listening to their Walkmen and showing them off.

7.5 THE OUTCOME OF TESTING

After a test is completed, the entrepreneur must still interpret the results of the test. But for the moment I shall leave it to Chapter 8 to discuss both the philosophical and practical problems associated with determining whether an entrepreneurial theory has been effectively refuted. For my present purposes, it is sufficient to accept that as a result of severe testing, an entrepreneurial theory may be corroborated or refuted.

An entrepreneurial theory is corroborated if it succeeds in resisting attempts to falsify it and if, in addition, it successfully predicts events that do not follow from competing theoretical explanations. It is not the number of tests which determines its degree of corroboration, but the severity of the tests the hypothesis has been subjected to and survived (see section 2.2.4). An entrepreneurial theory which yields a profit is tentatively corroborated. Corroboration only relates to past performance – it indicates comparative success in solving customer problems up to some time t. Thus, corroboration does not imply that an entrepreneurial theory is verified or justified in any sense, for it may be falsified in the future by different tests, including more precise versions of previous tests. (Nor can the entrepreneur's *choice* of a well-corroborated theory as a basis for action ever be justified on the grounds that it guarantees success or a high probability of success.) Indeed, if the conjecture has resisted refutation, the entrepreneur will provisionally accept that theory but will also investigate the possibility of subjecting the theory to more severe tests.

If for any given market problem the entrepreneur has developed two or more trial solutions (i.e. theories) in parallel, the entrepreneur will choose, other things being equal, the theory which after testing is better corroborated because that theory has higher information content (i.e. it says more) and has withstood more severe testing. In accordance with their *rules for acceptance of theories*, therefore, falsificationist entrepreneurs rationally choose the best-corroborated theory because it is more useful both as a basis for practical action and as an explanation of interesting phenomena. If all the entrepreneur's theories put forward to solve the same problem are actually refuted, the entrepreneur will choose the theory which is the better approximation to the truth (or to put it in philosophical lingo, the entrepreneur will prefer the theory which possesses a higher degree of verisimilitude or truth-likeness).[18]

An entrepreneurial theory which fails severe market tests is refuted. (The *rules for rejection* of entrepreneurial theories are discussed in the next section.) Though it is not essential to the matter, refutation often manifests itself in entrepreneurial losses. However, entrepreneurial losses – in the opportunity cost sense – do not mean that the entrepreneur's firm will disappear immediately or that the venture cannot be a success in the longer-term. Short periods of technical insolvency may be overcome by borrowing to meet any cash-flow deficiency (Burton 1983: 21–24). By interpreting the results of failed tests, the entrepreneur may learn from previous mistakes and avoid making them in the future. On the basis of poor test results, the entrepreneur may decide: to continue with the venture as planned or to discontinue it; to slow down, accelerate, redirect, or reorganise the new product development process; to conduct new kinds of tests which generate more knowledge; or to change the scale of operation or to postpone or to resequence proposed tests (Block and MacMillan 1985: 188). In interpreting results, however, entrepreneurs must be alert to potential immunising stratagems that may be employed to continue 'sinking good money after bad' (see section 6.3.2).

The refutation of an entrepreneurial theory may not just be the result of a temporary difficulty, however. Refutations may result in the entrepreneur being continually unable to cover contractual fixed costs, such as interest payments, from the revenue received. In such a case, the entrepreneur will go bankrupt and the creditors will become the owners of the firm's assets. In a different situation, refutation may mean that the entrepreneur earns sufficient receipts to cover contractual fixed and variable costs but not depreciation (in the economic sense of consumption of capital assets). The entrepreneur will not go bankrupt, but as the physical capital used to produce the new product wears out, the entrepreneur will not have made provision for funds to replace it. The enterprise is likely to be wound up voluntarily. A third case occurs when the entrepreneur receives sufficient revenue to cover contractual costs and depreciation charges, but does not obtain a rate of return greater than that which could be earnt elsewhere. The entrepreneur is not covering opportunity costs which include entrepreneurial quasi-wages and the interest forgone on the money capital employed in the enterprise (Burton 1983: 16). Here again, the enterprise is likely to be liquidated voluntarily because the owners are likely to shift their capital to where they can expect a higher return on their investment.

In the following sections, I explain the implications of refutation and corroboration in more detail. In the next section, it is argued that the number of tests that the entrepreneur will conduct following the discovery of an apparent counter-example will depend upon the particular school of falsificationism to which the entrepreneur subscribes. This discussion involves integrating falsificationism more intensively with a version of methodological individualism. In section 7.7 it is shown that, in the event of several corroborative tests, entrepreneurs may expect diminishing returns to arise from conducting more tests of the same type, which reduces the utility of further testing. Section 7.8 examines the economic costs of testing entrepreneurial conjectures. Economic costs have implications for the type, number and order of tests that the entrepreneur will decide to undertake.

7.6 THE SPEED WITH WHICH AN ENTREPRENEUR REJECTS A THEORY

The speed of response with which falsificationist entrepreneurs modify their conjectures if they fail particular tests depends to a large extent on the particular brand of falsificationism to which they subscribe.[19] The following discussion distinguishes between three brands of falsificationism – dogmatic, naive and sophisticated (see Table 7.3). Different brands imply different conceptions of what constitutes counterevidence and a refutation, and they also imply quite different rules for rejecting theories.

Dogmatic falsificationist entrepreneurs (DF entrepreneurs hereafter) believe that those theories which are false can be *proved* false by a *finite* number of market observations (cf. Lakatos 1970: 103). For

Table 7.3 Different brands of falsificationism

	Dogmatic falsificationism	*Naive methodological falsificationism*	*Sophisticated methodological falsificationism*
Proof	All theories equally fallible; they can never be proved or even made probable.	All theories equally fallible, unprovable and improbabilifiable.	All theories equally fallible, unprovable and improbabilifiable.
Refutation	False theories can be conclusively disproved by hard facts.	All theories equally undisprovable.	All theories equally undisprovable.
Status of observed facts	Infallible, provable (i.e. weak justificationism).	Fallible, unprovable and theory-laden (i.e. non-justificationism).	Fallible, unprovable and theory-laden (i.e. non-justificationism).
Rules for theory acceptance	Strict: a theory is acceptable if it is factually disprovable.	Liberal: any theory which can be interpreted as experimentally 'falsifiable' is acceptable.	A theory is acceptable if at least some of its novel predictions are corroborated.
Rules for elimination	Theories rejected once they are conclusively disproved.	A theory is rejected when it is *decided* that it is 'falsified' in the light of background theories, which are themselves fallible, however.	Even when it is decided that a theory is 'falsified', it is not rejected until it is superseded by a new and better theory.
The power of tests to lead to a direct rejection	Potentially deadly.	Powerful.	Less powerful by themselves in the absence of a better theory.
Relative speed of rejection	Fast.	May not be as fast as dogmatists but faster than sophisticated falsificationists.	A slow and often frustrating process.
Growth of knowledge	Linear: an alternating series of bold conjectures and empirical refutations.	Linear: an alternating series of bold conjectures and empirical refutations.	Not necessarily linear: varied types of interaction between theoretical development and empirical tests are possible.

instance, they believe that they can discover a certain number of hard facts about the market which will conclusively show their theories of latent demand to be wrong.[20] They do not expect to make any observational errors (cf. Lakatos 1970: 98–99). Not surprisingly, DF entrepreneurs believe that their theories can be refuted by a single market test since refutations are clear-cut and unambiguous. Once their ideas are disproved, DF entrepreneurs immediately and un-conditionally reject these ideas. For them, the rejection of a theory coincides with its refutation. Thus, they are able to respond speedily to the refutation of their hypotheses and the failure of their plans.

Naive falsificationist (NF) entrepreneurs also specify stringent rejection rules. If their ventures miss a critical milestone, they will abandon their current strategies even though they recognise that there is a risk that their current strategies are still correct (Type I error). However, because they regard both the theory-to-be-tested and the facts-to-do-the-testing as equally conjectural and fallible, NF entrepreneurs do prescribe some safety controls in order to reduce the chance of Type I errors resulting from experimental mistakes (cf. Lakatos 1970: 107). One such control is the attempted repetition of a market test where this is practicable in terms of competitive conditions, cost and timing. Hence, NF entrepreneurs are slower to respond to counter-examples than DF entrepreneurs.

Unlike other versions, *sophisticated* falsificationist (SF) entre-preneurs are more lenient with respect to theoretical innovations and young, fast-growing ventures.[21] They separate the *rejection* of a theory or idea from its *refutation*, so that even when they believe an idea to be refuted, they can continue to work on it to try to improve it: '[R]efuted theories may reveal hidden true consequences' (Nola 1987: 454). Because they are aware of the problems raised by the Duhem–Quine thesis described in Chapter 8, SF entrepreneurs believe that it requires a large number of market tests to eliminate an entrepreneurial theory. They claim that the evaluation of an entre-preneurial idea must pay attention to its longer-term performance and potential and not just its performance at a particular date: 'It is the *evolution* of a theory over long periods of time and not its shape at a particular moment that counts in our methodological appraisals' (Feyerabend 1975a: 183; original emphasis). They appreciate that the evaluation of an innovative idea or entrepreneurial venture takes place in real time, and they therefore try to avoid abandoning an entrepreneurial theory too hastily. In their opinion, new ideas require a 'breathing space'.[22]

Consequently, in line with their *rules for rejection of hypotheses*, SF entrepreneurs maintain that 'falsification' (in the sense of an apparent discrepancy between a prediction and an observed market event) is a necessary condition for doing away with an entrepreneurial theory, but it is not a sufficient condition. In general, SF entrepreneurs will not abandon a theory, even if it appears to clash with a few observations or market facts, until they have a new and better idea (Lakatos 1970: 116–122; cf. Popper 1974: 1035). Before rejecting an old hypothesis about consumers' most urgent unsolved problems, therefore, SF entrepreneurs must have a new hypothesis in reserve (cf. Popper 1959: 87). But generating new entrepreneurial theories of latent demand which anticipate and produce new market facts may take an indefinite amount of time, so that SF entrepreneurs may continue to develop a refuted idea (and to base their actions upon it) in spite of adverse evidence. The upshot is that they often take quite a long time before they will reject a once-corroborated theory which has since been refuted.

This section has inquired further into the question of how much contrary evidence and time different entrepreneurs require before they will reject a theory. It has been shown that different methodologies proceed at different speeds so that, other things being equal, entrepreneurs subscribing to different methodologies may respond to the same decision situation in different ways.[23] Consequently, even if two or more entrepreneurs were to possess exactly the same conjectures at some time t, the rate at which they would change their stocks of knowledge in the light of experience might differ. DF entrepreneurs require only so much time to undertake one critical test, whereas SF entrepreneurs need more time to conduct a larger number of tests (of their particular theories, competing theories and of their background knowledge). In summary, therefore, DF entrepreneurs exhibit the greatest elasticity of response to prima facie refutations. Furthermore, NF entrepreneurs exhibit a greater elasticity of response than do SF entrepreneurs to the discovery of an alleged counter-example.

7.7 DIMINISHING RETURNS FROM REPEATED CORROBORATIVE TESTS

For many falsificationist entrepreneurs, the degree of corroboration C awarded to an entrepreneurial theory will increase with the number of successful tests, but at a decreasing rate. Such entrepreneurs will usually (and subjectively) attribute greater significance to the first corroboration of a theory than to subsequent ones: once an entrepreneurial theory is well corroborated, successful repetitions of previous tests (within the same field of application) will be expected to raise the degree of corroboration very little (cf. Popper 1959: 269; 1963: 240).[24] These entrepreneurs thus argue that there is something resembling a law of diminishing (epistemic) returns from repeated tests:

$$C(H, E_1) > C(H, E_2) > C(H, E_3) \ldots$$

where H is a new hypothesis, and E_1, E_2, E_3 ... are favourable reports of the outcome of the first test, second test, and so on (Watkins 1978a: 356).[25]

After a sufficient number of severe tests, the additional corroboration accorded to a theory by another test would be considered to be zero. At this stage the entrepreneur tentatively accepts the truth of the test results, so that performing the test again would be of little value. Of course, depending on the *economic costs* of testing, the entrepreneur may decide to cease testing after the first or second corroborative instance – well before epistemic returns drop to zero. An entrepreneur is aware of the opportunity costs in experimentation and stops repeating a test when the severity (and hence learning value) of repetitions of that test is less than the severity of any other test.

However, not all falsificationist entrepreneurs will share the view that repeated corroborative tests yield steadily diminishing returns. Building such diversity into the GK theory of entrepreneurship is consistent with a more sophisticated version of methodological individualism. For example, some entrepreneurs may think that there is a discontinuous, 'one-step' function of the sort described by Musgrave: 'before "sufficiently many" repetitions of the same test have been performed, each one has the same severity; after "sufficiently many" repetitions, the severity of all future ones is zero' (1975: 251). Suppose that an entrepreneur decides that doing the same experiment three times is 'sufficiently often'.[26] Then, the entrepreneur will consider that neither the first nor the second execution of the same market test, if passed, corroborates her idea at all. Only upon the completion of three successful market experiments does she regard her theory as corroborated. Once the results of the three market tests are incorporated into her background knowledge,[27] the entrepreneur will regard further market tests of the same kind as having no learning value or corroborative power. The degree of severity of such tests will thus be expected to decline sharply to nil. Such entrepreneurs do *not* gradually integrate their test results into background knowledge. Rather, at a specific juncture (i.e. when a 'sufficient' amount of testing has been completed), they decide to treat a particular item of market knowledge as unproblematic because the correctness of the market test results is no longer questioned for the time being (cf. Radnitzky and Andersson 1978a: 5). This particular aspect of the 'one-step' treatment of corroborative power is also compatible with behavioural theories of choice which incorporate aspiration levels.

7.8 ECONOMIC COSTS OF TESTING

The testing of entrepreneurial conjectures is a resource-consuming process taking place in real time. Cost is a key factor in the entrepreneur's choice of type, amount, severity and sequencing of testing. The integration of economic constraints into the testing of entrepreneurial ideas is admittedly an underdeveloped aspect of the GK theory of entrepreneurship in its current state. (However, the costs of making Type I and Type II errors are discussed in section 8.2.2.) This deficiency is a reflection of the origins of the new theory: the fact that philosophical theories of scientific rationality have ignored the importance of economic costs in decision-making (Wible 1984–85: 271–276). Elaborating the consequences of cost for the testing of entrepreneurial conjectures is a priority item on the agenda for future research. Only then will we see to what extent a consistent choice-bound definition of opportunity cost (such as that developed by the LSE cost theorists and the Austrians) can be integrated into the GK theory of entrepreneurship, especially given the former's subjectivist implications for the testing of entrepreneurial conjectures.[28] The following discussion is limited to a few hints relevant to potential lines of inquiry.

The first point to be made is that the testing of conjectures entails opportunity costs: in testing one set of conjectures, entrepreneurs forgo opportunities to test competing sets (Earl 1986a: 22). The cost of testing one set of conjectures therefore reflects the entrepreneur's own evaluation of the epistemic utility (or learning value) that he or she anticipates having to forgo as a result of choosing to test that particular set rather than another (Buchanan 1973: 15). The cost associated with a test must reflect all the opportunities sacrificed by the entrepreneur in conducting that test. Consequently, the entrepreneur can estimate cost with reference to the forgone alternative use of resources (including his or her time) which are to be employed in designing and implementing the test and in interpreting its results. These resources might otherwise be applied in areas of the venture which increase revenues immediately rather than the entrepreneur's knowledge. 'Opportunity costs cannot be treated simply as known money costs, but must be considered as estimates of forgone alternative revenues' (Wiseman 1989: 41).

The undesirable, indirect consequences of testing must also be included in the entrepreneur's estimate of the cost of a test. For example, the entrepreneur may expect that customers sacrificed by an experimental price increase may never (or only with great difficulty) be recaptured from rival products which they might otherwise never have tried were it not for the experiment. This is especially pertinent if we consider the following hypothetical case which, for the purposes of this thought experiment, assumes that the decision-maker does not face any structural uncertainty. Suppose that an entrepreneur knows for certain that the demand Q for her new product is a negative linear function of its own price P. That is, $Q = \alpha - \beta P + e$, where Q is the quantity demanded, P is the price of this good, α and β are the model parameters, and e is the error term which conforms to the normal assumptions. (Of course in reality entrepreneurs can never be sure whether they have a true model or not.) The error term indicates that although certain about the form of the demand curve, the entrepreneur is aware that there are a large number of unmeasurable, random factors that affect the demand relationship and that cause temporary deviations.

Suppose that the entrepreneur wishes to test her theory about the size of the coefficients α and β. If the entrepreneur tests this theory by engaging in a deliberate programme of price experimentation, she must recognise that the learning value (i.e. knowledge gained) from charging different prices will vary. According to econometric theory, the variance of the estimated parameters is minimised by taking the most extreme values of P possible.[29] The entrepreneur should therefore test her theory by using two test markets, one in which P is set arbitrarily close to zero and another in which it is set arbitrarily high. Of course, no entrepreneur would actually use this test because it would be extremely expensive. In particular, since the elasticity of the entrepreneur's demand curve approaches infinity near the price axis, a very high experimental price in one test market would imply a massive anticipated loss of customers and thus enormous forgone revenues. Thus, the prices which would most severely test the entrepreneur's theory about the parametric specifications of her demand function are very likely to differ from the prices that would be charged to increase the entrepreneur's short-run profits (cf. Rothschild 1973: 1300; 1974).

The unwanted consequences of particular tests may thus be such that the costs of these tests are prohibitively high. Consequently, some entrepreneurs may deliberately choose *not* to undertake particular types of tests of their theories prior to launching their ventures or implementing their ideas. For example, they may choose to bypass the test-market stage altogether (and employ other methods of testing) because test marketing is expected to result in immense adverse strategic effects. The process of exposing entrepreneurial theories to test marketing may improve the entrepreneur's understanding of the difficulty of the market problem being faced. But any market experimentation also simultaneously makes some knowledge at least partially available to other entrepreneurs (Loasby 1982b: 243). There exists the possibility that competitors will be alerted to the profit potential of a particular market opportunity and that they will adopt immediate strategies which sabotage the entrepreneur's own plans (Hills 1981: 30). Consequently, an entrepreneur's property rights to his or her idea (i.e. the rights to control, benefit from and to transfer an idea) may be attenuated if, having discovered the entrepreneur's intentions, competitors decide to try to exploit the idea themselves. It is because of such threats of competitive response that other approaches to test marketing, such as the pre-emptive roll-out or limited introduction, have been adopted in order to neutralise potential reactions of rivals (see Aaker and Day 1980: 545; Achenbaum 1974: 4-50).

Furthermore, it may be the case that entrepreneurs decide that very little formal market research (including test marketing) is required in a particular field because they have intimate knowledge of the market in which they intend to launch their new product. However, it should be noted that this is possible only because they have carried out many piecemeal market tests on previous occasions, that is, because their theories have been tested continually by long-term experience with end-users and with the dynamics of customer problems. In addition, entrepreneurs must ensure that arguments about the dispensability of formal market research do not end up being employed to provide a dogmatic justification for insulating an entrepreneurial idea from eliminative criticism.

A related point is that the cost of testing a theory will depend upon the entrepreneur's previous experience (and background knowledge) in having conducted tests of the same or of a similar kind. It can be expected that the direct costs of testing will decline if the entrepreneur conducts repetitions of the same test. There are likely to be economies of scale and of scope in the testing of entrepreneurial conjectures. However, more *precise* repetitions of the same test may imply higher costs. For example, if considerable extra costs are associated with increasing sample size, repeating an otherwise identical test with a larger sample of potential customers will be more costly, other things being equal, than the original test.

From an epistemological perspective, an important point is that entrepreneurial estimates of the costs of testing are conjectures of a higher order than entrepreneurial conjectures about latent demand, production and governance. They are *meta*conjectures. To be included at this level are also each entrepreneur's conjectures about how cost changes as the type and number of tests change; conjectures on how the cost of testing a particular theory depends upon its degree of falsifiability and the severity of the tests to which it can be subjected; and conjectures on how evaluation costs depend upon the novelty, uncertainty and competitive pressures associated with the venture.

The nature of the relationship between the cost of testing a particular theory and the severity of specific tests cannot be given *a priori*. It may be that the more severe a test of a particular theory, the more it costs to conduct the test, other things being equal. But entrepreneurs need not necessarily consider a more severe test of *one* theory to be more costly than a less severe test of *another* theory. For it may be less expensive to conduct a severe test (e.g. an advertising copy test) of a bold hypothesis pertaining to a general class of subjects (e.g. all males) than it is to undertake a less severe test of a weaker hypothesis pertaining to some subset of that general class (e.g. those males with an internal locus of control). Such a situation could arise if there are substantially greater costs in identifying members belonging to that particular subset (e.g. the costs of applying Rotter's (1966) I-E scale to identify a sample of males with an internal locus of control) or if greater adverse selection problems are involved.

If entrepreneurs presume that the costs of testing tend to increase dramatically as they move from one critical testing stage to the next, then they may adopt sequential screening procedures: 'To select is to reject, and it is sometimes easier [and I may add, cheaper] to eliminate the many than to choose the one' (Loasby 1976: 52; parenthesis added).[30] For example, much can be learned from subjecting a new product to the threat of elimination by concept testing and consumer product testing before going to the expense of test marketing. The method of selection by successive elimination is appropriate under conditions in which the success of any proposed idea is improbable in the light of the entrepreneur's *a priori* expectations (i.e. background knowledge) and in situations where the costs of pinpointing potentially successful ventures are high or infinite, but the costs of identifying defective projects are low.

The sequencing of critical tests will in turn depend upon the entrepreneur's metaconjectures about the relation between the costs and benefits of each screen. The potential benefits of a screen include the saving in testing and product development costs achieved by eliminating ideas which would eventually be rejected at later stages of the new product development process.[31] The entrepreneur's choice of sequence also depends upon his or her metaconjectures about the extent to which the output of one screening stage improves the effectiveness and efficiency of subsequent testing stages (Loasby 1976: 51–52).

7.9 THE EVOLUTIONARY NATURE OF THE ENTREPRENEUR'S LEARNING PROCESS

Popper's (1972) evolutionary theory of knowledge can be applied to explain the evolutionary and endogenous nature of the entrepreneur's learning process. This involves extending and analysing in more detail the sequence of conjecture and refutation described in previous sections. See Figure 7.3. The process starts when an entrepreneur perceives an initial problem (P^1). The initial problem could be produced by the failure of the entrepreneur's existing theory to predict particular market events and the associated breakdown of his or her plans. The entrepreneur could also define the initial problem as a market problem which arises from the apparent disparity between the current achievements and aspirations of buyers and sellers.[32] In the early stages, the entrepreneur may have only a vague idea about the problem, and much time and effort may be spent in trying to define it more precisely. Hence, the entrepreneur's learning process does not need to be jump-started by disequilibrating events which have taken place outside the system, that is, by exogenous disturbances.

An array of entrepreneurial conjectures and plans (the *matrix* TS_1) is formed, each conjecture put forward by the entrepreneur as a tentative solution to the original problem (P_1). The number and variety of solutions proposed are limited only by the entrepreneur's creativity and imagination. At the next stage, each trial solution is controlled by a process of attempted error-elimination (EE_1), the character of which depends upon the entrepreneur's learning methodology. Evaluative error-elimination may occur, among others, by way of a private thought experiment or by way of interpersonal testing within the firm or the market (e.g. alpha and beta testing, start-up finance testing, test marketing – see section 7.3). In general, the process of error-elimination consists in comparing and assessing rival entrepreneurial conjectures in terms of how well they solve their (market) problems, that is, P_1. Some entrepreneurial conjectures will be eliminated quickly, whereas other tentative solutions may prove more successful and may ultimately be subject to severe market testing at a later stage. A falsification implies that the entrepreneur should develop a better trial solution because his or her conjecture or plan in its present form cannot solve all its problems: 'For to regard a theory [say, TS_i] as falsified is to be aware of a problem [$P_i + 1$] whose solution will require some sort of theoretical innovation [$TS_i + 1$]' (Musgrave 1971a: 33; parentheses added).

A new problem situation or set of problems (P_2), which may be far removed from the original problem (P_1), will thus as a rule emerge from the evolutionary sequence of conjecture and exposure to refutation. Hence, the entrepreneur's learning process is not a cycle because, in general, subsequent problem situations differ from previous ones. Rather, the learning sequence is a type of cybernetic feedback process, as can be seen from Figure 7.3.[33]

$$
\begin{array}{ccccccc}
P_1 & \rightarrow & TS_1 & \rightarrow & EE_1 & \rightarrow & P_2 \\
P_2 & \rightarrow & TS_2 & \rightarrow & EE_2 & \rightarrow & P_3 \\
P_3 & \rightarrow & TS_3 & \rightarrow & EE_3 & \rightarrow & P_4 \\
\cdot & & \cdot & & \cdot & & \cdot \\
\cdot & & \cdot & & \cdot & & \cdot \\
\cdot & & \cdot & & \cdot & & \cdot \\
P_n & \rightarrow & TS_n & \rightarrow & EE_n & \rightarrow & P_{n+1}
\end{array}
$$

Figure 7.3 The evolutionary and endogenous process of learning

The evolution of the entrepreneur's knowledge can be illustrated by means of the following somewhat oversimplified reconstruction of a real-world entrepreneur's problem situation and its modification over time:[34]

P_1 = to obtain resources to produce a new magazine;

TS_1 = business plan: budget for the *purchase* of a large piece of capital equipment;

EE_1 = refuted by testing in the factor market (i.e. capital market) because of an unacceptable financial structure;

P_2 = to devise a plan with an acceptable financial structure so as to obtain finance from a bank;

TS_2 = revised plan: budget for the *lease* of the equipment at conventional rates;

EE_2 = refuted again by testing in the capital market because of unacceptable cash-flow projections;

P_3 = to devise a plan with acceptable cash-flow projections;

TS_3 = revised plan: budget involves *borrowing* equipment from the supplier for the first nine months of operation;

EE_3 = resists refutation in the capital market for the time being. . . .

A new problem situation requires the entrepreneur to invent new trial solutions (i.e. revised conjectures and plans) which are then subjected to further testing. The process continues indefinitely, so that a series of new problems and new conjectures gradually brings about progress in the entrepreneur's knowledge. How much the entrepreneur has learned is reflected in the gap between the entrepreneur's original problem (P_1) and the subsequent problems (P_n) that he or she intends to solve.[35] The greatest advances give rise to an unexpected revolutionary change in the entrepreneur's conception of the problem.

Thus, the entrepreneur's learning process essentially consists in going from problems to deeper problems and subproblems. In solving any particular market problem, the entrepreneur discovers new problems, as well as their ramifications and interconnections: 'Problems, after they have been solved and their solutions properly examined, tend to beget problem-children: new problems, often of greater depth and ever greater fertility than the old ones' (Popper 1972: 287). Consequently, the entrepreneur's learning process is conceivably without end; it does not grind to a halt in some final equilibrium state. As I shall show in section 9.6, these points also relate to the continuity of the market process and to the fact that problems are created endogenously by the market process itself.

Even if an entrepreneur's imaginative conjecture fails a critical test completely, the entrepreneur must at least learn something about the inherent difficulties involved (thereby accounting for why obvious solutions do not work). The entrepreneur must also begin to understand the minimum conditions which must be fulfilled by any adequate solution to the problem, such as the minimum product requirements of consumers or the bottom-line financial structures acceptable to investors. In this way, unsuccessful attempts to solve a problem may be crucial to the development of successful ones: '(P)roducts that fail act as important probes into user space that can capture important information about what it would take to make a brand new effort successful, which sometimes makes them the catalyst for major reorientations' (Maidique and Zirger 1985: 306).[36]

The above account should not be interpreted to imply that entrepreneurs always learn the best lesson from their market tests. Even when entrepreneurs are learning from the refutation of their previous conjectures, some of their tentatively corroborated prior knowledge is simultaneously being rendered obsolete by discontinuities in the entrepreneurial environment. Such obsolescence of knowledge gives rise to new problem situations as the entrepreneur's old theories fail to predict or to explain market circumstances adequately (cf. Lachmann 1971b: 46). Thus, as in science, even the most successful theory will eventually break down and so produce new problems.

According to this model of endogenous learning, entrepreneurs may fail to solve the problems (e.g. P_1) which they set out to solve but succeed in solving other important problems (say, P_5). For example, with its Thermo-Fax (TS_1), the 3M Company failed to solve adequately the problems of customers in its original target market: namely, the problems encountered by researchers in copying library documents (P_1). In light of this experience, however, the company redesigned the product (TS_2) for the office market (P_2), and it was highly profitable (Block and MacMillan 1985: 187). Another example at the corporate level is Sony Corporation's failure to exploit Philips's laser disc technology (TS_1) in the development of a home videodisc system (P_1) which had both a recording capability as well as a playback facility. In 1977, after it failed crucial technical tests (EE_1), Sony's project was put on hold but not abandoned. Some months later, Philips successfully redefined the problem as that of developing a compact disc for audio play (P_2). Sony was able to resurrect its programme in a modified form (TS_2) for the solution of this new problem (P_2), unlike American manufacturers who had completely given up the new technology. The project was a resounding success: Sony became a dominant force in the market for CD players (Kanter and Fonvielle 1987: 14).

Sometimes too entrepreneurs may succeed in solving the problems that they set out to solve *and* then in using the solution concepts to solve quite different problems which were not envisaged to start with. In other words, they are able to solve two different problems without necessarily changing their existing solution concepts. Such 'concept-stretching' is a vehicle by which entrepreneurs can extend the life cycle of their existing solution concepts (as embodied in their products).[37] The concept-stretching method involves widening generic product concepts to cover customer problems, usage contexts and markets that are alien to those problems, contexts and markets which were intended.[38] Entrepreneurs design a product (TS_1) to solve a particular set of customer problems (P_1). That the product concept has the potential to solve other sets of customer problems and subproblems (P_2) may have been entirely unexpected and unintended at the time the entrepreneur and others originally developed the product.

The marketing literature contains quite dramatic cases of firms which have successfully applied this 'concept-stretching' strategy. For example, General Foods discovered interesting new customer problems to be solved by its easy-to-prepare gelatin dessert product, 'Jell-O'. A completely flavourless 'Jell-O' was marketed to women consumers: once the powdered gelatin was dissolved in a liquid, it could be used as a means to strengthen fingernails. In addition, a variety of vegetable-flavoured Jell-O was also promoted to current dessert users as a base for salads. Similarly, Arm and Hammer found new uses for its product, baking soda, by promoting it as a refrigerator deodoriser. Yet another classic example is Listerine, originally sold as a mild external antiseptic, now sold as a breath-freshening mouthwash. Furthermore, DuPont extended the product life cycle of nylon by concept-stretching strategies (Levitt 1986: 188–193). It should also be noted that concept-stretching can go on when the entrepreneurial team is not aware of it (for example, when consumers find new uses for a product which the manufacturer has not yet discovered).

The GK theory of entrepreneurship has had very little to say about how entrepreneurs arrive at their hypotheses because the analysis is limited mainly to the context of evaluation, and by and large it excludes the psychological context of discovery (see section 1.5). However, before I conclude this section, it is worth highlighting briefly some of the implications of the GK theory for the generation of entrepreneurial conjectures.

An important point is that, as in scientific discovery, the generation of new hypotheses is problemistic: the entrepreneur has a particular problem to solve and that problem galvanises the entrepreneur into creating potential solutions. The implication is that the entrepreneur's aim structure exerts an influence over the generation of imaginative conjectures. Entrepreneurs engage in purposeful activity; their actions are consciously designed to achieve certain practical aims. Consequently, '[c]onscious action oriented to a certain state of the market cannot possibly be conceived as a "random event"' (Lachmann 1977: 150–151). This to some extent accounts for similar discoveries being made simultaneously by entrepreneurs working independently of one another.

Having a problem to solve also means that entrepreneurs have some knowledge based on previous experience (such knowledge constitutes the *background* of P_i). The approaches to exploration that entrepreneurs adopt are in particular influenced by their experiences of prior mistakes. In learning from past errors, entrepreneurs try to eliminate the possibility of, or to reduce the frequency of, trial solutions of a type which have previously been unsuccessful. Thus, their prior experimental knowledge, however vague, 'serves as a guide, and eliminates complete randomness' (Popper 1974: 1061).

Thus, entrepreneurs do not react to problems in a completely random fashion with chance-like trial solutions (cf. Popper 1972: 245). Entrepreneurs are not aimless in their attack on a problem. Their trials are *blind* rather than purely random (Campbell 1974: 421–422). Though blind to the solution of the problem, however, the trials are '. . . *not* always quite blind to the *demands* of the problem: the problem often determines the range from which the trials are selected' (Popper 1976c: 47; emphasis added). Hence, it is not appropriate to model entrepreneurial discovery as a stochastic process as do Nelson and Winter (1982) in their Markov chain approach.[39]

NOTES

1   For Popper's most extensive analysis of the severity of tests, see Popper (1963: 388–391). See too: Popper (1963: 112, 220, 240, 256, 287–288); and Musgrave (1974b: 576–578; 1975: 249–252).

2   In this context, 'severity' is not identical with Popper's strict definition of the severity of a test. 'Severity' is here being used metaphorically as an index of the harshness of the selection pressures and of the objectivity of criteria that are being employed by individuals participating in the tests.

3   See Weiss (1981: 48–51) for an illuminating discussion of the relative harshness of the testing environments to which independent startups (funded by external venture capitalists) and corporate ventures (funded by internal capital markets) are subjected.

4   The multidivisional (M-form) firm has an internal structure in which operating and strategic decision-making are clearly separated – the group responsible for the latter monitoring the performance of the group responsible for the former. On the other hand, in the traditional functionally organised (U-form) enterprise, decision-making authority for both the development of long-run strategy and for daily operating tactics are highly centralised in one executive group. Coordination of the functional areas is also carried out by the centralised management. Williamson hypothesises that conglomerate firms of the M-form type will have special advantages in screening investment proposals because top managers have superior knowledge of a narrow range of possible opportunities. It is predicted that such firms are thus able to allocate capital to high-yield opportunities more effectively. See Williamson (1975: 143–148) and Williamson and Bhargava (1972). For a critical review of Williamson's work on the M-form firm, see Hill (1985). See Armour and Teece (1978) for a corroborative empirical test of Williamson's 'M-form hypothesis' in the petroleum industry.

5   Applying the GK approach to the screening of entrepreneurial ideas by venture capitalists is an item on the agenda for future research. See section 11.1.

6   Alpha testing, on the other hand, involves the product being tested in-house by the manufacturing staff of the entrepreneur's firm. Because the product is only tested inside the firm's traditional boundaries, with the result that the critical appraisal of potential customers is excluded, this form of testing must be considered to be less 'severe' than beta testing.

7   This section (including Figure 7.1) owes an obvious debt to Kirzner (1963: 18–22).

8   Each of these critical tests is discussed in Block and MacMillan (1985), and the final column of Table 7.2 draws heavily on this work. Of course an extensive literature exists in strategic management and strategic marketing which is a rich source of material on methods for appraising markets. For instance, see: Ansoff (1984); Day, Shocker and Srivastava (1979); Hughes (1978); Porter (1980, 1985); Rowe, Mason and Dickel (1986); Shocker and Srinivasan (1974); Wheelen and Hunger (1989); and Woodruff (1976). Surprisingly, however, apart from the literature on new product development and the diffusion of innovation, marketing theory has paid little attention to new business ventures and entrepreneurship (Hills 1984: 51).

9   For a complete treatment of concept testing, see McGuire (1973: 330–375) and Moore (1982). Hills (1981) discusses and illustrates in detail a concept-testing methodology for evaluating new ventures.

10 But it should be noted that piecemeal physical engineering may not be

universally applicable at all stages of new product development. Loasby (1976: 37) observes that the manufacture of aircraft engines requires building a full-scale prototype at an early stage.

11 This procedure of course presupposes that multiple competing approaches are available for evaluation in the first place; that is, it assumes that entrepreneurs adopt a policy of theoretical pluralism (see section 6.2.2).

12 At another juncture, Popper writes: '[T]he critical method, though it will use tests wherever possible, and preferably practical tests, can be generalised into ... the critical or rational attitude' (Popper 1976c: 115). In an economic context, this more general concept of objectivity can therefore also include the appraisal of entrepreneurial ideas by venture capitalists, technological and management consultants and other transactors in the market process. It also relates to the objective surrogates of entrepreneurial theories which are discussed in section 7.4.

13 The terms 'test marketing' and 'market testing' are used interchangeably in the marketing literature. However, because the latter term is defined more generally in this book (in the sense of the market as an environment for testing entrepreneurial conjectures at any stage of development), only the term 'test marketing' will be used to refer to tests specifically conducted in the marketplace prior to commercialisation. For an excellent overview of piecemeal methods of test marketing, including a discussion of potential difficulties, see Achenbaum (1974) and the references cited therein. Other good discussions which emphasise experimental aspects of test marketing include: Achenbaum (1964); Appelbaum and Spears (1950); Banks (1965); Cadbury (1975); Cox and Enis (1969); Davis (1970, 1972); Gold (1964); Klompmaker, Hughes and Haley (1976); Lipstein (1961, 1964); Scanlon (1978); Venkatesan and Holloway (1971); and Wilson (1971).

14 For a detailed survey of complex experimental designs in test marketing, see Banks (1965, 1974) and Henderson and Hoofnagle (1974). See too Achenbaum's description of the 'checkerboard' design test and his discussion of in-store tests (1974: 4–47 to 4–49, 4–51).

15 There is a burgeoning literature suggesting that a sound business plan is essential for securing funding from venture capitalists: Gumpert and Timmons (1982); Haslett and Smollen (1985); Kravitt et al. (1984); Mancuso (1983); Rich and Gumpert (1985a, 1985b); Timmons (1980); Timmons and Gumpert (1982); and Timmons, Smollen and Dingee (1990).

16 The appraisal of objective surrogates, such as business plans, by venture capitalists is examined in Harper (1992: 320-334, 368ff.).

17 On the whole, this phase of the development of the innovation was characterised by the kind of dogmatism which can often precede criticism: '[Our marketing people] said it wouldn't sell, and it embarrassed me to be so excited about a product most others thought would be a dud. But I was so confident the product was viable that I said I would take personal responsibility for the project' (Morita 1986: 81). At a later stage, however, interpersonal criticism superseded the dogmatic phase, as indicated by Morita's (1986: 81–82) description of how he revised his conception of the usage situations in which the Walkman would be enjoyed.

18 The idea of verisimilitude sounds promising, in that it enables entrepreneurs

to compare the relative truth-content and falsity-content of competing theories which have been shown to be false. However, the idea of verisimilitude is not exploited further in this book because it turns out not to be operational. For further discussions in the area, see Popper (1963: 223–236; 1972: chs 2, 5) and Ackermann (1976: 89–92).

19 More generally, the speed with which an entrepreneur responds to error (R_e) and revises his or her theory depends upon the entrepreneur's philosophy of knowledge and learning methodology (M), the specificity of the entrepreneur's human capital investment in existing theories (H) and the urgency of the problem or immediacy of the predicted event (I). Thus:

$$R_e = f\ (M, H, I).$$

20 Thus, DF entrepreneurs are indeed meek justificationists in disguise. Although they acknowledge the fallibility of all entrepreneurial ideas, DF entrepreneurs cling to the notion that there is an infallible rock bottom of observational knowledge which can be used to provide a final justification (conclusive proof) of a refutation of their theories (cf. Lakatos 1970: 95–99).

21 A distinguishing characteristic of SF entrepreneurs has already been mentioned in section 6.2.4: namely, that in testing their theories, they are not just interested in 'refuting' instances or in the 'refutation' of their hypotheses; they also aim to corroborate at least some of their novel predictions (i.e. to corroborate the excess empirical content of their theories). In other words, they are interested in discovering novel market facts rather than just empirical refutations.

22 As an aside, it is pertinent to note that two psychological profiles of entrepreneurial characteristics hint at some elements of sophisticated methodological falsificationism (Timmons et al. 1977; Welsh and White 1977; 1978; 1981). In particular, they emphasise an entrepreneur's tolerance of ambiguity and persistence in solving problems, which correspond loosely to what I refer to as a recognition of the inconclusiveness of refutations and entrepreneurial tenacity against anomalies, respectively. These profiles specifically state that a characteristic of successful entrepreneurs is the ability to tolerate the ambiguity associated with seeking solutions to problems. Entrepreneurs are not expected to be intimidated by having to make decisions in ambiguous situations (which characterise logical refutations) (Welsh and White 1981: 508–509). What is more, entrepreneurs are considered to be persistent problem-solvers: they are unlikely to be satisfied by the first indications of success; they keep on trying for improvements because experiments never come out perfectly. They are described as possessing an intense level of determination for overcoming hurdles; in terms of the growth-of-knowledge (GK) theory, they are not deterred by solitary anomalies, and they try to improve their tentative solutions in spite of setbacks.

23 The *Entrepreneurial Learning Methodology Inventory* (*ELMI*) described in Chapter 10 suggests how researchers could identify entrepreneurs who adhere to different methodologies, including different versions of falsificationism.

24 Both in science and in the marketplace, absolutely identical repetitions of a

test are impossible. Spatio-temporal parameters at least will change, and this might affect the results. Furthermore, repetitions which agree in every detail except for their spatio-temporal parameters are extremely unusual. 'So possibly relevant spatio-temporal parameters always vary, and possibly relevant non-spatio-temporal parameters usually vary also' (Musgrave 1975: 248). Like scientists, entrepreneurs use their background knowledge to determine whether a proposed market experiment counts as a repetition of a previous experiment. In particular, negligibility assumptions in the entrepreneur's background knowledge assert that particular parameters which do change will not alter the results of the test.

25 For criticism of Popper's treatment of diminishing returns from repeated tests, see: Grünbaum (1978); Musgrave (1975); O'Hear (1975) whose argument is, however, based on a misinterpretation of 'background knowledge'; and Watkins (1978).

26 How many tests is sufficient is a matter of convention: it depends on the entrepreneur's specific methodology (e.g. brand of falsificationism) and the characteristics of the particular test situation.

How often an experiment should be repeated depends on a variety of factors: the complexity of the experiment, the number of possibly relevant variations, the ambiguity or otherwise of the first results, the ease of repetitions, the theoretical importance of the experiment, and so on.
(Musgrave 1975: 252)

27 More correctly, the entrepreneur integrates into her background knowledge not the particular results of her market experiments but the low-level universal (corroborating) hypothesis that she will obtain the typical test result p whenever the specified experimental conditions are met (cf. Musgrave 1971a: 2; 1974b: 590; 1975: 251). Consequently, the prediction p, which originally could only be derived from the entrepreneur's theory T under test, now follows from the entrepreneur's new background knowledge. Thus, further tests of p no longer constitute severe tests of T because p is no longer regarded as unlikely in the light of the entrepreneur's new *a priori* expectations or background knowledge.

28 See: Buchanan (1969); Buchanan and Thirlby (1973); Kirzner (1986a); Littlechild (1978b); Pasour (1978, 1980); Vaughn (1980); and Wiseman (1980, 1989).

29 For example, if it is assumed that each disturbance distribution has the same variance, σ^2, and that the distributions are independent, then it can be shown that the variance of β^* is given by: var $(\beta^*) = \sigma^2/\Sigma p^2_t$ where $\Sigma p^2_t = \Sigma(p_t - \bar{p})^2$. The term Σp^2_t in the denominator essentially expresses the variation in the observed values of P (in fact it is the sample variance before scaling). Thus, the equation implies that the variance of β^* depends inversely on Σp^2_t and that a relatively *low* variance of β^* is produced by a relatively *wide* spread of values of the explanatory variable P (Stewart 1976: 34). And in the hypothetical case discussed in the text, the spread of values of P is maximised by setting the price in one test market arbitrarily close to zero and the price in another market arbitrarily high.

30 In the section from which this quotation is taken, Loasby (1976: 51-52) is summarising Gallagher's (1971) unpublished doctoral thesis, part of which

describes a formal scheme for sequentially screening innovations in the chemical industry. This paragraph and the next draw heavily from Loasby's discussion.

31 The saving is really one of *net* costs because many ideas which would eventually be rejected at later stages could still have substantial positive spin-offs for the development of other projects which turn out to be successful.

32 See too section 6.2.1 on the problem-sensitivity of entrepreneurs. Although Klein (1977: 141–142) distinguishes between dilemmas and problems ('minor dilemmas'), the GK conception of problems is sufficiently wide to encompass both of Klein's categories. This becomes clear when one considers Klein's (1977: 142) characterisation of dilemmas: 'when dealing with a dilemma, the important factor is explaining why an existing theory is not satisfactory'. Similarly, following Popper, I acknowledge that problems can involve the breakdown of existing theories.

33 It should be noted that the arrow symbol '→' in Figure 7.3 does *not* mean the relation of logical deducibility or analytical implication. Each arrow between the P_i and the T_i can loosely be interpreted as meaning 'evokes' or 'is followed by'. An arrow between the T_i and the EE_i should be read as 'is subjected to' or 'is controlled by'. Finally, each arrow between the EE_i and the P_i means 'gives rise to'.

34 This example was inspired by Block and MacMillan (1985).

35 Cf. Popper (1972: 144, 165, 169, 287–288). If the new problem P_2 turns out to be merely a disguised version of the initial problem P_1, then the entrepreneur's tentative solution TS_1 has only succeeded in *shifting* the problem. More precisely, it has led to a *degenerating* problem shift, and the entrepreneur will reject that theory as an inadequate solution to the problem.

36 Block (1989), Block and MacMillan (1985), Maidique and Zirger (1985), Sahal (1981) and Whyte (1975) all emphasise this theme in their studies of the development of new technological ventures. They argue that success in innovation depends on learning from past failures.

37 The original source on 'concept-stretching' is Lakatos's work on quasi-empirical mathematics (1963–64: 314–318, 324–336). In the following discussion, the term 'concept-stretching' is being used metaphorically and in a different sense from that of Lakatos.

38 In using the concept-stretching method, the entrepreneur must avoid inductivist pitfalls. Concept-stretching entrepreneurs do not seek to infer general theories from particular events or individual observations.

39 In addition, randomness and the associated notion of probabilistic independence in a sequence of (replicated) trials is not applicable because of *structural* uncertainty: the entrepreneur does not have a complete list of the courses of action and outcomes that are possible. 'There must be a definite, *given* order if we want to speak of randomness' (Popper 1974: 1061; emphasis added). See section 3.2.

8

REFUTATIONS: CAUSES AND DIFFICULTIES

If one maps out a programme of formulating and testing hypotheses on a decision tree, one must recognise that a refutation is not an event – it is a decision.

(Loasby 1987: 11)

In the following section I examine the causes of the refutation of entrepreneurial theories from the point of view of the observing economic theorist. This point of view, of course, may or may not coincide with the explanations formed by economic agents themselves to account for the refutation of their own conjectures. To simplify the discussion, it is assumed for the moment that the responsibility for a refutation can be pinned on the entrepreneur's theory itself rather than on any supplementary hypotheses made in order to test that theory. In later sections, however, I explain why identifying the source of a refutation is by no means a straightforward matter, neither for the economist nor for the entrepreneur. These sections emphasise in particular the perspective of the entrepreneur and discuss in detail the problems facing entrepreneurs in deciding whether their theories have been effectively refuted.

8.1 THE CAUSES OF REFUTATION

In general, an entrepreneurial theory is refuted because it fails to correspond to, and to include, all the actual developments which are relevant to the market problem that the entrepreneur is trying to solve. More specifically, entrepreneurial theories may be refuted by unforeseen endogenous disturbances or by purely exogenous changes. Because human decisions are indeterminate and impossible to predict in complete detail, it is inevitable that some entrepreneurial conjectures will be rendered obsolete and refuted (see section 3.2). 'The pattern of knowledge never stands still' (Lachmann 1977: 36).

As has already been discussed in section 5.1, in the face of a complex and structurally uncertain environment, entrepreneurs develop theories in order to be able to predict, to explain and to control market events. Because the market is a complex system and because their rationality is limited, entrepreneurs treat the market as a decomposable system since they cannot consider all the necessary interdependencies and interactions. For example, entrepreneurs may limit their conjectures to the actions of incumbent entrepreneurs in their particular industry and in concentrically related industries, but they may fail to consider the activity of potential competitors in unrelated industries. However, '[m]ajor innovations are very likely to violate the bounds of decomposability, including, very often, the bounds within which the critical invention is made' (Loasby 1976: 41). Mutations in consumer demand, in particular, are unlikely to be captured.

Consequently, the implication of limited rationality and entrepreneurial fallibility is that an entrepreneur's theory may well be a misspecification of economic phenomena. It may thus be susceptible to refutation, because plans based on the theory will have unintended outcomes arising from the neglect of significant interaction effects. (More formally, the entrepreneur's theory and plans may implicitly contain false negligibility assumptions.) For example, the entrepreneur's model of governance costs may be misspecified – which leads the entrepreneur to draw inappropriate boundaries around the firm. (In some cases, entrepreneurs may even fail to take transaction costs into account at all (Picot 1986: 4).) The result is that transactions are internalised which would have been conducted more cheaply via the market, given the actual low level of specificity of the inputs involved. Alternatively, the production of some idiosyncratic intermediate goods may be subcontracted on a frequent basis when they should have been manufactured in-house so as to avoid small-numbers bargaining problems. The inefficient setting of firm boundaries may give rise to higher governance costs than the entrepreneur expected. Revenue may fail to cover the sum of production and governance costs, so that entrepreneurial losses may ensue.

Another possibility is that the entrepreneur's model of consumer demand is misspecified. For example, assume that the actual demand relationship for an entrepreneur's good is a first degree (i.e. linear) function relating quantity demanded Q_d to both the level of advertising expenditure A and consumers' disposable income Y. The true model then has three parameters, α, β_1, β_2:

$$Q_d = \alpha + \beta_1 A + \beta_2 Y + e$$

Assume too that, as is often the case in economic relationships, both explanatory variables (A, Y) are themselves positively correlated.

Suppose, however, that the entrepreneur imagines that demand is characterised by a linear function between quantity demanded Q and advertising expenditure A alone, so that the entrepreneur unknowingly omits the consumer income variable Y from her model (i.e. consumer income is mistakenly hypothesised to have absolutely no influence on demand, and β_2 is wrongly forced to be zero *a priori*). The entrepreneur's conjectured demand function thus has only two parameters, its intercept α^* and its slope β_1^*:

$$Q_d = \alpha^* + \beta_1^* A + e.$$

In attempting to explain why market events happen, the entrepreneur may then ascribe to her firm's advertising outlays sales changes which are really the result of variations in consumer income.[1] The entrepreneur's guess of the size of the advertising coefficient is likely to be inflated because it captures the separate effect of the omitted variable Y on quantity demanded. In econometric terminology, the entrepreneur's estimate of the true slope parameter β_1 will contain an upward bias because β_2 and Cov (A, Y) are both of the same sign: that is, the true coefficient of the omitted variable and the correlation between the omitted and the included explanatory variable are both positive. As a consequence, the entrepreneur will hold false conjectures about the effectiveness of advertising (i.e. the marginal sales productivity of an advertising dollar as measured by the estimated slope parameter β_1^*).

On the basis of this misspecified model of demand, the entrepreneur may overpredict the quantity demanded generated by the chosen level of advertising expenditure and may therefore supply the wrong quantity of the good. As a result, actual sales (Q^a) may be less than expected (Q^e). Actual revenue may fail to cover all production and governance costs, so that entrepreneurial losses may result. '[A]n actor's mistakes which result from acting on the basis of false knowledge, even when the givens have not changed, will directly and endogenously cause changes in the future givens' (Boland 1982: 183). In this case, entrepreneurial actions based on a misspecified model of demand are likely to result in serious unintended and unwanted changes in the entrepreneur's financial position – which may impose constraints upon future decisions. Oversupply and entrepreneurial losses may lead the entrepreneur to discover that she made the wrong decision on the advertising budget. Depending upon her learning methodology, she may accordingly revise her model of the demand function – although the previous refuting evidence may be of little help in specifying future demand curves.

It should be noted, however, that on the basis of the misspecified model the entrepreneur could have fortuitously set an advertising budget such that actual quantity demanded was equal to that expected – so that the entrepreneur's theory would coincidentally appear to resist falsification. In this case, the entrepreneur's model of consumer demand would be falsely corroborated by the market test (see section 8.2.1).

In the following discussion, I emphasise three sources of refutation: internal inconsistency of the theory itself; incompatibility with the theories of other entrepreneurs; and unexpected exogenous changes.[2]

One cause of the refutation of entrepreneurial theories – which does not arise from false conjectures about the decisions of other market participants – is that the theory is internally inconsistent. 'A plan if it is to make sense must be based on one self-consistent scheme of expectations' (Shackle 1949: 111). An entrepreneurial theory is inconsistent if the chain of reasoning by which the entrepreneur progresses from one conjecture to another is logically invalid. Conclusions will then not follow logically from statements which represent the premises of the entrepreneur's argument. More specifically, internal inconsistency arises if the end to be realised (e.g. the exploitation of a profit opportunity) is incompatible with other ends being pursued by the entrepreneur; if the entrepreneur's own actions to realise the primary end have unintended and undesirable byproducts which eliminate the profit opportunity;[3] if the entrepreneur has false knowledge of the different means which are technically suitable (in terms of quantity and quality) for attaining that end; and if, in spite of believing that he or she has inadequate (access to) means, the entrepreneur attempts to achieve that particular end anyway (cf. Schutz 1943: 142).

An example of an internally inconsistent entrepreneurial theory would be one that predicts that a positive profit is to be obtained by making speculative purchases at today's high price in the expectation that the price will fall tomorrow. As a real-world example, internal inconsistencies in strategy were partly responsible for the failure of the Ford Motor Company's Edsel in the mid-1950s (see Brooks 1963; Hartley 1986: ch. 13; Reynolds 1967). The theory was to supply a medium-priced car embodying heavy horsepower and high-speed performance to young, upwardly-mobile executives and professional families. However, the means made available to produce and to distribute the new car – especially in terms of time and personnel – were inadequate to the ends desired. Production was rushed to market the Edsel on schedule, which resulted in poor quality control and the Edsel earning the reputation of being a 'lemon'. In addition, an array of models increased quality control difficulties. A further internal inconsistency is that Ford had insufficient management personnel to staff the separate division set up to market the Edsel. The establishment of a separate division also added to the fixed costs of operation and raised the break-even point to a very high level. In addition, Ford and Mercury (two of the five divisions within the Ford Motor Company) extended their product lines, thereby cannibalising the market in which the new Edsel was supposed to be positioned.

Two main types of inconsistency can be identified. Diachronic inconsistency refers to incompatibility between the elements in an entrepreneurial plan which pertain to actions over time (past, present and future), whereas synchronic inconsistency relates to incongruity between various items of knowledge pertaining to actions, objects and events at any given point in time.[4]

Though necessary, the internal consistency of an entrepreneurial theory is not of course a sufficient condition for resisting falsification. Unintended consequences can still arise even if the entrepreneur's theory is internally consistent, because an internally consistent theory can still be false. Assuming that the entrepreneur's theory is internally coherent, the refutation of that theory reveals that the entrepreneur's plan is incompatible with the plans of other market participants (i.e. other entrepreneurs, factor-owners and consumers) or that there have been exogenous changes which were not foreseen by any market participants (Hayek 1937).

In a society founded on specialisation and exchange, entrepreneurial conjectures are primarily concerned with the actions of other market participants (Richardson 1960; Shand 1984: 70). An entrepreneurial theory involves the entrepreneur forming conjectures about other entrepreneurs' conjectures (or making predictions about predictions). In forming her buying, selling and investment plans, the entrepreneur cannot avoid making conjectures about the future actions of those from whom she intends to buy and those to whom she intends to sell. However, these conjectures imply that the entrepreneur must also ultimately form conjectures about the future actions of potential rival entrepreneurs whose buying, selling, and investment decisions compete with her own (Kirzner 1973: 11).

The entrepreneur's decision to invest is based on the assumption that future revenue will more than cover the costs of production and governance. When that future period is reached, however, consumers may not be prepared to pay the expected price for the quantity supplied. The entrepreneur's plans are not compatible with those of consumers.[5] The entrepreneur has held false conjectures about the most urgent unsolved problems of consumers, which are being addressed more satisfactorily by the products offered by rival entrepreneurs. Because their theories of latent demand are very often false, entrepreneurs often underestimate the marketing costs involved in reaching their target markets and in explaining to potential customers how a new product is related to the solution of one of their particular problems.

Even in principle (let alone in practice), it is impossible for the entrepreneur to possess corroborated knowledge of the future actions of other entrepreneurs because these actions are not predetermined and are being conceived at the same time as the entrepreneur is deciding upon his or her own course of action (see section 3.2.1). Other relevant decisions may already have been taken by rivals but will not be known to the entrepreneur in the absence of collusion, espionage or headhunting key personnel. In disequilibrium, therefore, some, if not many, entrepreneurs will have their conjectures falsified because the actual actions of other entrepreneurs differ from those which they had specifically envisaged or which were indirectly implied by their own conjectures (cf. Hayek 1937: 38; Kirzner 1979b: 23). Hence, falsificationist entrepreneurs are conscious of the tentative nature of their conjectures and recognise the possibility that their conjectures will be falsified by the autonomous imaginations of other entrepreneurs.[6]

An interesting example of inconsistency among entrepreneurial plans relates to a segment of the computer data storage industry: the Winchester disk-drive industry. Both entrepreneurs and venture capitalists ignored the logical implications of their individual decisions on start-up and investment (Sahlman and Stevenson 1985: 80). Forty-three different manufacturing ventures were started up in an industry segment that could be expected in the long run to sustain perhaps four firms. The result was a much greater intensity of competition than predicted, rampant price-cutting, a sharp fall in margins, and rapid proliferation of better or cheaper technologies which displaced existing technologies. All of these forces combined to put intense pressure on the financial resources of disk-drive firms. An industry shakeout ensued, as well as a tremendous decline in the stock prices of some of the leading disk-drive firms (Sahlman and Stevenson 1985: 88–90).

Another instance of inconsistent entrepreneurial plans relates to the case of quadraphonic sound systems in the home audio market. Competing firms offered incompatible four-channel systems ('matrix' and 'discrete' technology), which hindered the development of a viable customer base. Their promotional efforts were diverted to making negative claims about rival quadraphonic systems, rather than to challenging stereo sound. Customer confusion and ambivalence about the entire product concept thus emerged, and audio retailers made little effort to market the new medium. In addition, rivalry between sponsors of matrix and discrete systems resulted in premature product introduction as each sought to prevent the other from building a network and pre-emptively establishing the quadraphonic standard (and thus obtaining the profits associated with the 'winning' technology). The relatively poor quality of early products compounded problems by seriously damaging the reputation of the new product category with consumers, retailers and recording artists.

Entrepreneurs may also hold false conjectures about the extent and efficiency of resources to which they have access (Lachmann 1943: 15). In this case, entrepreneurs' plans are incompatible with the plans of resource-owners (capitalists, suppliers of labour and landowners). These false conjectures are also ultimately falsified by the actions of other entrepreneurs, however. If entrepreneurs are unable to secure factors of production at a cost at which they can profitably employ those factors, the reason is that factor-owners are able to sell their services to other entrepreneurs (not necessarily restricted to any particular industry) who can afford to make higher bids for resources because they are more successful at solving consumers' problems (cf. Rothbard 1970: 601).

Strictly speaking, consistency (or inconsistency) is a purely objective logical relation which holds only between propositions, statements or theories. Thus, the proposition, 'the entrepreneur's action is inconsistent' is false or meaningless because the entrepreneur's action is not a proposition or a conjunction of propositions (cf. Lakatos 1970: 99). Only statements of actions (as specified, for example, by entrepreneurs in their business plans or by omniscient observing economists) can be consistent or inconsistent. Similarly, the fact that there is a lack of consistency within and between particular entrepreneurial theories is a logical fact, which holds irrespective of whether or not any economic agent has recognised this inconsistency (cf. Popper 1972: 299). Consequently, even if economic agents fail to notice that their ideas contradict each other (i.e. Hayekian intertemporal disequilibrium), such disequilibrium will still exist.

There is yet another source of refutation that could arise even in the extremely unlikely (though theoretically conceivable) event that individual plans are mutually compatible: namely, a lack of correspondence between consonant individual plans and the actual external events. Even if all the individual plans of the entrepreneurs and consumers dovetail perfectly, so that there was a potential set of external events (or objective data) which would enable all the plans to be materialised and to resist refutation,[7] the actual events may not correspond to the unanimous expectations of all market participants (Hayek 1937: 39–43). Circumstances which are not part of their plan of action but which are relevant to their decisions may turn out to be different from what they anticipated (1937: 42). Such unforeseen exogenous changes may include acts of nature, such as drought, floods, earthquakes, hurricanes, eruptions, fires and accidents. It is a characteristic of exogenous disturbances that agents do not themselves bring about these changes by the very act of carrying out their plans (O'Driscoll and Rizzo 1985: 100). They are factors that are unambiguously unforeseen by all market participants. As a result of the exogenous change, the actual price–quantity configurations of inputs and outputs supplied and demanded (as well as the actual constellation of other elements of the marketing mix) will differ from the equilibrium levels implied by the inter-compatible plans.

It should be noted that if plans are not perfectly coordinated, it is not meaningful to refer to unexpected exogenous changes in objective data as a source of refutation of entrepreneurial theories.[8] 'Indeed, in a subjectivist framework, a change in the objective data can only be defined *relative* to a state of coincidence of expectations, irrespective of whether there is any absolute change' (Böhm 1986: 25; original emphasis). If expectations are not compatible, actual market events may corroborate the conjectures of some entrepreneurs and falsify the expectations of others. Hence, there is no basis for identifying a change in the objective data. Those entrepreneurs able to carry out their plans correctly anticipated the market event, so that from their subjective point of view, no change has occurred: expected and actual outcomes do not diverge (Hayek 1937: 40). However, the successful fulfilment of entrepreneurs' market plans does not necessarily imply that their knowledge is correct; and the theories of those entrepreneurs whose market plans fail are not necessarily false, a point which Hayek does not emphasise. It is these matters that I shall now consider in the next section.

8.2 DIFFICULTIES IN DETERMINING WHETHER A CONJECTURE HAS BEEN REFUTED

In this section I consider the major difficulties which entrepreneurs encounter in determining whether their conjectures have been effectively refuted. One difficulty is that the empirical evidence, which entrepreneurs use to critically evaluate their conjectures, is itself impregnated with hypotheses and is therefore fallible (section 8.3). The theory-laden nature of evidence is actually only part of a much more comprehensive problem. The main difficulty which I investigate is the Duhem–Quine irrefutability thesis (section 8.4). The implication of the thesis is that determining whether an entrepreneurial conjecture is false is by no means an unambiguous matter. '[E]rror correction may be faltering and incomplete' (Loasby 1982a: 122), because the testing of entrepreneurial ideas – both prior to commercialisation and in the marketplace – cannot be conclusive.

However, before I analyse the Duhem–Quine thesis and other difficulties, it is convenient to look at the types of mistakes that entrepreneurs can make in interpreting the results of their experiments. In particular, I first discuss false refutations and false corroborations (section 8.2.1) and then examine these decision errors in more detail by means of an analogy from statistical inference (section 8.2.2).

8.2.1 False refutations and false corroborations

The decision to reject or not to reject an idea is made under structural uncertainty. An important consequence of entrepreneurial fallibility is that entrepreneurs are liable to make errors in determining whether a conjecture has been effectively falsified and are prone to making mistakes in their relative appraisals of competing theories.[9] There are definite, but unknown, possibilities of making two types of error: false refutations and false corroborations. A false refutation involves the entrepreneur rejecting a conjecture in the mistaken belief that it has been effectively refuted by empirical testing when in fact the conjecture is basically sound. False refutations may arise in at least two ways. First, the entrepreneur may conduct an inappropriate test (which may involve applying criteria reflecting product or technical standards that are not relevant to consumer requirements), so that the conjecture is refuted but only by the wrong test. For example, Loasby (1976: 55) pinpoints inappropriate screening criteria as having led the ICI Paints Division to fail to exploit an opportunity to commercialise a new type of paint. A new paint had been developed, which, when applied to wet plaster, could be immediately peeled away from the wall as a sheet. Because this product characteristic did not match scientists' technical standards, the paint was rejected, even though the technical standard did not reflect the needs of do-it-yourself householders. However, a similar paint was successfully marketed by a competitor. It has been suggested that this type of false refutation results from an incorrect definition of the (customer) problem. Had the problem been correctly specified and the appropriate test undertaken, the conjecture might well not have been falsified.

A second case of false refutations arises if the appropriate test is undertaken but the entrepreneur interprets the results incorrectly. The entrepreneur interprets the test results as implying that the conjecture has been refuted (i.e. the entrepreneur regards the conjecture as false) whereas a more accurate interpretation of the results is that the conjecture has been corroborated.

Classic examples of false refutation concern some of the greatest commercial success stories of all time. For instance, the inappropriate screening procedures of the Victor Talking Machine Company meant that it dismissed the innovative opportunity represented by radio (but RCA did recognise the opportunity) (Hanan 1969b). Furthermore, numerous companies turned down the opportunity to develop Chester Carlson's new process of electrophotography (later called xerography) which would in years to come revolutionise office copying (Dessauer 1971; Jewkes *et al.* 1959; Quinn 1979: 20). Included among those who failed to perceive the novel promise of this new idea are the managers of IBM, Remington Rand and Eastman Kodak. The invention was eventually licensed and developed into the first marketable xerographic copier by a small photo-paper firm called

Haloid Company, which grew to become the giant multinational, Xerox Corporation.

Thus, a theory which has on a previous occasion been falsely refuted may be reinstated (i.e. corroborated) at a later date. But a once-refuted theory which is subsequently corroborated need not necessarily have been wrongly refuted in the original instance. A refuted entrepreneurial idea may be retested and corroborated, perhaps because new or changed conditions make it now seem more promising or appropriate (this is in contrast to biological evolution, where previously rejected mutations cannot be recalled when conditions change (cf. Nozick 1974: 317)). For example, entrepreneurial theories concerning particular items of fashion which were popular many years ago, and which were finally refuted at some stage, may be retested in later years and be corroborated.

False corroboration arises when entrepreneurs complete their transactions at the terms which they had predicted, thereby capturing lucrative profit opportunities, even though their plans are based on conjectures, the falsity of which they could only have discovered by experimenting with alternative trading configurations. Consequently, the successful execution of plans in the market does not ensure that the entrepreneur is in fact not mistaken. False corroboration also occurs when the entrepreneur allows a false conjecture which should have been refuted by successive stages of screening and testing to progress to commercialisation. The entrepreneur believes a conjecture to be corroborated by a test, whereas the theory is in fact false.

Corfam represents a dramatic example of false corroboration. Corfam was a new material which DuPont had developed to replace leather for shoe uppers. In order to test the market acceptance for this new material, more than 15,000 pairs of shoes made from Corfam were subjected to consumer-use testing before full-scale introduction. 'No product has been more thoroughly market tested prior to coming to market than Corfam'.[10] The new product was a mighty failure, however. Among the key factors which account for its lack of success can be included researchers' misinterpretation of the results of market testing. In particular, evidence that a significant (8 per cent) proportion of consumers in the sample experienced some discomfort was deemed not to be a serious threat to their theory of latent demand. In hindsight, such a decision to reject possible refuting evidence was unwise, especially given that the new material did not mould to the foot as does leather, and given also that it was expensive. After seven years of huge losses estimated as high as

$US100m, DuPont abandoned the venture and sold the process and selling rights to Polimex-Sekop, a Polish government-owned manufacturing operation (Hartley 1986: 210).[11]

False corroborations can occur because a theory which is false may still lead the entrepreneur to an indefinite number of consequences (i.e. predictions) which are in fact true (cf. Magee 1973: 42). This problem is especially vexatious for economic decision-makers who act on the basis of a misspecified model of the world:

> Among the many difficulties that can occur with a misspecified model, one of the most trying is the possibility that such a model can make correct predictions over some range of policies. The *apparent confirmation* in this 'misspecification trap' can prevent the decision maker from pursuing an improved model that would reveal superior alternatives remote from current policy.
>
> (Cohen and Axelrod 1984: 30; emphasis added)

In a structurally uncertain environment, the path of the entrepreneur is littered with 'misspecification traps'. Entrepreneurs may unwittingly omit relevant explanatory variables from their models of the world and may unknowingly disregard qualitative changes in one or more variables; and they may unintentionally include irrelevant explanatory variables or may even inadvertently specify an incorrect relationship between the relevant variables. And yet in spite of these errors, entrepreneurs may still be successful in their predictive activities within a certain domain of application, and they may interpret their theories as being corroborated.

Chance and compensating errors also play a role in false refutations and false corroborations. A false refutation can arise from a windfall loss (i.e. bad luck). Similarly, a false corroboration can arise from sheer chance. Windfall gains are generated by unanticipated changes which lead to a market test result which appears to corroborate the entrepreneur's vision, even though the apparent corroboration was due to factors which were no part of the entrepreneur's set of conjectures (see Kirzner 1979b: ch. 10, esp. 177–180).

For example, consider the case of an entrepreneur who unknowingly holds the false conjecture that on any week-day it is possible to make a profit by selling Japanese magazines on a particular street corner in central Munich. Suppose that in order to test that conjecture, the entrepreneur undertakes a market trial, and that the entrepreneur's expectations seem to be corroborated: on the day of the market test a sufficient number of magazines are sold at a price which yields a profit. For the sake of argument, suppose that the entrepreneur had absolutely no expectation whatsoever that on this particular day there was going to be an international fair on electronics at the Munich exhibition centre, at which a substantial proportion of the delegates were Japanese. (In Shacklean terms, the trade fair is associated with an absolute maximum potential surprise.) In addition, assume that if it had not been for the fair, no Japanese magazines would have been sold. In such a case then the market profit is captured by sheer luck on the part of the seller and cannot be attributed to superior vision unique to the entrepreneur.

However, had the entrepreneur realised that there *might* be an international function attended by Japanese guests (that is, if the entrepreneur's conjectures did not *exclude* the possibility of an inter-national event), the corroboration of the entrepreneurial idea could not be attributed completely to sheer chance:

> [A]ny windfall realized receipts to which any degree of poten-tial surprise less than the absolute maximum . . . was attached, ought not to be classified as due to pure luck; but any part of the windfall realized receipts which had carried the absolute maximum potential surprise ought to be so classified.
>
> (Shackle 1969: 268)

Furthermore, it is conceivable that a false conjecture fails to be refuted by a market test because its errors offset each other (i.e. there is a compensation of errors in different directions). I will consider these issues in more detail in my discussion of the Duhem–Quine thesis (especially in section 8.4.1).

8.2.2 An analogy

The two types of errors discussed above correspond to Type I and Type II errors in the classical Neyman–Pearson theory of statistical inference (see Lehmann 1959 for a detailed treatment). False refuta-tion is tantamount to Type I error, which is the mistaken decision to reject a true hypothesis, and false corroboration parallels Type II error, which is the mistaken decision to accept (or not to reject) a false hypothesis.[12] Type II error also includes premature introduction of new solution concepts which might have been commercially successful under different circumstances (e.g. quadraphonic sound systems). In general, the entrepreneur has no way of setting up a market test that is not to some extent exposed to the risk of both types of error.[13]

Before I proceed further, it is important to emphasise that the use of this analogy from statistical theory should not be taken to imply that entrepreneurs operate under conditions of parametric uncertainty in which the probabilities of each type of decision error can be precisely calculated and manipulated at will. Structural uncertainty implies that entrepreneurs cannot have the knowledge (neither prior nor posterior) which would be basic to the calculation of such probabilities (see section 3.2.1). Consequently, entrepreneurs do not employ a weighted averaging process in setting up their tests, and they do not make their decisions in terms of well-defined loss (or utility) functions. They are not able to compare the expected losses for alternative pairs of probabilities of Type I and Type II errors, so that an optimal pair can be chosen. Having given this caveat, I can now consider the implications of this analogy for characterising the entrepreneur's decision problem.

Entrepreneurs adopting a compensatory (as opposed to a priority-based) choice model will emphasise the *trade-off* between their errors of rejecting good ideas and their errors of accepting bad ideas. In so far as they perceive an inverse relation between the likelihood of making Type I and Type II errors, entrepreneurs can reduce the chance of one type of error only by increasing the chance of the other type of error. For any given experimental set-up, different entrepreneurs will hold different views on whether they are less or more likely to mistakenly dismiss a hypothesis than to mistakenly accept one.

In addition, individual entrepreneurs may form their own conjectures about the relative economic consequences of each type of decision error. The cost of making a Type I error consists of the forgone profit from failing to introduce an innovation that would have been tremendously successful. The cost of making a Type II error is the economic loss incurred from approving a new product idea which eventually fails in the marketplace. Consequently, if the error of rejecting a good idea (Type I error) is expected to be costly relative to the error of failing to reject a bad idea (Type II error), the entrepreneur will try to design a test which involves a lower chance of the first kind of error. For example, by lowering the reservation level for a particular screening criterion (e.g. the post-trial purchase intention score in a product test), the entrepreneur may expect to reduce the chance of a good idea being rejected (Type I error) and to increase the chance of a bad idea being accepted (Type II error) (cf.

Sah and Stiglitz 1986: 722). The same effect could also be achieved by lowering the level of the minimum consensus which is required for accepting an action-scheme in an entrepreneurial team of a fixed size (cf. Sah and Stiglitz 1988: 451, 455–459).

If, on the other hand, the total net cost of Type I error is imagined to be less than that of Type II error, it is rational for the entrepreneur to attempt to set up the test in such a way that the possibility of the first kind of error is greater than that of the second. (Conservative entrepreneurs in particular will conjecture that the cost of failing to acknowledge a truth is less than the cost of accepting a falsehood.) The entrepreneur may adopt a stringent rejection rule which is anticipated to imply a greater chance of a Type I error than of a Type II error. An example would be to reject all ventures which do not have a high supposable return on investment.

It seems reasonable to propose that an entrepreneur may have vague hunches about which type of decision error is likely to be the more costly. But it may well be the case that the entrepreneur has absolutely no idea about the potential cost of drawing an incorrect conclusion from a test. It should at least be clear that the entrepreneur cannot be sure of the profit opportunity forgone as a result of a Type I error because the rejected venture is never fully realised (not by that particular entrepreneur, in any case). And if the entrepreneur were convinced (rightly or wrongly) about the profit opportunity attached to a particular commercial venture, then, provided he or she were not frustrated by a lack of resources, the entrepreneur would not pass up the chance of taking advantage of the pure profit possibility: 'One does not refrain from exploiting a truly perceived opportunity for pure gain' (Kirzner 1979b: 169; see too 1983b: 64–65). As a result, the entrepreneur would not reject the project in the first place and so would not commit the Type I error (though the profit opportunity could turn out to be only apparent, so that the entrepreneur would end up making a Type II error).

Of course, in setting up a test, entrepreneurs do not have to apply a compensatory model of choice. They can adopt other types of choice models, such as a *priorities-based* (lexicographic) method of taking decisions. In a particular variant of this latter model, the entrepreneur will rank Type I and Type II errors in order of importance (e.g. in terms of their cost implications) and will set maximum tolerable levels of conjectured possibility for each. For the testing schemes under consideration, the entrepreneur will then estimate the possibility of each type of error in the appropriate sequence and will only choose a test set-up which satisfies both aspiration levels. They thereby avoid considering trade-offs of the conventional kind between Type I and Type II errors.

Attribution theory can provide an explanation for why we would expect entrepreneurs to have a greater fear of Type II error than of Type I error and to rank the former ahead of the latter in their priority systems. Suppose that entrepreneurs try to conduct themselves in a way that impresses other economic agents, such as investors and other stakeholders in their ventures, and that they accordingly try to evoke external attributions (i.e. attributions to external causes) to negative outcomes associated with their ventures. If other economic agents can be assumed to explain an entrepreneur's mistakes and failures in accordance with attribution theory (e.g. Weiner 1974 and van Raaij 1985), they will attribute mostly external causes to forgoing a profit – as happens, for example, when an entrepreneur fails to approve a good idea (Type I error). In contrast, other people will be expected to give mainly internal attributions (i.e. to blame the entrepreneur) for incurring a loss due to approving a bad idea (Type II error), irrespective of the size of the loss. The reason for these inferences of causality is that economic agents take the status quo as a reference point: the maintenance of the status quo is less attributable to a person than is a change from the existing state of affairs. Consequently, forgoing a profit due to a Type I error is similar to maintaining the status quo and is thus more externally attributed (cf. Thaler's (1980) discussion of the endowment effect). In contrast, incurring a loss as a result of a Type II error implies a deviation from the status quo, and thus the entrepreneur is held responsible for that divergence.

8.3 THE THEORY-LADEN NATURE OF EVIDENCE

One difficulty which entrepreneurs encounter in determining whether a theory has been falsified is that the facts gathered to expose the theory to refutation are selected and determined by the theory itself, so that all evidence is to some extent theory-laden.[14] '[F]actual statements . . . either *contain* theoretical assumptions or *assert* them by the manner in which they are used' (Feyerabend 1975a: 31; original emphasis).

Almost all the claims, including test-statements, that an entrepreneur makes about the world are essentially theoretical in character.

Entrepreneurs are theorising all the time, even when they are making the most trivial singular statements in ordinary speech (cf. Popper 1959: 423). For example, if the entrepreneur observes that 'm consumers paid producer b a price of $\$n$ for x units of good y at time t', then the description of this market event may at first appear to be theory-free. However, even this low-level, seemingly innocuous description transcends experience, because by describing something as a 'price' the entrepreneur is attributing to it properties which go beyond direct observation of this market event. That is, 'price' is a theoretical term: assigning a definite numerical value for the price presupposes that there is a medium of exchange, a store of purchasing power and a unit of account in which prices for transactions can be expressed. The price reflects the ratio of exchange of good y for money. 'Money is money precisely because it is generalised purchasing power. It is "generally acceptable in exchange" – a phrase which implies the existence of underlying general laws' (Hollis and Nell 1975: 108). That is, 'price' and 'money' are universal terms, and universals always describe a law-like behaviour or a systematic relationship. Similarly, the basic terms 'producer' and 'consumer' in the test-statement above presuppose a particular allocation of economic roles or functions. These terms apply to economic agents who have dispositions to act in a certain regular manner (e.g. to sell and to consume, respectively) (cf. Popper 1959: 424–425). Indeed, whenever entrepreneurs specify observation statements which contain one or more terms designating such economic concepts as price, cost, profit, capacity, production and consumption, those statements will always depend upon theory (cf. Hollis and Nell 1975: 108–109).[15] For entrepreneurs, there is no domain of brute atomic facts.

In addition, the interpretation of data always depends upon, and presupposes, the entrepreneur's point of view and the problems that he or she is trying to solve. Difficulties of interpretation are exacerbated when empirical data are not available in a form which corresponds to the entrepreneur's theoretical constructs. Problems of aggregation may then be involved (cf. Caldwell 1982: 241–242; 1984c: 493).

In attempting to test their theories in terms of observed predictions, therefore, falsificationist entrepreneurs encounter a paradox, because these very observations are profoundly conditioned by their preconceived theories: 'even the careful and sober testing of our ideas by experience is in its turn inspired by ideas; experiment is planned action in which every step is guided by theory' (Popper 1959: 280). The research design, the specific testing procedure to be used, the test market to be selected, the criteria to be employed, the data processing techniques used and the evidence to be gathered, are not derived independently from the theory. For example, the specific design of a concept test, including the choice of method by which to present the product benefit to potential consumers (e.g. as a written description, a picture, or a mock-up of the product), reflects theoretical presumptions, and these presumptions may produce evidence in their own support. The entrepreneur will have to grapple with the problem that the form of the concept presentation can have a dramatic influence on the respondents' reactions to the concept, so that it may be difficult to determine precisely what has been measured (Haley and Gatty 1968, 1971; Tauber 1972). There is always the possibility that respondent reaction to a defective concept presentation might be misleading (Aaker and Day 1980: 531).

In a phrase, all entrepreneurial knowledge is theory-impregnated. But it should be noted that although economic facts are not theory-free, they may sometimes be *theory-neutral*, in the sense that they are consistent at some level with a number of entrepreneurial theories which conflict with each other at some higher level of abstraction:[16]

> Yes, facts are to a greater or lesser extent theory laden, but they need not be wholly constituted by the theories that they are adduced to support. . . . In short, facts have at least some independence from theories if only because they may be true although the particular theory in question is false. . . . Once we grant that completely, certain knowledge is denied to us, there is nothing inherently uncomfortable about the profoundly theoretical nature of our very way of looking at facts in the real world.
>
> (Blaug 1980: 42)

As a consequence, economic agents who maintain quite different theories, including different theories about method (i.e. different methodologies), can sometimes reach a high degree of agreement as to what the facts of a market situation are. That is, intersubjective agreement over factual claims about market conditions is in principle possible (cf. Popper 1959: 104). For example, two or more members of an entrepreneurial team may accept specific evidence as relevant for deciding between their competing viewpoints. Economic agents who share the same methodological theories are more likely to arrive at agreement concerning market facts than agents who use differing methods, but methodological agreement is neither a necessary nor a sufficient condition for such intersubjectivity (cf. McLaughlin 1971: 465).

8.4 THE DUHEM–QUINE THESIS

Working out why one's plans cannot be carried out in the market (i.e. identifying the source of a refutation) is by no means a straightforward and unambiguous matter. The major difficulty that confronts entrepreneurs in interpreting the results of their market experiments arises from the Duhem–Quine irrefutability thesis (hereafter referred to as the DQ thesis). This thesis states that it is impossible to falsify conclusively a single hypothesis because it is always necessary to test an individual hypothesis in conjunction with various auxiliary hypotheses (or theoretical assumptions or background knowledge).[17]

The DQ thesis can be elaborated with the help of elementary logical symbolism. From section 4.2, it will be recalled that by means of the principle of *modus tollens* , entrepreneurs can argue from the falsity of their predictions against the truth of their premises:

$$[(T \rightarrow P) \cdot ({\sim} P)] \rightarrow ({\sim} T)$$

where T is a particular entrepreneurial idea or theory, P is the entrepreneur's prediction (e.g. about the existence of a profit opportunity) and the symbols $\rightarrow$, $\cdot$ and $\sim$ mean 'imply', 'conjoined with' and 'not', respectively.[18]

However, the structure of a market experiment is more complicated than the above schema would suggest. It is not just the entrepreneur's particular theory (T) alone which is tested or confronted with experiment, but the theory in conjunction with any supporting hypotheses (A) that the entrepreneur makes (Amsterdamski 1975: 92–93). Expressed symbolically, an entrepreneur faces the following situation whenever his or her plans cannot be carried out in the market without disappointment:

$$[(T \cdot A \rightarrow P) \cdot ({\sim} P)] \rightarrow {\sim} (T \cdot A)$$

where T is the specific idea which the entrepreneur is testing, A is the entrepreneur's set of background assumptions and $T \cdot A$ is their conjunction.

Thus, the result of testing entrepreneurial plans in the market is not conclusive. The individual entrepreneur cannot be certain whether the theory itself (T) or only the auxiliary conditions (A) have been refuted in the falsifying experiment.[19] When actual market events diverge from what they predicted, entrepreneurs learn that something is wrong in their stocks of knowledge. They know that they cannot hold on to their entire conjectural framework ($T \cdot A$) if it clashes with apparently respectable market evidence, because to do so would be to violate the law of contradiction. They know that at least one of their hypotheses ought to be modified, but they do not know what is to be modified, nor do they know how many hypotheses need to be corrected, for they could all be false. In summary, entrepreneurs cannot pin down the 'cause' or the source of the apparent failure of their plans. The most that an entrepreneur can say is that the conjunction of his or her particular theory (T) with a particular set of supplementary hypotheses (A) is in trouble.

The DQ thesis thus implies that, with sufficient imagination, an entrepreneur can always save any cherished idea from refutation whenever his or her plans are disappointed by market participation:[20]

> Any statement can be held true come what may, if we make drastic enough adjustments elsewhere in the system. . . . Conversely, . . . no statement is immune to revision.
>
> (Quine 1980: 43)

Whenever plans cannot be carried out, the extent of adjustment required by the entrepreneur is usually not just limited to changing a couple of assumptions. If an entrepreneur modifies one or more assumptions because of some conflict with market experience, then this modification will require adjustments to some other assumptions in order to restore internal consistency in the entrepreneur's system of knowledge. 'Reëvaluation of some statements entails reëvaluation of others, because of their logical interconnections' (Quine 1980: 42). Thus, the ramifications of failing to realise an entrepreneurial plan extend far beyond the original set of conjectures and expectations upon which that plan was based.

Similarly, given the rationality assumptions put forward in Chapter 4, it is not possible for the entrepreneur to rescue some treasured conjecture from falsification by merely adding one or more new auxiliary hypotheses to his or her existing stock of knowledge. Elementary logic demonstrates that simply adding an extra premise to the entrepreneur's theoretical system does not get rid of any of the original consequences (including past predictions about market events). In particular, it does not eliminate the consequence (prediction) which was refuted by market testing (cf. Musgrave 1974b: 592). Thus, the entrepreneur will have to modify or discard any premises which logically entail the falsified prediction. Logic will also compel the entrepreneur to reject any already accepted hypotheses which contradict the new auxiliary hypothesis which has been introduced to save the conjecture in question from refutation.

The question arises as to how much of the entrepreneur's stock of knowledge is confronted by any single market experiment. In particular, must the DQ thesis lead entrepreneurs to a holistic view of the market tests which they conduct?[21] Taken to its radical extreme, a holistic version of the DQ thesis would imply that every market test of an entrepreneurial plan is a test of *all* the entrepreneur's knowledge:

> [O]ur statements about the external world face the tribunal of sense experience not individually but only as a corporate body.
> (Quine 1980: 41)[22]

However, as a matter of logic, each market test cannot be a challenge to the totality of the entrepreneur's knowledge because not all the entrepreneur's knowledge is necessary for deriving a particular plan, and therefore, not all of it is tested when the entrepreneur tests that plan. 'The ramifications of falsifications may be considerable, but they do not lead *everywhere*' (Musgrave 1971a: 4; original emphasis). Large chunks of the entrepreneur's knowledge may be irrelevant to any particular market test. Consequently, there is some decomposability in the systems of theories and assumptions with which entrepreneurs confront the empirical world. For example, entrepreneurs with a background in physics who are starting up a high-tech venture are able to avoid testing their physical theories of dynamic systems along with their entrepreneurial theories of latent demand, of governance and of production, even though they may apply their physical theories, however inappropriately, to explain the movement of the market system and to find supposed laws of motion pertaining to it.

8.4.1 An example

A simple example will help to make the implications of the Duhem–Quine thesis clear.[23] Hopefully, this example will at least suffice to show that the testing of plans in the market inevitably entails bringing in a substantial baggage of additional assumptions.

Suppose that an entrepreneur wishes to test a hunch (H_T) about the market:

H_T There is a latent demand for at least 1000 units per day of a new low-cholesterol ice-cream product at a unit price of DM 4.50 within the Englischen Garten in Munich during the summer months of 1995.

From this hypothesis (and others), the entrepreneur deduces the prediction (P) that she can sell more than 1000 items of the new characteristics-bundle at a price of DM 4.50 over the specified time period within the Englischen Garten. In order to test her target conjecture (H_T), the entrepreneur also necessarily ends up testing it in conjunction with auxiliary conjectures about, among other things, the appropriate design of the market experiment, the distribution channel and promotional devices that would be effective, the personal characteristics of sellers and competitors' activities. The types of additional hypotheses ($A_1, \ldots, A_m$) that the entrepreneur needs to introduce in order to reason from her main hypothesis (H_T) to its prediction (P) can be itemised as follows:[24]

A_1 Five sellers, each with a mobile refrigerating system, are an effective distributional and promotional channel for this market experiment.

A_2 Each member of my salesforce has the personal characteristics – experience, ability, efficiency, motivation, persistence, tact and appearance – required for the successful marketing of my new ice-cream product.

A_3 A test market conducted in fine weather conditions during the month of July between the hours of 10a.m. and 4p.m. on a day of the weekend is a representative test.

A_4 The production team will be able to deliver the specified quality of the new ice-cream product on schedule.

A_5 The information system set up to record the results of the test market is adequate.

A_6 The sets of market data to be collected are appropriate measures of sales and of price.

In addition, the entrepreneur introduces *ceteris paribus* conditions ($C_1, \ldots, C_n$) that encompass a potentially infinite number of excluded environmental changes which could conceivably occur while the market test is being conducted (though in practice, entrepreneurial hypotheses underlying *ceteris paribus* conditions are typically not made explicit):

C_1 Competitors' marketing programmes will not change during the period of the test.

C_2 Consumers' incomes will not change during the period of the test.

C_3 The prices of substitutes and complements will not change during the period of the test.

C_4 The population of potential consumers in the region will not change during the period of the test.

C_5 Consumers' tastes will not change during the period of the test.

Thus, the entrepreneur must specify an elaborate 'experimental hook-up' between the particular idea that she is seeking to realise and the concrete market experiment. Such an experimental hook-up consists of a hierarchy of auxiliary assumptions $(A_1, \ldots, A_m; C_1, \ldots, C_n)$ which relates the target hypothesis (H_T) to the particular market test. The entrepreneur's chain of deduction for deriving the testable prediction P is thus:

- Major premise: If H_T (and $A_1, \ldots, A_m, C_1, \ldots, C_n$) are true, then P is true (i.e. over 1000 units of the new product can be sold at a price of DM 4.50 on a summer's day within the Englischen Garten in Munich during 1995);
- Minor premise: H_T (and $A_1, \ldots, A_m, C_1, \ldots, C_n$) are true;
- Conclusion: Therefore P is true.

Should the entrepreneur's cluster of hypotheses be refuted by testing in the market, there is nothing to prevent the entrepreneur from sticking to her target hypothesis (H_T) and arguing that the latent demand for the new ice-cream product does indeed exist, but that poor sales resulted because one of the cooperating assumptions was false: namely, the distribution channel used was inappropriate, or one or more of the salespeople were unexpectedly unpleasant and inept, or the information system was not working as expected or the weather conditions were surprisingly unfavourable. (The entrepreneur could also invoke a number of other immunising stratagems – see section 6.3.2.) Furthermore, the disappointing test results may be due to any conjunction of these factors. Thus, even if substantial unsold (and unintended) inventories are generated by market participation, the entrepreneur need not necessarily modify her original expectations concerning the willingness of other participants to buy her new product.

The question remains as to what exactly is deemed to be refuted by the particular market test: the entrepreneur's target conjecture and/or one or more of the auxiliary conditions? As with any refutation, the entrepreneur must interpret the results to draw her own conclusions. The entrepreneur's decision will depend on the 'interpretation of experience, i.e. on creative acts of the mind' with the result that 'knowledge yielded will be imperfect' (Lachmann 1959: 71). Furthermore, in order to test each hunch about the source of the refutation (e.g. the hypothesis that her plan could not be carried out because of the inefficacy of the distribution channel), the entrepreneur will need to take many other theories and assumptions for granted which may themselves be misleading.

It should be noted that entrepreneurs cannot even get around the DQ problem by using statistical analysis, which could be applied, for example, if they wanted to test their conjectures about how potential customers will react to different prices that they may charge (see Harper 1992: 275–278). For when conducting a statistical test, one is not testing a target hypothesis in isolation, but the hypothesis in combination with a large network of cooperating hypotheses.[25] In the case of statistically testing conjectures about the form of the demand function for a new product, this network of hypotheses could include: assumptions about the vector of relevant explanatory variables, relationships between them and appropriate measures of them; assumptions about the stability of economic relationships; auxiliary hypotheses regarding the appropriate time lag structures involved; assumptions about the generation of the error term; and assumptions underlying the use of any particular statistical test.

The difficulties of interpretation created by the DQ problem are not limited solely to refutations. Apparent corroborations of entrepreneurial conjectures are also subject to the same difficulties. When an entrepreneur's theory is apparently corroborated by market events, it is not possible to demonstrate conclusively that there is nothing wrong with the theory. It may be, for instance, that reporting mechanisms used in testing entrepreneurial plans in the market are inadequate and are providing false information which inspires overconfidence in the venture's prospects.

Indeed, this factor can be credited to a large extent for the rapid rise and fall of the Osborne Computer company, which marketed the first portable business computer (see Hartley 1986, ch. 16). The venture seemed to be enjoying overwhelming corroborative evidence by the end of the first one and half years of its operation. Accounting profits appeared to be rising rapidly, surpassing all expectation, and shipments of the product were soaring. However, lack of internal monitoring controls resulted in supposed profits being suddenly exposed at a later date instead as crippling losses. In spite of early reports that pre-tax profits for the first half of the February 1983 quarter were $US300,000 greater than company projections, later figures showed a $1.5m loss for the whole quarter which soon after was revised to a loss of $5m (The final statement for the fiscal year ended February 1983 reported a loss of more than $12m) The firm had no efficient controls for monitoring inventories of finished products or for monitoring expenses. As a result, excessive inventories of old stock had built up which managers did not even know existed, expenses had run rampant, liabilities had not been recorded, and inadequate bad debt reserves and warranty reserves had been set up. Later that year the company was forced to seek protection from creditors under the US bankruptcy code.

8.4.2 Possible strategies entrepreneurs can use to respond to apparent refutations and the Duhem–Quine problem

A mixture of entrepreneurial judgment, common sense and instinct is required to cope with the DQ problem. There is no general policy for dealing with DQ situations. For each particular situation, entrepreneurs must exercise judgment in deciding which of the policies described below is to be preferred (cf. Lakatos 1970: 106ff.; 1971a: 126). Individual entrepreneurs may also have hunches about what parts of their own sets of conjectures are at fault and should therefore be made the target of the *modus tollens* .[26] Even prior to testing plans in the market, entrepreneurs are likely to have vague ideas about which types of market events would refute their target hypotheses and which would lead to a questioning of their background knowledge. Whatever the circumstances, entrepreneurs must recognise that 'it is a matter of risky conjecture to which part of a theory we attribute the responsibility for a refutation' (Popper 1974: 1010). It should also be noted that there is no hard and fast rule about which parts of an entrepreneur's set of conjectures and expectations must be retained in the event of a refutation. Some entrepreneurs may make profitable advances by modifying what they and others had previously considered to be obviously unproblematic ideas.

Entrepreneurs can employ a variety of possible strategies in response to the apparent failure of their plans and related DQ problems.[27] The following list is neither exhaustive nor exclusive and is itself open to entrepreneurial initiative. The entrepreneur can:

1. challenge the original derivation of his or her prediction (e.g. P : 'There is a profit opportunity in the space–time region k') by showing that P does not in fact follow logically from the conjunction of his or her target hypothesis (T) and the auxiliary assumptions (A);
2. only modify his or her theory (T) with minor changes;
3. reject T (i.e. dramatically revise his or her basic theory) and keep the set of supplementary hypotheses (A);
4. stick to the theory (T) and reject one or more of the cooperating hypotheses (A);
5. reject his or her entire set of conjectures (i.e. *both* the specific theory T and the supplementary hypotheses A) and devise an altogether new set ($T' \cdot A'$);
6. try to identify any parts of his or her set of conjectures which are independent of the failed plan (and hence, which are not involved in the refutation of that plan by market testing), thereby reducing the scope of the DQ problem.

How entrepreneurs deal with the apparent failure of their plans depends upon their boldness and their learning methodology, and the peculiarities of the market context in which their plans have failed. For any particular decision situation, entrepreneurs can be expected to differ both in the *scope* of responses they are willing to try and in the *order* in which they will actually attempt various types of solution (cf. Musgrave 1971a: 34–35). Other things being equal, such diversity of response will of course be reflected in different patterns of entrepreneurial behaviour.

In the following discussion, I distinguish between three particular learning methodologies (conventionalism, Popper's falsificationism and Lakatos's methodology), and I explain the different ways in which entrepreneurs who adhere to different methodologies will respond to the discovery that their plans have apparently failed testing in the market. This discussion serves to categorise entrepreneurs in terms of their 'typical' behavioural characteristics.

Entrepreneurs who subscribe to *conventionalist* methodology prefer uncritical, conservative responses to apparent refutations and the DQ problem. They will only try the least drastic, *ad hoc* solutions and will never consider more extensive alterations to their plans, even after earlier revisions have failed. They attempt to safeguard their theories against refutation, even if their dogmatic tactics to evade refutation reduce the scope of what they can say about the world. A conventionalist strategy aims to restore consistency by disturbing the total theoretical system as little as possible: it merely keeps the edge of the entrepreneur's corpus of knowledge 'squared with experience' (Quine 1980: 44–46). Consequently, conventionalist entrepreneurs make minor *ad hoc* adjustments to their sets of conjectures, for example, by attributing the responsibility for their failed plans to one or more of the supplementary hypotheses that they made in order to test those very plans in the market (strategy 4 above).

In contrast, *falsificationist* entrepreneurs consider that strategy 4 must not be pursued each time that a plan fails a market test, because if it were, 'no test could count as a real test (since the hypothesis could escape refutation)' (Popper 1974: 1035). Bold, falsificationist entrepreneurs will tend to revise their basic theories or will try to devise entirely new conjectural frameworks when they experience *repeated* disappointment in the market (strategies 3 and 5, respectively). However, these entrepreneurs are most unlikely to develop a completely new set of first principles every time their plans are frustrated, because if they were to do so, they would never be able to see a venture through to completion and would be forever returning to the drawing board. Thus, falsificationist entrepreneurs generally aim to scrutinise and to retest their stocks of knowledge in a more or less piecemeal fashion.

In the event of a refutation of their plans, falsificationist entrepreneurs tend to retain the better-corroborated parts of their stocks of knowledge and to modify the more speculative hypotheses. For example, entrepreneurs may attribute the failure of their plans solely to their new theories about *market demand* which they have proposed to explain their lower-level, well-corroborated hypotheses about particular *market segments* (cf. Popper 1959: 76–77). This implies that in order to be at least moderately successful in determining the source of a refutation, entrepreneurs must have had some previous empirical successes: they must have been able to carry out some of their plans without disappointment and must have succeeded in concluding some profitable transactions. At least some of their ideas must be temporarily corroborated by market testing if they are

₁o have any hope of learning from refutations. A continuous series of refutations would leave individual entrepreneurs at a loss in dealing with the Duhem problem: they would have no clue about what parts of their knowledge they should blame for their failed plans (cf. Popper 1963: 243–244).

In spite of the DQ problem, some entrepreneurs are still pretty successful in attributing, even if only tentatively, the failure of their plans to distinct parts of their systems of knowledge. 'It is possible in quite a few cases to find which hypothesis is responsible for the refutation; or in other words, which part, or group of hypotheses, was necessary for the derivation of the refuted prediction' (Popper 1963: 239).

The falsificationist methodology stipulates that the modifications which entrepreneurs make to their own stocks of knowledge in order to accommodate refutations must not be *ad hoc* (see section 6.3.2). This applies to both minor and major changes to their sets of conjectures and expectations. Regardless of which chunks of their knowledge they decide to replace (T or A or both), the new parts ($T'$and/or A') must be such that their new conjectural frameworks do not convey less empirical information about the world than did their previous frameworks.

Lakatosian entrepreneurs use other ways to try to get around the DQ problem. They divide their sets of conjectures (or research programmes, to use Lakatos's terminology) into two parts: a hard core and a protective belt. What is relevant in the present context is that under certain conditions, they *never* attribute failed plans to their hard-core assumptions and procedures, thereby protecting these conjectures from refutation and elimination. (In contrast, the Popperian entrepreneur never makes a dogmatic decision to designate some theory T as a privileged part of an irrefutable hard core. Falsificationist methodological rules explicitly forbid using stratagems which spare any part of one's system of knowledge from empirical challenge.) Lakatosian entrepreneurs always shift the blame for refutations to other parts of their explanatory and predictive frameworks, namely, the protective belts of auxiliary hypotheses which they are prepared to adjust, readjust or even entirely replace in the face of anomalous market evidence (see Lakatos 1970: 133, 184–188). Thus, if T belongs to the hard core, the entrepreneur always retains T and replaces A whenever his or her plans are refuted – provided that the entrepreneur can consistently predict some novel facts about the market, and can successfully execute some new plans, on the basis of the revised set of conjectures. Hence, in the event of a refutation by market testing, the Lakatosian entrepreneur adopts a variant of strategy 4 above, with the proviso that the entrepreneur will only stick to T and protect it from refutation for as long as his or her conjectural framework is occasionally successful in its novel predictions. (The number of times their plans fail is irrelevant to how Lakatosian entrepreneurs appraise their own sets of conjectures (cf. Koertge 1978: 261).) In addition, the modification of auxiliary hypotheses in the entrepreneur's protective belt must not be arbitrary: it must be inspired by the positive heuristic of the entrepreneur's research programme. This heuristic consists of a long-term plan for coping with anomalous market evidence.

An important implication of Lakatos's approach is that two entrepreneurs with almost identical research programmes, the first of whom has assigned an assumption to the hard core while the second has placed the same assumption in the protective belt, will respond differently to the failure of a plan that is based upon a set of conjectures which includes the assumption in question. The first entrepreneur will normally never revise this assumption, whereas the second entrepreneur may modify the assumption slightly or dispense with it altogether. The kinds of decisions and plan revisions that they will make in the wake of refutations are thus likely to differ.

This discussion brings to a close (for now at least) the GK theory at the level of the individual entrepreneur. In the next chapter, I take some very initial steps in developing a GK theory of the market process.

NOTES

1 The entrepreneur in this example can be thought of as applying a *covariation* principle to market information from multiple observations over time, in line with Kelley's (1967) attribution theory which describes the attribution process in an analysis of variance (ANOVA) framework.
2 An important item on the agenda for further research would be to supplement this *a priori* categorisation of the causes of refutation with real-world case studies from business history. In particular, it would be appropriate to investigate which causes are more important for each of the types of test described in section 7.3.
3 The outcome of an entrepreneurial action may not only be unintended, but it may also be the opposite of what was intended: 'through the workings of an entire system effects may be very different from, and even opposed to, intentions' (Arrow 1968: 376). For example, suppose that an entrepreneur in Kirzner's model identifies a profit opportunity arising

from imperfect coordination between factor markets and product markets (i.e. disequilibrium). In order to exploit the opportunity, the entrepreneur undertakes buying and selling of inputs: such false trading (contracting at disequilibrium prices) may have income effects which not only nullify the equilibrium towards which the market was being directed but which also eliminate the profit opportunity (cf. Loasby 1982a: 114, 116).

4 For further discussion on diachronic and synchronic relations in theoretical systems, see Kay (1982: 18–20, 23–29).

5 For a discussion of how government intervention (especially an expansionary monetary policy) can give rise to false entrepreneurial conjectures about consumer intentions, see Hayek (1931) and Mises (1949: 392, 787ff.).

6 Inadequate knowledge of the intentions of rival entrepreneurs is a crucial epistemic problem facing entrepreneurs in atomistic competition – a problem that has been discussed in detail by Richardson (1960).

7 In order for agents' action programmes to be mutually compatible over time, they must all be based on the expectation of the same set of external events. The reason is that, if the conjectures of the individual entrepreneurs conflicted, there is no conceivable single set of external facts which would enable each entrepreneur to carry out his or her plan, that is, there is no possible way that all entrepreneurial conjectures could resist falsification.

8 It is interesting to note that Lachmann diverges from Hayek's more thorough subjectivist position. Lachmann argues that *both* unexpected exogenous change and the *in*consistency of plans are *necessary* conditions, but that neither is a *sufficient* condition, for the perpetuation of the market process (1971b: 48; 1977: 151). Clearly then, Lachmann does not exclude the possibility of unexpected exogenous change without perfect coordination of individual plans: '[s]uch inconsistency [of plans] is a permanent characteristic of a world in which unexpected change is expected to occur' (1971b: 48–49; parenthesis added).

9 Not only are entrepreneurs fallible, but so too are consumers. It is quite conceivable that an innovation may still fail test marketing and commercialisation because the innovation is simply too novel and fails to find consumer acceptance even though it would (according to some tentatively accepted 'objective' criterion employed by an omniscient observer) meet consumers' requirements more satisfactorily than existing products. In these circumstances I would argue that this is indeed a refutation of the new idea (i.e. it is not a false refutation). The refutation is as effective as any other type of refutation even though the innovation 'objectively' meets consumer requirements better than rival product offerings. Successful entrepreneurship involves creative imagination constrained to what is possible in the market.

10 Mr B. Rossi, editor of a trade journal, quoted from a secondary source in Hartley (1986: 205) (originally quoted in 'Another Nylon?', *Forbes* October 15, 1964).

11 Hartley (1986: 213–214) pointedly raises the question whether the decision to drop Corfam might not in fact have been a false rejection (i.e.

Type-I error) after all, given that: (a) the Polish firm not only manufactured for domestic production but also successfully exported the material to shoe manufacturers in the USA; and that (b) US semiconductor firms were using it to make silicon wafers.

12 In the light of *sophisticated* falsificationist methodological rules, it would be better to modify the common terminology 'reject' and 'accept'. The corresponding terms 'inconsistent with the data' and 'consistent with (or not inconsistent with) the data' would be preferable from the point of view of sophisticated falsificationism.

13 Now is an opportunity to clear up a mistake in the discussion of statistical inference in Blaug's (1980, 20–22) otherwise excellent book on the methodology of economics. Blaug defines the Neyman–Pearson theory of statistics as a 'method of statistical inference that instructs us to set the chance of Type I error . . . at some arbitrary small figure and then *to maximize the chance of Type II error . . . for the given Type I error*' (1980: 266; emphasis added). This is obviously erroneous (the same mistake is repeated on p. 21). The source of Blaug's error lies in his misconception about the 'power' of a statistical test, which he defines as consisting of *mistakenly* accepting the null hypothesis (i.e. Type II error). Of course, the power of a test is not this at all: the power of a test is typically defined as the probability of *correctly* rejecting the null hypothesis when it is in fact *false* (i.e. power = 1 - probability of Type II error). The standard practice in econometrics is to set the probability of a Type I error at 1 or 5 per cent and to use a test statistic that would make the probability of Type II error as small as possible. Consequently, '[w]ithin a class of tests, one is said to be the best if it has the *maximum* power (*minimum* probability of Type II error) among all tests with size (probability of Type I error) less than or equal to some particular level' (Engle 1984: 777; emphasis added). Hence, Cross's (1984: 91) criticism that 'most econometric tests ignore Type-II errors' is also ill-founded, although it is conceded that the exact probability of this kind of error is usually not known (see Gorman 1984: 263).

14 This issue of the theory-impregnation of market test results can be incorporated into the Duhem–Quine problem described in the next section. It is discussed here separately for reasons of expository convenience. It should also be noted that one must not mistake the argument that facts are theory-laden for the argument that they are often or always value-laden (see Musgrave 1983).

15 It must be noted that Hollis and Nell criticise the ideas of empirical testability and falsification in economics. Their argument is based upon the justificationist misconception that the empirical testing of theories requires observed data free of all interpretation. Given that theory-free facts are not available, they propose a non-empiricist approach to methodology to replace positivism. However, there is an alternative to positivist versions of empiricism which they fail to recognise: Popper's non-justificationist methodology. Indeed, at least forty years earlier, Popper raised many of their points about the difficulties of empirically testing theories, but Hollis and Nell do not refer at all to Popper's ideas in their text. Their discussion in Chapter 4 of the inseparability of facts

and theories, for example, is largely anticipated by Popper (1959: appendix *X, esp. 420–426).

16 To claim the existence of theory-neutral facts, however, is not to imply that some facts are neutral between *all* theories (since they would then effectively be theory-free facts) (McLaughlin 1971: 460).

17 The thesis derives originally from the work of the French physicist, Pierre Duhem (1954: 183–190) and from that of the American philosopher, Willard van Orman Quine (1980: ch. 2). For an excellent collection of papers about the DQ thesis, see Harding (1976). For further discussion of Duhem's argument, see Grünbaum (1963: ch. 4, section A) and Lowinger (1941: 132–140). For more on Quine's version of the thesis, see Orenstein (1977) and Shahan and Swoyer (1979). For a discussion about weak and strong interpretations of the DQ thesis and about its relationship to falsificationism, see Lakatos (1970: 184–189). Even Popper himself endorses the irrefutability thesis (1959: 50, 70, 108; 1963: ch. 10; 1974: 1035). See too the end of section 2.2.4. Nevertheless, some commentators continue to claim that Popper denies the existence of the Duhem problem (see, for example, Worrall 1978: 69).

18 In words: 'If P is derivable from T, and if P is false, then T is also false.'

19 The DQ problem is not just a problem for entrepreneurs. It also frustrates applied economists: 'The inability to pin down the source of falsity (of a conclusion) in the *set* of premises . . . is probably *the* major obstacle in testing economic theories' (Boland 1977: 100; original emphasis).

20 Grünbaum (1960) criticises versions of the DQ thesis which assert that any hypothesis can always be saved from refutation by modifying auxiliary hypotheses. (See too Harding 1976.) The version of the DQ thesis which has withstood criticism so far, however, is that it is impossible to demonstrate that a set of amendments to auxiliary hypotheses *cannot* be made to rescue the particular hypothesis from refutation (Cross 1982: 322).

21 Popper of course finds that 'the holistic dogma of the "global" character of all tests or counter examples is untenable' but admits that 'we can often test only a large chunk of a theoretical system, and sometimes perhaps only the whole system, and that in these cases, it is sheer guesswork which of its ingredients should be held responsible for any falsification' (1963: 239).

22 Duhem's (1954: 187) version of the irrefutability thesis merely states that we cannot test an isolated hypothesis but only a whole group of hypotheses. In contrast, with assertions such as '[t]he unit of empirical significance is the whole of science', Quine (1980: 41–42) appears to be putting forth a radical, holistic version of the irrefutability thesis according to which every empirical test is a test of *all* our statements about the external world'. Recognising the obvious errors in this extreme view, Musgrave (1971a: 3) comes to Quine's defence by claiming that '[a]n eminent logician like Quine cannot be supposed to have advocated a thesis which violates the most elementary facts about deductive logic'. He provides a reinterpretation of Quine's message which does not suffer from these logical difficulties. More recently, Quine himself has clarified his own viewpoint, and to a limited extent, he has moderated his position: 'All we really need

to say in the way of holism . . . is that empirical content is shared by the statements of science *in clusters* and cannot for the most part be sorted out among them. Practically the relevant cluster is indeed *never* the whole of science; there is a grading off ' (Quine 1980: viii; emphasis added).

23 In future research, it may be fruitful to use the framework of the DQ thesis to provide a rational reconstruction of the difficulties that real-world entrepreneurs and managers have encountered in interpreting the results of market research. Two potential cases from business history (already discussed briefly earlier in this chapter) which could be candidates for such analysis are DuPont's Corfam and Ford's Edsel. Both of these classic failures involved intense product planning, and each relied heavily on marketing research, the results of which, in hindsight, are likely to have been misinterpreted. The wrong conclusions were drawn concerning the new product introductions, with devastating consequences.

24 This list is by no means exhaustive. Entrepreneurs can never be sure that they have specified all of the auxiliary hypotheses which are relevant to any particular market test of their plans. They may unwittingly take for granted the truth of one or more important auxiliary hypotheses which are in fact false.

25 On the other hand, economic agents in the literature on 'rational learning' appear to be methodologically misguided in the light of the DQ thesis because they do not recognise the conjointness of the statistical tests of their econometric models. Though of course, these economic agents are concerned more with *estimating* relationships than with *testing* economic hypotheses.

26 Cf. Popper (1959: 76, note 2): 'It is often only the scientific instinct of the investigator (influenced, of course, by the results of testing and retesting) that makes him guess which statements . . . he should regard as innocuous, and which he should regard as being in need of modification'.

27 For a novel decision-theoretic analysis of an agent's responses to the Duhem–Quine problem, see Koertge (1978: esp. 255, 259, 263). (This reference was especially useful for the writing of this section.) For each option (v) available, it is suggested that the agent estimate expected epistemic utility $E(u)$. This is a product of:

 (i) the informative content of the outcome, if the option were successful (ic); and
 (ii) the probability that the option will be successful (p).

Thus:

$$E(u_v) = ic_v \times p_v.$$

Although I am not convinced by a decision-theoretic analysis based on expected utility, I think there is some scope for taking this simple idea and applying non-probabilistic theories of subjective choice (e.g. Shackle's approach).

9

SOME INSIGHTS INTO
THE MARKET PROCESS

INTRODUCTION

In this chapter, I briefly draw out some preliminary implications of the growth-of-knowledge (GK) approach for how the market process operates. In particular, I examine the character of this learning process, how it is organised, the criteria by which it screens new ideas, the origins of this process, and its comparative performance. I also make some observations regarding the continuity of the market process.

In this discussion I make use of the notion of a learning process or mechanism. A learning mechanism[1] is a problem-solving process which involves particular means of generating trials (e.g. rival entrepreneurial ideas) and particular methods of eliminating errors (i.e. particular methods of controlling trials). More specifically, the functions of a learning procedure are:

- to provide incentives for identifying new problems and opportunities;
- to provide incentives to formulate tentative solutions (i.e. entrepreneurial theories) to perceived problems and to thereby spur the exploitation of possible opportunities;
- to provide a pool of resources upon which participants can draw in the solution of problems and the exploitation of opportunities;
- to provide information on the costs and benefits of using resources in the solution of problems (i.e. to provide criteria by which to evaluate competing tentative solutions);
- to provide a selection environment in which tentative solutions are subjected to critical testing (i.e. the environmental test of fitness);
- to eliminate inferior tentative solutions, and to selectively permit some innovative ideas to survive;

• and to coordinate individual plans and actions aimed at solving problems and exploiting opportunities.

In this discussion, I characterise the market process as a Popperian (non-justificationist) learning procedure which involves a sequence of conjecture (theory formation) and refutation (theory modification and replacement). The *ex ante* prospect of profit creates an incentive for identifying new problems and for developing solutions to them. The price mechanism provides information for evaluating tentative solutions, and factor and product markets operate as testing environments for proposed new solutions. Entrepreneurial losses and business failure serve to screen out inferior solutions, whereas *ex post* entrepreneurial profits reward solutions better suited to their problem situations.

The market process can be conceived as an evolutionary, self-organising process involving the growth of knowledge, which bears important similarities to the progress of scientific knowledge. To the extent that the market system is a Popperian falsificationist learning process, knowledge in the market evolves by means of Darwinian *selection* rather than Lamarckian *instruction* (cf. Popper 1972: 144; 1976c: 167). The neoclassical conception of the market, on the other hand, is Lamarckian rather than Darwinian. The growth of market knowledge in a Lamarckian learning process is repetitive and cumulative (see section 2.2.3).

In Part II I have outlined a theory of the sophisticated falsificationist entrepreneur. Such a theory provides a basis, consistent with methodological individualism, upon which to construct a theory of the market system. However, it is argued that the market *system* itself is a sophisticated falsificationist learning mechanism, even if none of the entrepreneurs operating within it is a falsificationist. The system imposes a binding constraint on market participants. As an illustration, suppose that some entrepreneurs are instrumentalists. Instrumentalist entrepreneurs regard their theories as simply instruments for making predictions about the market. They believe that the degree of realism of their assumptions is irrelevant to the validity of their theories. Consequently, instrumentalist entrepreneurs who consciously accept false assumptions may never revise their theories, in spite of refuting evidence. (They are even slower than conventionalist entrepreneurs to react to recalcitrant data.) Thus, even though instrumentalist entrepreneurs may knowingly hold false theories and may be consistently making losses, they may continue to cling to their theories.

However, entrepreneurial losses transmit a warning signal to other stakeholders in the enterprise who will react to the new information. (The speed with which they will react will depend upon their own methodologies.) If certain entrepreneurs fail to respond rationally to the results of market tests, then other market participants can be counted on to look after their own self-interest. Suppliers and creditors start to look elsewhere, employees begin to quit, and owners will eventually shift their money capital into other businesses where the prospective rates of return are higher. The entrepreneur's last-ditch attempts to obtain more funds from the capital market in order to cover fixed contractual costs, especially interest payments, will be unsuccessful. The entrepreneur's access to resources will dry up. Bankruptcy will ensue. Hence, the market system has eliminated a false entrepreneurial theory, even though the individual entrepreneur clinging to that theory may not have discarded it.

9.2 THE ORGANISATION OF CONJECTURE AND REFUTATION IN THE MARKET ECONOMY

Certain aspects of the spontaneous organisation of the modern market economy impinge upon the process of conjecture and refutation that characterises the market process. The organisation of conjecture and refutation is important because, in order to determine what criteria the market applies in screening and refuting entrepreneurial conjectures, we must first identify who are doing the refuting and how they are organised.

9.2.1 The organisation of conjecture

A fundamental feature of the organisation of the modern market economy is that certain persons initiate the production of new goods (conceived as characteristics-bundles) which will be used to solve the problems of other persons. In general, consumers do not initiate production by entering prior contracts with producers (see Yu 1981).[2] The reason is that consumers cannot predict their own future problem situations or their intensity, and they do not know the quantities and qualities of the goods that they will demand to solve these problems. They may also be uncertain about their ability to pay in future periods (Knight 1964: 240–241). Consequently, consumers leave it to entrepreneurs to create new products, to determine quality, and to set prices. Thus, with the exception of second-hand consumer goods markets, the final consumer is excluded from the price-making function and the production process and is confined to an exchange economy (Lachmann 1986: 121–122).

Entrepreneurs thus attempt to predict and to control the decisions of consumers without prior agreement or commitment on the part of consumers. Individual entrepreneurs believe that they can foresee the wants of substantial groups of consumers with more precision than individual consumers can predict their own wants. Accordingly, entrepreneurs direct production in line with their perceptions of the situation-specific demands of groups of consumers. This involves the consolidation of risks and of uncertainties (the 'law of large numbers') (Knight 1964).

Another important feature of the organisation of conjecture is that entrepreneurs are not known in advance. The individuals responsible for conceiving new conjectures are not preselected. The individuals who participate in the process of conjecture are generally those who believe themselves to be sufficiently creative to discover opportunities presented by potential lacunae in social coordination. As a result, many entrepreneurs may take part in the solution of any particular market problem. Consequently, the organisation of conjecture often results in a multiplicity of entrepreneurial ideas being put forward as possible solutions to similar market problems.

From a historical perspective, this organisation of conjecture is a recent phenomenon. Less than a century ago in European economies, market transactions typically involved haggling over prices between buyers and sellers, and individual consumers participated in the production process by exercising their choice regarding product characteristics, such as size and style (Lachmann 1986: 122). The modern organisation of conjecture has efficiency advantages. By confining production and pricing decisions to entrepreneurs, it reduces the transaction costs to consumers in specifying their requirements and bargaining over prices. Furthermore, the production and marketing of standardised characteristics-bundles also reduce the sum of production and transaction costs to producers, because they facilitate the exploitation of potential economies of scale.

The foregoing discussion on the organisation of conjecture must be subject to qualification, however. In particular, the above scenario may not be typical of industrial markets, especially markets for durable capital goods. In such markets, industrial customers may provide innovative manufacturers with information about the existence of particular customer problems. They may also supply producers with many fresh ideas about appropriate solutions – including the general types of solutions to be embodied in new industrial products, functional specifications of new products, and possibly even field-tested new product designs (von Hippel 1976a; 1977a; 1982b: 413–415).[3]

However, even when industrial customers take the initiative to request new products and to supply new product ideas, the entrepreneur must still test the potential solution concepts presented by customers, since they themselves may hold false theories about their own most important latent needs. Their real problems may be very different from the problems that they have identified and articulated. Furthermore, the entrepreneur will only develop those customer ideas which are conjectured to offer the most profit potential (von Hippel 1982b: 410). It is still vital that the entrepreneur test the ideas against the reality of the marketplace. In particular, the entrepreneur must check that each problem and its associated solution concept are not so situation-specific that market demand is limited to the original customer who initiated the product idea or request.

9.2.2 The organisation of refutation

Although *individual* consumers are price-takers who do not participate in the production process, entrepreneurs are ultimately subject to the *aggregated* economic power of consumers to refute their theories:[4]

> [T]he consumer is cast in the role of a judge or arbitrator, though not necessarily one possessing absolute or infinite wisdom. As judge, the consumer assigns by his spending pattern the rewards or penalties for specific productive efforts. Entrepreneurs and resource-owners (the consumers in their alternative roles) must adapt themselves to the consumers' verdicts.
>
> (Hildebrand 1951: 20)

In the case of process innovations, for instance, entrepreneurs select from the uncompleteable schema of technologically feasible methods those which they imagine are most suitable for supplying the bundles of product characteristics which consumers demand most urgently. Whether such process innovations are or are not appropriate is provisionally decided by entrepreneurs themselves (e.g. via in-house prototype testing) but it is consumers in their purchasing decisions who ultimately decide the success or failure of entrepreneurs' conjectures.[5]

Having identified consumers as the economic agents who ultimately refute entrepreneurial theories, one can then ask *which* consumers are responsible for the screening and refutation of any particular entrepreneurial idea: all potential consumers, the subset of consumers targeted by the entrepreneur, or actual consumers (who may not necessarily be the same as those targeted). In principle, the consumption of all products is connected, either directly or indirectly, by substitution or complementary effects. Consequently, it could be argued that all consumers are potentially involved in the decision to buy or not to buy an entrepreneur's new product, and that they are therefore responsible for the screening and refutation of entrepreneurial conjectures. However, in light of the fact that falsificationist entrepreneurs specify their target markets beforehand in order to speed up their own learning, I would argue that a target market's abstention from buying a new product is a refutation of an entrepreneur's conjecture, even if the product is unexpectedly consumed by another set of consumers not targeted. Sales of an entrepreneur's product to consumers not targeted may result in a false corroboration of the entrepreneur's theory of latent demand, because the sales are the result of luck and not superior entrepreneurial imagination. The *ex post* results were not part of the entrepreneur's *ex ante* conjectures.

It can be seen that the refutation of entrepreneurial conjectures is a highly decentralised activity which does not involve an organised group or collective body representing consumers. Rather it results from a sufficiently large number of targeted consumers individually deciding not to purchase an entrepreneur's product offering (though possible interactions between individuals' demands and consumption decisions are acknowledged).

9.3 CRITERIA BY WHICH THE MARKET SCREENS ENTREPRENEURIAL CONJECTURES

The criterion by which the market screens an entrepreneurial conjecture is the degree to which it solves the most urgent problems of consumers *relative* to the degree attained by theories provided by competing entrepreneurs. The market thus operates in a manner similar to the way that 'natural selection operates on each organism within its contemporary network of competing or complementary organisms' (Loasby 1984a: 76). The market test is of relative effectiveness in particular problem situations.

The market demand for a new product is the outcome of the interaction and combination of the subjective valuations of a multitude of individual consumers. Each consumer judges whether the new characteristics-bundle solves the most urgent of his or her as yet unsolved problems. Each consumer compares the net implications of the entrepreneur's new idea with those of other ideas offered by rival entrepreneurs (see section 5.4). Refutation arises if these valuations result in enough target consumers abstaining from purchasing the entrepreneur's new product.

It is argued below that *ex ante* the prospect of positive profits is important in providing a stimulus to the formation and implementation of entrepreneurial conjectures. *Ex post*, however, entrepreneurial loss (negative profit) is considered to be the more important criterion by which the economic system filters out false entrepreneurial theories. *Ex post* profits serve to reward entrepreneurs whose theories are better approximations of consumers' latent demands.

9.3.1 The role of entrepreneurial losses in the refutation of false knowledge

The economics literature on the profit-and-loss system in a market economy tends to focus exclusively on the role of profits without examining entrepreneurial losses. Mises (1949) deplored the idea of analysing entrepreneurial profit without simultaneously investigating its corollary, entrepreneurial loss.[6] Standard microeconomic analysis of profit treats losses conceptually as negative profits. Although this treatment is formally adequate, it fails to emphasise the importance of entrepreneurial loss in the growth of knowledge – namely, its role in the identification and elimination of entrepreneurial errors. Treating entrepreneurial losses as negative profits also masks the asymmetric nature of the process of change occurring in the market economy. In particular, asymmetry arises if a change of a given magnitude in a determinant of economic behaviour does not have an equal but opposite effect if it is a decrease rather than an increase.

Entrepreneurial losses are fundamentally important to the evolutionary functioning of the market economy: 'A social order based on private control of the means of production cannot work without entrepreneurial action and entrepreneurial profit and, of course, entrepreneurial loss' (Mises 1980: 149). More specifically, the main function of entrepreneurial losses is to shift the control of capital (and other resources) away from those entrepreneurs who employ capital goods inefficiently and who fail to produce the characteristics-bundles most intensely demanded by consumers. Entrepreneurs with false theories who repeatedly suffer losses, eventually become bankrupt and are finally eliminated by the market process from their entre-preneurial positions (Mises 1980: 108; Rothbard 1970: 469). They are replaced by other entrepreneurs who can better serve consumers and who hold theories which have so far resisted refutation by the market. At the level of the market, the main role of entrepreneurial loss is that it provides consumers in aggregate with an instrument for refuting false entrepreneurial conjectures about the most pressing of their as yet unsatisfied needs (i.e. latent demands).

At the time of the decision to invest in a productive process, the entrepreneur cannot know for certain what the market exchange value of the end-product will be at the date it will be available for sale (Cantillon 1931; Shackle 1955: 81). The market is a process, and the state of the market is changing continuously. The future constellation of demand and supply is uncertain and non-determinate. Entre-preneurial loss arises if: the entrepreneur makes overly optimistic predictions about the future revenue stream from the sale of the new product; the entrepreneur pays prices for the factors of production which are too high from the point of view of the future state of the market; or the entrepreneur underestimates the governance costs incurred in organising the relevant transactions. More formally, entre-preneurial loss (EL) arises if the sum of total production (PC) and governance costs (GC) exceeds the total revenue (R) obtained from selling the new product over the relevant time period: given that $PC + GC > R$, $EL = R - (PC + GC)$.

Thus, the value of the end attained is less than the value of the means applied in the pursuit of that end. *Ex post* entrepreneurial loss means that the entrepreneur's *ex ante* conjectures are not fulfilled. Entrepreneurial losses are the unintentional result of entrepreneurs using inadequate theories to derive their anticipations about the future state of the market. Entrepreneurial loss reveals that the entrepreneur's conjectures are either internally inconsistent or incompatible with the plans of other entrepreneurs and consumers. It indicates that the entrepreneur has intensified 'a maladjustment, through allocating factors where they were overvalued as compared to the consumers' desire for their product' (Rothbard 1970: 468).

9.3.2 The role of *ex post* entrepreneurial profits in the corroboration of entrepreneurial theories

The emergence of entrepreneurial profit is an *ex post* tentative corroboration of the entrepreneur's theory. (Though it should be noted that *windfall* profits may give rise to *false* corroborations – see section 8.2.1.) Entrepreneurial profit means that the predictions the entrepreneur derived from his or her system of knowledge were more correct than other participants' predictions. At the *ex ante* stage, the entrepreneur bought inputs which, in the light of his or her conjectures about the future state of the market, were underpriced. *Ex post* profit means that the entrepreneur's expectations resisted attempts at falsification. Consequently, profit arises whenever the sum of total production and governance costs is less than the revenue received by the entrepreneur from selling the new product.

This approach stands in contrast to the usual treatment of entrepreneurial profit. Profit is typically equated with the perception or discovery of the 'truth', i.e. the *verification* of entrepreneurial knowledge. For example, Kirzner argues that 'on the one hand, (profit) is generated by ignorance; on the other, it provides the incentive for realising the truth' (1979b: 156). From a Popperian perspective, however, it is logically impossible for either scientists, entrepreneurs or the market system to be able to prove that theories are true, although they might be true. Entrepreneurs and other transactors in the market process are only able to isolate false knowledge, and even then not conclusively. The capturing of profit does not prove that an entrepreneur's theory is true. Entrepreneurial profit performs a role only in the *corroboration* of an entrepreneurial theory, which is not the same as a proof of its truth (see section 2.2.4).

It should also be emphasised that profit is only an *ordinal* measure: it is a sign of an entrepreneurial theory's success compared with competing theories up to a point in time. A profit result means that the particular entrepreneurial theory was a better tentative solution to a specific market problem than other theories:

> The market process does not lead to definitive truth; it provides an environment for the testing of conjectures, both new and old, an environment in which novel conjectures, if corroborated, may bring rich rewards.
>
> (Loasby 1984a: 76)

Ordinality implies that profit is an inherently qualitative measure, which in turn means that its significance must be interpreted.

Ex post profit is merely a measure of an entrepreneurial theory's fitness to survive market tests conducted so far. It is only an indication of the theory's successful *past* performance in addressing the most urgent needs of consumers and says nothing about future performance. An important feature of profit is that it relates only to past corrections of maladjustment. Profit is simply an index that maladjustments have been rectified by the entrepreneur. The bigger the profit captured by the entrepreneur, the greater the previous underlying maladjustment (Kirzner 1973: 224–225; Mises 1980: 119; Rothbard 1970: 468).

Structural uncertainty and real time mean that there is no guarantee that the entrepreneur's predictions will continue to be more correct than other entrepreneurs' predictions in the future. The tentative nature of corroboration means that the theory is still exposed to refutation and may be falsified at any moment. The theory will be continually subject to new tests, the outcome of which cannot be known beforehand. A profit today does not prevent the entrepreneur's theory being superseded by a better theory tomorrow. Nor does it prevent the emergence of entrepreneurial losses. The capturing of profit gradually communicates more and more information to more and more market participants (Kirzner 1973: 228–229). Eventually, profit disappears when the maladjustment is entirely removed (Mises 1980: 119).

Ex post entrepreneurial profit is the instrument by which consumers in aggregate corroborate entrepreneurial theories which have so far best served them. Profits perform an important function in shifting the control of productive activities to those entrepreneurs who have so far had the best ideas on how to employ resources for the best possible satisfaction of consumers (Mises 1980: 123). Profit results in an increase in money capital and hence it increases the entrepreneur's command over factors of production.

9.4 THE MARKET PROCESS AS A SPONTANEOUSLY EVOLVED LEARNING MECHANISM

The competitive market process is a *spontaneously evolved* set of institutions which facilitates the testing of entrepreneurial conjectures and the generation of new structural knowledge. The fact that the market process is a learning mechanism which is spontaneous in origin means that it has been created from forces within the system (i.e. its structure is endogenous). It has formed itself through a process of selective evolution – it is a self-organising system. Unlike *pragmatic* learning mechanisms, such as the firm, the market has not been consciously designed and set up by an external designing agency. Rather the market is the unintended and unpredictable result of the pursuit of private interests by numerous and dispersed individuals (Lachmann 1971a: 81; Ullmann-Margalit 1978: 271). Thus, it is 'the result of human action, but not . . . of any human design' (Ferguson 1966).

The spontaneous origin of the market process has implications for the nature of this learning mechanism. Different learning mechanisms involve different means for problem-solving, different ways of generating trials, and different methods of eliminating errors.

Because complex institutions which endure tend to be decomposable (Loasby 1976: 31; Simon 1969: 90–92), a spontaneous learning mechanism will usually prevail even if the particular elements and the number of elements in the system change. Hence, the competitive market process will survive even if some entrepreneurs, their organisations or even whole industries are eliminated because they adhere to falsified theories.[7] That the majority of entrepreneurial theories may be refuted by the market and that the market system can generally adjust smoothly to business errors, are signs of the durability and success of the market order.

Pragmatic learning mechanisms, such as firms, are designed to serve the purposes of the person who set them up (or they serve the purposes of those currently in control of the institution). The commanding authority (e.g. top management) establishes what problems are to be solved, and determines which new venture proposals to accept or reject, and which existing ventures to develop and discontinue. Herein lies the most fundamental difference between pragmatic and spontaneous learning mechanisms because, unlike the former, spontaneous learning processes do not have apredefined hierarchy of objectives or a particular purpose. That is, there is no prior specification either of the problems to be solved or of the types of knowledge to be generated. A spontaneously evolved learning mechanism assists the discovery and solution of a multitude of interrelated problems which are not known in their entirety to any single person or group of people (Hayek 1973: ch. 2; 1978: 183).

Another characteristic of a spontaneous learning mechanism is that it improves the chances of unknown entrepreneurs. It is preferable that entrepreneurs are not selected beforehand, because in a world of structural uncertainty it is not possible to determine in advance which individuals will conceive the best ideas. A decentralised spontaneous learning process, such as the competitive market, disperses the task of discovering future knowledge to a multitude of unknown entrepreneurs. No other real-world institution does a better job of ensuring that unknown entrepreneurs, who have the imagination to experiment with new methods and the knowledge suited to the solution of particular problems, will be attracted to those problems (Hayek 1949: 95; 1976, ch. 10; 1978: 184). Furthermore, the competitive process allows for the possibility that the discoverer of an opportunity can participate in its exploitation.

In a hierarchical pragmatic learning procedure, on the other hand, one person or group of persons (e.g. the CEO or top management team) selects specific individuals and directs them in their generation of knowledge. Individuals may be excluded from the learning process. Furthermore, the person who conceives an opportunity may be excluded from participating in its exploitation.

The degree of complexity of the problems addressed by a spontaneous learning process is not limited to that which can be handled by a single person or group of people, all of whom are boundedly rational. (In this connection, the degree of complexity refers to the number of problems, their diversity and their interactions.) The knowledge and methodological rules applied in the process of learning, conjecture and refutation are those of all the entrepreneurs in the self-organising market system. A spontaneously evolved learning process is capable of generating knowledge that is not able to be created consciously. Complex problems can be solved spontaneously that are not able to be solved deliberately by pragmatic learning mechanisms (Hayek 1945: 527).

9.5 THE PERFORMANCE OF THE MARKET PROCESS IN GENERATING AND TESTING NEW CONJECTURES

The comparative success and durability of the market process are attributable to it performing the functions of a learning mechanism (identified earlier) more effectively than other competing institutions. According to Hayek (1973: 38), this function is confined to the coordination of expectations and plans. However, the function of the competitive market process is not limited to coordination: 'In a world where we are inevitably ignorant about some of the past and present, let alone the future, *the co-ordination of activities is less important* than the perception of new problems and opportunities, and adaptation to them' (Loasby 1976: 191–192; emphasis added).

Not only does the competitive market process perform a function by providing a stimulus to discover new problems through the prospect of positive profits; it also encourages the generation of a multiplicity of entrepreneurial theories and a diversity of experimentation:

> The virtue of competition lies not in constraining all similar agents to the same action, but in encouraging them to behave differently. . . . The argument for competition rests on the belief that people are likely to be wrong.
>
> (Loasby 1976: 191–192)

Hence, the competitive market process has evolved as an appropriate institutional response to structural uncertainty. Given that entrepreneurial conjectures are liable to be false,[8] the multiplicity and variety of entrepreneurial theories generated in the competitive process increase the possibility of at least one new idea resisting refutation, and they thereby help to avoid the disaster of a false monolithic structure made up of centrally imposed theories of latent demand, production and governance. This in turn increases the market system's chances of survival.

In addition to performing a useful function in eliciting a wide spectrum of entrepreneurial theories, the competitive market process also provides a selection environment in which entrepreneurial theories can be exposed to critical testing and potential refutation by consumers. From a Popperian perspective, the progress of knowledge requires the refutation of false knowledge. Similarly, the market process necessarily involves refuting some false conjectures:

> [T]he generally beneficial effects of competition must include disappointing or defeating some particular expectations or intentions.
>
> (Hayek 1978: 180)

> It is one of the chief tasks of competition to show which plans are false.
>
> (Hayek 1976: 117)

As described in earlier chapters, entrepreneurs submit their new ideas for appraisal by the market. The competitive process then assesses these entrepreneurial theories according to the double-edged criteria of *ex post* (though not necessarily maximum) profit and loss: the former operating to tentatively corroborate entrepreneurs' theories which have to date been superior to those of their competitors, the latter revealing the inadequacy of inferior entrepreneurial ventures.

The refutation of entrepreneurial theories is sometimes incorrectly upheld as evidence of market failure. But it is the entrepreneur and the capitalist who bear the losses from refutation: the entrepreneur through the loss of reputation capital and the capitalist by the direct financial disutilities resulting from loss. The market process performs a useful function in refuting false theories of latent consumer demands and false theories of how best to satisfy them. Falsification by the market involves the refutation of false structural knowledge, that is, false knowledge of the ends worth pursuing and the means available. It makes possible an advance of knowledge.

Another important point is that the refutation of entrepreneurial conjectures and any associated losses and business failures arise even in the most efficient markets which are not hampered by distortionary government policies (see Mises 1949: 390–391). Indeed, the failure of loss-making enterprises actually yields positive systemic consequences for the functioning of the market as a whole (Burton 1983: 20). In a centrally planned economic system, a central plan which is based upon false knowledge of what consumers want (should that be considered desirable) may not come under direct testing. Hence, there is no negative feedback mechanism, no systematic way of correcting errors.

It is claimed by some authors that as much new structural knowledge will be generated by the competitive market process as by any other learning procedure. They argue that entrepreneurial opportunities in a market system tend to be discovered (see, for example, Kirzner 1979b: 9, 32, 130, 170). Certainly, we have already identified several features of spontaneous learning mechanisms which suggest that the market process will be more effective in generating new knowledge and testing new conjectures than pragmatic institutions, such as the centrally planned economy. However, the outcome of a problem-solving mechanism is by its very nature unpredictable (Scriven 1959). And because the knowledge generated by a learning process cannot be specified in advance, it is not possible to determine how effective the process is in creating knowledge that might be generated:

To know whether a . . . process is optimal, we would need
to know the very information whose discovery is the object of
that process. . . . [I]f we could independently ascertain the
information, the . . . process in question would be superfluous.

(O'Driscoll and Rizzo 1985: 110)

By drawing an analogy with Gödel's theorem (which states that it is
impossible to prove the consistency of a formal system within the
system itself), it can be argued that neither the superiority of established scientific procedures nor the superiority of the market process
can be proved scientifically (Hayek 1978: 180–184).

9.6 SOME IMPLICATIONS FOR THE CONTINUITY OF THE MARKET PROCESS

The GK approach also yields a number of interesting insights into
the continuity of the market process. In particular, it can help lay
the groundwork for explaining how the market process can be perpetuated by purely endogenous forces, that is, it can make some
contribution towards accounting for the endogenous dynamics of the
market process. Indeed, it can provide a way of describing the sorts
of endogenous economic changes which constitute the competitive
market process. It offers an alternative to the conventional approach
which portrays the market solely as a process of equilibrating
adjustments to exogenous shocks.

In my earlier discussion at the level of the individual entrepreneur
(especially section 7.9), I showed that an entrepreneur's learning
process is both ongoing and non-determinate and that it is pervaded
by endogenous changes. Given that the market process is generated
by the interaction in the market of individual decision-makers as they
learn from their new experiences and revise their plans, it follows that
the market process too is made up of a series of endogenous changes
taking place over time.

The GK approach implies that the market process is driven by
an endogenous momentum and that it would not converge towards
a final state of equilibrium even in the absence of exogenous
changes. At no point does the growth of knowledge advance towards
a predetermined end state; the growth of knowledge is in principle
unpredictable and open-ended.[9] Consequently, disequilibrium is
something endogenous to the operation of the market process itself,
that is, it is endogenously created change. Both the equilibrating

and disequilibrating aspects of the actual market process must be included within any explanation of its continuity. The GK approach therefore rejects claims that by its very nature the market process possesses a *strict* tendency toward an *overall* equilibrium. And it also implies a departure from the standard analytical method which treats disequilibrating events as the result of only exogenous forces (Machlup 1958).

Thus, the GK vision of the market process is closer in spirit to the Lachmannian version of market process theory than it is to the second of the two variants described by Kirzner (1992: 42–43). First, equilibrating and disequilibrating changes are considered to be so interconnected that they are not capable of being analysed separately; and second, 'the presence of the disequilibrating changes renders it impossible for market participants to identify with clarity the steps that need to be taken to achieve equilibrium' (Kirzner 1992: 43).

A key point of the GK approach is that the market process itself produces the problems which entrepreneurs may discover and attempt to solve. This can best be demonstrated by generalising the evolutionary model of learning depicted in Figure 7.3 in Chapter 7. As can be seen from this figure, the problems (P_i) are endogenously produced by the foregoing sequence of past problems (P_{i-n}), trial solutions (TS_{i-n}) and tests of trial solutions (EE_{i-n}). In addition, each phase contains the seeds of the next phase, so that the market process exhibits dynamic continuity – that is, each sequence is connected to the previous sequence and to the next, and the interaction effects of entrepreneurial adjustments within and between sequences may be significant. Indeed, the market process *consists* of the continuous generation, discovery and tentative solution of new market problems. It thereby generates within itself the changes to which entrepreneurs must adjust. New entrepreneurial opportunities are continuously created endogenously by the actions of market participants and especially by the unplanned consequences of these actions. Hence, it is not necessary to introduce new problems and opportunities exogenously by a continual sequence of autonomous changes (e.g. in consumer tastes, resource availabilities or technological possibilities) in order to sustain the market process and to provide scope for on-going entrepreneurial discovery.

According to the GK theory, even if entrepreneurs were to solve a market problem to the universal satisfaction of target consumers, they would create, in solving that particular problem, many other new problems which would need to be solved. Unexpected new problems (P_i) may emerge as the often unintended byproducts of entrepreneurial solutions (TS_{i-n}) to previous market problems (P_{i-n}). Every entrepreneurial action, even the most meticulously planned, will generally give rise to at least some unintended and unavoidable consequences, thereby creating new market problems, new needs, new value scales (i.e. consumer tastes), and further possible opportunities for entrepreneurial profit. Consequently, entrepreneurship may be simultaneously both a coordinating force and a disequilibrating force.

Similarly, the GK approach does not treat changes in tastes, technology and resources as necessarily exogenous to the market system. Rather these changes are portrayed as the result, whether designed or unintended, of entrepreneurs' profit-seeking responses (TS_i) to perceived market problems. In trying to formulate profitable solutions to new problems, entrepreneurs may develop new technologies and discover new uses for inputs. Their activities may also (often unwittingly) lead to changes in consumer preferences.

Furthermore, the *GK* theory claims that, at any time, there are countless market problems and entrepreneurial opportunities that remain undiscovered and unsolved. In contrast to Kirzner's theory,[10] the GK approach claims that market problems and profit opportunities are *not* destined to be discovered and exploited. Potential profit opportunities may exist without ever being actualised or realised. They certainly do not 'cry out' to be perceived and corrected, as Kirzner (1973: 127) assumes. In this connection, the GK approach therefore rejects what Popper (1963) refers to as the 'theory of manifest truth': that it is the nature of truth that it will reveal itself or will be revealed by us sooner or later, given sufficient time. Following Popper, the GK programme emphatically rejects this optimistic epistemology as untenable and false. Such a rejection implies that entrepreneurs may never hit on the truth, as it is in fact hard to come by. Entrepreneurs may fail to discover errors (both their own and those of others) and to revise their plans so that they are consistent with the actual state of the market. They may fail to learn the correct facts of their situations. Furthermore, as discussed previously, entrepreneurs can never know with certainty that they have found the truth, even if they have found it (and nor can the observing economist!).

Because entrepreneurs will always face the challenge of discovering new market problems, so that they can never completely exhaust the opportunities which exist at any time, there will always be scope for entrepreneurship regardless of exogenous changes in the basic data of the market (cf. Popper 1963: 352; 1972: 116–119, 160–161).

As a final comment, it is worth remarking that the GK conception of market processes has much in common with the new evolutionary paradigm which emphasises non-equilibrium as a source of spontaneous self-organisation (Prigogine 1985: 108; Buchanan and Vanberg 1991: 168). It constitutes a *non-teleological* conceptualisation of the market process – it is non-teleological in that it rejects the notion that the market process gravitates towards a conceptually definable, pre-existing equilibrium.[11] Rather, it emphasises innovative entrepreneurial dynamics and the truly creative, open-ended and evolving nature of the market process. Accordingly, market problems (the P_i) are not predetermined or pre-ordained but they are continuously generated by the actual pattern and sequence of economic agents' trials (the TS_i) and tests (the EE_i). In line with a non-teleological perspective, the market process is conceived as being non-deterministic, irreversible, and path-dependent. Relatively minor entrepreneurial events may decide the particular path along which the market process evolves.

This concludes my brief attempt to develop some implications of the GK approach for the operation of the market process. The next two chapters develop an agenda for further work within the GK programme.

NOTES

1 By the use of the term 'mechanism', I certainly do not wish to imply that learning mechanisms are systems which have necessarily been designed and set up – although some are (see Section 9.4). Furthermore, another misconception to be avoided is that the workings of a learning mechanism are like that of a machine which can be improved by introducing appropriate modifications. See Shand (1984: 64). For my purposes, the terms 'mechanism', 'procedure', 'process' and even 'system' are employed synonymously.

2 In the terminology of the Arrow–Debreu framework, there is an absence of futures markets: entrepreneurs typically cannot sell the new goods which they plan to produce until after they have produced them.

3 For case studies in which industrial customers have been a source of successful new products, see: Maidique and Zirger (1985: 302–303); and von Hippel (1976a, 1976b, 1977a, 1977b, 1978, 1982a, 1982b). For a discussion of the conditions under which the so-called 'customer-active paradigm' is applicable, see von Hippel (1982b: 416–420).

4 But venture capitalists, wholesalers and retailers are also involved in the screening and refutation of entrepreneurial conjectures during intermediate stages of the testing process.

5 It should also be noted that the actual power of consumers to refute entrepreneurial ideas is not absolute. Given the existence of a market mechanism, one of the prerequisites for absolute consumer sovereignty is that the assumptions of the perfect competition model are not infringed.

6 This discussion of entrepreneurial profits and losses refers to real profits and losses, of course.

7 Of course, a pragmatic learning mechanism, such as a firm, can also survive in spite of the elimination of some of its parts, such as the closure of particular plants, the removal of particular divisions, the selling of subsidiaries, or the substitution of in-house transactions with subcontracting. The firm can survive if parts of it break off and if its boundaries are redefined. The nexus of contracts comprising the firm is constantly changing.

8 This proposition stands in contrast to Kirzner's claim that entrepreneurial conjectures are likely to be correct.

9 Surprisingly, a footnote in one of Kirzner's earliest writings is most relevant to the ideas advanced here (even though Kirzner is using the term 'purist' pejoratively):

> Of course, the purist may point out that there are *always* unknown technological possibilities that future generations will discover. From this point of view a market system might be described as *always in a state of disequilibrium* with respect to the infinity of knowledge that is beyond human reach.
>
> (Kirzner 1963: 258; emphasis added)

This insight, however, has to my knowledge never been elaborated in any of Kirzner's subsequent work.

10 For example:

> Despite this realization [that ignorance may block *immediate* exploitation of a profit opportunity], our instinct still assures us that the opportunity *will sooner or later* be discovered and exploited. ... Our instinctive feeling of assurance that profitable opportunities *will* be noticed should not lead us to treat this tendency as being so powerful as to be *instantaneously* realized.
>
> (Kirzner 1979b: 32–33; emphasis added)

There can never be a guarantee that anyone will notice that of which he is utterly ignorant; the most complete rationality of decision making in the world cannot ensure search for that the existence of which is wholly unsuspected. *Yet we submit that few will maintain that initial ignorance concerning desirable opportunities costlessly available can be expected to endure indefinitely.* We recognize, surely, that human beings are motivated to notice that which it is to their benefit to notice. ... This omnipresent human alertness makes it *inconceivable* that market participants can be expected *indefinitely* to continue to pay more for an item than they in fact need to; or that they can be expected *indefinitely* to continue to accept less in payment for an item than they are in fact able to command. We are *convinced* that specifically unpredictable acts of discovery will *add up to a systematic erosion* of unjustified price differentials.

(Kirzner 1992: 48; emphasis added)

Without the 'rationality' assumption *tending to assure gradual spontaneous discovery of relevant market truths*, economists would have no basis upon which to account for the systematic character of market processes.

(Kirzner 1992: 204; emphasis added)

On this topic, see too Kirzner (1973: 228ff.) and Böhm (1992: 100–101).

11 For a short critique of Buchanan and Vanberg's (1991) non-teleological perspective, including their claim that Kirzner's theory is still fettered by the 'subliminal' teleology implicit in notions of equilibration, see Kirzner (1992: 16-21).

Part III

AGENDA AND CONCLUSIONS

10

A POTENTIAL EMPIRICAL TEST OF THE NEW THEORY

The present work is acknowledged to be exploratory. It aims to outline and to extend the foundations for a theory of entrepreneurship. The development of the growth-of-knowledge (GK) programme is conceived to progress along two lines: the first empirical (described in the present chapter), the second theoretical (the next chapter).

Empirical work is required to determine whether the GK theory of entrepreneurship represents an empirically progressive problem shift: that is, whether some of its excess empirical content is corroborated. This can only be determined by independent empirical testing of the new theory's novel predictions. This chapter specifies a potential crucial test for the GK theory of entrepreneurship.

Critics may claim (wrongly) that the GK theory of entrepreneurship is not scientific because it is not operationalised in a sufficiently falsifiable way, because it cannot be applied in practical analyses of observed economic behaviour, or because it is concerned with entrepreneurs' learning methodologies which are themselves not observable.

Such criticisms can be rebutted by a number of counterarguments. First, any pragmatic difficulties associated with identifying entrepreneurial characteristics are not limited solely to testing the GK theory but are also encountered in testing at least two rival theories of entrepreneurship. Casson acknowledges that the qualities his theory predicts are required of an entrepreneur are exceptionally difficult to screen, even though Casson explicitly aims to provide a predictive theory of entrepreneurial behaviour (Casson 1982: 29, 329–333, 358–360; Vaughn 1983: 991–992). Kirzner (1983b: 65–68) too expresses uncertainty in identifying with precision the personal and psychological qualifications associated with successful entrepreneurial alertness. According to Kirzner, not even entrepreneurs themselves (let alone observing economists) are aware that they possess entrepreneurial insight.

Second, the GK theory *is* testable (in any case, more so than at least two of its rivals). It is acknowledged that a new theory that attributes sophisticated falsificationism to entrepreneurs must, for the sake of logical consistency, in turn specify precisely the conditions under which the theory itself would be refuted. (In more sophisticated terms, the new theory must anticipate how its excess empirical content could be corroborated.) The development of the GK programme requires progressing beyond exclusively *a priori* speculation about entrepreneurs' theories of method. This chapter proposes a new technique for identifying the learning methodologies of individual entrepreneurs which at the same time reduces the need for economic researchers to make external rationalisations of observed entrepreneurial behaviour. Once the learning methodologies of a sample of entrepreneurs have been identified, it is possible to conduct statistical tests of the GK theory's predictions which posit a relationship between entrepreneurial performance and entrepreneurial learning methodologies.

10.1 OPERATIONALISATION OF THE THEORY AND EMPIRICAL TESTING

The predictions of the GK theory of entrepreneurship are formulated in rather imprecise terms. Although the new theory has not yet been the subject of a systematic empirical investigation, its predictions could conceivably be tested by introducing additional postulates. The specification of all these auxiliary hypotheses exceeds the scope of the present work; it is a task which belongs on the agenda for future development of the GK programme.

This chapter will therefore be limited to a potential approach for testing the new theory's predictions about requisite entrepreneurial qualities. It will be recalled that a novel prediction of the GK theory is that the entrepreneur's learning methodology is a useful predictor of the performance of the entrepreneur and/or the venture (call this prediction P1). More specifically, the GK theory predicts that the performance of sophisticated falsificationist entrepreneurs is significantly better than the performance of entrepreneurs who adhere to other learning methodologies (prediction P2). The prediction P2 has greater empirical content and thus has a higher degree of testability than the prediction P1. If we (as economic theorists) are to follow Popper's methodological recommendation by formulating our theories as sharply as possible so as to expose them most unambiguously to refutation, then the prediction P2 is to be preferred to P1. Accordingly, the remainder of this chapter is devoted towards testing P2.

Since prediction P2 is a directional hypothesis, a one-tailed test is required. The corresponding null and alternative hypotheses can be defined as follows:

Null hypothesis H_0: there are no differences between the performance of sophisticated falsificationist entrepreneurs and the performance of entrepreneurs who adhere to other learning methodologies.

Alternative hypothesis for the one-tailed test H_1: sophisticated falsificationist entrepreneurs perform better than other entrepreneurs.

The new theory would be falsified (in the naive sense) if the empirical test did not lead to the rejection of the null hypothesis in favour of the alternative hypothesis at the previously set level of significance, that is, if it were concluded that sophisticated falsificationist entrepreneurs do not have (stochastically) better performance track records than other entrepreneurs.

It should be noted that the philosophical basis of the modern (i.e. Neyman-Pearson) theory of statistical inference is naive methodological falsificationism (Blaug 1980: 20–22; Lakatos 1970: 109). The specification of the rejection rules by which statistically interpreted evidence may be rendered inconsistent with the theory under test is a matter of convention, of decision. Even if, in the light of these rules we decided to interpret the empirical evidence as conflicting with the GK theory, the theory itself would not be falsified in the sense that it was conclusively disproved; the prediction (H_1) could still be true. More specifically, any statistical test could yield a value of the test statistic that would lead to H_0 being accepted when in fact it was false. The probability of committing such a Type II error would be β, and it would be determined by the particular statistical test, the selection of the level of significance (i.e. the probability of making a Type I error, α), and the size of the sample (Siegel and Castellan 1988: 9–11). In general, there is a danger of committing a Type II error (or Type I error) in any statistical test.

Only a naive falsificationist economist would reject the GK theory if it were falsified by the empirical test described in this chapter. Falsification in the naive sense (i.e. contradiction by accepted empirical evidence) would not, from the vista of sophisticated methodological falsificationism, be seen as a sufficient condition for eliminating the GK theory of entrepreneurship (see Chapter 2). That is, a sophisticated falsificationist economist would not conflate the alleged refutation of the GK theory with its rejection. The sophisticated falsificationist would only reject the GK theory if its 'refuting instances' corroborated a new and better theory at the same time. In the meantime, it would be perfectly rational to continue working upon the GK theory and trying to improve it.

The research approach would involve a survey, conducted by personal interview and mail questionnaire, of individual entrepreneurs who have launched high-technology startup companies.[1] In the case of businesses started by teams, the principal founder would be asked to participate. The sample of innovative entrepreneurs would be drawn from the files of new venture proposals submitted to well-known venture capital firms. Cooperating venture capitalists may also be willing to make their due diligence files, investment proposals and closing documents available. By selecting ventures belonging to the portfolios of professionally managed venture capital firms, the researcher would be able to gain access to the names, addresses and telephone numbers of entrepreneurs, and would be able to obtain data on the years of startup, the types of product, market and industry involved, and the stages of investment of their ventures.

According to statistical theory, the sample size is determined by the desired level of significance, the allowed estimate of error and the variance of the population. However, in this study the researcher would not know the parameters of the venture population from which the sample would be drawn. Not even the total size of the population of high-tech startups would be known, let alone the variability within that population. Sample standard deviations for the variables involved are not even available from previous comparable surveys. Thus, it would not be possible to apply statistical theory to determine sample size. Furthermore, given that this empirical investigation would only be a pilot survey, the sample-size decision is likely to be driven by pragmatic considerations, such as research cost and feasibility.[2]

Such sampling methods as stratified sampling would be necessary in order to ensure adequate representation of each type of entrepreneur.

The USA would provide the best setting in which to obtain a sample and to undertake the study, because of the multitude of high-tech startups in that country.

At a preliminary stage, it would be necessary to screen the ventures carefully in order to ensure that all sample members are actually independent, technological startups and *not* ordinary new businesses (such as retailing or publishing ventures), corporate startups (i.e. new business activities within established firms), management buyout proposals or part-time businesses. The intent would be to obtain startup businesses which were founded in the same year and to obtain performance data for the first five-year period following startup. It is important that the sample be drawn from the population of ventures launched in the same time period, because such firms would be subject to the same business cycle conditions, similar opportunities for merger and acquisition, and similar venture capital market conditions. For similar reasons, sampling should also aim to minimise the heterogeneity of the startups with respect to the markets, industry, technology and products involved. Sample members should serve similar markets and emphasise industrial rather than consumer product markets.

A structured questionnaire would be used in the survey. The questionnaire would be divided into two major sections. The first section would investigate the performance of the entrepreneur's venture (the dependent variable). The second section would involve an *Entrepreneurial Learning Methodology Inventory* (*ELMI*) for identifying the entrepreneur's learning methodology (the independent variable). The *ELMI* would in turn be divided into two parts. The proposed questionnaire will now be described in more detail.

10.2 SECTION ONE OF THE QUESTIONNAIRE

The first section of the questionnaire would be conducted by personal interview. In this section, interviewees would be asked to provide quantitative data on the dependent variable of the model to be tested, that is, the actual performance of their own ventures. Because the data would be obtained by retrospective reporting, errors and biases (such as response bias) may exist to some degree. Venture capitalists could thus be called upon at a later date to check the performance data reported by the entrepreneur.

The performance data required would be based upon objective measures of venture success during a specified five-year period: each venture's status and aspects of its financial performance.[3] In order to test the predictions of the GK theory, the study must not limit itself exclusively to surviving ventures, which has been the scope of some empirical investigations into the determinants of market and financial performance (e.g. the Strategic Planning Institute's PIMS programme, Biggadike 1979, Weiss 1981). Accordingly, the questionnaire would first request information about the state of the entrepreneur's venture: Did the venture continue operation as an independent firm throughout the first five years after its founding? Was the venture acquired or merged during that period?[4] Did the venture undergo bankruptcy reorganisation? Was the venture discontinued as a result of commercial failure during the first five years after startup (without having been acquired or merged)?

For those ventures which survived as independent firms for at least five years after startup,[5] several financial performance variables would be sought, including four measures of revenue (sales value, rate of sales growth, sales per employee and turnover of assets) and five measures of profitability (absolute profits, return on investment, return on sales, time periods required to reach profitability and positive cash-flow). (The data could originally be gathered in absolute dollar form and could then be converted into the various financial ratios.) Each entrepreneur would be requested to supply this information on his or her venture's performance on a year-by-year basis throughout the five-year period after initial launching.[6] Both revenue and profitability variables would need to be used because of the lack of agreement in the management science literature on the most appropriate measure of performance for entrepreneurial ventures at an early stage in their life-cycle (Buzzell *et al.* 1975; MacMillan *et al.* 1985; Stuart and Abetti 1987; Weiss 1981).

Five categories of new-venture performance would be used. These categories would be based upon the venture's survival and each measure of financial performance within the first five years of its operation. The five categories would be as follows:

- *Highly successful* (++): the venture has attained profitability at an early stage (e.g. within three years); it has thereafter achieved substantial returns commensurate with its 'risk'; it may have reached or be near cash-flow breakeven; it has had an exceptional rate of sales growth in the early years; and it has built sales at a much faster rate than investments or the number of employees.
- *Successful* (+): the venture has reached profitability, but its overall

level of performance (including the sales growth rate and the time period to profitability), though satisfactory, is not as impressive as that of the highly successful venture.

- *Marginal* (0): the venture is just surviving; the rate of sales growth has been poor; and the venture is only just breaking even.
- *Unsuccessful* (-): the venture has continued to record severe losses over the first five years of its operation; it has not reached breakeven; sales levels remain very low or it has undergone bankruptcy reorganisation.
- *Highly unsuccessful* (- -): the venture was dissolved because of commercial failure within five years of its founding, and it was neither merged nor acquired.

Some allocation method would need to be developed by which to assign ventures to the five categories of new venture performance. Numerical ranges would have to be defined for different levels of financial performance, such as for 'substantial' returns, and 'exceptional', 'satisfactory' and 'poor' rates of sales growth.

Thus, in the pilot survey the dependent variable (i.e. the performance of the entrepreneur's venture) would only be measured in an ordinal scale and not in an interval scale. Ventures in one performance category would therefore not just be different from other ventures in other categories of that ordinal scale, they would also stand in some kind of relation to them. The performance of one class would be either better or worse than that of another class. In addition, all the ventures in any one category would be considered equivalent with respect to their performance track records. It should be noted that each venture would *not* be assigned an overall performance score which is a real number.

In the case of a Chi-square test for two independent samples, it may be necessary to collapse the categories of new ventures into just three groups (successful (++, +), marginal (0) and unsuccessful (-, - -)) if there were fewer than five ventures in any cells. However, the statistical test described in section 10.4 would not require such conditions to be fulfilled.

10.3 SECTION TWO OF THE QUESTIONNAIRE

At the end of the personal interview (Section One), entrepreneurs would be provided with Section Two of the questionnaire, which they would be asked to mail to the researcher upon completion. Having obtained in Section One the information required to measure the dependent variable, the questionnaire would then turn to the independent variable, that is, the entrepreneur's learning methodology. Section Two of the questionnaire would comprise a test instrument called the *Entrepreneurial Learning Methodology Inventory (ELMI)*.[7] Because entrepreneurial learning methodologies have not as yet been the subject of an empirical investigation, no operational measures of learning methodologies exist. Even within the fields of the sociology and philosophy of science there is a surprising paucity of literature on characterising the methodologies of individual scientists.

Thus, in the pilot study the inventory would need to be specially designed to be able to distinguish between sophisticated falsificationist entrepreneurs and entrepreneurs who subscribe to other learning methodologies. In order to simplify this measurement instrument, it would be assumed that an individual entrepreneur possesses only one methodology and that he or she applies the same methodology to all problem situations. In follow-up empirical investigations, the instrument could be refined to discriminate between a wider range of distinct learning methodologies that could potentially be employed by entrepreneurs: e.g. naive and sophisticated falsificationism, conventionalism, instrumentalism, naive and sophisticated inductivism, apriorism and scepticism. These entrepreneurial learning methodologies would only be very broad characterisations of their corresponding theories of scientific method.

To counter any potential charge that I am overselling the capabilities of the *ELMI*, it is important to highlight at the outset the limitations of any instrument which is designed to identify entrepreneurial learning methodologies. A truly critical method of testing economic theories must recognise that experimental and survey techniques for collecting and interpreting data are themselves fallible. In a survey using the *ELMI*, data would be collected by means of entrepreneurs' self-reports of their own learning methodologies. Any self-report research method, however, is subject to a number of limitations. For instance, a major problem with self-reports on learning methodologies is that entrepreneurs are not in the habit of thinking about, and articulating upon, matters related to their own learning methodologies. (As mentioned in section 4.3, however, a notable exception is Soros (1987, 1992) who explicitly indicates that Popper's philosophy has influenced his entrepreneurial decision-making in financial markets.) Their second-order learning methodologies are often tacitly applied to their first-order entrepreneurial conjectures. The *ELMI* would require entrepreneurs to verbalise their interpretation of information beyond a level that they would normally do, although the closed-response question format would ameliorate this situation to some extent.

Consequently, the possibility exists that entrepreneurs will report that they subscribe to a particular learning methodology, whereas their actual behaviour is consistent with another. For example, entrepreneurs may indeed believe that they derive their beliefs inductively from observation even though induction is not applied. Or they may believe that they learn from their successes when in fact they learn from their mistakes. When propounded by entrepreneurs, the specified methodology may thus be a misrepresentation of what they actually do.

Even scientists' accounts of their own theories of method are unreliable.[8] A notorious case is Newton's own reconstruction of how he made scientific discoveries and his associated disavowal of hypotheses (*'hypotheses non fingo'*). Historical research reveals that the method of Baconian induction, which Newton himself said he employed to logically derive his theory of celestial mechanics from observations (namely, Kepler's laws), could not have been the method that he actually employed (Duhem 1954: 193; Popper 1963: 185ff.; 1972: 197–202). (Pirating a term from Marx, Lakatos (1971a: 96) referred to such phenomena as the problem of 'false consciousness'.) Darwin is also a case in point. Darwin said of himself that he 'worked on true Baconian principles, and without any theory collected facts on a wholesale scale' (Darwin 1888: 83). But in private letters he admitted that he held 'an old belief that a good observer really means a good theorist' (Darwin and Seward 1903).[9]

Thus, the capabilities of the preliminary version of the *ELMI* should not be overestimated. It would also not be surprising if few practising entrepreneurs consistently employ falsificationist learning strategies. Indeed, empirical evidence indicates that a substantial proportion of practising scientists do not even follow falsificationist methodological rules across a variety of inference tasks.

Having placed these caveats on the *ELMI*, I can now proceed to describe my proposals for an *ELMI* in more detail. The *ELMI* would attempt to define an entrepreneur's learning methodology with respect to a three-dimensional grid (see Figure 10.1). Each dimension would reflect a different aspect of how the entrepreneur goes about learning about the world. The instrument would attempt to order an entrepreneur's learning methodology on three axes: degree of non-justificationism (nj), degree of empiricism (e), and degree of rationalism (r).[10] Each entrepreneur's learning methodology is a combination of all three dimensions. An entrepreneur's learning methodology cannot be described adequately by just one or two of the three dimensions. For example, two entrepreneurs who are both non-justificationists will have very different learning methodologies if one of them is also a rationalist while the other is not. Thus, the learning methodology of entrepreneur i must be represented by a vector comprising the entrepreneur's score along each of these three dimensions:

$$M_i = (nj_i, e_i, r_i)$$

and where the set of all learning methodologies, M, has two members:

$$M = \{\text{sophisticated falsificationism, other learning methodologies}\}$$

The horizontal axis of the grid is the most important dimension for distinguishing entrepreneurial learning methodologies (see Figure 10.1). It represents the degree to which the entrepreneur's learning methodology is non-justificationist. The non-justificationist nature of an entrepreneur's learning methodology increases as one moves to the east of the zero origin. A high scorer is an adherent of non-justificationism and consequently rejects the thesis that there is any foundation of certainty in knowledge. Non-justificationism (and its counterpart, justificationism) were described in detail in Chapter 2. The non-justificationist claims that all knowledge is conjectural and that we cannot prove that knowledge is true, even if it is true. The growth of knowledge is conceived to be (r)evolutionary or discontinuous. Non-justificationist methodologies include sophisticated falsificationism – defined broadly to include Lakatos's methodology of scientific research programmes – and Kuhn's conception of scientific research. (Non-justificationist uses of Bayesian techniques would not be included at this preliminary stage.) The relationship between entrepreneurial learning methodologies is depicted schematically in Figure 10.2.

In contrast, a low score on the horizontal indicates justificationism. Justificationists identify knowledge solely with assertions which are proven to be true (or highly probable, in the case of neo-justificationists). Consequently, they attempt to justify their beliefs and specify an epistemological authority (such as the intellect or sense experience) by which knowledge-claims must be validated in order to be accepted as genuine knowledge. Thus, genuine knowledge can and must be based upon a particular authoritative, epistemological foundation. Apart from the sceptics, justificationists also generally claim that the growth of knowledge is cumulative and continuous. Inductivism, conventionalism, dogmatic falsificationism (as Lakatos (1970: 96) uses the term) and scepticism are methodologies which are consonant with justificationism.

The vertical axis represents the extent to which the entrepreneur's learning methodology is empiricist. The higher the score on this dimension, the more empirical the learning methodology represented. Empiricist learning methodologies emphasise the role of experience, empirical testing, practical experimentation and empirical evidence in the growth of knowledge (especially in the rejection of theories or their tentative acceptance). They reject the claim that knowledge can be valid *a priori*, that is, valid prior to observational experience. Experience-based learning methodologies include falsificationism (dogmatic, naive and sophisticated), inductivism and conventionalism.

In contrast, low scores on the vertical dimension indicate non-empirical learning methodologies which emphasise the indubitable power of *a priori* reasoning, abstract conceptualisation and metaphysical speculation for acquiring knowledge. These methodologies extol the intellect above experience. Apriorism is an example of a non-empirical learning methodology. Apriorists deny the importance of empirical falsifications and corroborations. Knowledge, it is argued, is the product of the active mind and can be gained without recourse to experience (although they may admit that knowledge of sorts can be gained from experience). Justificationist apriorists[11] reject the notion that the only way in which knowledge-claims about the real world (so-called synthetic propositions) can be checked is to engage in empirical testing. The apriorist holds that some synthetic propositions need not and cannot be tested: they are inherent in the structure of our thinking, so that we would be incapable of making sense of a world in which these propositions were not factually or materially true. Thus, justificationist apriorists hold for certain that some synthetic propositions are *a priori* valid (so-called primary axioms) (Popper 1972: 47, 93–94). Starting from these axioms, the apriorist is able to derive further certain knowledge by pure deductive reasoning. Hence, the process of setting one's conjectures against empirical observation, of checking one's assumptions against reality,

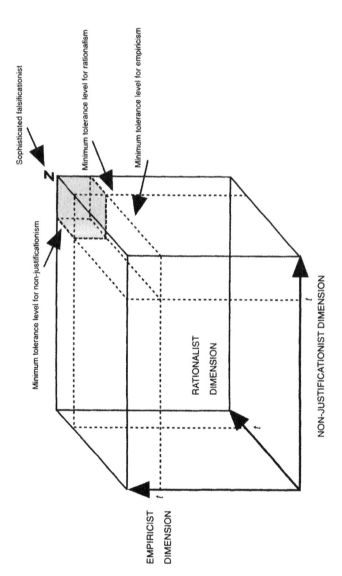

Figure 10.1 The three dimensions of the *Entrepreneurial Learning Methodology Inventory*

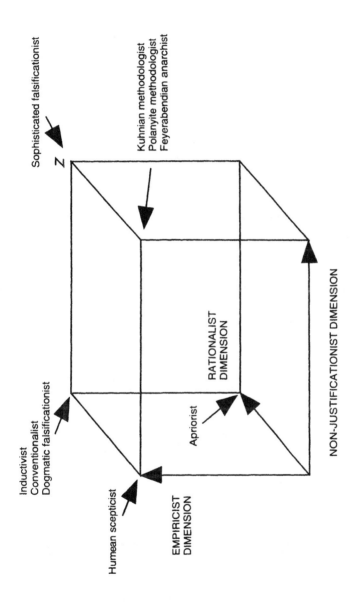

Figure 10.2 The relationship between various learning methodologies

is regarded as totally superfluous. Any 'testing' is limited to checking that the argument does not violate the rules of deductive logic, that is, to ensuring that the stated conclusions (or predictions) do in fact follow necessarily from the premises (Stewart 1979: 20, 239). Because apriorist entrepreneurs form their conjectures independently of real-world data, their conjectures (and the patterns of their behaviour) are unaffected by any changes in real-world data.

The next step is to superimpose a third axis upon this schema which represents the extent to which the entrepreneur's learning methodology is rationalist (in the broadest sense of the term). The degree of rationalism intensifies as one shifts further away from the zero origin. Entrepreneurs who score highly on this dimension subscribe to a rationalist learning methodology: they have reasons for their choices of action and use logic in their reasoning. Their actions are not random or haphazard. They employ rational evaluation criteria. They regard changing from one theory to another to be a rational change that is governed by logical rules. They recognise that strictly logical deductions enable them to infer (i.e. to transmit truth) but not to prove (establish truth). Justificationist rationalists seek to employ either deductive logic or an inductive logic in order to attempt to prove or to verify their theories, whereas non-justificationist rationalists rely solely upon deductive logic for disproving or for refuting their theories (however inconclusively). Non-justificationist empiricist rationalists deduce the implications (predictions) of their ideas and attempt to test them against empirical evidence. They recognise the logical validity of the *modus tollens* principle of propositional inference and apply only disconfirmatory reasoning in hypothesis testing. Non-justificationist rationalism also claims that rational decisions can be made in the absence of proven or probable knowledge. All brands of falsificationism, inductivism and apriorism are methodologies which belong to the rationalist tradition.

In contrast, a low score on the third dimension denotes irrationalism. An irrationalist sees decisions and the growth of knowledge as driven mainly or wholly by psychological, sociopsychological and political factors, rather than by rational arguments or causes. Included here are people's needs for self-justification and external justification, the power of persuasion, 'bandwagon effects', shared values and shared ideological commitments. Logical reasoning is not implicated in theory-choice. Changing one's beliefs is conceived to be more akin to a conversion experience than a rational choice.

They deny that there are always independent rational standards for comparing competing theoretical frameworks. One particular type of irrationalism, justificationist or Humean scepticism, claims that rational decision-making is only possible if one has proven knowledge about alternative courses of action; and since there is and can be no proven knowledge, it is argued that rationality itself is impossible. '[T]he end of justificationism' means 'the end of rationality' (Lakatos 1970: 178). Early Kuhnian methodology, Polanyi's post-critical philosophy and Feyerabend's methodological anarchism have also been polemically described as irrationalist learning methodologies (Lakatos 1970: 93–94), though Kuhn (1970b: 234) himself rejects being labelled an irrationalist.

On the basis of the GK theory of entrepreneurship, only a sophisticated falsificationist entrepreneur could possibly score highly on all three of the dimensions of the *ELMI*. With specific reference to the non-justificationist dimension, sophisticated falsificationist entrepreneurs would be expected to have a tendency to emphasise the tentativeness of knowledge, the impossibility of justifying their beliefs, the impossibility of deriving valid generalisations from particular instances, the importance of feedback and independent criticism, the theory-laden nature of observations, learning from mistakes and the objectivity of market problems. Their approach to problem-solving would be systematic rather than *ad hoc*. They would be expected to adopt critical policies towards their own conjectures, testing them by active experimentation and avoiding immunising strategies.

Although they would think conceptually about their ventures and would actively generate imaginative conjectures in response to specific problems, sophisticated falsificationist entrepreneurs would also be expected to receive high scores on the empiricist dimension, indicating a determination to learn primarily from experience. This dimension would be likely to manifest itself in an emphasis upon practical experience rather than just abstract thinking, upon practical experiments rather than only on thought experiments, and upon piecemeal experiments rather than holistic experiments. More concretely, they would be expected to stress the significance of in-depth analyses of market potential and to emphasise the importance of market tests which involve end users in the problem-solving process (e.g. beta tests during early stages of the venture). They also place a premium upon experimental knowledge with respect to the relevant technology and market. They would specify *ex ante* the precise conditions according to which the *ex post* performance of their start-ups is to be assessed, and they would assume that unintended consequences of a venture are inevitable. If there were discrepancies between their conjectures and the evidence, they would critically re-evaluate their business concepts and plans and would re-examine the evidence.

The sophisticated falsificationist would also be reported to rely heavily upon logical reasoning and rational evaluation (the rationalist dimension). They would employ rational standards for evaluating competing new product concepts and alternative strategies and policies. They would use deductive logic (specifically, disconfirmatory reasoning) in testing their entrepreneurial conjectures. They would emphasise that they change their conjectures for logical reasons rather than as a result of psychological, sociopsychological and political factors. They would not require proven knowledge about alternatives in order to make rational decisions. They would seek to develop business plans which are logically consistent (i.e. which do not violate the axioms of logic) and which are based on realistic assumptions.

It should be noted that in the pilot study the *ELMI* would simply be used as the basis for a nominal or classificatory scale and not for an ordinal scale. The *ELMI* would serve to partition the whole sample of entrepreneurs into a set of two non-empty, mutually exclusive subclasses.[12] The first group (*SF*) would comprise sophisticated falsificationist entrepreneurs, whereas the second (*OT*) would consist of entrepreneurs who adhere to other learning methodologies (hereafter referred to simply as 'other entrepreneurs' or 'other types of entrepreneurs'). The numerical scores for each dimension received by the individual entrepreneurs would *not* be used in the statistical tests.

In order to identify to which subclass in the binary scale each entrepreneur belongs, it would only be necessary to determine whether an entrepreneur is or is not a sophisticated falsificationist. This could be achieved by obtaining the entrepreneur's score with respect to each of the three dimensions (non-justificationism, empiricism and rationalism). As has already been mentioned, sophisticated falsificationism can be described as a methodology which is strictly non-justificationist, highly empirical (i.e. experience-based) and undeniably rational. Entrepreneurs with data points near point Z (in the upper right background corner in Figure 10.1) would be conjectured to be sophisticated falsificationists. Minimum tolerance levels for each dimension (t_{nj}, t_e, t_r) would have to be set, below which the entrepreneur would not be regarded as a sophisticated falsificationist. A high positive score (i.e. greater than the minimum threshold) for every dimension (nj, e, r) would be required for an entrepreneur to be designated a sophisticated falsificationist (i.e. data points would have to intercept within the shaded region in Figure 10.1). If the entrepreneur were to receive a score below the tolerance level for one or more dimensions, the entrepreneur would be allocated to the classification of 'other entrepreneurs' (i.e. data points intercepting outside the shaded region in Figure 10.1). The classification of each entrepreneur could thus be summarised simply by the following decision rule:

For entrepreneur i,
if $nj_i > t_{nj}$, $e_i > t_e$, $r_i > t_r$,

then M_i = sophisticated falsificationism,
else M_i = other learning methodologies;

where

nj_i, e_i, r_i = the individual entrepreneur's scores with respect to the non-justificationist, empiricist and rationalist dimensions, respectively; and

t_{nj}, t_e, t_r = the minimum tolerance levels for each dimension.

The *ELMI* would be divided into two parts, each part concerned with determining the entrepreneur's learning methodology with respect to these three dimensions. Part A would require entrepreneurs to indicate the extent to which they agree or disagree with a number of simple statements on the nature of knowledge and its acquisition. Part B would contain a decision scenario in which entrepreneurs would be directed to describe how they would account for, and how they would respond to, contrary evidence which conflicts with their conjectures about the market, competition and technology.

10.3.1 Part A of the *Entrepreneurial Learning Methodology Inventory*

Part A of the survey instrument would require entrepreneurs to complete a long series of questions designed to assess some aspect of their learning methodology. Each closed-response question would probe a different aspect of one of the three dimensions.[13] Detailed aspects of each dimension were described above. Differently phrased but essentially duplicate questions could also be employed to check for the reliability of responses. The response options would be presented on a Likert scale (see Table 10.1). Entrepreneurs would be asked to indicate their degree of agreement or disagreement with a variety of statements related to each dimension. To obtain an entrepreneur's score for a particular dimension, the entrepreneur's responses to individual questions related to that dimension would need to be summarised by a total score or some measure of central tendency.[14]

Table 10.1 includes a battery of possible Likert-scaled questionnaire items. These statements have been derived from the GK theory presented in this work, the philosophy of science and the literature on the development process for new products and ventures. Part A of the *ELMI* would need to be further refined on the basis of a small number of semi-structured, personal interviews with entrepreneurs and innovation experts (such as venture capitalists). Thorough pretesting conducted by personal interviews with a small but representative sample would also need to be undertaken in order to check the repeated use of this instrument. In particular, it would be necessary to ensure that potentially important aspects of each dimension are not omitted from the *ELMI*, to check that the vocabulary is simple, direct and familiar to participating entrepreneurs, and to identify and to correct for ambiguous, loaded or double-barrelled questions and statements. It should also be noted that items in Table 10.1 are not necessarily presented in a form directly consistent with the particular dimensions to which they relate. Individual statements which are negatively correlated with their respective dimensions are denoted by an asterisk (*).

The *ELMI* would have to be designed to check for a variety of biases, especially those introduced by closed-response questions. One approach could be to include an instruction sheet immediately preceding the closed-response questions of Part A of the *ELMI*. This sheet would require entrepreneurs to describe (in general terms if they wished) an actual historical case in which they had encountered some contradiction between market evidence and their own expectations regarding the feasibility of their venture. Open-ended questions would then direct entrepreneurs to describe how they made their judgments in a fairly concrete manner. The instruction sheet could be formulated along the following lines.

From your own experience, choose an *important* situation in which market information suggested that one or more of your business assumptions might be wrong. You may have faced the situation in the past or be currently dealing with it.

How did you learn of the discrepancy between the market information and your assumptions?

With reference to your own venture, what did you do (if anything) when you discovered that the latest market information or market event did not agree with your hunch about market opportunities? Describe as specifically as possible how you went about dealing with the discrepancy from start to finish.

Did the discrepancy recur? If so, how did you react? If not, how would you have reacted if it had recurred?

In general, how do you go about solving unexpected problems encountered during the new product development process (e.g. poor results from beta-testing the prototype)?

What do you think is your greatest strength as a learner? What is your greatest weakness?

The researcher would then attempt to summarise their replies in methodological and epistemological terms in order to identify each entrepreneur's underlying learning methodology.[15]

10.3.2 Part B of the *Entrepreneurial Learning Methodology Inventory*

As mentioned earlier, entrepreneurs are unlikely to be able to articulate their learning methodologies explicitly. Some may even have difficulty answering the closed-response questions above. However, the manner in which entrepreneurs respond in real time to unintended consequences reveals much about their methodologies (cf. Boland 1982: 184). For this reason, Part B of the *ELMI* would aim to indirectly determine entrepreneurs' learning methodologies by investigating their responses to a decision scenario which describes a venture that has failed to achieve important milestones.

A major advantage of the decision scenario approach is that it provides all participants with a standardised problem situation. The same decision scenario is evaluated by every participant in the study. Thus, it is possible to control (at least to some extent) for the inputs

Table 10.1 Part A of the *Entrepreneurial Learning Methodology Inventory*

	Disagree strongly		Neither agree nor disagree		Agree strongly
1. To answer each question in Part A, please circle one choice (1 to 5) that best describes how you learn or how you define knowledge. A five-point scale is provided with each point being defined as follows:					
1 = disagree strongly					
2 = disagree somewhat					
3 = neither agree nor disagree					
4 = agree somewhat					
5 = agree strongly					
The aim of the questionnaire is to describe how you learn, not to evaluate your learning ability.					
THE NON-JUSTIFICATIONIST DIMENSION					
I do not regard new market information as real knowledge unless I know for certain that it is true or probably true.*	1	2	3	4	5
In order to say that I have learnt something about the market, I must know for certain that what I have found out is 100 per cent correct.*	1	2	3	4	5
It is impossible to prove conclusively that new market information is correct, even if it is correct.	1	2	3	4	5
Once I have established hard facts about the market (e.g. about who will buy, how much and how often), these facts will never be disproved or overturned.*	1	2	3	4	5
Learning about a market consists of acquiring a growing body of hard facts.*	1	2	3	4	5
Different entrepreneurs making similar observations of similar market or technological developments will produce similar entrepreneurial ideas.*	1	2	3	4	5
My conviction that my entrepreneurial hunch is correct is strengthened by observing numerous or repeated market events which confirm my idea.*	1	2	3	4	5
The more information I can acquire which confirms my entrepreneurial hunch, the more probable it is that my entrepreneurial hunch is correct. *	1	2	3	4	5

By observing the price of a product at a particular time and place, I am able to draw valid conclusions about the behaviour of that product's price over all time and wherever it is sold.*	1	2	3	4	5
By generalising from observations of product sales in a limited number of representative test markets, I could arrive at valid conclusions about the total size of the market for that new product.*	1	2	3	4	5
I do not have the information required for calculating probabilities of different rates of return.	1	2	3	4	5
At the time of choosing between alternative pricing policies, I do not know all the possible outcomes that could result from any given policy.	1	2	3	4	5
There is no guarantee that what has been experienced in the past will persist in the future.	1	2	3	4	5
Feedback from other people is usually not constructive or useful.*	1	2	3	4	5
Successful entrepreneurs have to turn a deaf ear to other people's concerns about the venture and new product if they want to get anywhere at all.*	1	2	3	4	5
I make good use of feedback regarding my business strategies and plans.	1	2	3	4	5
I encourage feedback from other members of the entrepreneurial team.	1	2	3	4	5
I seek feedback from expert outside sources during the development process (e.g. accountants, venture capitalists, industry association members, potential customers).	1	2	3	4	5
Every new product should attempt to solve a customer problem.	1	2	3	4	5
I learn most from active attempts to solve practical and definite problems.	1	2	3	4	5
Any knowledge I have about the market, competition or technology is tentative and can be overturned at any moment by new developments.	1	2	3	4	5
There is no secure foundation to one's knowledge about the market, competition and technology.*	1	2	3	4	5

My knowledge of the market consists of hard facts, established conclusively by experience.*	1	2	3	4	5
My knowledge of the market consists of hard facts, established conclusively by abstract reasoning.*	1	2	3	4	5
I search for secure assumptions on which to base my business strategies and plans. *	1	2	3	4	5
I learn from my mistakes.	1	2	3	4	5
The only way I can learn something about the market is to find a flaw in my present understanding of it.	1	2	3	4	5
I consciously search for mistakes in my understanding of the market.	1	2	3	4	5
Other members of the entrepreneurial team are usually to blame for the disappointing results of our venture.*	1	2	3	4	5
Each modification of an existing product benefits from what we have learned from earlier models.	1	2	3	4	5
Knowledge gained from my failures is often instrumental in achieving subsequent successes.	1	2	3	4	5
It is very hard to learn from one's successes.	1	2	3	4	5
I learn from my successes.*	1	2	3	4	5
I solve problems in a trial-and-error manner.	1	2	3	4	5
Any observations I make about market developments are coloured by my own point of view and preconceptions.	1	2	3	4	5
My gathering and analysis of market data or information is not biased by my preconceptions and expectations.*	1	2	3	4	5
Profit opportunities are real, they 'exist' in some sense.	1	2	3	4	5
I ignore information which conflicts with my assumptions, plans or strategies, because I am positive that I am right while everyone else is wrong.*	1	2	3	4	5
I can use market data to corroborate my assertions about the market potential for my new product, provided the data was obtained from market studies conducted after I made my assertion.	1	2	3	4	5

I can use data collected by other people to support my projections of market potential for my new product, provided I did not originally use the same data in developing my projections.*	1	2	3	4	5
I can discover hard facts about the market which conclusively show my previous assumptions and expectations to be wrong. *	1	2	3	4	5
My assumptions and expectations about the market can never be conclusively disproved.	1	2	3	4	5
If my strategy does not agree with the latest market information, I must reject my strategy.*	1	2	3	4	5
If my venture misses an important milestone, I must reject my strategy, even if there is a risk that my original strategy is still correct.*	1	2	3	4	5
Even if my strategy conflicts with the facts, I will not abandon it unless I have a better strategy with which to replace it.	1	2	3	4	5
If my venture fails on a single occasion to achieve a predetermined performance target (e.g. the completion of product development), I will immediately change my business strategy and plans.*	1	2	3	4	5
The evaluation of a new venture must pay attention to its long-term performance and potential and not its performance at a particular date.	1	2	3	4	5
For new ventures, there is no need for predetermined go/no-go checkpoints or milestones at which to re-evaluate the entire venture.*	1	2	3	4	5
The difference between a successful and an unsuccessful venture is just a matter of the persistence of the entrepreneur to carry on single-mindedly.*	1	2	3	4	5
Sometimes rapid and radical adjustments in new products are required to salvage an otherwise troubled venture.	1	2	3	4	5
I regard a marketing plan as a system for classifying the market into distinct subsets of customers.*	1	2	3	4	5

Whenever my plan does not fit the facts, I am most likely to disregard the facts.*	1	2	3	4	5
Whenever my plan does not fit the facts, I am most likely to discard the plan immediately.*	1	2	3	4	5
Whenever my plan does not fit the facts, I am most likely to critically re-evaluate the plan and to re-examine the facts.	1	2	3	4	5
If a professional market study suggested that my venture was not economically viable, I would generally reject the results on the grounds that all survey findings and market research firms are notoriously unreliable.*	1	2	3	4	5
A setback for a new technical product is a temporary situation which is correctable over time with more money.*	1	2	3	4	5
Whenever my expectations for sales growth are severely disappointed by actual results, I will cautiously make minor *ad hoc* alterations to my strategies and plans so as to avoid jumping to conclusions.*	1	2	3	4	5
Whenever my expectations for sales growth are severely disappointed by actual results, I will make major revisions to my entire business strategy or will even try to devise an entirely new one.	1	2	3	4	5
I do not get worried whenever sales orders fall significantly below target levels because my assumptions and strategy still hold despite the discrepancy between expected and actual performance.*	1	2	3	4	5
I do not consider evidence of errors or mistakes to be a criticism of the realism of my assumptions and would not therefore change my business strategy.*	1	2	3	4	5
A business plan attempts to provide a realistic description of the venture's environmental conditions and should be based upon realistic assumptions.	1	2	3	4	5
I am solely concerned with the practical success of adopting a business strategy as a basis for action, not at all with whether the underlying assumptions are realistic or not.*	1	2	3	4	5

If I discover information which
conflicts dramatically with my
assumptions, I will not change my
business plan because I knew my
assumptions were unrealistic when I
developed the plan. The assumptions
were merely a convenient and practical
way to simplify developing the plan.*

1	2	3	4	5
Disagree strongly		Neither agree nor disagree		Agree strongly

THE EMPIRICIST DIMENSION

I set performance targets of a fairly
precise nature by which to compare
actual results with my original
expectations.

1	2	3	4	5

Detailed performance objectives
and projections are inappropriate for
innovative start-ups because they are
totally unreliable and bear little relationship
to actual results.*

1	2	3	4	5

I try out my ideas to see whether they
work and how they work.

1	2	3	4	5

Starting a new entrepreneurial venture
is essentially an experiment.

1	2	3	4	5

Implicit in a venture are a number
of hypotheses or assumptions about
the market, technology and
competition that can be tested only
by experience.

1	2	3	4	5

The development of a new product or
venture should be broken down into
manageable stages rather than
completed in one go according to a
predetermined business plan.*

1	2	3	4	5

A large-scale production plant can
be successfully planned by way of
blueprints.*

1	2	3	4	5

Small-scale product-use tests do not tell
us anything about the reactions of end
users to the new product.*

1	2	3	4	5

There is no venture or new product
which has not had any setbacks or
unexpected and undesirable effects.

1	2	3	4	5

Market testing for a new product is only of value if it is carried out in the national market as a whole.*	1	2	3	4	5
Market experiments (e.g. to find out the effects of a significant price change) are useless because it is impossible to repeat them under precisely similar market conditions.*	1	2	3	4	5
In my field, it is better not to involve end users in the product development process because it delays product introduction, reveals the product to competitors, and costs extra money.*	1	2	3	4	5
It is important to have in-depth and frequent interaction with potential customers throughout the development process, even at the risk of revealing some strategic information.	1	2	3	4	5
In my field, beta testing of the prototype (product-use tests at the customer's site) is too costly, too risky, and too time-consuming.*	1	2	3	4	5
In my field, it is better to bypass the market-testing stage.*	1	2	3	4	5
I continually test my assumptions by active experimentation, even at very early stages of the venture.	1	2	3	4	5
I avoid testing assumptions made in the business plan because I would not get passed square one if I did.*	1	2	3	4	5
I actively seek out market information prior to startup.	1	2	3	4	5
I do not place much importance on in-depth analyses of market potential.*	1	2	3	4	5
I rely primarily upon my intuitive feel for estimating market potential.*	1	2	3	4	5
An entrepreneurial team does not need to be knowledgeable about formal market evaluation methods.*	1	2	3	4	5
Informal approaches to assessing markets are better than formal market evaluation methods.*	1	2	3	4	5
In-depth market analysis is really only useful for meeting the requirements of potential investors.*	1	2	3	4	5

Market analysis is only useful for forecasting sales.*	1	2	3	4	5
Market analysis can be useful for evaluating the entire business concept.	1	2	3	4	5
Because I really believed in my venture idea, I did not need to conduct a market study.*	1	2	3	4	5
Many entrepreneurs could avoid failure through better market analysis prior to startup.	1	2	3	4	5
An entrepreneur must have previous experience in the relevant technology and/or market before launching a new venture.	1	2	3	4	5
Industrial customers lack the technical sophistication required to be able to point out successful new product ideas.*	1	2	3	4	5
During the new product development process, I rely mostly upon experiments carried out mentally ('thought experiments') rather than upon practical experiments which are too costly.*	1	2	3	4	5
I learn mainly from practical experience rather than abstract thinking.	1	2	3	4	5
No one really knows if an innovative product will be economically viable until it encounters the realities of the marketplace.	1	2	3	4	5
Venture success generally requires not one but several well-managed trial products.	1	2	3	4	5
I developed my new product ideas and business strategy quite independently of market information.*	1	2	3	4	5

Disagree strongly		Neither agree nor disagree	Agree strongly		

THE RATIONALIST DIMENSION

I use logical reasoning when deciding between alternative explanations of new market developments.	1	2	3	4	5
I use logical reasoning when deciding between alternative policies.	1	2	3	4	5
Reason and logic play only a minor role in my decision-making.	1	2	3	4	5

If I do not have full information about alternative courses of action, I cannot make a rational decision.*	1	2	3	4	5
Even though I do not have perfect knowledge about some alternatives, I can still make a rational decision.	1	2	3	4	5
Deciding to continue with a troubled venture is a matter of irrational faith.*	1	2	3	4	5
Deciding to continue with a troubled venture is not irrational because there is always the possibility that the project will turn out to be a commercial success resulting in large profits.	1	2	3	4	5
My decisions are not random or haphazard. I have reasons for my choices.	1	2	3	4	5
It is perfectly rational to persevere with a troubled venture, even when things look almost hopeless, and to try to transform it into a successful venture.	1	2	3	4	5
A business plan does not need to be logically sound.*	1	2	3	4	5
The only way I can assess a proposed policy (e.g. on pricing) is to find out how many members of the entrepreneurial team support it.*	1	2	3	4	5
My evaluation of a particular policy is not determined by the number of team members who support the policy.	1	2	3	4	5
The best I can do is to imitate the most successful entrepreneurs.*	1	2	3	4	5
There are rational criteria by which I can evaluate new product concepts.	1	2	3	4	5
Any decision to switch from manufacturing one product to manufacturing another is an instinctive reaction which cannot be governed by the rules of reason.*	1	2	3	4	5
The development of a new venture is a rational process.	1	2	3	4	5

2. *Indicate whether you agree or disagree that the following arguments employ correct reasoning.*

(Please note that the correctness of reasoning does NOT depend upon the factual truth of the assumptions made in each argument.)

	NO	YES
If A is true, then B is true; B is true. Therefore, A is true.*	N	Y
If there is an increase in demand for the component, its price will rise; the price of the component has risen. Therefore, demand for the component has increased.*	N	Y
If A is true, then B is true; B is not true. Therefore, A is not true.	N	Y
If there is an increase in demand for the component, its price will rise; the price of the component has not risen. Therefore, demand for the component has not increased.	N	Y
If A is true, then B is true; A is true. Therefore, B is true.	N	Y
If there is an increase in demand for the component, its price will rise; demand for the component has increased. Therefore, the price of the component is going to rise.	N	Y
If A is true, B is true; A is not true. Therefore, B is not true.*	N	Y
If there is an increase in demand for the component, its price will rise; demand for the component has not increased. Therefore, the price of the component is not going to rise.*	N	Y

into each entrepreneur's decision process. Although the approach is still exposed to the errors and biases that may accompany self-reporting, its application to entrepreneurial problem-solving would be likely to satisfy many of the criteria specified by Ericsson and Simon (1980) as necessary for reliable self-reports. (For further discussion on the use of decision scenarios, see Fredrickson and Mitchell 1984: 412–413.)

In line with the approach, entrepreneurs would be presented with a single decision scenario or problem. The scenario would describe in detail a hypothetical venture to introduce a new industrial product which is planned to result in a significant reduction in the user's production costs (cost of materials etc.) and/or transaction costs (costs of monitoring product quality etc.). Table 10.2 provides an illustration of the type of decision scenario that would be appropriate.[16] The decision scenario would involve reporting on experimental evidence which contradicts the entrepreneurial team's assumptions of the venture. The venture itself would neither be a meteoric success nor a spectacular failure. An appropriate candidate for a decision scenario would be a venture belonging to that category of investments which venture capitalists label pejoratively as 'the living dead': portfolio companies which fail to yield a return on investment corresponding to expectation and which never achieve sufficient operating profit to exist independently, but which also never quite fail.

Having read the scenario, entrepreneurs would then respond to an accompanying series of Likert-scaled questions asking them to describe how they would respond if their own ventures (had) faced the same situation. Table 10.2 presents examples of the kinds of questions which could be asked. The items would be designed to assess the degree of non-justificationism, empiricism and rationalism involved in the entrepreneur's decision process by investigating the methods and criteria that the entrepreneur would employ to evaluate and to screen out alternative courses of action. It is important that the entrepreneurial team in the scenario be reported to pursue immunising stratagems to an *intermediate* degree in order to safe-guard their venture. The entrepreneurial team in the scenario would be sufficiently imaginative to invent convincing *ad hoc* explanations of poor performance. Subsequent questions to determine the degree to which responding entrepreneurs immunise their ventures would ask them to indicate whether they would be *more* or *less* tolerant (than is the entrepreneurial team in the scenario) of evidence of counterexamples to their assumptions. By the method of selection by sequential elimination, the aim would be to screen out entrepreneurs who apply immunising stratagems above some level of tolerance, as they could not be sophisticated falsificationist entrepreneurs. In the questions relating to the decision scenario (Table 10.2), response options which represent immunising stratagems are denoted by an asterisk.

Table 10.2 Part B of the *Entrepreneurial Learning Methodology Inventory*

PART B: THE DECISION SCENARIO

At the start-up stage

Innovatech Company is an instrument venture that is developing a highly innovative microprocessor-based device for controlling certain aspects of production in the printing industry. The venture has been in business a short time (just under a year). At this startup stage, the venture possesses the following characteristics. A detailed business plan (including market analysis) has been completed and has subsequently received backing from a syndicate comprising one established venture capital firm and four other investors. The venture has been founded by an energetic entrepreneurial team with extensive experience with the targeted market and industry. The team is functionally balanced and has had prior experience of working together. An experienced partner of the venture capital firm (the lead investor) is on the venture's board, which plans to meet monthly.

The venture targets an existing market which is at the high growth stage and which is in a buoyant industry. According to the entrepreneur's calculations of user benefit, it is estimated that it would take less than twelve months for the product to pay for itself in decreased production costs. Potential customers have expressed interest in the device. The founders have offered to supply the final product to two potential customers at a discount price (should they decide to purchase when it becomes available) if they would provide written evaluations of the prototype after it has been installed on a trial basis in their plants. The prototype is still under beta testing.

The venture draws on proprietary technology which is already under development (i.e. the device has been produced to the point of a functioning prototype). Because of its technology advantages, the venture is expected to be insulated from competition during the first two to three years of operation.

The financial projections for five years ahead have been worked through with the venture capitalist and are considered to be realistic. The potential return on investment (around 40 per cent compounded annually, after tax) is considered to more than compensate for the level of risk. A high (50–55 per cent) gross margin on revenues is anticipated which will act as a buffer against unexpected losses (i.e. downside risk).

The level and timing of future infusions of capital have been planned to match the developmental needs of the venture and the accomplishment of significant milestones. The second round of funding is planned to occur in twelve months' time. The major goals or benchmarks set by the venture captitalist which are to be achieved by the next funding stage include: completing beta-testing; getting the product ready to market; making some initial sales to demonstrate that a real demand exists for the product; and establishing the manufacturing feasibility for the product.

First application for additional funding

Ten months later, the venture requires a second round of financing. The cash-flow burn rate has been much higher than projected in the business plan, cash resources have been exhausted, the next payroll cannot be met and losses are accumulating. Two milestones have been achieved. First, manufacturing feasibility has been established after significant technical bugs were ironed out which delayed product development (especially the incorporation of modifications for individual customers). Second, beta testing of the prototype has been completed, and the test results are satisfactory.

Otherwise the venture is seriously behind schedule in the achievement of milestones in the business plan. The company is still not producing revenues. No firm orders have yet been received, although the founders are convinced that one of the two beta-site customers will soon place an order once its individual specifications are met. Technical hitches have frustrated product modifications to meet the needs of one potential customer. There has also been some turnover of technical personnel which has disrupted the startup effort.

For one reason or another, monthly board meetings did not take place, and the venture capitalist is ill-informed about the venture's situation. The venture team manages to convince the venture capitalist that they recognise the cause of the problem: technical problems have hampered production, and the firm has been unable to ship because of these technical difficulties. A larger investment and more time are needed to generate the critical early sales. The reinvestment decision is recommended by the same venture capital partner who made the original investment decision. The venture captialist's reinvestment decision was made under significant time constraints, and he did not repeat the thorough screening process that he had undertaken at the startup stage. Given that this is the first application for additional funding, the venture capital firm is prepared to make a further investment provided that several changes are instituted. The venture team is willing to make changes and revise the business plan.

The most important benchmarks which were agreed upon by both parties are: to gain a foothold in the market, to build sales, to increase manufacturing capacity and to reach break-even. The next funding round is timetabled for twelve months ahead.

QUESTIONS RELATING TO THE SCENARIO

Please circle *one* number (1 to 5) on each line to indicate *how likely* it is that you would consider each explanation or take each particular action.

	Very unlikely		Neither likely nor unlikely		Very likely

1. How likely is it that you would *seriously consider* each of the following explanations to account for the failure to reach the milestones described in the scenario situation?

(a) my original projections about the timing of sales were overly optimistic	1	2	3	4	5
(b) unpredictable external events	1	2	3	4	5
(c) bad luck *	1	2	3	4	5
(d) our assumptions about market needs were mistaken	1	2	3	4	5
(e) slow market growth	1	2	3	4	5
(f) industrial customers are simply deferring their purchase decisions *	1	2	3	4	5
(g) the market is not as receptive as first thought	1	2	3	4	5
(h) it is just a delay in the market's learning of the new product *	1	2	3	4	5
(i) the product is not supplying the benefits it was supposed to confer	1	2	3	4	5
(j) the venture has missed the target market	1	2	3	4	5
(k) the venture is ahead of its time *	1	2	3	4	5
(l) technical difficulties have given rise to unanticipated delays in product development and made shipping impossible	1	2	3	4	5
(m) inadequate execution by the management team of the original entrepreneurial idea	1	2	3	4	5
(n) normal seasonal fluctuation in this market sector *	1	2	3	4	5

(o) the market sector and/or the economy is in a recession	1	2	3	4	5
(p) lack of experience with the target market	1	2	3	4	5
(q) purchasing managers lack the sophistication required to recognise the product's technical superiority *	1	2	3	4	5
(r) the price is too high	1	2	3	4	5
(s) a technological advance or market shift has made the product obsolete	1	2	3	4	5
(t) potential market size and/or share is not as large as projected but is still economically feasible	1	2	3	4	5
(u) product is not sufficiently competitive in the market	1	2	3	4	5
(v) marketing strategy is wrong	1	2	3	4	5
(w) inadequate financial controls	1	2	3	4	5
(x) inadequate marketing	1	2	3	4	5
(y) potential market size and/or share is not big enough to be economically viable	1	2	3	4	5
(z) the product is too unique, novel or state of the art *	1	2	3	4	5

2. How likely is it that you would *seriously consider* taking each of the following actions in response to the missed milestone?

(a) wait and see	1	2	3	4	5
(b) teach the market	1	2	3	4	5
(c) add a new member to the venture team or replace personnel	1	2	3	4	5
(d) change the business concept and/or marketing strategy	1	2	3	4	5
(e) change the assumptions of the business plan but leave the strategy intact *	1	2	3	4	5
(f) examine the growth rate for forward orders and the composition of the order books	1	2	3	4	5

(g)	seek outside advice and assistance	1	2	3	4	5
(h)	re-examine the entire business concept critically	1	2	3	4	5
(i)	make personal contact with potential customers	1	2	3	4	5
(j)	undertake market research	1	2	3	4	5
(k)	expand marketing effort *	1	2	3	4	5
(l)	reduce price	1	2	3	4	5
(m)	switch target markets *	1	2	3	4	5
(n)	modify or reposition the product	1	2	3	4	5
(o)	switch products *	1	2	3	4	5
(p)	switch technologies *	1	2	3	4	5
(q)	stay in the original market	1	2	3	4	5
(r)	ramp up manufacturing *	1	2	3	4	5
(s)	develop second-generation product *	1	2	3	4	5
(t)	broaden market	1	2	3	4	5
(u)	restructure company	1	2	3	4	5
(v)	diversify products	1	2	3	4	5
(w)	begin major expansion of company *	1	2	3	4	5
(x)	discontinue venture	1	2	3	4	5
(y)	alter initial selling method and/or distribution	1	2	3	4	5

Second application for additional financing

Eight months later, a second cash crisis develops. The company has now been in business two-and-a-quarter years. None of the milestones that were agreed upon when the extra capital was first injected have been reached. Although the product is in fact being produced, only a few initial sales and some orders have been made, and both actual sales and orders have failed to reach projected levels. Actual revenues have yet to reach the first target level set at the startup funding stage (now eighteen months ago). The level of sales volume is substantially below breakeven. Inventories are building up.

In addition, the venture is more vulnerable to competitive attack than first thought. An unanticipated competitor has announced its intentions to enter the market. The competitor has simultaneously developed a similar device which employs alternative non-patented technology which supplies user benefits in a cheaper way. It is estimated that the competitor's action could result in up to a 50 per cent loss of planned market share for the firm.

The reasons put forward by the venture team to explain the 'time lags' encountered by the venture are: the lack of success in accomplishing prior developmental objectives have frustrated the subsequent progress of the company; purchase decisions are being deferred because the venture missed the annual budget year of its industrial customers and because the sanction of managers at higher levels in client organisations is required before purchase decisions can be made; and the market is confused since the competitor has made an announcement of a similar device that it intends to introduce.

The venture team suggests that the appropriate response to its difficulties is for the venture capitalist to provide it with funds to be utilised for a major expansion in the company's marketing effort.

FURTHER QUESTIONS RELATING TO THE SCENARIO

	Very unlikely		Neither likely nor unlikely		Very likely

3. How likely is it that you would *seriously consider* taking each of the following actions?

(a) wait and see	1	2	3	4	5
(b) teach the market	1	2	3	4	5
(c) add a new member to the venture team or replace personnel	1	2	3	4	5
(d) change the business concept and/or marketing strategy	1	2	3	4	5
(e) change the assumptions of the business plan but leave the strategy intact *	1	2	3	4	5
(f) examine the growth rate for forward orders and the composition of the order books	1	2	3	4	5
(g) seek outside advice and assistance	1	2	3	4	5
(h) re-examine the entire business concept critically	1	2	3	4	5
(i) make personal contact with potential customers	1	2	3	4	5
(j) undertake market research	1	2	3	4	5
(k) expand marketing effort *	1	2	3	4	5
(l) reduce price	1	2	3	4	5
(m) switch target markets *	1	2	3	4	5
(n) modify or reposition product	1	2	3	4	5

(o)	switch products *	1	2	3	4	5
(p)	switch technologies *	1	2	3	4	5
(q)	stay in the original market	1	2	3	4	5
(r)	ramp up manufacturing *	1	2	3	4	5
(s)	develop second-generation product *	1	2	3	4	5
(t)	broaden market	1	2	3	4	5
(u)	restructure company	1	2	3	4	5
(v)	diversify products	1	2	3	4	5
(w)	begin major expansion of company *	1	2	3	4	5
(x)	discontinue the venture	1	2	3	4	5
(y)	alter initial selling method and/or distribution	1	2	3	4	5

In order to construct the decision scenario, a range of pilot interviews would be undertaken with innovation experts and entrepreneurs at the instrument development stage. The emphasis of the interview would be upon identifying critical milestones which new, high-tech ventures typically fail to reach. It would also explore and describe the different types of actions that entrepreneurs often take when significant milestones are not attained.

In addition, the technique of simultaneous verbal protocols is an approach which could be used as a basis to develop Part B of the *ELMI*. (For a review of this method, see Schweiger 1983.) Verbal protocols are a method for using verbal responses as empirical data in the testing of hypotheses. By this method, it may be possible to identify the sequences in which entrepreneurs interpret refuting evidence, the criteria that they apply for evaluating their ventures and ultimately the detailed aspects of each of the dimensions for distinguishing entrepreneurial learning methodologies. Simultaneous verbal protocols can be used to trace the processes involved in problem-solving activities (Schweiger 1983). The method simply involves asking entrepreneurs to verbalise their conscious thought processes in the course of solving a specific, concrete problem (such as evidence of counterexamples which do not fit the entrepreneurs' plans). The deliberations of entrepreneurs would be tape-recorded as they each evaluate their own ventures in the light of evidence which suggests that their ventures are in difficulty. Their verbalisations would then be transcribed and codified according to some pre-designed scheme for classifying entrepreneurs' thought units into methodological categories.

Significant pretesting would need to be conducted in order to ensure that the scenario represents a realistic decision context for entrepreneurs. Thus, participants would be asked to rate on a five-point scale how typical the scenario situation is in their own experiences of start-up ventures.

Pretesting would also be needed to detect any major biases that may be present in the instrument. In order to check for biases introduced by closed-response questions, participating entrepreneurs would be asked to describe as specifically as possible how they would explain and actually deal with the situation in the scenario, and they would be directed to record their approach on a worksheet. The worksheet would be completed after reading the decision scenario but before reading the questions relating to it. In addition, in order to discourage a normative response, participants would be told that there are no correct answers, and they would be requested to specify the actions which they would actually take and not to describe how they think they should behave.

10.4 THE STATISTICAL TEST

This empirical study would employ two independent samples: sophisticated falsificationist entrepreneurs, and entrepreneurs who adhere to other learning methodologies. The usual parametric technique for testing whether two independent samples have been drawn from the same population is a t test applied to the means of the two groups. In this empirical investigation, however, parametric tests, such as the t test, would be inapplicable for a variety of reasons. Apart from its small sample size, the study would violate the restrictive assumptions about the population which are associated with parametric tests. In addition, because the data for the dependent variable would be measured by an ordinal scale (i.e. the five categories of venture performance), the data would fail to meet the measurement requirements of parametric tests.[17]

Consequently, only non-parametric statistical tests for two independent samples should be employed in this empirical investigation. Because the difference in central tendency (i.e. difference in location rather than in dispersion or skewness) between the two samples would be the focus of the hypotheses being tested, tests which are most sensitive to differences in location should be selected. A further requirement would be that the test be appropriate for larger samples and ordinal measurement. Thus, in this case, either the

Mann–Whitney U test or the Kolmogorov–Smirnov two-sample test (for a one-tailed test) would be applicable. However, the Mann–Whitney U test would be more appropriate because of its ability to distinguish between two populations with relatively small differences in central tendency but significantly different frequency distributions in the upper and lower performance categories (Sandberg 1986: 104).

The Mann–Whitney U test (1947) is a conservative non-parametric test for two independent samples.[18] It is one of the most powerful non-parametric tests and an excellent alternative to the parametric t test. The Mann–Whitney test needs only to assume that the observations are independent and that the data (in this case, on venture performance) represent a distribution which has underlying continuity (Gibbons 1985: 140, 148; Siegel 1956: 25, 116, 123).

The null and alternative hypotheses were defined in section 10.1. These hypotheses can now be restated more specifically with reference to the Mann–Whitney U test. In the case of prediction P2, the null hypothesis (H_0) is that the population of sophisticated entrepreneurs (X) and the population of other types of entrepreneurs (Y) have identical distributions. That is, if x is one entrepreneur sampled from the population X and y is one entrepreneur sampled from the population Y, then the null hypothesis is that the probability that x's performance is better than y's performance is equal to one-half. Thus: $H_0: P(x > y) = \frac{1}{2}$. The alternative hypothesis (H_1), against which H_0 is tested, is that sophisticated falsificationist entrepreneurs have (stochastically) better performance track records than entrepreneurs who are not sophisticated falsificationists. Thus: $H_1: P(x > y) \neq \frac{1}{2}$.[19]

We would reject H_0 if the probability of the sophisticated falsificationist entrepreneur's performance being better were greater than one-half. The GK theory of entrepreneurship would then have resisted refutation by this particular test: some of its excess empirical content would have been corroborated. It would have led to the discovery of novel facts. The GK theory would be refuted *by this particular empirical test* if it were decided that the data did not support the rejection of H_0 in favour of H_1 at the prespecified level of significance.

In later empirical investigations, the intent would be to test the association between entrepreneurs' degree of sophisticated falsificationism and the degree of economic success of their ventures. To this end, non-parametric measures of correlation, such as the

Spearman rank-order correlation coefficient, would be applied.[20] This measure of association makes no assumption about the shape of the population from which the data are obtained. However, the Spearman rank-order correlation coefficient does require that both variables be measured in at least an ordinal scale. It would therefore be necessary to refine the *Entrepreneurial Learning Methodologies Inventory* to measure the *degree* of an entrepreneur's sophisticated falsificationism. (The closer the entrepreneur's data point is to point Z in the upper-right background corner of Figure 10.1, the greater the degree to which the entrepreneur's learning methodology is sophisticated falsificationist.) Statistical tests would also be undertaken to determine the significance of any correlation that may be observed in the sample.

This chapter has described a potential empirical test of the GK theory of entrepreneurship. Only by such testing will it be possible to determine whether the new theory is empirically as well as theoretically progressive. The next chapter outlines directions for further theoretical development within the GK research programme and comments upon the fruitfulness of the new programme.

NOTES

1 For previous empirical research into the prefunding factors which may predict the success or failure of technological startups, see: Cooper and Bruno (1977); Roure and Maidique (1986); Stuart and Abetti (1987) and Van de Ven *et al.* (1984). See too Maidique (1986) for a general discussion of key success factors in high-technology ventures. The literature on the success of new products and technological innovations is much more extensive. See: Cooper (1979a, 1979b, 1980, 1983); Maidique and Zirger (1984: 192–193; 1985); Mowery and Rosenberg (1979); Myers and Marquis (1969); and Rothwell *et al.* (1974).

2 At this point, it is worth noting that previous studies into the prefunding factors which may influence the performance of high-tech new ventures rarely discuss how they arrive at their sample sizes. Sample sizes are typically small. For example, see: Roure and Maidique (1986) – eight high-tech companies from the electronics industry; Sandberg and Hofer (1987) – seventeen new ventures, not all high-tech; Stuart and Abetti (1987) – twenty-four technical ventures, both independent and corporate; Van de Ven *et al.* (1984) – thirteen software firms. One exception is Cooper and Bruno's (1977) longitudinal study, which is based upon an investigation of 250 high-technology firms founded on the San Francisco peninsula during the 1960s. They regarded their study as a census of the population of high-tech startups for that location and period.

3 The relative success of a new venture can be measured in various ways. For a discussion of the different dimensions by which previous research has defined venture success, see Stuart and Abetti (1987: 217–218). For a discussion of the definition of failure, see Sharma and Mahajan (1980: 81).

4 Firms which had been acquired or merged would be eliminated from the sample because acquisition is often a vehicle for both successful and unsuccessful new firms (cf. Cooper and Bruno 1977: 18).

5 All the surviving firms would have been operating in the market for that time-span and could therefore be regarded as successful to some extent. In this study, however, survival would not be the only measure of performance.

6 Because the performance data would be limited to this time span, only the initial performance of a venture and not its long-term performance would be measured. It must be noted that, in the absence of an inductive logic, early success or profitability does not necessarily guarantee continued success or profitability (Biggadike 1979: 105; Stuart and Abetti 1987: 219).

7 This instrument should not be confused with the Learning Style Inventory of Kolb, Rubin and McIntyre (1979). Their inventory is a simple self-description test for characterising how a participant learns, and it is based upon a psychological and largely *inductive* theory of experiential learning. The structure and detail of their inventory is not appropriate for testing the predictions of the GK theory of entrepreneurship. For a somewhat rudimentary application of the Learning Style Inventory to entrepreneurship, see Bailey (1986).

8 Though the following examples are drawn from the natural sciences, the methodological pronouncements of social scientists (including economists) may also bear little relationship to their own actual behaviour. Kaplan (1964: 3–11) neatly distinguishes between 'logic-in-use' and 'reconstructed logic' to describe this dichotomy between what scientists themselves actually do and what they say they do.

9 Both of Darwin's quotes in this paragraph were taken second-hand from Medawar (1969: 11).

10 Within the justificationist philosophical programme, the terms 'rationalism' and 'empiricism' typically refer to rival theories on the source of knowledge and the method by which knowledge is acquired. Justificationist rationalism (especially seventeenth-century classical intellectualism) claims that pure reason by itself, without appeal to sense perception, can provide certain knowledge. Certain knowledge can be derived from certain propositions (axioms about which one cannot be wrong) by means of strictly logical deductions. On the other hand, justificationist empiricism (e.g. the logical positivist movement in the twentieth century) claims that all knowledge is derived from experience. It seeks to construct certain knowledge inductively from a small set of factual propositions which are also indubitable (see Chapter 2). However, no conflict between the dimensions of empiricism and rationalism is implied by the *Entrepreneurial Learning Methodology Inventory*. These terms are used in a broad sense (discussed more fully

in subsequent paragraphs), not in their narrow justificationist sense. Thus, it is indeed possible to be strictly empiricist without being justificationist. Empiricist methodologies are not necessarily justificationist; they need not be based upon the sensationalist assumption that genuine knowledge can only be derived through the senses (Agassi 1966). For instance, empiricism underlies Popper's non-justificationist philosophy of science: '[T]here is no clash between my theory of non-induction and either rationality, or empiricism, or the procedure of science' (1972: 5).

11 To my knowledge, all apriorist learning methodologies are justificationist. Justificationist apriorism implies that our intellect is invariably successful in imposing its interpretation upon the world and that the theories created by our minds must be true *a priori* (Popper 1963: 191–192). I do not know of a purely apriorist learning methodology which is also non-justificationist.

12 In the follow-up empirical investigation, entrepreneurs could be classified according to a more extensive categorisation of learning methodologies. Scores with respect to each dimension could be classified as either high or low. Given that there are three dimensions, there would then be potentially eight ($2 \times 2 \times 2 = 8$) major categories of learning methodologies (each corner of the cube in Figure 10.1). The point of interception of the entrepreneur's scores with respect to each of the three dimensions would determine into which of the eight learning-methodology categories the entrepreneur would be assigned. Similarly, if scores for each dimension were classified as either low, medium or high, then there would be twenty-seven potential classes of learning methodologies ($3 \times 3 \times 3 = 27$).

13 The Cronbach alpha for each dimension could later be calculated to test the reliability of the measurements for each dimension. Principal component factor analysis (Varimax rotation) could also be undertaken to test whether the responses to individual items loaded onto factors with combinations similar to those designed to reflect the dimensions of an entrepreneur's learning methodology.

14 The most appropriate measure for describing the central tendency of scores in an ordinal scale is the median (Siegel 1956: 25). However, under some important assumptions, it may be more convenient to obtain the arithmetic mean. Before the arithmetic mean could be calculated from the ordinal data, responses to individual items would have to be scored by assigning values from one ('disagree strongly') to five ('agree strongly'). In the case of statements which are negatively related to the dimension in question, it would be necessary to correct for the scoring direction by assigning a scale value of one to 'agree strongly ' and so on.

15 The disadvantage of such an unstructured, open-ended question approach as a general basis for the *ELMI* would be that each historical case would be evaluated solely by the entrepreneur who reported it and by no other participants in the study. Without a set of common or standardised historical cases, it would not be possible for the researcher to assess the extent to which an entrepreneur's response to a counter-

344

example is a function of the historical case as well as of his or her methodology.

16 Table 10.2 is merely provided as a sketch of a possible scenario. Greater institutional detail would need to be obtained from interviews with industry experts at the instrument development stage and from a literature review of the selected industry.

In developing the instrument, the researcher may also find helpful empirical psychological research into the way decision-makers respond to failure. In particular, for the design of laboratory experiments on escalation, see Conlon and Wolf (1980), McCain (1986), Staw (1976) and Tegar (1980).

The literature on early warning indicators of business failure may also be consulted: Argenti (1976a, 1976b); R. G. Cooper (1975, 1979a, 1979b, 1980, 1983); and Sharma and Mahajan (1980). In addition, the following works would provide a useful basis for developing a more detailed scenario: Block and MacMillan (1985); De Sarbo, MacMillan and Day (1987); Greiner (1972); MacMillan *et al.* (1985: 121); Maidique and Zirger (1985); Rich and Gumpert (1985b: 157–158); Robinson (1987); Roure and Maidique (1986: 295–296) and Ruhnka and Young (1987).

17 For a discussion of the inappropriateness of parametric statistical tests in the context of new venture performance, see Sandberg (1986: 103–105). The parametric statistical model associated with the normal distribution assumes that independent observations are drawn from normally distributed populations with equal variances. It also requires that the observations are measured in the strength of at least an interval scale (Siegel and Castellan 1988: 20, 33, 103). The assumptions of normal distributions and equal variances within the two independent populations would be dubious in the context of empirically testing the GK theory: no empirical research has been undertaken into the survival rate of, or into the distribution of performances of, new high-tech ventures led by sophisticated falsificationist entrepreneurs and other types of entrepreneurs.

18 Another version of this test is referred to as the Wilcoxon (1945) rank-sum test. Even though the Mann–Whitney U test and the Wilcoxon two-sample test appear to test different hypotheses, they are actually equivalent and provide tests of the same null hypothesis but from a different perspective (Gibbons 1985: 148; Marascuilo and Serlin 1988: 228, 236). Although the Wilcoxon format reflects the basic theory more directly, the Mann–Whitney procedure is easier to apply and to computerise, and it can be adapted to the estimation of a confidence interval for the median difference (i.e. the difference in location) (Sprent 1989: 87, 93; Marascuilo and Serlin 1988: 240). For useful discussions of the Mann–Whitney/Wilcoxon test, the reader should refer to Lehmann (1975), Mann and Whitney (1947), Siegel (1956), Siegel and Castellan (1988) and Wilcoxon (1945).

19 A less general way of stating the null hypothesis is that the median performance of X is equal to the median performance of Y: H_0: $\theta_x = \theta_y$. Similarly, the alternative hypothesis may also be stated in terms

of medians: $H_1: \theta_x > \theta_y$. It should be noted that in this case the alternative hypothesis specifies only that there is a difference in medians, that is, it specifies that the two samples come from populations with distributions which differ only in location (Gibbons 1985: 149; Siegel and Castellan 1988: 137; Sprent 1989: 87–90). Like the null hypothesis, the alternative hypothesis assumes that the variances of the distributions are equal (i.e. homoscedastic).

20 The usual parametric measure of correlation, the Pearson product-moment correlation coefficient, would not be applicable because the set of data would not meet its requirement that both variables (in this case, venture performance and the entrepreneur's sophisticated falsificationism) be measured in at least an equal-interval scale (Siegel and Castellan 1988: 225).

11

AGENDA FOR FURTHER DEVELOPMENT OF THE THEORY, AND CONCLUSIONS

This chapter charts possible new courses for further theoretical development and offers some concluding thoughts on the new programme. As part of developing the growth-of-knowledge (GK) theory of entrepreneurship, I provide a couple of suggestions on which lines of research may promise to be fruitful. The theory can be expected to develop in at least three directions: at the level of individual decision-making, the level of the entrepreneurial team or firm, and the level of public policy. As for the first of these, theoretical development could entail the application of GK rationality to decision-making by other transactors in the market process, such as venture capitalists (section 11.1). As for the firm, the theory could be expanded by developing a theory of the firm as a Popperian learning mechanism or a Lakatosian research programme (section 11.2). The third line of inquiry would involve drawing out the public policy implications of the GK theory (section 11.3). (It is also anticipated that the theory will develop at the level of market processes – some suggestions were provided in Chapter 9.) I will briefly discuss each of these suggested directions for future research in turn.

11.1 THE SCREENING OF ENTREPRENEURIAL IDEAS BY VENTURE CAPITALISTS

The GK approach could be extended to the learning procedures of other transactors in the market process, such as venture capitalists, who evaluate entrepreneurial ideas and who face difficulties of interpretation. The procedures that venture capitalists employ will affect the realisation of entrepreneurial ideas and hence the pattern of market adjustment and the growth of knowledge. '[T]he ability to get *financial* backing emerges as probably *the* most crucial factor in embarking on any entrepreneurial project' (Ronen 1983b: 142; emphasis added). Venture capital has become an increasingly important medium for financing the realisation of entrepreneurial ideas which entail setting up innovative companies at the frontier of new technologies and markets.[1] 'It plays an essential role in the entrepreneurial process' (Tyebjee and Bruno 1984a: 1051). The connection between entrepreneurship and venture capitalists' decision-making is intensified still further when one recalls Mises' point that an entrepreneurial element is inherent in all human action: 'in any real and living economy every actor is always an entrepreneur and speculator' (1949: 252).

The process of interpersonal criticism within the external venture capital market is especially pertinent as an object of study because independent venture capitalists have been relatively successful in investing in innovative business startups (Dixon 1989; Joint Economic Committee 1985; Sandberg and Hofer 1982; Timmons and Bygrave 1986). It has been suggested that the source of venture capitalists' success is the evaluation procedures and the rigorous selection criteria that they employ. Indeed, venture capitalists undertake intensive screening and analysis of the projects in which they invest. During the pre-investment phase, business proposals are subjected to successive stages of scrutiny: prescreening, screening, evaluation, and structuring and pricing the investment proposal. Thus, venture capitalist decision-making may be the paragon of critical rationalism in the context of the growth of market knowledge. Furthermore, venture capitalist screening is of particular importance because such appraisal is typically a prerequisite to further screening by other resource owners and transactors in the economic process: the acquisition of venture capital is often required to finance the formation of contracts with other factors of production (labour, land, machinery, plant and equipment).

Venture capital is also interesting from a theoretical perspective. Apart from a few exceptions (Baaken 1989; Chan 1983; Cooper and Carleton 1979; Khan 1987; Meade 1978; Tyebjee and Bruno 1984a), a theoretical approach to the decision-making of venture capitalists has not received much emphasis in the literature of economics, management and finance. Most literature on venture capital is highly descriptive and lacks an explicit theoretical foundation. Thus, venture capitalist decision-making emerges as an appropriate subject for the application of the general theoretical framework developed in Parts 1 and 2 of this book.[2]

348

The GK approach would concentrate on the role of venture capitalists in the appraisal of innovative entrepreneurial ideas. The aim would be to develop a model of venture capitalist screening as a basis for explaining the methods and selection criteria that venture capitalists apply in evaluating innovative entrepreneurs and their novel ideas. It would be necessary to explain a number of factors: the sequence of screening stages employed by venture capitalists; the particular nature of the appraisal of entrepreneurial ideas by venture capitalists; the role of objective surrogates (such as business plans) in the venture screening process; and the employment of experts in the appraisal of entrepreneurial ideas. It would also be important to examine the difficulties which venture capitalists encounter in evaluating the performance of projects in their current portfolios and in deciding whether to make follow-on investments. It would also be useful to inquire into the reasons why venture capitalists reject entrepreneurial ideas.

Any GK model of venture capitalist screening that is developed could then be assessed in the light of previous empirical research which has studied the evaluation of business proposals by venture capitalists. The next step would be to subject the model itself to severe empirical testing.

11.2 ENTREPRENEURIAL TEAMS AND FIRMS

The GK theory of entrepreneurship has been presented at the level of the individual entrepreneur. The GK approach can also be extended to the conception of the entrepreneurial team or firm. Such an approach introduces a theory of learning into the theory of the firm. Pioneering attempts at depicting the firm in terms of concepts from theories of the growth of scientific knowledge have been advanced by Earl (1984: ch. 5; 1987) and Loasby (1971, 1976, 1983). The GK approach complements, and extends beyond, the literature on corporate culture which originated with Selznick (1957) and which has subsequently been championed by organisational sociologists.[3] The approach provides 'a theoretical basis for the existence of corporate cultures and strategies, not merely another language for characterizing them' (Earl 1987: 19). It provides a framework for synthesising recent developments in the strategic management literature, organisation theory and behavioural economics.

However, there is still much scope for the development of these fruitful ideas for explaining entrepreneurial and business behaviour. To date, the emphasis has been upon firms as Kuhnian paradigms, which are well outside the Popperian philosophical tradition.[4,5] In contrast, it is possible to portray the firm as a Popperian inquiring system or an entrepreneurial research programme which is akin to a scientific research programme within Lakatos's methodology. (As mentioned in section 2.3, Lakatos's methodology is itself '"Popperian" in a wider sense', representing a 'creative shift' in Popper's programme (Worrall 1978: 65).)

The GK approach treats the firm as a set of rules for problem-solving. In addition, a business strategy is argued to reflect a particular theoretical perspective on the (business) world. A business strategy is depicted, not as a single objective or isolated plan, but as a complex of conjectures which possesses organic unity, heuristic power and continuity. In Lakatosian terms, the business strategy of a firm is its entrepreneurial research programme. The descriptive hard core of such a programme is constituted by the central assumptions held by the entrepreneurial team about the nature of the firm's business. The normative hard core comprises the methodological decision rules which supplement the firm's objectives and guide the generation and selection of new entrepreneurial ventures. The protective belt of an entrepreneurial research programme is the malleable boundary of the firm which can be redefined (e.g. by divesting peripheral business activities) in order to stave off a potential threat to the core line of business.

Like Ansoff's (1965) classic model of corporate strategy, the GK approach would assume that an entrepreneurial team relies upon comprehensive logical analysis in determining strategy. Like Ansoff, it would present a rational rather than a sociopsychological model of business growth.[6] (Indeed, the GK approach can provide an objective reconstruction of sociopsychological, Kuhnian models of the firm.) Firms would be portrayed as undertaking their strategic activities (e.g. market development, diversification, divestiture) in a rational way.

The GK approach to entrepreneurial teams and firms would seek to offer solutions to an array of important problems: How does the structure or architecture of firms affect entrepreneurship (including the screening of entrepreneurial ideas)? Why and how do entrepreneurs work as a team? What adjustments might they have to make to their individual strategies in order to be able to work together? How are decisions implemented in firms managed jointly by more than one entrepreneur? Why do businesses in the same or similar situations[7] choose different paths to growth? Why and how do entrepreneurs' strategic choices change over time? In particular, why and how do entrepreneurial firms shift away from their original core lines of business? Why do patterns of strategic behaviour persist in the face of new leadership? What does an entrepreneurial firm need in order to achieve orderly and profitable growth? Why are some failing ventures in a firm 'immunised' from elimination but not others? Why do large firms 'spin off' some new businesses as separate enterprises?[8] How does a coalition of entrepreneurs learn in an environment of structural uncertainty? How does an entrepreneurial team coordinate its problem-solving activities (including the selection of market problems, new ideas and experiments)? What guides the generation and application of localised knowledge within a multi-entrepreneur firm?

The long-run evolution of corporate strategies away from original core lines of business is an important subject for further research. This could be analysed by means of Remenyi's (1979) theory of 'core demi-core interaction'. Remenyi extends Lakatos's analysis by adding several new elements which attempt to capture the dynamic and evolutionary nature of scientific disciplines. In contrast to Lakatos's model which portrays the emergence of competing research programmes as external to the dominant SRP, Remenyi's model allows for the internal generation of recalcitrant hypotheses which may grow more visible as the demi-core of an established subdiscipline (which is in the protective belt of the main discipline) is driven into open conflict with the discipline's hard core.[9] This approach can be used to explain how new entrepreneurial ideas or ventures can be developed within a firm even though they conflict with its core business activities.

In order to develop a theory of the long-run evolution of business strategy and structure, it may also be possible to combine the GK approach with theories of corporate development (e.g. Chandler 1962, 1977; Chandler and Daems 1980; Scott 1973).[10] The theory may assist in analysing the character and timing of firms' responses to new situations. Furthermore, the GK approach (and especially the Lakatosian view of the firm) may provide a methodology by which the business historian can reconstruct the internal history of business enterprises and it may thus provide a rational explanation of the growth of actual entrepreneurial firms.

Although the GK approach does not examine the transaction

cost or agency cost properties of alternative governance structures, it could extend transaction cost theory if it were grafted on as a theory of learning. At present, the transaction cost literature does not emphasise the differential efficiency of alternative learning mechanisms in eliminating errors and in facilitating the progress of knowledge.[11]

It should be recognised that at multiple levels within a firm, individuals are pursuing problem-solving activities of their own. Even within an entrepreneurial team, individual members have their own agendas. In order to take account of internal decision-making processes in entrepreneurial teams, it may be possible to integrate the GK approach with the literature on committees, hierarchies and polyarchies (Nalebuff and Stiglitz 1983; Sah 1991; Sah and Stiglitz 1985, 1986, 1988).

At this juncture it should be mentioned that the approach may diverge to some extent from the GK programme as specified formally in Chapter 1. In particular, depending upon how these suggestions are implemented, it may conflict with the principle of methodological individualism (see HC1 and PH3 in section 1.4). While it should be kept to a minimum, such a conflict should not worry us unduly at this early stage in the programme's development. As Blaug (1980: 51) comments, methodological individualism is a commendable heuristic postulate, but one which should not be adhered to at all costs if it would halt the investigation of collective entities (e.g. venture teams and firms) which cannot as yet be reduced to the decision-making of individuals.

The GK approach could also be used to compare the differences between various hierarchically organised learning mechanisms, that is, alternative intra-firm arrangements for instituting the generation and interpersonal criticism of ideas. Different hierarchical learning mechanisms provide different incentives and employ different techniques for identifying new market problems and for generating solutions to them. Different learning mechanisms employ different criteria by which to evaluate alternative solutions and different practical rules for rational action. The necessary and sufficient conditions for the elimination of unsatisfactory solutions (including failing ventures) vary between learning mechanisms, so that the response of a decision-maker to a refutation by market experiment differs: in one institutional context, it may be irrational to develop an entrepreneurial or strategic idea further, whereas in another it may be rational to persist with it.

More specifically, it may be possible to apply the GK approach to such issues as the comparative institutional assessment of Japanese and Western industrial corporations. In particular, the approach may be used to compare selection processes within Japanese and Western enterprises: how ideas are screened and revised during the process of product innovation and strategy formulation. For example, hard-core assumptions about strategic activity are likely to differ between Japanese and Western firms. Strategic activity is regarded as a sequential, partitioned process (comprising successive stages of problem identification, strategy formation and strategy implementation) within Western corporations. In contrast, strategic evolution is implicitly assumed by the Japanese to be a parallel, dynamically interdependent process. Ansoff (1984: Section 6.4; 1987: 508) claims that this assumption is the direct result of the Confucian theory of knowledge which is embedded in Japanese culture.[12]

11.3 PUBLIC POLICY IMPLICATIONS

Another suggested line of inquiry is to tease out the public policy implications of the GK conception of entrepreneurship and of the market process. Rather than investigate all the factors which determine entrepreneurial activity and learning from a GK perspective, the focus will be upon those tractable variables which can be readily affected by public policy. The aim is to identify and explain the determinants of entrepreneurship which are most relevant to public policy. Among other things, I would expect to find a detailed analysis of the institutional framework and of economic policy (especially regulations).[13]

The GK theory of entrepreneurship is not institution-neutral. As it stands, the theory is linked to a particular set of economic, political and social parameters. It is mainly concerned with the outcomes that can emerge within a market economy or the private sector of a mixed economy. However, the theory could be extended to a wider variety of institutional contexts.

The institutional and constitutional framework includes the particular type of political and economic organisation of the society in question, the degree of decentralisation in economic decision-making and the particular system of property rights. It is expected that the specific set of institutional conditions in which entrepreneurship is conducted will have a significant effect upon entrepreneurship itself (Baumol 1990, 1993). Thus, the supply of entrepreneurship is endogenous to the institutional context in which it is exercised. The task of this line of inquiry would be to explain *how* and *to what extent* entrepreneurship depends upon the institutional framework.

The institutional framework determines the degree to which entrepreneurs and others are free to pursue their respective interests, to try to discover new problems and opportunities, to find ways of solving and exploiting them, to achieve rewards and to engage voluntarily in transactions with each other. In particular, the legal framework determines the degree of contractual freedom granted to entrepreneurs and other individuals. The legal framework is the product of both conscious design and of spontaneous ordering processes.

Regulatory constraints differ from the institutional framework in that they are situation-specific and less enduring. They are directly amenable to change through the policy-making process. They arise from what are perceived and expected to be unsatisfactory market outcomes. Thus, regulations are intended to modify the constellation of inputs utilised, outputs consumed and their prices, quantities and qualities from what they would otherwise be in the absence of governmental intervention.

It is expected that the GK programme will contribute most to the analysis and design of institutional structures (i.e. the rules of the game). Consequently, it could be used to address a number of fundamental questions: What should be the role of government in the economy? To what extent, if any, can government encourage or release entrepreneurial endeavour? What set of general principles should be considered in examining institutions and policies which impinge on entrepreneurship? What is the normative yardstick against which they should be evaluated? Which institutional conditions provide the best environment for entrepreneurship to flourish? How does the institutional framework affect the supply and allocation of entrepreneurial talent? How does it affect spontaneous and deliberate problem-solving on the part of entrepreneurs? The approach taken should be comparative-institutional. It would be interesting to apply the GK theory in order to explain why some economies induce only sluggish entrepreneurial responses (following economic liberalisation, for instance) whereas others are characterised by rapid and vibrant entrepreneurship.

In addition, it would also be important to investigate whether the GK programme can say anything about the mix, design and sequencing of specific public policies. What mix of policies gives the greatest spur to arbitrage, speculation and innovation? Is the GK approach capable of being 'operationalised' in a policy setting? The GK approach could have very practical implications for policy-makers if it could help identify the prerequisites for an entrepreneurial environment. For what set of policy problems, if any, does the GK approach have a comparative advantage relative to other approaches?

In section 9.1, I defined a learning procedure as a problem-solving process which entails particular means of generating trials (competing entrepreneurial conjectures) and particular methods of eliminating errors (ways of controlling the trials). This simple notion can be used as a basis for analysing the impact of public policy on entrepreneurship and competitive market processes. In particular, it suggests that when formulating and evaluating individual public policies it is important to take account of their effects on the following sorts of factors: the incentives for entrepreneurs to identify new market problems and opportunities; the pattern of entrepreneurial conjectures formulated as tentative solutions to perceived market problems; the nature of the critical tests and severity of the selection pressures to which entrepreneurial ideas are subjected (i.e. the process of exposure to refutation); the refutation and elimination of entrepreneurial conjectures; the distribution of rewards from successful problem-solving; and the coordination of individual entrepreneurs' endeavours. Consequently, any government intervention which disturbs the *ex ante* prospect of profit, the informational content of market prices, the testing function of factor and product markets, and the eliminative power of *ex post* entrepreneurial losses and business failure, will have some non-negligible effect upon entrepreneurial activity.

The GK approach may help us identify the types of regulatory impediments and specific policies which most inhibit the operation of competitive entrepreneurial processes. Ideally, for any given country in a given time period, we would like to be able to rank regulations and other policies according to the direction and magnitude of their impacts upon the level of entrepreneurial activity. (However, because of the open-ended nature of market processes and the fact that we may never know what might have been discovered by entrepreneurs in the absence of a particular policy, such judgements are likely to be fraught with difficulties – Kirzner 1985: 119–149.) The range of policies that could be studied includes regulation, competition policy (including regulation of mergers, takeovers and trade practices), macroeconomic policy (both fiscal and monetary), policies relating to state-owned enterprises, human resources policies (e.g. education, immigration, research, science and technology policies), and social (welfare) policy.

In its application to policy, the GK approach would emphasise the inherent structural uncertainty facing policy-makers in their decision situations – there is always the danger that they are working with a misspecified model. Accordingly, the fallibility of policy decisions and the possibility of Type I and Type II errors would play a key role in the analysis. The sequencing of public policies would be designed to capture the benefits of learning from mistakes committed in earlier stages. The GK approach would avoid the 'pretence of knowledge' that tends to permeate policy advice based upon mainstream economics. The approach would also require policy-makers and regulators to specify *ex ante* the possible outcomes which would suggest that a proposed policy had failed. It would stress the need for policy-makers and their advisers to be forever vigilant of the unintended consequences of policy initiatives.

11.4 CONCLUDING THOUGHTS

It is now widely recognised that processes of learning are crucial to most phenomena which economic theorists seek to explain. For too long, however, economists have paid only lip service to this fact and have resorted to makeshift devices. This book is the first systematic attempt to build a dynamic theory of entrepreneurial learning based upon Popper's ideas on the growth of knowledge. The thoroughgoing application of Popper makes a significant contribution towards upgrading the treatment of knowledge and learning in economic theory.

One of the objectives of Part III has been to appraise the GK theory of entrepreneurship. According to the standards of Lakatos's (1970: 119) methodology of scientific research programmes, it can be argued that the GK theory (which is the first in a series) is scientific because it is at least theoretically progressive. Novel predictions can be deduced from the new theory which are not derivable from competing theories of the entrepreneur. Some of these predictions are both temporally and logically novel (cf. Musgrave 1974a, 1978). The new theory makes predictions which conflict with those of previous theories of entrepreneurship as well as predicting phenomena, about which rival theories remain silent.

The logical novelty of the new theory includes its explanation of entrepreneurial learning. By formally building in explicit conjectures about the entrepreneur's methodology and the nature of entrepreneurial knowledge, the new theory lays the groundwork for explaining entrepreneurial learning and the endogenous dynamics of the market process. Even though they characterise the entrepreneur as a type of learner, at least two previous theories (namely, those of Kirzner and Casson) fail to elucidate the entrepreneur's learning methodology and/or implicitly rely upon inadequate justificationist theories of knowledge and learning. They are not able to explain entrepreneurial learning in the market context on the basis of entrepreneurial alertness or judgment alone. As a result, their conception of entrepreneurial knowledge is not wholly dynamic.

The study has also outlined a test by which the excess empirical content of the GK theory could potentially be corroborated. This test will involve obtaining new kinds of evidence at the micro-analytic level (such as that acquired by the *Entrepreneurial Learning Methodology Inventory*). Only independent empirical testing can determine whether the GK theory of the entrepreneur represents an empirically progressive as well as a theoretically progressive problem shift. It may take some time before the GK programme is seen not only to predict but also to produce genuinely novel facts, that is, to lead to the actual discovery of some hitherto unexpected facts.

I make no pretensions to having produced a theoretical system that can compete with the neoclassical (microeconomic) research programme. At this stage in its development, the GK programme does not by any means offer a complete and coherent alternative to the neoclassical programme. But the GK approach has the potential to solve problems for which neoclassical economics is ill-suited. It provides a fresh approach to crucial issues that have largely been ignored by mainstream theory; let us not forget that there is *no* neoclassical theory of entrepreneurship. Some commentators may argue that there is no reason to abandon or to do research outside the neoclassical research programme until a 'really convincing' replacement is in place (Blaug 1980: 186). However, I regard such a blinkered strategy as inhibiting the growth of knowledge in economic theory. A replacement to neoclassical theory will only emerge if a number of new theories is offered for extensive theoretical development and empirical trials.

Popper and Lakatos emphasise the importance to the growth of knowledge of proposing a sufficient number of competing theories of sufficient variety (Lakatos 1970: 121; Popper 1963: 313). Given the absence of a well-corroborated economic theory of the entrepreneur, the development and testing of rival theoretical systems in this area should be regarded as a priority on the agenda of economic research. The GK theory is one such candidate which has just entered the competitive arena. The fruitfulness of the GK research programme itself can only be decided as further theoretical and empirical work within it is undertaken. The long-term survival of the GK programme, as for all theoretical innovations, will ultimately depend upon its performance relative to that of competing theory-sequencies – its ability to solve problems better than its rivals.

Given that there is an entrepreneurial element in all decision-making, and that this theory sheds new light on what constitutes entrepreneurship, it follows that the GK approach has profound ramifications for our very conception of economic decision-making. Consequently, the GK approach may have effects which extend well beyond its original and intended target. Indeed, the approach could be applied to a wide spectrum of economic behaviour and could lead to the development of new theories of demand (consumer behaviour), of the firm, of investment, and even of the business cycle.

The GK theory is a fertile approach which makes bold new predictions about entrepreneurial behaviour and the character of the market process. It deserves to be developed further and tested empirically so that we can have a real opportunity to find out its strength. I am optimistic about its prospects.

NOTES

1 Venture capital is defined here as equity provided to highly uncertain – not necessarily high-tech – activities, and it is primarily associated with financing small, potentially high growth, innovative companies at an early stage of their development.
2 See Harper (1992: chs 10, 11) for an initial attempt at such an application.
3 See: Burker (1983); Jelinek, Smircich and Hirsch (1983); Kilmann, Saxton and Serpa (1985, 1986); Lorsch (1986); O'Toole (1979); Pettigrew (1979); Schwartz and Davis (1981); and Tunstall (1986).
4 Some models in the strategic management literature also provide an account of Kuhnian 'normal' strategic behaviour in organisations. In what Ansoff calls *ad hoc* management models, for example,

the perspective is psycho-sociological. Managers are very much in evidence and they drive the firm to high performance *norms*. But they do this within a sympathetic *historical culture*, and are therefore able to gain a supportive *consensus* for their decisions. While the power of inertia is strong, managers use this power by sticking to *incremental changes*, consistent with historical behavior of the firm.

(Ansoff 1987: 509; emphasis added)

Two examples are Quinn's (1978, 1980b) model of logical increment-alism and Mintzberg's (1973, 1978, 1980) model of strategic behaviour. Mintzberg's model emphasises that although individual managers make their decisions locally without an overall plan of the firm, decisions by different managers will be consistent with one another because they depend upon a shared pattern of experience of the strategic history of the firm. A similar theme has been developed by Nelson and Winter (1982) and Loasby (1989: 202– 206). For other examples of incremental, 'normal' strategic processes, see Fredrickson and Mitchell (1984: 401).

5 Although outside the GK programme, an interesting task would be to apply the rhetorical approach (Klamer 1984; Klamer, McCloskey and Solow 1989; McCloskey 1983, 1986) to the process of strategy formulation in the firm. According to this view, strategy formation would be regarded as a social activity in which CEOs seek to persuade other top managers, middle management and the board of directors by means of rhetorical devices. The process of strategy formation would then be seen to involve managers trying to convince – by argument – an audience of the quality of their own strategic vision. Particular use could be made of Klamer's metaphor of such a communication process as a process of *negotiation* (Klamer *et al.* 1989: ch. 17).

6 In contrast to Kuhnian strategic management models, Ansoff's model assumes that managers will lead the firm into new, *non*-incremental strategic domains whenever technological, socioeconomic or political discontinuities make this necessary for the future success and survival of the firm. It also assumes that organisational inertia will not impede change (Ansoff 1987: 509–510). Like Popper (1976b), Ansoff is rejecting the 'myth of the framework'.

Other models of strategy formulation which characterise the strategic process as highly rational, systematic and comprehensive are: Andrews (1971), Grant and King (1982), Hofer and Schendel (1978), Lorange and Vancil (1977), Steiner (1979) and Thompson and Strickland (1978).

It should be noted that Ansoff's (1984) later work goes beyond a purely rational model of strategic planning to include sociopsychological and political dimensions.

7 The similarity of circumstance is of course from the viewpoint of the observing economist.

8 Venture 'spin-offs' should be distinguished from the specialised form of 'spin-outs'. In the case of venture spin-offs, the parent firm maintains trade relations with the fledgling start-up and participates in capitalisa-tion through a minority position (Allen 1985: 40). In the case of venture spin-outs, the parent organisation does not separate itself from

the organisational subunit but simply changes its status, by forming an independent subsidiary, for example. The existing organisational subunit is removed from the structure of the parent corporation but the ownership conditions remain the same (Hanan 1969a; 1976: 129ff.; Nathusius 1979: 237).

9 Remenyi's (1979) approach also focuses on the role of conflict resolution within this evolutionary process: in particular, the role of academic and institutional defence mechanisms of a discipline in combating rival theories and core-threatening anomalies.

10 See too the literature on the development process in new and small entrepreneurial firms: Buchele (1967); Charan, Hofer and Mahan (1980); Churchill and Lewis (1983); A. C. Cooper (1979, 1981); Galbraith (1982); Greiner (1972); Hofer and Schendel (1978); and Kimberly and Miles (1980). See too Penrose (1959). These models typically describe the development of the firm as an internal process of linear and incremental growth (Jarillo 1989: 135; Lorenzoni and Ornati 1988: 41–42). In contrast, 'external-growth' models describe an entirely different pattern of growth for entrepreneurial firms: the use of external resources to grow beyond the limits set by the firm's current financial, technological and managerial resources.

11 However, the transaction cost literature does recognise that opportunism may inhibit the discovery of new problems. Keller's (1989) book on General Motors suggests that cultural factors may also impinge upon the extent to which knowledge of problems is transmitted within the firm. According to Keller, GM managers attempted to conceal problems that they had discovered. When working in a Japanese environment as part of a joint venture, they were astounded at how Japanese managers regarded problems as opportunities which are to be shared with other managers in the organisation. For a further examination of how differences in (expected) opportunistic behaviour may affect comparative organisational structures in the US and Japan, see the chapter by Casson and Nicholas in Casson (1990a: 105–124).

12 On the role of Confucian ethics in Japanese firms, see Dore (1973). On the process of learning within Japanese companies, see too Abegglen and Stalk (1985), Aoki (1990), Aoki and Rosenberg (1989), Imai, Nonaka and Takeuchi (1985), Kono (1984), Moroshima (1982), and Yoshino (1968). Aoki (1986) and Itoh (1987) also examine how Japanese learning mechanisms coordinate activity directed at solving problems.

13 As a guide, see Harper (1994b) for an analysis of public policy and entrepreneurship from an Austrian perspective.

BIBLIOGRAPHY

Aaker, D.A. and Day, G.S. (1980) *Marketing Research: Private and Public Sector Decisions*, New York: John Wiley & Sons.

Abegglen, J.C. and Stalk, G. (1985) *Kaisha, The Japanese Corporation*, New York: Basic Books.

Achenbaum, A.A. (1964) 'The Purpose of Test Marketing', in R.M. Kaplan (ed.) *The Marketing Concept in Action*, Chicago, Ill.: American Marketing Association.

—— (1974) 'Market Testing: Using the Marketplace as a Laboratory', in Ferber (1974), 4-31 to 4-54.

Ackermann, R.J. (1976) *The Philosophy of Karl Popper*, Amherst, Mass.: University of Massachusetts Press.

Adams-Webber, J.R. (1979) *Personal Construct Theory: Concepts and Applications*, Chichester: Wiley.

Adorno, T.W., Albert, H., Dahrendorf, R., Habermas, J., Pilot, H. and Popper, K. (1976) *The Positivist Dispute in German Sociology*, London: Heinemann, First German edition (1969).

Agassi, J. (1959) 'Corroboration versus Induction', *British Journal for the Philosophy of Science* 9, 311–317.

—— (1961) 'The Role of Corroboration in Popper's Methodology', *Australasian Journal of Philosophy* 39, 82–91.

—— (1964) 'The Nature of Scientific Problems and Their Roots in Metaphysics', in Bunge (1964a), 189–211.

—— (1966) 'Sensationalism', *Mind* 75, January, 1–24.

—— (1969) 'The Novelty of Popper's Philosophy of Science', *International Philosophical Quarterly* 8, 442–463.

—— (1971a) *Faraday as a Natural Philosopher*, Chicago, Ill.: University of Chicago Press.

—— (1971b) 'The Standard Misinterpretation of Skepticism', *Philosophical Studies* 22(4), June, 49–50.

—— (1975) 'Institutional Individualism', *British Journal of Sociology*, 26, 144–155.

Aitken, H.G.J. (1965a) 'Entrepreneurial Research: The History of an Intellectual Innovation', in Aitken (1965b), 3–19.

—— (ed.) (1965b) *Explorations in Enterprise*, Cambridge, Mass.: Harvard University Press.

—— (1965c) 'Points of View', in Aitken (1965b), 23–29.

361

Akerlof, G.A. and Dickens, W.T. (1982) 'The Economic Consequences of Cognitive Dissonance', *American Economic Review* 72, 307–319.

Albert, H. (1967) *Marktsoziologie und Entscheidungslogik: Ökonomische Probleme in soziologischer Perspektive*, Neuwied am Rhein: Luchterhand.

Alchian, A.A. (1950) 'Uncertainty, Evolution, and Economic Theory', *Journal of Political Economy* 57 (June), 211–221.

—— (1953) 'Biological Analogies of the Firm: Comment', *American Economic Review* 42(4), 600–603.

—— (1984) 'Specificity, Specialization, and Coalitions', *Zeitschrift für die gesamte Staatswissenschaft* 140(1), 34–49.

Alderson, W. (1971) 'Advertising Strategy and Theories of Motivation', in A.S.C. Ehrenberg and F.G. Pyatt (eds) *Consumer Behaviour: Selected Readings*, Harmondsworth, England: Penguin Books.

Allen, D.N. (1985) 'An Entrepreneurial Marriage: Business Incubators and Startups', in Hornaday, Shils, Timmons and Vesper (1985), 38–60.

Amsterdamski, S. (1975) *Between Science and Metaphysics, Boston Studies in the Philosophy of Science*, Volume 35, Dordrecht: Reidl Publishing Co.

Anderson, E. and Schmittlein, D. (1984) 'Integration of the Sales Force: An Empirical Examination', *The Rand Journal of Economics* 15, 385–395.

Anderson, T.L. and Hill, P.J. (undated) 'The Contractual Nature of Entrepreneurship', mimeo.

Andrews, K.R. (1971) *The Concept of Corporate Strategy*, Homewood, Ill.: Dow Jones–Irwin.

Ansoff, H.I. (1965) *Corporate Strategy: An Analytic Approach to Business Policy for Growth and Expansion*, New York: McGraw-Hill.

—— (1984) *Implanting Strategic Management*, New York: Prentice-Hall International.

—— (1987) 'The Emerging Paradigm of Strategic Behavior', *Strategic Management Journal* 8, 501–515.

Aoki, M. (1986) 'Horizontal vs. Vertical Information Structure of the Firm', *American Economic Review* 76(5), December, 971–983.

—— (1990) 'Toward an Economic Model of the Japanese Firm', *Journal of Economic Literature* 28, March, 1–27.

Aoki, M. and Rosenberg, N. (1989) 'The Japanese Firm as an Innovating Institution', in T. Shiraishi and S. Tsuru (eds) *Economic Institutions in a Dynamic Society*, London: Macmillan Press, 137–154.

Appelbaum, W. and Spears, R.F. (1950) 'Controlled Experimentation in Marketing Research', *Journal of Marketing* 14, January, 505–517.

Apter, D.E. (ed.) (1964) *Ideology and Discontent*, New York: Free Press.

Argenti, J. (1976a) *Corporate Collapse: The Causes and Symptoms*, New York: John Wiley & Sons, Inc.

—— (1976b) 'How Can You Tell If They Are Going Bust?', *Accountancy* 87, October, 42–44.

Argyris, C. and Schon, D. (1983) *Reasoning, Learning and Action*, San Francisco, Calif.: Jossey-Bass.

Armour, H.O. and Teece, D.J. (1978) 'Organizational Structure and Economic Performance: A Test of the Multidivisional Hypothesis', *Bell Journal of Economics* 9(1), 106–122.

Aronson, E. (1968) 'Dissonance Theory: Progress and Problems', in R.P. Abelson *et al.*, (eds), *Theories of Cognitive Consistency: A Sourcebook*, Chicago, Ill.: Rand McNally.

—— (1979) *The Social Animal*, third edition, San Francisco, Calif.: W.H. Freeman.

Arrow, K.J. (1959) 'Towards a Theory of Price Adjustment', in M. Abramovitz (ed.) *The Allocation of Economic Resources*, Stanford, Calif.: Stanford University Press, 1959, 41–51.

Arrow, K.J. (1968) 'Economic Equilibrium', in D.L. Sills (ed.), *International Encyclopedia of the Social Sciences* 4, 376–388.

—— (1974) *The Limits of Organization*, New York: W. W. Norton & Co.

Arrow, K.J. and Hahn, F.H. (1971) *General Competitive Analysis*, San Francisco, Calif.: Holden Bay.

Arrow, K.J. and Hurwicz, L. (1958) 'On the Stability of the Competitive Equilibrium, I', *Econometrica* 26, 522–552.

Arrow, K.J., Block, H.D. and Hurwicz, L. (1959) 'On the Stability of the Competitive Equilibrium, II', *Econometrica* 27, 82–109.

Austin Smith, R. (1966) *Corporations in Crisis*, New York: Anchor Books/Doubleday.

Baaken, T. (1989) *Bewertung technologieorientierter Unternehmensgründungen*, Berlin: Erich Schmidt Verlag.

Bacharach, M.O.L. (1986) 'The Problem of Agents' Beliefs in Economic Theory', in Baranzini and Scazzieri (1986), 175–204.

Bailey, J.E. (1986) 'Learning Styles of Successful Entrepreneurs', in Rondstadt, Hornaday, Peterson and Vesper (1986), 199–210.

Baird, C.W. (1987) '*The Economics of Time and Ignorance*: A Review', in Rothbard (1987b), 189–206.

Banks, S. (1965) *Experimentation in Marketing*, New York: McGraw-Hill.

—— (1974) 'Experimental Design and Control', in Ferber (1974), 2-472 to 2-498.

Bannister, D. and Fransella, F. (1980) *Inquiring Man: The Psychology of Personal Constructs*, second edition, Harmondsworth: Penguin Books.

Bannister, D. and Mair, J.M.M. (1968) *The Evaluation of Personal Constructs*, New York: Academic Press.

Baran, P. and Sweezy, P. (1966) *Monopoly Capital*, New York: Monthly Review Press.

Baranzini, M. and Scazzieri, R. (1986) *Foundations of Economics: Structures of Inquiry in Economic Theory*, Oxford: Basil Blackwell.

Barnard, C. (1968) *The Functions of the Executive*, Cambridge, Mass.: Harvard University Press.

Barreto, H. (1989) *The Entrepreneur in Microeconomic Theory: Disappearance and Explanation*, London: Routledge.

Bartlett, F.C. (1932) *Remembering*, New York: Cambridge University Press.

Bartley, W.W., III (1964) 'Rationality versus the Theory of Rationality', in Bunge (1964a), 3–31.

—— (1976) 'On Imre Lakatos', in Cohen, Feyerabend and Wartofsky (1976), 37–38.

363

—— (1982) 'The Philosophy of Karl Popper: Part III. Rationality, Criticism and Logic', *Philosophia* 11, February, 121–221.

—— (1984) *The Retreat to Commitment*, second edition, revised and enlarged, La Salle, Ill.: Open Court. First edition 1962.

Baumol, W.J. (1965) *Economic Theory and Operations Analysis*, second edition, Englewood Cliffs, N.J.: Prentice-Hall, Inc.

—— (1968), 'Entrepreneurship in Economic Theory', *American Economic Review*, Papers and Proceedings, 58, 64–71.

—— (1990) 'Entrepreneurship: Productive, Unproductive, and Destructive', *Journal of Political Economy* 98(5), Part 1, October, 893–921.

—— (1993) *Entrepreneurship, Management, and the Structure of Payoffs*, Cambridge, Mass.: MIT Press.

Bausor, R. (1982) 'Time and the Structure of Economic Analysis', *Journal of Post Keynesian Economics* 5(2), 163–179.

Bazerman, M.H., Beekun, R.I. and Schoorman, F.D. (1982) 'Performance Evaluation in a Dynamic Context: A Laboratory Study of the Impact of a Prior Commitment to the Ratee', *Journal of Applied Psychology* 67(6), December, 873–876.

Becker, G.S. (1971) *Economic Theory*, New York: Knopf.

Begley, T.M. and Boyd, D.P. (1987) 'Psychological Characteristics Associated with Performance in Entrepreneurial Firms and Smaller Businesses', *Journal of Business Venturing* 2(1), 79–93.

Belk, R.W. (1974) 'An Exploratory Assessment of Situational Effects in Buyer Behavior', *Journal of Marketing Research* 11, May, 156–163.

—— (1975a) 'The Objective Situation as a Determinant of Consumer Behavior', *Advances in Consumer Research* 2, 427–437.

—— (1975b) 'Situational Variables and Consumer Behavior', *Journal of Consumer Reasearch* 2(Dec.), 157–164.

Berger, B. (1991) *The Culture of Entrepreneurship*, San Francisco, Calif.: ICS (Institute for Contemporary Studies) Press.

Bergson, H. (1910) *Time and Free Will*, London: George Allen & Unwin. Translated by F.L. Pogson.

Best, M.H. (1990) *The New Competition: Institutions of Industrial Restructuring*, Oxford: Polity Press.

Biggadike, R. (1979) 'The Risky Business of Diversification', *Harvard Business Review*, May-June, 103–111.

Birner, J. (1985) 'Review of Lawrence A. Boland's (1982) "The Foundations of Economic Method"', *British Journal for the Philosophy of Science* 36, June, 215–221.

Blaseio, H. (1986) *Das Kognos-Prinzip. Zur Dynamik sich-selbstorganisierender wirtschaftlicher und sozialer Systeme*, Volkswirtschaftliche Schriften, Heft 364, Berlin: Duncker & Humblot.

Blaug, M. (1980) *The Methodology of Economics: Or How Economists Explain*, Cambridge: Cambridge University Press.

—— (1985) 'Comment on D. Wade Hands, "Karl Popper and Economic Methodology: A New Look"', *Economics and Philosophy* 1, 286–288.

Block, Z. (1982) 'Can Corporate Venturing Succeed?', *Journal of Business Strategy* 3(2), Fall, 21–33.

—— (1989) 'Damage Control for New Corporate Ventures', *The Journal of Business Strategy*, March–April, 22–28.

Block, Z. and MacMillan, I.C. (1985) 'Milestones for Successful Venture Planning', *Harvard Business Review*, September–October, 184–188.

Bloor, D. (1971) 'Two Paradigms for Scientific Knowledge?', *Science Studies* 1, 101–115.

—— (1974) 'Popper's Mystification of Objective Knowledge', *Science Studies* 4, 65–76.

Blume, L. and Easley, D. (1982) 'Learning to be Rational', *Journal of Economic Theory* 26, 340–351.

Blume, L., Bray, M.M. and Easley, D. (1982) 'Introduction to the Stability of Rational Expectations Equilibrium', *Journal of Economic Theory* 26, 313–317.

Boettke, P.J. (ed.) (1994) *The Elgar Companion to Austrian Economics*, Aldershot: Edward Elgar Publishing.

Boettke, P.J., Kirzner, I.M., and Rizzo, M.J. (eds) (1994) *Advances in Austrian Economics*, 1, Greenwich, Connecticut: JAI Press.

Böhm, S. (1986) 'Time and Equilibrium: Hayek's Notion of Inter-temporal Equilibrium Reconsidered', in Kirzner (1986b), 16–29.

—— (1992) 'Conversation: Austrian Economics and the Theory of Entrepreneurship: Israel M. Kirzner Interviewed by Stephan Böhm on 2 May 1989', *Review of Political Economy* 4 (1): 95–110.

Böhm-Bawerk, E. von (1959) *Capital and Interest*, Volume Two, *The Positive Theory of Capital*, South Holland, Ill.: Libertarian Press. Translated by G. D. Huncke and H. F. Sennholz.

Boland, L.A. (1977) 'Testability in Economic Science', *The South African Journal of Economics* 45(1), 93–105.

—— (1978) 'Time in Economics vs. Economics in Time: the "Hayek" Problem', *Canadian Journal of Economics* 11, 240–262.

—— (1979a) 'A Critique of Friedman's Critics', *Journal of Economic Literature* 17 (June), 503–522.

—— (1979b) 'Knowledge and the Role of Institutions in Economic Theory', *Journal of Economic Issues* 13(4), 957–972.

—— (1980) 'Friedman's Methodology vs. Conventional Empiricism: A Reply to Rotwein', *Journal of Economic Literature* 18, 1555–1557.

—— (1982) *The Foundations of Economic Method*, London: George Allen & Unwin.

—— (1986a) 'Methodology and the Individual Decision Maker', in Kirzner (1986b), 30–38.

—— (1986b) *Methodology for a New Microeconomics. The Critical Foundations*, Boston, Mass.: Allen & Unwin.

Boland, L.A. and Newman, G. (1979) 'On the Role of Knowledge in Economic Theory', *Australian Economic Papers* 18(June), 71–80.

Borland, C. (1974) 'Locus of Control, Need for Achievement and Entre-preneurship', Doctoral Dissertation, The University of Texas at Austin.

Bosch, A., Koslowski, P., and Veit, R. (eds) (1990) *General Equilibrium or Market Process: Neoclassical and Austrian Theories of Economics*, Tubingen: Mohr.

Boulding, K.E. (1956) 'General Systems Theory – The Skeleton of Science', *Management Science* 2(3), 197–208.

—— (1966a) 'The Economics of Knowledge and the Knowledge of Economics', *American Economic Review, Papers and Proceedings* 56(2), May, 1–13.

—— (1966b) 'The Ethics of Rational Decision', *Management Science*, Series B, 12, 161–169.

—— (1978) *Ecodynamics: A New Theory of Societal Evolution*, Beverly Hills, Calif.: Sage Publications.

—— (1981) *Evolutionary Economics*, Beverly Hills, Calif.: Sage Publications.

Bray, M.M. (1982) 'Learning, Estimation and the Stability of Rational Expectations', *Journal of Economic Theory* 26, April, 318–339.

—— (1983) 'Convergence to Rational Expectations Equilibrium', in R. Frydman and E.S. Phelps (eds) *Individual Forecasting and Aggregate Outcomes*, Cambridge: Cambridge University Press.

Bray, M.M. and Kreps, D.M. (1987) 'Rational Learning and Rational Expectations', in G.R. Feiwel (ed.) *Arrow and the Ascent of Modern Economic Theory*, New York: New York University Press.

Bray, M.M. and Savin, N.E. (1986) 'Rational Expectations Equilibrium, Learning, and Model Specification', *Econometrica* 54(5), September, 1129–1160.

Brennan, T.J. (1984) 'Is Economics Methodologically Special?', in Samuels (1984), 127–140.

Brewer, A. (1990) *Marxist Theories of Imperialism: A Critical Survey*, second edition, London: Routledge.

Brockhaus, R.H. (1975) 'I-E Locus of Control Scores as Predictors of Entrepreneurial Intentions', *Proceedings*, New Orleans: Academy of Management.

—— (1980) 'The Effect of Job Dissatisfaction on the Decision to Start a Business', *Journal of Small Business Management* 18(1), 37–43.

—— (1982) 'The Psychology of the Entrepreneur', in Kent, Sexton and Vesper (1982), 39–57.

Brockhaus, R.H. and Horwitz, P.S. (1986) 'The Psychology of the Entrepreneur', in Sexton and Smilor (1986), 25–48.

Brockhaus, R.H. and Nord, W.R. (1979) 'An Exploration of Factors Affecting the Entrepreneurial Decision: Personal Characteristics vs. Environmental Conditions', *Proceedings of the National Academy of Management.*

Brockner, J. and Rubin, J.Z. (1985) *Entrapment in Escalating Conflicts*, New York: Springer-Verlag.

Brooks, J.N. (1963) *The Fate of the Edsel and Other Business Adventures*, New York: Harper and Row.

Brown, E.K. (1981) 'The Neoclassical and Post-Keynesian Research Programs: The Methodological Issues', *Review of Social Economy* 39(2), 111–132. Reprinted in Caldwell (1984a), 438–459. (Page references are to the original.)

Buchanan, J.M. (1969) *Cost and Choice: An Inquiry in Economic Theory*, Chicago, Ill.: University of Chicago Press.

—— (1973) 'Introduction: L.S.E Cost Theory in Retrospect', in Buchanan and Thirlby (1973), 1–18.

Buchanan, J.M., and Faith, R.L. (1981) 'Entrepreneurship and the

Internalization of Externalities', *Journal of Law and Economics* 24(1), April, 95–111.

Buchanan, J.M. and Thirlby, G.F. (eds) (1973) *L.S.E. Essays on Cost*, Birkenhead: Willmer Brothers.

Buchanan, J.M. and Vanberg, V.J. (1991) 'The Market as a Creative Process', *Economics and Philosophy* 7: 167–186.

Buchele, R.B. (1967) *Business Policy in Growing Firms: A Manual for Evaluation*, San Francisco, Calif.: Chandler Pub. Co.

Buck, R.C. and Cohen, R.S. (1971) *Boston Studies in the Philosophy of Science* 8, PSA 1970 – In Memory of Rudolf Carnap, Proceedings of the 1970 Biennial Meeting, Philosophy of Science Association, Dordrecht-Holland: D. Reidel Publishing Company.

Buckley, W. (ed.) (1968) *Modern Systems Research for the Behavioral Scientist. A Sourcebook*, Chicago, Ill.: Aldine Publishing Co.

Bunge, M. (ed.) (1964a) *The Critical Approach to Science and Philosophy: Essays in Honor of Karl R. Popper*, New York: The Free Press of Clencoe.

—— (1964b) 'Phenomenological Theories', in Bunge (1964a), 234–254.

Burke, T.E. (1983) *The Philosophy of Popper*, Manchester: Manchester University Press.

Burker, W. (ed.) (1983) 'Special Issue on Organizational Culture', *Organizational Dynamics*, Autumn.

Burton, J. (1983) 'Picking Losers . . . ?', *Hobart Paper*, 99, London: Institute of Economic Affairs.

Butters, G.R. (1977) 'Equilibrium Distributions of Sales and Advertising Prices', *Review of Economic Studies* 44(3), no.138, 465–491.

Buzzell, R.D., Gale, B.T. and Sultan, R.G.M. (1975) 'Market Share – A Key to Profitability', *Harvard Business Review*, January-February, 97–105.

Cadbury, N.D. (1975) 'When, Where and How to Test Market', *Harvard Business Review*, May–June, 96–105.

Caldwell, B.J. (1980a) 'A Critique of Friedman's Methodological Instrumentalism', *Southern Economic Journal*, October, 366–374. Reprinted in Caldwell (1984a), 225–233.

—— (1980b) 'Positivist Philosophy of Science and the Methodology of Economics', *Journal of Economic Issues*, March, 53–76.

—— (1982) *Beyond Positivism: Economic Methodology in the Twentieth Century*, London: George Allen & Unwin.

—— (ed.) (1984a) *Appraisal and Criticism in Economics. A Book of Readings*, Boston, Mass.: Allen & Unwin.

—— (1984b) 'Economic Methodology in the Post-Positivist Era', in Samuels (1984), 195–205.

—— (1984c) 'Some Problems with Falsificationism in Economics', *Philosophy of the Social Sciences* 14, 489–495.

—— (1991) 'Clarifying Popper', *Journal of Economic Literature* 29 (March), 1–33.

Caldwell, B.J. and Böhm, S. (eds) (1993) *Austrian Economics: Tensions and New Directions*, Boston, Mass.: Kluwer Academic Publishers.

Campbell, D.T. (1969) 'Reforms as Experiments', *American Psychologist*, April, 409–429.

—— (1974) 'Evolutionary Epistemology', in Schlipp (1974), 413–463.

Cantillon, R. (1931) *Essai sur la nature du commerce en général*, London: Royal Economic Society. Edited and translated by H. Higgs.

Capek, M. (1971) *Bergson and Modern Physics*, Dordrecht, Holland: D. Reidel.

Casson, M.C. (1982) *The Entrepreneur*, Oxford: Martin Robertson & Company.

—— (1987a) 'Entrepreneurship', in J. Eatwell, M. Milgate and P. Newman (eds) *The New Palgrave: A Dictionary of Economics*, London: Macmillan, 1987.

—— (1987b) *The Firm and the Market: Studies on Multinational Enterprise and the Scope of the Firm*, Oxford: Basil Blackwell.

—— (1990a) *Enterprise and Competitiveness: A Systems View of International Business*, Oxford: Clarendon Press.

—— (ed.) (1990b) *Entrepreneurship*, Aldershot: Edward Elgar Publishing.

—— (1991) *The Economics of Business Culture: Game Theory, Transaction Costs, and Ecomomic Performance*, Oxford: Clarendon Press.

Chalmers, A.F. (1982) *What is This Thing Called Science?*, second edition, Milton Keynes: Open University Press. First edition 1978.

Chan, Y.S. (1983) 'On the Positive Role of Financial Intermediation in the Allocation of Venture Capital in a Market with Imperfect Information', *Journal of Finance* 38(5), December, 1543–1568.

Chandler, A.D., Jr. (1962) *Strategy and Structure: Chapters in the History of the Industrial Enterprise*, Cambridge, Mass.: MIT Press.

—— (1977) *The Visible Hand: The Managerial Revolution in American Business*, Cambridge, Mass.: Belknap Press.

Chandler, A.D., Jr. and Daems, H. (eds) (1980) *Managerial Hierarchies: Comparative Perspectives on the Rise of the Modern Industrial Enterprise*, Cambridge, Mass.: Harvard University Press.

Charan, R.W., Hofer, C.W. and Mahan, J.H. (1980) 'From Entrepreneurial to Professional Management: A Set of Guidelines', *Journal of Small Business Management* 19, 1–10.

Choi, Y.B. (1993) *Paradigms and Conventions: Uncertainty, Decision Making and Entrepreneurship*, Ann Arbor, Mich.: University of Michigan Press.

Churchill, N.C. and Lewis, V.L. (1983) 'The Five Stages of Small Business Growth', *Harvard Business Review* 3, 30–50.

Coats, A.W. (1976) 'Economics and Psychology: The Death and Resurrection of a Research Programme', in Latsis (1976b), 43–64.

—— (1983) 'The Revival of Subjectivism in Economics', in Wiseman (1983b), 87–103.

Coddington, A. (1982) 'Deficient Foresight: A Troublesome Theme in Keynesian Economics', *American Economic Review* 72(3), 480–487.

Cohen, M.D. and Axelrod, R. (1984) 'Coping with Complexity', *American Economic Review* 74(1), 30–42.

Cohen, R.S., Feyerabend, P.K. and Wartofsky, M.W. (eds) (1976) *Essays in Memory of Imre Lakatos*, Boston Studies in the Philosophy of Science, 39, Dordrecht: D. Reidel Publishing Co.

Cole, A.H. (1965) 'An Approach to the Study of Entrepreneurship', in Aitken (1965b), 30–44.

—— (1968) 'The Entrepreneur: Introductory Remarks', *American Economic Review* 58, 60–63.

Colodny, R. (ed.) (1966) *Mind and Cosmos: Explorations in the Philosophy of Science*, The University of Pittsburgh Series in the Philosophy of Science, Volume III, Pittsburgh, Pa.: University of Pittsburgh Press.

Comegys, C. (1976) 'Cognitive Dissonance and Entrepreneurial Behavior', *Journal of Small Business Management*, January.

Conlon, E.J. and Wolf, G. (1980) 'The Moderating Effects of Strategy, Visibility and Involvement on Allocation Behaviour: An Extension of Staw's Escalation Paradigm', *Organizational Behaviour and Human Performance* 26(2), October, 172–192.

Converse, P.E. (1964) 'The Nature of Belief Systems in Mass Publics', in Apter (1964), 206–261.

Cooper, A.C. (1979) 'Strategic Management: New Ventures and Small Business', in Schendel and Hofer (1979), 316–327.

—— (1981) 'Strategic Management: New Ventures and Small Business', *Long Range Planning* 14(5), 39–45.

Cooper, A.C. and Bruno, A.V. (1977) 'Success Among High-Technology Firms', *Business Horizons*, April, 16–22.

Cooper, I.A. and Carleton, W.T. (1979) 'Dynamics of Borrower-Lender Interaction: Partitioning Final Pay-Off in Venture Capital Finance', *Journal of Finance* 34(2), May, 517–529.

Cooper, R.G. (1975) 'Why New Industrial Products Fail', *Industrial Marketing Management*, 4, January, 315–326.

—— (1979a) 'The Dimensions of Industrial New Product Success and Failure', *Journal of Marketing* 43, Summer, 93–103.

—— (1979b) 'Identifying Industrial New Product Success: Project NewProd', *Industrial Marketing Management* 8, 124–135.

—— (1980) 'Project NewProd: Factors in New Product Success', *European Journal of Marketing* 14(5/6), 277–292.

—— (1983) 'A Process Model for Industrial New Product Development', *IEEE Transactions on Engineering Management*, EM-30, (1), February, 2–11.

Cox, K.K. and Enis, B.M. (1969) *Experimentation for Marketing Decisions*, Scranton, Pa.: International Textbook Co.

Cross, R. (1982) 'The Duhem–Quine Thesis, Lakatos and the Appraisal of Theories in Macroeconomics', *Economic Journal*, June, 320–340. Reprinted in Caldwell (1984a), 284–304.

—— (1984) 'Monetarism and Duhem's Thesis', in Wiles and Routh (1984), 78–99.

Currie, D.A. and Peters, W. (1980) *Contemporary Economic Analysis*, Volume Two, *Papers Presented at the Conference of the Association of University Teachers of Economics 1978*, London: Croom Helm.

Currie, M. and Steedman, I. (1990) *Wrestling with Time: Problems in Economic Theory*, Manchester: Manchester University Press.

Cyert, R.M. and March, J.G. (1963) *A Behavioral Theory of the Firm*, Englewood Cliffs, N.J.: Prentice Hall.

Dahlman, C.J. (1979) 'The Problem of Externality', *Journal of Law and Economics* 22(1), 141–162.

Dahrendorf, R. (1968) *Essays in the Theory of Society*, Stanford, Calif.: Stanford University Press.

Darwin, F. (1888) *The Life and Letters of Charles Darwin*, London: J. Murray. (Includes an Autobiographical chapter.)

Darwin, F. and Seward, A.C. (1903) *More Letters of Charles Darwin: A Record of His Work in a Series of Hitherto Unpublished Letters*, London: J. Murray.

Davidson, P. (1980a) 'The Dual-Faceted Nature of the Keynesian Revolution: Money and Money Wages in Unemployment and Production Flow Prices', *Journal of Post Keynesian Economics* 2(Spring), 291–307.

—— (1980b) 'Post Keynesian Economics: Solving the Crisis in Economic Theory', *The Public Interest*, Special Issue, 151–173.

—— (1991) 'Is Probability Theory Relevant for Uncertainty? A Post Keynesian Perspective', *Journal of Economic Perspectives* 5(1), Winter, 129–143.

Davidson, P. and Davidson, G.S. (1984) 'Financial Markets and Williamson's Theory of Governance: Efficiency versus Concentration versus Power', *Quarterly Review of Economics and Business* 24(4), 50–63.

Davis, E.J. (1970) *Experimental Marketing*, London: Nelson.

—— (1972) 'Market Testing and Experimentation', in Worchester (1972), 494ff.

Day, G.S., Shocker, A.D., and Srivastava, R.K. (1979) 'Customer-Oriented Approaches to Identifying Product-Markets', *Journal of Marketing* 43, Fall, 8–19.

De Sarbo, W., MacMillan, I.C., and Day, D.L. (1987) 'Criteria for Corporate Venturing: Importance Assigned by Managers', *Journal of Business Venturing* 2(4), 329–350.

Debreu, G. (1959) *Theory of Value*, New York: Wiley.

Dennis, K. (1986) 'Boland on Friedman: A Rebuttal', *Journal of Economic Issues* 20(3), 633–660.

Denzau, A.T., and North, D.C. (1994) 'Shared Mental Models: Ideologies and Institutions', *Kyklos* 47 (1): 3–31.

Dessauer, J. (1971) *My Years with Xerox*, New York: Doubleday & Co.

Dewey, J. (1903) *Studies in Logical Theory*, Chicago, Ill.: University of Chicago Press.

Dickson, P.R., (undated) 'The Missing Link', mimeo.

Dietrich, M. (1994) *Transaction Cost Economics and Beyond: Towards a New Economics of the Firm*, London: Routledge.

Dimson, E. (1978) 'Financing the Smaller Company', *Long Range Planning* 11(6), December, 9–13.

Dixon, R. (1989) 'Venture Capitalists and Investment Appraisal', *National Westminster Bank Quarterly Review*, November, 2–21.

Dolan, E.G. (ed.) (1976) *The Foundations of Modern Austrian Economics*, Kansas City, Kan.: Sheed and Ward.

Dominguez, J.R. (1974) *Venture Capital*, Lexington, Mass.: Lexington Books.

Dore, R. (1973) *British Factory, Japanese Factory: The Origins of National Diversity in Industrial Relations*, Berkeley, Calif.: University of California Press.

BIBLIOGRAPHY

Drucker, P.F. (1973) 'On Managing the Public Service Institution', *The Public Interest*, No.33, Fall, 43–60.

Dugger, W.M. (1979) 'Methodological Differences between Institutional and Neoclassical Economics', *Journal of Economic Issues* 13(4), 899–909.

Duhem, P. (1954) *The Aim and Structure of Physical Theory*, Princeton, N.J.: Princeton University Press. First French edition 1906.

Earl, P.E. (1983a) 'The Consumer in his/her Social Setting – A Subjectivist View', in Wiseman (1983b), 176–191.

—— (1983b) *The Economic Imagination. Towards a Behavioural Analysis of Choice*, Armonk, N.Y.: M.E. Sharpe.

—— (1984) *The Corporate Imagination: How Big Companies Make Mistakes*, Armonk, N.Y.: M.E Sharpe.

—— (1986a) 'A Behavioural Analysis of Demand Elasticities', *Journal of Economic Studies* 13(3), 20–37.

—— (1986b) *Lifestyle Economics: Consumer Behaviour in a Turbulent World*, Brighton: Wheatsheaf.

—— (1987) *Scientific Research Programmes, Corporate Strategies, and the Theory of the Firm*, Occasional Papers, 1/87, Information Research Unit, Dept. of Economics, University of Queensland, Brisbane.

—— (ed.) (1988a) *Behavioral Economics*, Volumes One and Two, Schools of Thought in Economics No.6, Aldershot: Edward Elgar.

—— (ed.) (1988b) *Psychological Economics: Development, Tensions, Prospects*, Boston, Mass.: Kluwer Academic Publishers.

—— (1990a) 'Economics and Psychology: A Survey', *The Economic Journal* 100, September, 718–755.

—— (1990b) *Monetary Scenarios: A Modern Approach to Financial Systems*, Aldershot: Edward Elgar.

—— (1992) 'On the Complementarity of Economic Applications of Cognitive Dissonance Theory and Personal Construct Psychology', in S.E.G. Lea, P. Webley, and B. Young (eds) *New Directions in Economic Psychology*, Aldershot: Edward Elgar, 49–65.

Easterbrook, W.T. (1965) 'The Climate of Enterprise', in Aitken (1965b), 65–79.

Eatwell, J., Milgate, M., and Newman, P. (1987) *The New Palgrave: A Dictionary of Economics*, London: Macmillan.

Ebeling, R.M. (1986) 'Toward a Hermeneutical Economics: Expectations, Prices and the Role of Interpretation in a Theory of the Market Process', in Kirzner (1986b), 39–55.

—— (ed.) (1991) *Austrian Economics: A Reader*, Hillsdale, Mich.: Hillsdale College Press.

Edwardes, M. (1983) *Back from the Brink: An Apocalyptic Experience*, London: Collins.

Edwards, P. (ed.) (1967) *The Encyclopedia of Philosophy*, New York: The Macmillan Co. and the Free Press.

Eichner, A.S. and Kregel, J.A. (1975) 'An Essay on Post-Keynesian Theory: A New Paradigm in Economics', *Journal of Economic Literature* 13(4), December, 1293–1314.

Ekelund, R.B., Jr., and Hébert, R.F. (1991) 'Dupuit's Characteristics-

Based Theory of Consumer Behavior and Entrepreneurship', *Kyklos* 44(1), 19–34.

Endres, A.M. (1988) 'Subjectivism, Psychology, and the Modern Austrians: A Comment', in Earl (1988b), 121–124.

Engle, R.F. (1984) 'Wald, Likelihood Ratio, and Lagrange Multiplier Tests in Econometrics', in Griliches and Intriligator (1984), 775–826.

Ericsson, K.A. and Simon, H.A. (1980) 'Verbal Reports as Data', *Psychological Review* 87, 215–251.

Fennell, G. (1978) 'Consumers' Perceptions of the Product-Use Situation', *Journal of Marketing*, April, 38–47.

Ferber, R. (ed.) (1974) *Handbook of Marketing Research*, New York: McGraw-Hill Book Co.

Ferguson, A. (1966) *An Essay on the History of Civil Society*, Edinburgh: Edinburgh University Press. Edited, with a Introduction, by D. Forbes. First published 1767.

Festinger, L. (1957) *A Theory of Cognitive Dissonance*, Stanford, Calif.: Stanford University Press.

Feyerabend, P. (1963) 'How to Be a Good Empiricist – A Plea for Tolerance in Matters Epistemological', in B. Baumrin (ed.) *Philosophy of Science. The Delaware Seminar*, Volume One, New York: John Wiley, 3–40.

—— (1970) 'Consolations for the Specialist', in Lakatos and Musgrave (1970), 197–230.

—— (1975a) *Against Method: An Outline of an Anarchist Theory of Knowledge*, London: New Left Books.

—— (1975b) 'How to Defend Society against Science', *Radical Philosophy* 11, 3–8.

—— (1978) *Science in a Free Society*, London: New Left Books.

Fisher, F.M. (1970) 'Quasi-Competitive Price Adjustment by Individual Firms: A Preliminary Paper', *Journal of Economic Theory* 2, 195–206.

—— (1972) 'On Price Adjustment Without an Auctioneer', *Review of Economic Studies* 39(1), January, 1–15.

—— (1973) 'Stability and Competitive Equilibrium in Two Models of Search and Individual Price Adjustment', *Journal of Economic Theory* 6, 446–470.

—— (1974) 'The Hahn Process with Firms but No Production', *Econometrica* 42(3), May, 471–486.

—— (1976) 'The Stability of General Equilibrium: Results and Problems', in M. J. Artis and A. R. Nobay (eds) *Essays in Economic Analysis (The Proceedings of the Association of University Teachers of Economics, Sheffield 1975)*, London: Cambridge University Press, 1976, 3–29.

—— (1981) 'Stability, Disequilibrium Awareness, and the Perception of New Opportunities', *Econometrica*, March 49(2), 279–317.

—— (1983) *Disequilibrium Foundations of Equilibrium Economics*, Econometric Society Publication No.6, Cambridge: Cambridge University Press.

—— (1987) 'Adjustment Processes and Stability', in J. Eatwell, M. Milgate and P. Newman (eds) *The New Palgrave: A Dictionary of Economics*, London: Macmillan.

Ford, H. (1923) *My Life and Work*, New York: Doubleday, Page & Co.

Fourgeaud, C., Gourieroux, C., and Pradel, J. (1986) 'Learning Procedures and Convergence to Rationality', *Econometrica* 54, July, 845–868.

Frank, P. (1932) *Das Kausalgesetz und seine Grenzen*, Vienna: J. Springer.

Fredrickson, J.W. (1984) 'The Comprehensiveness of Strategic Decision Processes: Extension, Observations, Future Directions', *Academy of Management Journal* 27(3), 445–466.

Fredrickson, J.W. and Mitchell, T.R. (1984) 'Strategic Decision Processes: Comprehensiveness and Performance in an Industry With an Unstable Environment', *Academy of Management Journal* 27(2), 399–423.

Freeman, E. and Skolimowski, H. (1974) 'The Search for Objectivity in Peirce and Popper', in Schlipp (1974), 464–519.

Frydman, R. (1982) 'Towards an Understanding of Market Processes: Individual Expectations, Learning and Convergence to Rational Expectations Equilibrium', *American Economic Review* 72(4), September, 652–668.

Fusfeld, D.R. (1980) 'The Conceptual Framework of Modern Economics', *Journal of Economic Issues* 14, March, 1–52.

Galbraith, J. (1982) 'The Stages of Growth', *Journal of Business Strategy* 3, 70–79.

Gallagher, W.M. (1971) 'The Evaluation and Control of Research and Development Projects', Ph.D Thesis, University of Stirling.

Gasse, Y. (1982) 'Elaborations on the Psychology of the Entrepreneur', in Kent, Sexton and Vesper (1982), 57–71.

—— (1986) 'The Development of New Entrepreneurs: A Belief-Based Approach', in Sexton and Smilor (1986), 49–60.

Georgescu-Roegen, N. (1971) *The Entropy Law and the Economic Process*, Cambridge, Mass.: Harvard University Press.

—— (1987) 'Entropy', in Eatwell, Milgate and Newman (1987), 153–156.

Gibbons, J.D. (1985) *Nonparametric Statistical Inference*, second edition, New York: M. Dekker Inc.

Giedymin, J. (1976) 'Instrumentalism and its Critique: A Reappraisal', in Cohen, Feyerabend and Wartofsky (1976), 179–208.

Gilad, B. (1982) 'On Encouraging Entrepreneurship: An Interdisciplinary Approach', *Journal of Behavioral Economics* 11(1), Summer, 132–163.

—— (1984) 'The Case of the "Partnership Approach" to Public Regulation', *Journal of Economic Psychology* 5, 265–280.

—— (1986) 'Entrepreneurial Decision Making: Some Behavioral Considerations', in Gilad and Kaish (1986), 189–208.

Gilad, B. and Kaish, S. (eds) (1986) *Handbook of Behavioral Economics*, Volume A, *Behavioral Microeconomics*, and Volume B, *Behavioral Macroeconomics*, Greenwich, Conn.: JAI Press.

Gilad, B.,Kaish, S., and Ronen, J. (1988) 'The Entrepreneurial Way with Information', in Maital (1988), 480–503.

Gold, J.A. (1964) 'Testing Test Market Predictions', *Journal of Marketing Research* 1, August, 8–16.

Gomes, G.M. (1982) 'Irrationality of "Rational Expectations"', *Journal of Post Keynesian Economics* 5, 51–65.

Gordon, D. and Hynes, A. (1970) 'On the Theory of Price Dynamics', in E.S. Phelps *et al.*, (eds) *Microfoundations of Income and Employment Theory*, New York: Norton.

Gorman, W.M. (1984) 'Towards a Better Economic Methodology?', in Wiles and Routh (1984), 260–288.

Grant, J.H. and King, W.R. (1982) *The Logic of Strategic Planning*, Boston, Mass.: Little, Brown and Company.

Greiner, L. (1972) 'Evolution and Revolution as Organizations Grow', *Harvard Business Review*, July–August, 37–46.

Griliches, Z. and Intriligator, M.D. (1984) *Handbook of Econometrics*, Volume Two, Amsterdam: North-Holland.

Groenveld, K., Maks, J.A.H., and Muysken, J. (eds) (1990) *Economic Policy and the Market Process: Austrian and Mainstream Economics*, Amsterdam: North-Holland.

Grossman, S.J. and Stiglitz, J.E. (1976) 'Information and Competitive Price Systems', *American Economic Review, Papers and Proceedings* 66(2), May, 246–253.

—— (1980) 'On the Impossibility of Informationally Efficient Markets', *American Economic Review* 70(3), June, 393–408.

Grünbaum, A. (1960) 'The Duhemian Argument', *Philosophy of Science* 2, 75–87.

—— (1962a) 'The Nature of Time', in R.G. Colodny (ed.) *Frontiers of Science and Philosophy*, Pittsburgh, Pa.: University of Pittsburgh Press.

—— (1962b) 'Carnap's Views on the Foundations of Geometry', P.A. Schlipp (ed.) *The Philosophy of Rudolf Carnap*, La Salle, Ill.: Open Court.

—— (1963) *Philosophical Problems of Space and Time*, New York: Knopf.

—— (1976) 'Ad Hoc Auxiliary Hypotheses and Falsificationism', *The British Journal for the Philosophy of Science* 27, 329–362.

—— (1978) 'Popper vs Inductivism', in Radnitzky and Andersson (1978b), 117–142.

Guilford, J.P. (1967) 'Some Theoretical Views of Creativity', in H. Helson amd W. Bevan (eds) *Contemporary Approaches to Psychology*, Princeton, N.J.: Van Nostrand, 419–459.

Gumpert, D.E., and Timmons, J.A. (1982) *Insider's Guide to Small Business Resources*, New York: Doubleday.

Gutman, J. (1982) 'A Means-End Chain Model Based on Consumer Categorization Processes', *Journal of Marketing* 46, Spring, 60–72.

Hahn, F.H. (1962) 'On the Stability of Pure Exchange Equilibrium', *International Economic Review* 3, May, 206–214.

—— (1970) 'Some Adjustment Problems', *Econometrica* 38, January, 1–17.

—— (1980) 'General Equilibrium Theory', *Public Interest*, special edition, 123–138.

—— (1987) 'The Auctioneer', in Eatwell, Milgate and Newman (1987), 136–138.

Hahn, F.H. and Negishi, T. (1962) 'A Theorem on Non-Tâtonnement Stability', *Econometrica* 30(3), July, 463–469.

Haley, R.I. (1968) 'Benefit Segmentation: A Decision-Oriented Research Tool', *Journal of Marketing* 32, July, 30–35.

Haley, R.I. and Gatty, R. (1968) 'The Trouble With Concept Testing', *Journal of Advertising Research*, June, 23–35.

—— (1971) 'The Trouble With Concept Testing', *Journal of Marketing Research*, May, 230–232.

Hamberg, D. (1963) 'Invention in the Industrial Research Laboratory', *Journal of Political Economy* 71(2), April, 95–115.

Hamilton, R.T. and Harper, D.A. (1994) 'The Entrepreneur in Theory and Practice', *Journal of Economic Studies* 21(6), 3–18.

Hanan, M. (1969a) 'Corporate Growth through Internal Spin-Outs', *Harvard Business Review*, November/December, 55–66.

—— (1969b) 'Corporate Growth through Venture Management. Innovative Team Approach Seeks Out New Business Opportunities and Plans the Company's Profitable Entry into Them', *Harvard Business Review*, January/February, 43–61.

—— (1976) *Venture Management: A Game Plan for Corporate Growth and Diversification*, New York: McGraw-Hill Inc.

Hands, D.W. (1985a) 'Karl Popper and Economic Methodology', *Economics and Philosophy* 1, 83–99.

—— (1985b) 'Second Thoughts on Lakatos', *History of Political Economy* 17(1), 1–16.

Hanson, N.R. (1958) *Patterns of Discovery. An Inquiry into the Conceptual Foundations of Science*, Cambridge: Cambridge University Press.

Harding, S.G. (ed.) (1976) *Can Theories Be Refuted? Essays on the Duhem–Quine Thesis*, Dordrecht: D. Reidel.

Harper, D.A. (1989) *Entrepreneurship and the Market Process*, Discussion Paper in Economics, Series A, Vol II, no. 220, Department of Economics, University of Reading.

—— (1992) 'Entrepreneurship and the Market Process: An Inquiry into the Growth of Knowledge', PhD thesis, University of Reading.

—— (1994a) 'A New Approach to Modeling Endogenous Learning Processes in Economic Theory', in Boettke, Kirzner and Rizzo (1994): 49–79.

—— (1994b) *Wellsprings of Enterprise: An Analysis of Entrepreneurship and Public Policy in New Zealand*, New Zealand Institute of Economic Research (NZIER) Research Monograph 64.

Hartley, R.F. (1985) *Marketing Successes. Historical to Present Day: What We Can Learn*, New York: John Wiley & Sons.

—— (1986) *Marketing Mistakes*, New York: John Wiley & Sons (first edition 1976).

Harvey, J.H. and Smith, W.P. (1977) *Social Psychology: An Attributional Approach*, Saint Louis, Mo.: C.V. Mosby Company.

Haslett, B. and Smollen, L.E. (1985) 'Preparing a Business Plan', in Pratt and Morris (1985), 22–32.

Hayek, F.A. (1931) *Prices and Production*, London: Routledge & Kegan Paul.

—— (1937) 'Economics and Knowledge', *Economica* (New Series), 4, 33–54. Reprinted in Hayek (1949), 33–56. (Page references are to the original.)

—— (1945) 'The Use of Knowledge in Society', *American Economic*

Review 35(4), 519–530. Reprinted in Hayek (1949), 77–91. (Page references are to the original.)

—— (1949) *Individualism and the Economic Order*, London: Routledge & Kegan Paul.

—— (1967) *Studies in Philosophy, Politics and Economics*, London: Routledge & Kegan Paul.

—— (ed.) (1971a) 'Principles or Expediency' in Hayek (1971b) Volume One, 29–45.

—— (ed.) (1971b) *Toward Liberty: Essays in Honor of Ludwig von Mises*, Volumes One and Two, Menlo Park, Calif.: Institute for Humane Studies.

—— (1973) *Law, Legislation and Liberty. A New Statement of the Liberal Principles of Justice and Political Economy*, Volume One, Rules and Order, London: Routledge & Kegan Paul.

—— (1976) *Law, Legislation and Liberty. A New Statement of the Liberal Principles of Justice and Political Economy*, Volume Two, The Mirage of Social Justice, London: Routledge & Kegan Paul.

—— (1978) *New Studies in Philosophy, Politics, Economics and the History of Ideas*, London: Routledge & Kegan Paul.

—— (1979) *Law, Legislation and Liberty. A New Statement of the Liberal Principles of Justice and Political Economy*, Volume Three, *The Political Order of a Free People*, London: Routledge & Kegan Paul.

Hébert, R.F. and Link, A.N. (1982) *The Entrepreneur: Mainstream Views and Radical Critiques*, New York: Praeger.

—— (1989) 'In Search of Entrepreneurship', *Small Business Economics* 1(1), 39–49.

Heider, F. (1944) 'Social Perception and Phenomenal Causality', *Psychological Review* 51, 358–374.

—— (1958) *The Psychology of Interpersonal Relations*, New York: Wiley.

Heilmayer, E. (ed.) (1983) *Workshop '83: Venture Capital für junge Technologieunternehmen*, Haar bei München: Verlag Mark & Technik.

Henderson, P.L. and Hoofnagle, W.S. (1974) 'Measuring the Effects of Store Promotions', in Ferber (1974), 4-324 to 4-344.

Heskett, J. (1976) *Marketing*, New York: Macmillan.

Hey, J.D. (1974) 'Price Adjustment in an Atomistic Market', *Journal of Economic Theory* 8, 483–499.

Hicks, J.R (1976) 'Some Questions of Time in Economics', in Tang, Westfield and Worley (1976), 135–152.

High, J. (1982) 'Alertness and Judgment: Comment on Kirzner', in Kirzner (1982a), 161–168.

—— (1986) 'Equilibration and Disequilibration in the Market Process', in Kirzner (1986b), 111–121.

Hildebrand, G.H. (1951) 'Consumer Sovereignty in Modern Times, *American Economic Review, Papers and Proceedings* 41, 19–33.

Hill, C.W.L. (1985) 'Oliver Williamson and the M-Form Firm: A Critical Review', *Journal of Economic Issues* 19(3), 731–751.

Hills, G.E. (1981) 'Evaluating New Ventures: A Concept Testing Methodology', *Journal of Small Business Management* 19(4), October, 29–41.

—— (1984) 'Market Analysis and Marketing in New Ventures: Venture Capitalists' Perceptions', in Hornaday, Tardley and Timmons (1984), 43–54.

Hippel, E. von (1976a) 'The Dominant Role of Users in the Scientific Instrument Innovation Process', *Research Policy* 5, 212–239.

—— (1976b) 'Users as Innovators', *Technology Review* 5, 212–239.

—— (1977a) 'The Dominant Role of the User in Semiconductor and Electronic Subassembly Process Innovation', *IEEE Transactions on Engineering Management* 24(2), May, 60–71.

—— (1977b) 'Successful and Failing Internal Corporate Ventures: An Empirical Analysis', *Industrial Marketing Management* 6, 163–174.

—— (1978) 'A Customer-Active Paradigm for Industrial Idea Generation', *Research Policy* 7(3), 240–266.

—— (1982a) 'Get New Products From Customers', *Harvard Business Review*, March–April, 117–122.

—— (1982b) 'Successful Industrial Products from Customer Ideas', in Tushman and Moore (1982), 409–423. Reprinted from the *Journal of Marketing*, January, 1978, 34–49. (Page references are to the reprint.)

Hofer, C.W. and Schendel, D. (1978) *Strategy Formulation: Analytical Concepts*, St. Paul, Minn.: West Publishing Co.

Hollis, M. and Nell, E.J. (1975) *Rational Economic Man. A Philosophical Critique of Neo-Classical Economics*, Cambridge: Cambridge University Press.

Hornaday, J.A., Tardley, Jr., F.A., and Timmons, J.A. (1984) *Frontiers of Entrepreneurship Research 1984*, Proceedings of the Fourth Annual Babson College Entrepreneurship Research Conference, Wellesley, Mass.: Center for Entrepreneurial Studies, Babson College.

Hornaday, J.A., Timmons, J.A., and Vesper, K.H. (1983) *Frontiers of Entrepreneurship Research*, Proceedings of the 1983 Conference on Entrepreneurship at Babson College, Wellesley, Mass.: Center for Entrepreneurial Studies, Babson College.

Hornaday, J.A., Shils, E.B., Timmons, J.A., and Vesper, K.H. (1985) *Frontiers of Entrepreneurship Research 1985*, Proceedings of the Fifth Annual Babson College Entrepreneurship Research Conference, Wellesley, Mass.: Center for Entrepreneurial Studies, Babson College.

Hoselitz, B.F. (1951) 'The Early History of Entrepreneurial Theory', *Explorations in Entrepreneurial History* 3(4), 193–220.

Hughes, G.D. (1978) *Marketing Management: A Planning Approach*, Reading, Mass.: Addison-Wesley Publishing Company.

Hughes, J. (1966) *The Vital Few*, Boston, Mass.: Houghton Mifflin.

Hull, D.L., Bosley, J.J., and Udell, G.G. (1980) 'Renewing the Search for the Heffalump: Identifying Potential Entrepreneurs by Personality Characteristics', *Journal of Small Business Management* 18(1), 11–18.

Ikeda, S. (1990) 'Market-Process Theory and "Dynamic" Theories of the Market', *Southern Economic Journal* 57(1): 75–92.

Imai, K., Nonaka, I., and Takeuchi, H. (1985) 'Managing the Product Development Process: How Japanese Companies Learn and Unlearn', in K.B. Clark, R.H. Hayes and C. Lorenz (eds) *The Uneasy Alliance:*

BIBLIOGRAPHY

Managing the Productivity-Technology Dilemma, Boston, Mass.: Harvard Business School Press, ch. 8.

Itoh, H. (1987) 'Information Processing Capacities of the Firm', *Journal of the Japanese and International Economies* 1(3), September, 299–326.

Jarillo, J.C. (1989) 'Entrepreneurship and the Strategic Use of External Resources', *Journal of Business Venturing* 4, 133–147.

Jarvie, I.C. (1976) 'Toulmin and the Rationality of Science', in Cohen, Feyerabend and Wartofsky (1976), 311–333.

Jelinek, M., Smircich, L., and Hirsch, P. (eds) (1983) 'Organizational Culture (Special Issue)', *Administrative Science Quarterly* 28, 331–499.

Jewkes, J., Sawers, D., and Stillerman, R. (1959) *The Sources of Invention*, second edition, London: Macmillan.

Johansson, J. (1975) *A Critique of Karl Popper's Methodology*, Stockholm: Scandinavian University Books.

Joint Economic Committee (1985) *Venture Capital and Innovation*, Study Prepared for the Use of the Joint Economic Committee of the United States, Washington, D.C.

Jones, E.E. and Davis, K.E. (1965) 'From Acts to Dispositions', in L. Berkowitz (ed.) *Advances in Experimental Social Psychology* 2, New York: Academic Press, 1965.

Jones, G.R. and Hill, C.W.L. (1988) 'Transaction Cost Analysis of Strategy-Structure Choice', *Strategic Management Journal* 9, 159–172.

Joskow, P. (1985) 'Vertical Integration and Long Term Contracts: The Case of Coal Burning Electric Generating Plants', *Journal of Law, Economics, and Organization* 1, 25–64.

Jussawalla, M. and Ebenfield, H. (eds) (1984) *Communication and Information Economics. New Perspectives*, Information Research and Resource Reports, Volume 5, Amsterdam: North-Holland.

Kanter, R.S. and Fonvielle, W.H. (1987) 'When to Persist and When to Give Up', *Management Review*, January, 14–15.

Kaplan, A. (1964) *The Conduct of Inquiry. Methodology for Behavioural Science*, Aylesbury: Intertext Books.

Kay, N.M. (1979) *The Innovating Firm: A Behavioural Theory of Corporate R & D*, London: Macmillan.

—— (1982) *The Evolving Firm: Strategy and Structure in Industrial Organisation*, New York: St. Martin's Press.

—— (1983) 'Optimal Size of Firm as a Problem in Transaction Costs and Property Rights', *Journal of Economics Studies* 10(2), 29–41.

—— (1984) *The Emergent Firm: Knowledge, Ignorance and Surprise in Economic Organisation*, London: Macmillan.

Keller, M. (1989) *Rude Awakening: The Rise, Fall, and Struggle for Recovery of General Motors*, New York: Morrow.

Kelley, H.H. (1967) 'Attribution Theory in Social Psychology', in D. Levine (ed.) *Nebraska Symposium on Motivation*, Lincoln, Nebr.: University of Nebraska Press.

Kelly, G.A. (1955) *The Psychology of Personal Constructs*, New York: Norton.

—— (1963) *A Theory of Personality. The Psychology of Personal Constructs*, New York: W. W. Norton and Co.

BIBLIOGRAPHY

Kent, C.A. (ed.) (1984a) *The Environment for Entrepreneurship*, Lexington, Mass.: Lexington Books, D. C. Heath and Company.

—— (1984b) 'The New Entrepreneurs', in Kent (1984a), 173–191.

Kent, C.A., Sexton, D.L., and Vesper, K.H. (eds) (1982) *Encyclopedia of Entrepreneurship*, Englewood Cliffs, N.J.: Prentice-Hall.

Kerin, R.A., Harvey, M.G., and Rothe, J.T. (1978) 'Cannibalism and New Product Development', *Business Horizons*, October, 25–31.

Kets de Vries, M.F.R. (1977) 'The Entrepreneurial Personality: A Person at the Crossroads', *Journal of Management Studies*, February, 34–57.

Khan, A.M. (1987) 'Assessing Venture Capital Investments with Non-compensatory Behavioural Decision Models', *Journal of Business Venturing* 2(3), 193–205.

Kilmann, R.H., Saxton, M.J., and Serpa, R. (eds) (1985) *Gaining Control of the Corporate Culture*, San Francisco, Calif.: Jossey-Bass Inc., Publishers.

—— (1986) 'Issues in Understanding and Changing Culture', *California Management Review* 28(2), Winter, 87–94.

Kimberly, J.R. and Miles, R.H. (1980) *The Organizational Life Cycle*, San Francisco, Calif.: Jossey-Bass Inc., Publishers.

Kirzner, I.M. (1962a) 'Rational Action and Economic Theory', *Journal of Political Economy* 70, 380–385.

—— (1962b) 'Rejoinder', *Journal of Political Economy* 71, 84–85.

—— (1963) *Market Theory and the Price System*, Princeton, N.J.: D. Van Nostrand Co.

—— (1971) 'Entrepreneurship and the Market Approach to Development', in Hayek (1971b), Volume Two, 194–208.

—— (1973) *Competition and Entrepreneurship*, Chicago, Ill.: University of Chicago Press.

—— (1979a) 'Comment. X-Inefficiency, Error, and the Scope for Entrepreneurship', in Rizzo (1979b), 140–152.

—— (1979b) *Perception, Opportunity, and Profit*, Chicago, Ill.: University of Chicago Press.

—— (1980) 'The "Austrian" Perspective on the Crisis', *The Public Interest*, Special Issue, 111–122.

—— (ed.) (1982a) *Method, Process, and Austrian Economics. Essays in Honor of Ludwig von Mises*, Lexington, Mass.: Lexington Books.

—— (1982b) 'The Theory of Entrepreneurship in Economic Growth', in Kent, Sexton and Vesper (1982), 272–277.

—— (1982c) 'Uncertainty, Discovery, and Human Action: A Study of the Entrepreneurial Profile in the Misesian System', in Kirzner (1982a), 139–160.

—— (1983a) 'Entrepreneurs and the Entrepreneurial Function: A Commentary', in Ronen (1983a), 281–290.

—— (1983b) 'The Primacy of Entrepreneurial Discovery', in *The Entrepreneur in Society*, CIS Policy Forums, St. Leornards, New South Wales: Centre for Independent Studies, 57–79. Originally published in Seldon (1980), 3–30.

—— (1984a) 'The Entrepreneurial Process', in Kent (1984a), 41–58.

—— (1984b) *The Role of the Entrepreneur in the Economic System*, CIS

379

Occasional Papers 10, St. Leornards, New South Wales: Centre for Independent Studies.

—— (1985) *Discovery and the Capitalist Process*, Chicago, Ill.: Chicago University Press.

—— (1986a) 'Another Look at the Subjectivism of Costs', in Kirzner (1986b), 140–156.

—— (ed.) (1986b) *Subjectivism, Intelligibility and Economic Understanding*, New York: New York University Press.

—— (1989) *Discovery, Capitalism and Distributive Justice*, Oxford: Basil Blackwell.

—— (1992) *The Meaning of Market Process: Essays in the Development of Modern Austrian Economics*, London: Routledge.

—— (ed.) (1994a) *Classics in Austrian Economics: A Sampling in the History of a Tradition*, Volume 1, *The Founding Era*, Volume 2, *The Interwar Period*, Volume 3, *The Age of Mises and Hayek*, London: William Pickering.

—— (1994b) 'Introduction' in Kirzner (1994a) Volume 1: ix–xxx.

Klamer, A. (1984) *The New Classical Macroeconomics: Conversations with New Classical Economists and Their Opponents*, Brighton: Wheatsheaf.

Klamer, A., McCloskey, D.N., and Solow, R.M. (eds) (1989) *The Consequences of Economic Rhetoric*, Cambridge: Cambridge University Press.

Klein, B., Crawford, R.G., and Alchian, A.A. (1978) 'Vertical Integration, Appropriable Rents, and the Competitive Contracting Process', *Journal of Law and Economics* 21(2), 297–326.

Klein, Burton H. (1977) *Dynamic Economics*, Cambridge, Mass.: Harvard University Press.

Klir, G.J. (ed.) (1972) *Trends in General Systems Theory*, New York: Wiley-Interscience.

Klompmaker, J.E., Hughes, G.D., and Haley, R.I. (1976) 'Test Marketing in New Product Development', *Harvard Business Review*, May–June, 128–138.

Knight, F.H. (1964) *Risk, Uncertainty and Profit*, New York: Augustus. M. Kelley (originally published 1921).

Koertge, N. (1975) 'Popper's Metaphysical Research Program for the Human Sciences', *Inquiry* 18(4), Winter, 437–462.

—— (1978) 'Towards a New Theory of Scientific Inquiry', in Radnitzky and Andersson (1978b), 253–278.

—— (1979) 'The Methodological Status of Popper's Rationality Principle', *Theory and Decision* 10, 83–95.

Kolb, D.A., Rubin, I.M., and McIntyre, J.M. (1979) *Organizational Psychology: An Experiential Approach*, third edition, Englewood Cliffs, N.J.: Prentice-Hall Inc.

Kono, T. (1984) *Strategy and Structure of Japanese Enterprises*, London: Macmillan.

Koopmans, T.C. (1957) *Three Essays on the State of Economic Science*, New York: McGraw-Hill Book Co.

Kover, A.J. (1967) 'Models of Man as Defined by Marketing Research', *Journal of Marketing Research* 4, May, 129–132.

Kravitt, G.I., Grossman, J.E., Keller, K.P., Mitra, K., Raha, E.A., and

Robbins, A.E. (1984) *How to Raise Capital. Preparing and Presenting the Business Plan*, Homewood, Ill.: Dow Jones-Irwin.

Krige, J. (1978) 'A Critique of Popper's Conception of the Relationship Between Logic, Psychology, and a Critical Epistemology', *Inquiry* 21, 313–335.

Krupp, S.R. (ed.) (1966) *The Structure of Economic Science. Essays on Methodology*, Englewood Cliffs, N.J.: Prentice-Hall, Inc.

Kuhn, T.S. (1970a) 'Logic of Discovery or Psychology of Research?', in Lakatos and Musgrave (1970), 1–23.

—— (1970b) 'Reflections on My Critics', in Lakatos and Musgrave (1970), 231–278.

—— (1970c) *The Structure of Scientific Revolutions*, International Encyclopedia of Unified Science, Volume Two, Number Two, Chicago, Ill.: University of Chicago Press, second edition. First edition 1962.

—— (1977a) *The Essential Tension. Selected Studies in Scientific Tradition and Change*, Chicago, Ill.: University of Chicago Press.

—— (1977b) 'Second Thoughts on Paradigms', in F. Suppe, ed., *The Structure of Scientific Theories*, second edition, Urbana, Ill.: University of Illinois Press, 459–482.

Lachmann, L.M. (1943) 'The Role of Expectations in Economics as a Social Science', *Economica* 10(February), 37, 12–23. Reprinted in Lachmann (1977), 65–80. Page references are to the orginal.

—— (1959) 'Professor Shackle on the Economic Significance of Time', *Metroeconomica* 11(September), 64–73. Reprinted in Lachmann (1977), 81–93. (Page references are to the orginal.)

—— (1971a) *The Legacy of Max Weber*, Berkeley, Calif.: The Glendessary Press.

—— (1971b) 'Ludwig von Mises and the Market Process', in Hayek (1971b), Volume 2, 38–52. Reprinted in Lachmann (1977), 181–193. (Page references are to the orginal.)

—— (1974) 'On the Central Concept of Austrian Economics: Market Process', Lecture given at Austrian Economics Conference, South Royalton, Vermont, June 1974. Reprinted in Dolan (1976), 126–132.

—— (1976a) 'From Mises to Shackle: An Essay on Austrian Economics and the Kaleidic Society', *Journal of Economic Literature* 14(March), 54–62.

—— (1976b) 'On Austrian Capital Theory', in Dolan (1976), 145–151.

—— (1977) *Capital, Expectations and the Market Process: Essays in the Theory of the Market Economy*, Kansas City, Kan.: Sheed Andrews & McMeel.

—— (1978a) 'An Austrian Stocktaking: Unsettled Questions and Tentative Answers', in Spadaro (1978a), 1–18.

—— (1978b) *Capital and its Structure*, Kansas City, Kan.: Sheed Andrews & McMeel (originally published in 1956 by Bell and Sons)

—— (1982) 'The Salvage of Ideas. Problems of the Revival of Austrian Economic Thought', *Zeitschrift für die gesamte Staatswissenschaft/Journal of Institutional and Theoretical Economics* 138, 629–645.

—— (1986) *The Market as an Economic Process*, Oxford: Basil Blackwell.

Lakatos, I. (1963–64) 'Proofs and Refutations', *The British Journal for the Philosophy of Science* 14, 1–25, 120–139, 221–245, 296–342.

—— (1968a) 'Changes in the Problem of Inductive Logic', in Lakatos (1968b), 315–417.

—— (ed.) (1968b) *The Problem of Inductive Logic. Proceedings of the International Colloquium in the Philosophy of Science, London: 1965,* Amsterdam: North-Holland Publishing Company.

—— (1970) 'Falsification and the Methodology of Scientific Research Programmes', in Lakatos and Musgrave (1970), 91–196.

—— (1971a) 'History of Science and its Rational Reconstructions' in Buck and Cohen (1971), 91–136.

—— (1971b) 'Replies to Critics', in Buck and Cohen (1971), 174–182.

—— (1974) 'Popper on Demarcation and Induction', in Schlipp (1974), 241–273.

—— (1978) *Philosophical Papers*, Volume One, 'The Methodology of Scientific Research Programmes'. Edited by J. Worrall and G. Currie, Cambridge: Cambridge University Press.

Lakatos, I. and Musgrave, A. (eds) (1970) *Criticism and the Growth of Knowledge*, Cambridge: Cambridge University Press.

Lancaster, K.J. (1966) 'A New Approach to Consumer Theory', *Journal of Political Economy* 74, April, 132–157.

Langlois, R.N. (1982), 'Austrian Economics as Affirmative Science: Comment on Rizzo', in Kirzner (1982a), 75–84.

—— (1984a) 'Internal Organisation in a Dynamic Context: Some Theoretical Considerations', in Jussawalla and Ebenfield (1984), 23–49.

—— (1984b) 'Kaleidic and Structural Interpretations of Uncertainty', paper prepared for a C.V. Starr Center-Liberty Fund Conference on O'Driscoll and Rizzo's *The Economics of Time and Ignorance*, November 3–6 (1984), Rye Brook, New York.

—— (1986a) 'Coherence and Flexibility: Social Institutions in a World of Radical Uncertainty', in Kirzner (1986b), 171–191.

—— (ed.) (1986b) *Economics as a Process. Essays in the New Institutional Economics*, Cambridge: Cambridge University Press.

—— (1986c) 'The New Insititutional Economics: An Introductory Essay', in Langlois (1986b), 1–26.

—— (1986d) 'Rationality, Institutions, and Explanation', in Langlois (1986b), 225–255.

Latsis, S.J. (1972) 'Situational Determinism in Economics', *The British Journal for the Philosophy of Science* 23, 207–245.

—— (1976a) 'The Limitations of Single-Exit Models: Reply to Machlup', *The British Journal for the Philosophy of Science* 27, 51–60.

—— ed.) (1976b) *Method and Appraisal in Economics*, Cambridge: Cambridge University Press.

—— (1976c) 'A Research Programme in Economics', in Latsis (1976b), 1–42.

—— (1983) 'The Role and Status of the Rationality Principle in the Social Sciences', in R.S. Cohen and M.W. Wartofsky (eds) *Epistemology, Methodology and the Social Sciences*, Boston Studies in the Philosophy of Science, 71, Dordrecht: D. Reidel Publishing Co.

Lehmann, E.L. (1959) *Testing Statistical Hypotheses*, New York: John Wiley & Sons, Inc.

—— (1975) *Nonparametrics: Statistical Methods Based on Ranks*, San Francisco, Calif.: Holden Day, Inc.

Leibenstein, H. (1968) 'Entrepreneurship and Development', *American Economic Review* 58, 72–83.

—— (1979) 'The General X-Efficiency Paradigm and the Role of the Entrepreneur', in Rizzo (1979b), 127–139.

Levenson, H. (1974) 'Activism and Powerful Others: Distinctions within the Concept of Internal-External Control', *Journal of Personality Assessment* 38, 377–383.

Levinson, P. (ed.) (1982) *In Pursuit of Truth: Essays on the Philosophy of Karl Popper on the Occasion of His 80th Birthday*, Brighton: Harvester Press.

Levitt, T. (1986) *Marketing Imagination*, second edition, New York: The Free Press. First edition 1983.

Lindsay, R.B. (1968) 'Physics – To What Extent is it Deterministic?', *American Scientist* 56, 93–111.

Lipstein, B. (1961) 'Tests for Test Markets', *Harvard Business Review*, March–April, 74–77.

—— (1964) 'The Design of Test Marketing Experiments', *Proceedings of the Forty-Seventh National Conference of the American Marketing Association*, Chicago, Ill.

Littlechild, S.C. (1977) 'Change Rules, O.K.?', an Inaugural Lecture delivered at the University of Birmingham on 28 May 1977.

—— (1978a) *The Fallacy of the Mixed Economy: An 'Austrian' Critique of Conventional 'Mainstream' Economics and of British Economic Policy*, Hobart Paper no.80, London: Institute of Economic Affairs.

—— (1978b) 'The Problem of Social Cost', in Spadaro (1978a), 77–93.

—— (1979a) 'Comment: Radical Subjectivism or Radical Subversion?', in Rizzo (1979b), 32–50.

—— (1979b) 'An Entrepreneurial Theory of Games', *Metroeconomica* 31, 145–165.

—— (1986) 'Three Types of Market Process', in Langlois (1986b), 27–40.

—— (ed.) (1990) *Austrian Economics*, Aldershot: Edward Elgar.

Loasby, B.J. (1971) 'Hypothesis and Paradigm in the Theory of the Firm', *The Economic Journal* 81, December, 863–885.

—— (1976) *Choice, Complexity and Ignorance. An Enquiry into Economic Theory and the Practice of Decision-Making*, Cambridge: Cambridge University Press.

—— (1982a) 'Economics of Dispersed and Incomplete Information', in Kirzner (1982a), 111–130.

—— (1982b) 'The Entrepreneur in Economic Theory', *Scottish Journal of Political Economy* 29(3), 235–245.

—— (1983) 'Knowledge, Learning and Enterprise', in Wiseman (1983b), 104–121.

—— (1984a) 'Entrepreneurs and Organisation', *Journal of Economic Studies* 11(2), 75–88.

—— (1984b) 'On Scientific Method', *Journal of Post Keynesian Economics* 6, 394–410.

—— (1984c) 'Professor Shackle's "To Cope with Time": A Discussion', in Stephen (1984), 80–83.

—— (1985) 'Profit, Expectations and Coherence in Economic Systems', *Journal of Economic Studies* 12 (1/2), 21–33.

—— (1986a) 'Marshall's Economics of Progress', *Journal of Economic Studies* 13(5), 16–26.

—— (1986b) 'Organisation, Competition, and the Growth of Knowledge', in Langlois (1986b), 41–58.

—— (1986c) 'Public Science and Public Knowledge', in Samuels (1984), 211–228.

—— (1987) *One Firm Spot in Which to Stand*, University of Stirling Discussion Papers in Economics, Finance and Investment, no. 130.

—— (1989) *The Mind and Method of the Economist: A Critical Appraisal of Major Economists in the 20th Century*, Aldershot: Edward Elgar.

—— (1991) *Equilibrium and Evolution: An Exploration of Connecting Principles in Economics*, Manchester: Manchester University Press.

—— (1994) 'Evolution within Equilibrium', in Boettke, Kirzner and Rizzo (1994): 31–47.

Lorange, P. and Vancil, R.A. (1977) *Strategic Planning Systems*, Englewood Cliffs, N.J.: Prentice-Hall.

Lorenzoni, G. and Ornati, O.A. (1988) 'Constellations of Firms and New Ventures', *Journal of Business Venturing* 3, 41–57.

Lorsch, J.W. (1986) 'Managing Culture: The Invisible Barrier to Strategic Change', *California Management Review* 28(2), Winter, 95–109.

Lowinger, A. (1941) *The Methodology of Pierre Duhem*, New York: Columbia University Press.

Lucas, R.E. (1975) 'An Equilibrium Model of the Business Cycle', *Journal of Political Economy* 83, December, 1113–1144.

Lutz, R.J. and Kakkar, P. (1975) 'The Psychological Situation as a Determinant of Consumer Behavior', *Advances in Consumer Research* 2, 439–455.

McCain, B.E. (1986) 'Continuing Investment Under Conditions of Failure: A Laboratory Study of the Limits of Escalation', *Journal of Applied Psychology* 71(2), 280–284.

McClelland, D. (1961) *The Achieving Society*, Princeton, N.J.: D. Van Nostrand.

McCloskey, D.N. (1983) 'The Rhetoric of Economics', *Journal of Economic Literature* 21, June, 481–517. Reprinted in Caldwell (1984a), 320–356.

—— (1986) *The Rhetoric of Economics*, Brighton: Wheatsheaf.

McGregor, D. (1960) *The Human Side of Enterprise*, New York: McGraw-Hill Inc.

McGuire, E.P. (1973) *Evaluating New-Product Proposals*, New York: The Conference Board, CBR 604.

McLaughlin, A. (1971) 'Method and Factual Agreement in Science', in Buck and Cohen (1971), 459–469.

MacMillan, I.C., Block, Z., and SubbaNarasimha, P.N. (1986) 'Corporate

Venturing: Alternatives, Obstacles and Experience Effects', *Journal of Business Venturing* 1(3), 177–191.

MacMillan, I.C., Siegel, R., and SubbaNarasimha, P.N. (1985) 'Criteria used by Venture Capitalists to Evaluate New Venture Proposals', *Journal of Business Venturing* 1, 119–128.

MacMillan, K. and Farmer, D. (1979) 'Redefining the Boundaries of the Firm', *Journal of Industrial Economics* 27(3), March, 278–285.

Machlup, F. (1958) 'Equilibrium and Disequilibrium: Misplaced Concreteness and Disguised Politics', *The Economic Journal* 68, March, 1–24.

Magee, B.M. (1971) *Modern British Philosophy*, London: Secker & Warburg.

—— (1973) *Popper*, London: Fontana/Collins.

Maidique, M.A. (1980) 'Champions and Technological Innovation', *Sloan Management Review* 21(2), Winter, 59–76.

—— (1986) 'Key Success Factors in High Technology Ventures', in Sexton and Smilor (1986), 169–180.

Maidique, M.A. and Hayes, R.H. (1984) 'The Art of High-Technology Management', *Sloan Management Review*, Winter, 17–31.

Maidique, M.A. and Zirger, B.J. (1984) 'A Study of Success and Failure in Product Innovation: The Case of the U.S. Electronics Industry', *IEEE Transactions on Engineering Management*, EM-31(4), November, 192–203.

—— (1985) 'The New Product Learning Cycle', *Research Policy* 14(6), 299–313.

Maital, S. (1988) *Applied Behavioral Economics*, Volumes One and Two, Brighton: Wheatsheaf.

Mancuso, J.R. (1983) *How to Prepare and Present a Business Plan*, Englewood Cliffs, N.J.: Prentice-Hall.

Mann, H.B. and Whitney, D.R. (1947) 'On a Test of Whether One or Two Random Variables is Stochastically Larger than the Other', *Annals of Mathematical Statistics* 18, 50–60.

Marascuilo, L.A. and Serlin, R.C. (1988) *Statistical Methods for the Social and Behavioral Sciences*, New York: W.H. Freeman & Co.

Marcet, A. and Sargent, T.J. (1989a) 'Convergence of Least-Squares Learning in Environments with Hidden State Variables and Private Information', *Journal of Political Economy* 97(6), December, 1306–1322.

—— (1989b) 'Convergence of Least-Squares Learning Mechanisms in Self-Referential Linear Stochastic Models', *Journal of Economic Theory* 48(2), August.

March, J.G., and Simon, H.A. (1958) *Organizations*, New York: John Wiley & Sons, Inc.

Marchi, N., de (1988a) 'Introduction', in de Marchi (1988c), 1–15.

—— (1988b) 'Popper and the LSE Economists', in de Marchi (1988c), 139–166.

—— (ed.) (1988c) *The Popperian Legacy in Economics*, Papers Presented at a Symposium in Amsterdam, December 1985, Cambridge: Cambridge University Press.

Margenau, H. (1966) 'What is a Theory?', in Krupp (1966), 25–38.

Marshall, A. (1961) *Principles of Economics*, ninth (variorum) edition, two volumes, London: Macmillan. Originally published 1890.

Masterman, M. (1970) 'The Nature of a Paradigm', in Lakatos and Musgrave (1970), 59–90.

Meade, J.E. (1971) *The Controlled Economy*, London: G. Allen & Unwin.

Meade, N. (1978) 'Decision Analysis in Venture Capital', *Journal of the Operational Research Society* 29(1), 43–53.

Medawar, P.B. (1967) *The Art of the Soluble*, London: Methuen.

—— (1969) *Induction and Intuition in Scientific Thought. (Jayne Lectures for 1968)*, Philadelphia, Pa.: American Philosophical Society.

Merton, R.K. (1948) 'The Self-Fulfilling Prophecy', *The Antioch Review*, Summer, 193–210. Reprinted in R.K. Merton, *Social Theory and Social Structure*, revised and enlarged edition, New York: The Free Press (1968).

Michaelis, E. (1985) *Organisation unternehmerischer Aufgaben – Transaktionskosten als Beurteilungskriterium*, Betriebswirtschaftliche Studien Rechnungs- und Finanzwesen, Organisation und Institution, Band 4, Frankfurt am Main: Peter Lang.

Miller, D. (ed.) (1983) *Popper Selections*, Princeton, N.J.: Princeton University Press.

Miller, G.A., Galanter, E., and Pribram, K.H. (1960) *Plans and the Structure of Behavior*, New York: Holt, Rinehart & Winston Inc.

Milsum, J.H. (1972) 'The Hierarchical Basis of General Living Systems', in Klir (1972), 145–187.

Mintzberg, H. (1973) 'Strategy-Making in Three Modes', *California Management Review* 16(2), 44–53.

—— (1978) 'Patterns of Strategy Formation', *Management Science* 24, 934–948.

—— (1980) *The Nature of Managerial Work*, Englewood Cliffs, N.J.: Prentice-Hall.

Mirowski, P. (1989) *More Heat Than Light. Economics as Social Physics: Physics as Nature's Economics*, Cambridge: Cambridge University Press.

Mises, L. von (1949) *Human Action. A Treatise on Economics*, New Haven, Conn.: Yale University Press (there is a third revised edition 1966 by Henry Regnery Company, Chicago).

—— (1980) *Planning for Freedom and Sixteen other Essays and Addresses*, fourth edition, South Holland, Ill.: Libertarian Press (first edition 1952).

Mitroff, I.I. (1974) *The Subjective Side of Science. A Philosophical Inquiry into the Psychology of the Apollo Moon Scientists*, Amsterdam: Elsevier.

Moore, W.L. (1982) 'Concept Testing', *Journal of Business Research* 10(3), 279–293.

Morgenstern, O. (1935) 'Volkommene Voraussicht und wirtschaftliches Gleichgewicht', *Zeitschrift für Nationalökonomie* 6(3). Reprinted in English in A. Schotter (ed.) *Selected Readings of Oskar Morgenstern*, New York: New York University Press (1976).

Morita, A. (1986) *Made in Japan: Akio Morita and Sony*, New York: E. P. Dutton.

Moroshima, M. (1982) *Why Has Japan 'Suceeded'?: Western Technology and the Japanese Ethos*, Cambridge: Cambridge University Press.

Mowery, D. and Rosenberg, N. (1979) 'The Influence of Market Demand Upon Innovation: A Critical Review of Some Recent Empirical Studies', *Research Policy* 8, 102–153.

Mulkay, M. and Gilbert, G.N. (1981) 'Putting Philosophy to Work: Karl Popper's Influence on Scientific Practice', *Philosophy of the Social Sciences* 11, 389–407.

Musgrave, A.E. (1971a) *Falsification and its Critics*, Paper Written for the IVth International Congress for Logic, Methodology, and Philosophy of Science, Bucharest, Romania.

—— (1971b) 'Kuhn's Second Thoughts (Review Article)', *British Journal of the Philosophy of Science* 22, 287–306.

—— (1974a) 'Logical Versus Historical Theories of Confirmation', *British Journal for the Philosophy of Science* 25, 1–23.

—— (1974b) 'The Objectivism of Popper's Epistemology', in Schlipp (1974), 560–596.

—— (1975) 'Popper and "Diminishing Returns from Repeated Tests"', *Australasian Journal of Philosophy* 53, 248–253.

—— (1976) 'Method or Madness? Can the Methodology of Research Programmes be Rescued from Epistemological Anarchism', in R.S. Cohen, P.K. Feyerabend and M.W. Wartofsky (eds), *Essays in Memory of Imre Lakatos*, Dordrecht, Holland: D. Reidel Publishing Company, 457–491.

—— (1978) 'Evidential Support, Falsification, Heuristics, and Anarchism', Radnitzky and Andersson (1978b), 181–201.

—— (1981) '"Unreal Assumptions" in Economic Theory: The F-Twist Untwisted', *Kyklos* 34(3), 377–387.

—— (1983) 'Facts and Values in Science Studies', in R.W. Home (ed.), *Science under Scrutiny*, Dordrecht: D. Reidel Publishing Company, 49–79.

Myers, S. and Marquis, D.G. (1969) *Successful Industrial Innovations*, National Science Foundation, Rep. NSF 69–17.

Nalebuff, B.J. and Stiglitz, J.E. (1983) 'Information, Competition and Markets', *American Economic Review, Papers and Proceedings* 73, May, 278–283.

Nathusius, K. (1979) *Venture Management: Ein Instrument zur innovativen Unternehmungsentwicklung*, Betriebswirtschaftliche Forschungsergebnisse, Band 81, Berlin: Duncker & Humblot.

Negishi, T. (1961) 'On the Formation of Prices', *International Economic Review* 2, January, 122–126.

Nelson, R.R. and Winter, S.G. (1982) *An Evolutionary Theory of Economic Change*, Cambridge, Mass.: Harvard University Press.

Nevins, A. and Hill, F. (1954) *Ford*, Volume One, *The Times, The Man, The Company*, New York: Scribner's.

—— (1957) *Ford*, Volume Two, *Expansion and Challenge*, New York: Scribner's.

Nevitt, P.K. (1983) *Project Financing*, London: Euromoney Publications.

Newell, A., Shaw, J.C., and Simon, H.A. (1958) 'Elements of a Theory of Human Problem-Solving', *Psychological Review* 65(May), 151–166.

Newton-Smith, W.H. (1981) *The Rationality of Science*, London: Routledge & Kegan Paul.

Nola, R. (1987) 'The Status of Popper's Theory of Scientific Method', *British Journal for the Philosophy of the Social Sciences* 38, 441–480.

Nottorno, M.A. and Wettersten, J. (eds) (1989) *Psychologism*, The Hague: Martinus Nijhoff.

Nozick, R. (1974) *Anarchy, State and Utopia*, Oxford: Basil Blackwell.

O'Donnell, L.A. (1973) 'Rationalism, Capitalism, and the Entrepreneur: The Views of Veblen and Schumpeter, *History of Political Economy* 5(Spring), 199–214.

O'Driscoll, G.P., Jr. (1979) 'Rational Expectations, Politics and Stagflation', in Rizzo (1979b), 153–176.

O'Driscoll, G.P., Jr. and Rizzo, M.J. (1985) *The Economics of Time and Ignorance*, Oxford: Basil Blackwell.

O'Hear, A. (1975) 'Rationality of Action and Theory-Testing in Popper', *Mind*, 273–276.

—— (1980) *Karl Popper*, London: Routledge & Kegan Paul.

O'Toole, J. (1979) 'Corporate and Managerial Cultures', in Cooper, C.L. (ed.) *Behavioral Problems in Organizations*, Englewood Cliffs, N.J.: Prentice-Hall.

Orenstein, A. (1977) *Willard van Orman Quine*, Boston, Mass.: Twayne.

Osgood, C.E. and Tannenbaum, P.H. (1955) 'The Principle of Congruity in the Prediction of Attitude Change', *Psychological Review* 62, January.

Paqué, K. (1985) 'How Far is Vienna from Chicago?. An Essay on the Methodology of Two Schools of Dogmatic Liberalism', *Kyklos* 38(3), 412–434.

Pasour, E.C. (1978) 'Cost and Choice –Austrian vs. Conventional Views', *Journal of Libertarian Studies* 2(4), 327–336.

—— (1980) 'Cost of Production: A Defensible Basis for Agricultural Price Supports?', *American Journal of Agricultural Economics*, May, 244–248.

Penrose, E.T. (1959) *The Growth of the Firm*, Oxford: Basil Blackwell.

Pettigrew, A. (1979) 'On Studying Organizational Cultures', *Administrative Science Quarterly* 24, December, 570–581.

Picot, A. (1986) 'Transaktionskosten im Handel. Zur Notwendigkeit einer flexiblen Strukturentwicklung in der Distribution', *Betriebsberater*, Beilage 13/1986, Heft 27/1986, 1–16.

Picot, A. and Schneider, D. (1988) 'Unternehmerisches Innovationsverhalten, Verfügungsrechte und Transaktionskosten', in D. Budäus, E. Gerum and G. Zimmermann (eds) *Betriebswirtschaftslehre und Theorie der Verfügungsrechte*, Wiesbaden, Gabler, 18–38.

Picot, A., Laub, U., and Schneider, D. (1988) 'The Transaction Cost Approach to Research in Innovative Business Start-Ups: Theory and Empirical Evidence', Manuscript.

—— (1989a) *Innovative Unternehmensgründungen: Eine ökonomisch-empirische Analyse*, Berlin: Springer-Verlag.

—— (1989b) 'Transaktionskosten und innovative Unternehmensgründung. Eine empirische Analyse', *Zeitschrift für Betriebswirtschaftliche Forschung* 41(5), 357–387.

Pilkington, A.E. (1976) *Bergson and His Influence*, Cambridge: Cambridge University Press.

Polanyi, M. (1958) *Personal Knowledge. Towards a Post-Critical Philosophy*, London: Routledge & Kegan Paul.

—— (1966) *The Tacit Dimension*, Garden City, N.Y.: Doubleday.

Popper, K.R. (1950) 'Indeterminism in Quantum Physics and in Classical Physics, Parts I and II', *The British Journal for the Philosophy of Science* 1, 117–133, 173–195.

—— (1959) *The Logic of Scientific Discovery*, London: Hutchinson. First German edition 1934.

—— (1960) *The Poverty of Historicism*, second edition. London: Routledge & Kegan Paul. First Edition 1957.

—— (1963), *Conjectures and Refutations. The Growth of Scientific Knowledge*, London: Routledge & Kegan Paul.

—— (1966a) *The Open Society and its Enemies*, Volume One, *The Spell of Plato*, fifth edition, London: Routledge & Kegan Paul. First edition 1945.

—— (1966b) *The Open Society and its Enemies*, Volume Two, The High Tide of Prophesy: Hegel, Marx and the Aftermath, fifth edition, London: Routledge & Kegan Paul. First edition 1945.

—— (1970) 'Normal Science and its Dangers', in Lakatos and Musgrave (1970), 51–58.

—— (1972) *Objective Knowledge. An Evolutionary Approach*, Oxford: Oxford University Press.

—— (1974) 'Replies to My Critics', in Schlipp (1974), 961–1197.

—— (1976a) 'The Logic of the Social Sciences', in Adorno *et al.* (1976), 87–104.

—— (1976b) 'The Myth of the Framework', in E. Freeman (ed.), *The Abdication of Philosophy. Philosophy and the Public Good. Essays in Honour of Paul Arthur Schlipp*, La Salle, Ill.: Open Court.

—— (1976c) *Unended Quest. An Intellectual Autobiography*, London: Fontana/Collins.

—— (1979a) 'Appendix 2: Supplementary Remarks', in K.R. Popper, *Objective Knowledge: An Evolutionary Approach*, revised edition, Oxford: Clarendon Press, 1979.

—— (1979b) *Die beiden Grundprobleme der Erkenntnistheorie: aufgrund von Ms. aus d. Jahren 1930–1933*, Tübingen, Mohr. Edited by T. E. Hansen. Written in 1930–32 but not published until 1979.

—— (1982) *The Open Universe: An Argument for Indeterminism, From the Postscript to 'The Logic of Scientific Discovery'*, London: Hutchinson.

—— (1983a) 'Introduction, 1982', in Popper (1983b), xix–xxxix.

—— (1983b) *Realism and the Aim of Science. From the Postscript to 'The Logic of Scientific Discovery'*, Totawa, N.J.: Rowan and Littlefield.

—— (1983c) 'The Rationality Principle', in Miller (1983), 357–365.

Popper, K. R., and Eccles, J.C. (1977) *The Self and its Brain*, Berlin: Springer-Verlag.

Porter, M.E. (1980) *Competitive Strategy: Techniques for Analyzing Industries and Competitors*, New York: The Free Press.

—— (1985) *Competitive Advantage: Creating and Sustaining Superior Performance*, New York: The Free Press.

Postrel, S.R. (1990) 'Competing Networks and Proprietary Standards: The

Case of Quadraphonic Sound', *Journal of Industrial Economics* 39(2), December, 169–185.

Pounds, W.F. (1969) 'The Process of Problem Finding', *Industrial Management Review* 11, 1–19.

Pratt, S.E. (ed.) (1982) *How to Raise Venture Capital*, New York: Charles Scribner's Sons.

Pratt, S.E. and Morris, J.K. (eds) (1985) *Pratt's Guide to Venture Capital Sources*, ninth edition, Wellesley Hills, Mass.: Venture Economics.

Prigogine, I. (1985) 'New Perspectives on Complexity', in S. Aida *et al. The Science and Praxis of Complexity*, Tokyo: The United Nations University, 107–118.

Quine, W.V.O. (1980) *From a Logical Point of View: Nine Logico-Philosophical Essays*, second edition, revised, with a new foreword by the Author, Cambridge, Mass.: Harvard University Press. First edition 1953.

Quinn, J.B. (1978) 'Strategic Change: "Logical Incrementalism"', *Sloan Management Review*, 20(1), Fall, 7–21.

—— (1979) 'Technological Innovation, Entrepreneurship, and Strategy', *Sloan Management Review* 20(3), Spring, 19–30.

—— (1980a) 'Managing Strategic Change', *Sloan Management Review* 21(4), 3–20.

—— (1980b) *Strategies for Change: Logical Incrementalism*, Homewood, Ill.: Dow Jones-Irwin.

—— (1985) 'Managing Innovation: Controlled Chaos', *Harvard Business Review*, May–June, 73–84.

Raaij, W.F. van (1985) 'Attribution of Causality to Economic Actions and Events', *Kyklos* 38(1), 3–19.

Radnitzky, G. (1976) 'Popperian Philosophy of Science as an Antidote Against Relativism', in Cohen, Feyerabend and Wartofsky (1976), 505–546.

Radnitzky, G. and Andersson, G. (1978a) 'Objective Criteria of Scientific Progress? Inductivism, Falsificationism, and Relativism', in Radnitzky and Andersson (1978b), 3–19.

—— (eds) (1978b) *Progress and Rationality in Science, Boston Studies in the Philosophy of Science* 58, Dordrecht: D. Reidel Publishing Co.

Rae, J.B. (1965) *The American Automobile*, Chicago, Ill.: University of Chicago Press.

Rapoport, A. (1968) 'Critiques of Game Theory', in W. Buckley (ed.), *Modern Systems Research for the Behavioral Scientist. A Sourcebook*, Chicago, Ill.: Aldine Publishing Co, 474–489.

Redlich, F. (1949) 'The Origin of the Concepts of "Entrepreneur" and "Creative Entrepreneur"', *Explorations in Entrepreneurial History* 1(2), 1–7.

Reekie, W.D. (1984) *Markets, Entrepreneurs and Liberty: An Austrian View of Capitalism*, Brighton: Wheatsheaf Books.

Reichenbach, H. (1938) *Experience and Prediction*, Chicago, Ill.: University of Chicago Press.

—— (1947) *Elements of Symbolic Logic*, New York: Macmillan Co.

—— (1956) *The Direction of Time*, Berkeley, Calif.: University of California Press. Edited by Maria Reichenbach.

Remenyi, J.V. (1979) 'Core Demi-Core Interaction: Toward a General Theory of Disciplinary and Subdisciplinary Growth', *History of Political Economy* 11(1), 30–63.

Reynolds, W.H. (1967) 'The Edsel Ten Years Later', *Business Horizons*, Fall, 39–46.

Rich, S.R. and Gumpert, D.E. (1985a) *Business Plans that Win $$$: Lessons from the MIT Enterprise Forum*, New York: Harper & Row.

—— (1985b) 'How to Write a Winning Business Plan', *Harvard Business Review*, May–June, 156–166.

Richardson, G.B. (1960) *Information and Investment. A Study in the Working of the Competitive Economy*, Oxford: Oxford University Press.

—— (1972) 'The Organisation of Industry', *Economic Journal* 82, 883–896.

Ricketts, M. (1987a) *The Economics of Business Enterprise. New Approaches to the Firm*, Brighton: Wheatsheaf Books.

—— (1987b) 'Rent Seeking, Entrepreneurship, Subjectivism, and Property Rights', *Journal of Institutional and Theoretical Economics* 143, 457–466.

Rifkin, J. (1980) *Entropy: A New World View*, New York: Viking Press.

Riordan, M.H. and Williamson, O.E. (1985) 'Asset Specificity and Economic Organisation', *International Journal of Industrial Organisation* 3, 365–378.

Rizzo, M.J. (1979a) 'Disequilibrium and All That: An Introductory Essay', in Rizzo (1979b), 1–18.

—— (ed.) (1979b) *Time, Uncertainty and Disequilibrium. Exploration of Austrian Themes*, Lexington, Mass.: Lexington Books, D.C.Heath & Co.

—— (1982) 'Mises and Lakatos: A Reformulation of Austrian Methodology', in Kirzner (1982a), 53–74.

Roberts, E.B. (1980) 'New Ventures for Corporate Growth', *Harvard Business Review* 58(4), July–August, 130–142.

Robinson, J. (1980) 'Time in Economic Theory', *Kyklos* 33(2), 219–229.

Robinson, P.J., Faris, C.W., and Wind, Y. (1967) *Industrial Buying and Creative Marketing*, Boston, Mass.: Allyn and Bacon.

Robinson, R.B. (1987) 'Emerging Strategies in the Venture Capital Industry', *Journal of Business Venturing* 2(1), 53–77.

Rokeach, M. (1960) *The Open and Closed Mind*, New York: Basic Books.

Ronen, J. (ed.) (1983a) *Entrepreneurship*, Lexington, Mass.: D. C. Heath & Co.

Ronen, J. (1983b) 'Some Insights into the Entrepreneurial Process', in Ronen (1983a), 137–174.

Ronstadt, R., Hornaday, J.A., Peterson, R., and Vesper, K.H. (1986) *Frontiers of Entrepreneurship 1986*, Proceedings of the Sixth Annual Babson College Entrepreneurship Research Conference, Wellesley, Mass.: Center for Entrepreneurial Studies, Babson College.

Röpke, J. (1977) *Die Strategie der Innovation: Eine Systemtheoretische Untersuchung der Interaktion von Individuum, Organisation und Markt im Neuerungsprozeß*, Tübingen, Mohr (Paul Siebeck).

Rorty, R. (1979) *Philosophy and the Mirror of Nature*, Princeton, N.J.: Princeton University Press.

Rosenstein-Rodan, P.N. (1934) 'The Role of Time in Economic Theory', *Economica*, February, 77–97.

Rothbard, M.N. (1970) *Man, Economy and State, A Treatise on Economic Principles*, 2 Volumes, Los Angeles, Calif.: Nash Publishing.

—— (1987a) 'Breaking Out of the Walrasian Box: The Cases of Schumpeter and Hansen', in Rothbard (1987b), 97–108.

—— (ed.) (1987b) *The Review of Austrian Economics*, volume one, Lexington, Mass.: Lexington Books, D. C. Heath & Co.

Rothschild, M. (1973) 'Models of Market Organization with Imperfect Information: A Survey', *Journal of Political Economy* 81(6), November–December, 1283–1308.

—— (1974) 'A Two-Armed Bandit Theory of Market Pricing', *Journal of Economic Theory* 9, 185–202.

Rothwell, R., Freeman, C., Horsley, A., Jervis, V.T.P., Robertson, A.B., and Townsend, J. (1974) 'SAPPHO Updated – Project SAPPHO Phase II', *Research Policy* 3, 258–291.

Rotter, J.B. (1966) 'Generalised Expectancies for Internal versus External Control of Reinforcement', *Psychological Monographs* 80(1), 1–28.

Roure, J.B. and Maidique, M.A. (1986) 'Linking Prefunding Factors and High-Technology Venture Success: An Exploratory Study', *Journal of Business Venturing* 1(3), 295–306.

Rowe, A.J., Mason, R.O., and Dickel, K.E. (1986) *Strategic Management: A Methodological Approach*, Reading, Mass.: Addison-Wesley Publishing Co.

Ruhnka, J.C. and Young, J.E. (1987) 'A Venture Capital Model of the Development Process for New Ventures', *Journal of Business Venturing* 2(2), 167–184.

Runde, J.H. (1988) 'Subjectivism, Psychology, and the Modern Austrians', in Earl (1988b), 101–120.

Russell, B. (1961) *History of Western Philosophy*, second edition, London: George Allen & Unwin. First published 1946.

—— (1977) *The Philosophy of Bergson*, Folcroft Pa.: Folcroft Library Editions. First published 1914.

Rutherford, M. (1984) 'Rational Expectations and Keynesian Uncertainty: A Critique', *Journal of Post Keynesian Economics* 6, 377–387.

Sah, R.K. (1991) 'Fallibility in Human Organizations', *Journal of Economic Perspectives* 5(2), Spring, 67–88.

Sah, R.K. and Stiglitz, J.E. (1985) 'Human Fallibility and Economic Organization', *American Economic Review, Papers and Proceedings* 75(2), May, 292–297.

—— (1986) 'The Architecture of Economic Systems: Hierarchies and Polyarchies', *American Economic Review* 76(4), September, 716–727.

—— (1988) 'Committees, Hierarchies and Polyarchies', *The Economic Journal* 98, June, 451–470.

Sahal, D. (1981) *Patterns of Technological Innovation*, Reading, Mass.: Addison-Wesley.

Sahlman, W.A. and Stevenson, H.H. (1985) 'Capital Market Myopia', in Hornaday *et al.* (1985), 80–104.

Salmon, W.C. (1967) *The Foundations of Scientific Inference*, Pittsburgh, Pa.: University of Pittsburgh Press.

Salop, S. and Stiglitz, J.E. (1977) 'Bargains and Ripoffs: A Model of

Monopolistically Competitive Price Dispersion', *Review of Economic Studies* 44(3), 138, 493–510.

—— (1982) 'The Theory of Sales: A Simple Model of Equilibrium Price Dispersion with Identical Agents', *American Economic Review* 72(5), December, 1121–1130.

Samuels, W.J. (ed.) (1984) *Research in the History of Economic Thought and Methodology, A Research Annual,* Volume Two, Greenwich, Conn.: JAI Press.

—— (ed.) (1989) *Institutional Economics,* three volumes, Aldershot: Edward Elgar.

Samuelson, P.A. (1941) 'The Stability of Equilibrium', *Econometrica* 9, 97–120.

—— (1942) 'The Stability of Equilibrium', *Econometrica* 10, 1–25.

—— (1947) *Foundations of Economic Analysis,* Cambridge, Mass.: Harvard University Press.

Sandberg, W.R. (1986) *New Venture Performance. The Role of Strategy and Industry Structure,* Lexington, Mass.: Lexington Books.

Sandberg, W.R. and Hofer, C.W. (1982) 'A Strategic Management Perspective on the Determinants of New Venture Success', in Vesper (1982), 204–237.

—— (1987) 'Improving New Venture Performance: The Role of Strategy, Industry Structure, and the Entrepreneur', *Journal of Business Venturing* 2(1), 5–28.

Scanlon, S. (1978) 'Test Marketing: Zeroing in on Profits', *Sales & Marketing Management,* March, 61–75.

Scheffler, M. (1967) *Science and Subjectivity,* Indianapolis, Ind.: The Bobbs-Merril Co.

Schendel, D.E. and Hofer, C.W. (1979) *Strategic Management: A New View of Business Policy and Planning,* Boston, Mass.: Little, Brown and Co.

Schlick, M. (1931) 'Die Kausalität in der gegenwärtigen Physik', *Die Naturwissenschaften* 19(7), 148–159.

Schlipp, P.A. (ed.) (1974) *The Philosophy of Karl Popper,* La Salle, Ill.: Open Court.

Schmalensee, R. and Willig, R. (1989) *Handbook of Industrial Organization,* Volumes One and Two, Amsterdam: North-Holland.

Schneider, Dieter (1985) *Allgemeine Betriebswirtschaftslehre,* second edition, Munich: Oldenbourg.

Schneider, Dietram (1988) 'Zur Entstehung Innovativer Unternehmen: Eine Ökonomisch-Theoretische Perspektive', Ph.D Dissertation, Technische Universität München.

Schumpeter, J.A. (1934) *The Theory of Economic Development: An Inquiry into Profits, Capital, Credit, Interest and the Business Cycle,* Cambridge, Mass.: Harvard University Press. Translated from the German by Redvers Opie.

—— (1947) 'The Creative Response in Economic History', *Journal of Economic History* 7(2), 149–159.

—— (1950) *Capitalism, Socialism and Democracy,* third edition, New York: Harper & Row. First edition 1942.

—— (1954) *History of Economic Analysis,* London: George Allen & Unwin.

—— (1965) 'Economic Theory and Entrepreneurial History', in Aitken (1965b), 45–64.

Schutz, A. (1943), 'The Problem of Rationality in the Social World', *Economica*, New Series, 10(May), 130–149.

—— (1967) *Collected Papers I: The Problem of Social Reality*, second unchanged edition, The Hague: Martinus Nijhoff. Edited by M. Natanson.

Schwartz, H. and Davis, S.M. (1981) 'Matching Corporate Culture and Business Strategy', *Organizational Dynamics*, Summer, 30–48.

Schweiger, D.M. (1983) 'Is the Simultaneous Verbal Protocol a Viable Method for Studying Managerial Problem Solving and Decision Making?', *Academy of Management Journal* 26(1), 185–192.

Scitovsky, T. (1952) *Welfare and Competition*, London: Allen & Unwin.

Scott, B.R. (1973) 'The New Industrial State, Old Myths and New Realities', *Harvard Business Review*, March–April, 133–148.

Scriven, M. (1959) 'Explanation and Prediction in Evolutionary Theory', *Science* 130, August, 447–482.

Seeman, M. and Evans, J.W. (1962) 'Alienation and Learning in a Hospital Setting', *American Sociological Review* 27(6), December, 772–781.

Seldon, A. (ed.) (1980) *The Prime Mover of Progress: The Entrepreneur in Capitalism and Socialism. Papers on 'The Rôle of the Entrepreneur'*, IEA Readings, 23, London: Institute of Economic Affairs.

Selznick, P. (1957) *Leadership in Administration*, Evanston, Ill.: Harper & Row.

Settle, T. (1974) 'Induction and Probability Unfused', in Schlipp (1974), 697–749.

Sevin, C.H. (1965) *Marketing Productivity Analysis*, New York: McGraw-Hill.

Sexton, D.L. and Smilor, R.W. (eds) (1986) *The Art and Science of Entrepreneurship*, Cambridge, Mass.: Ballinger Publishing Co.

Shackle, G.L.S. (1949) *Expectation in Economics*, Cambridge: Cambridge University Press.

—— (1955) *Uncertainty in Economics and Other Reflections*, Cambridge: Cambridge University Press.

—— (1958) *Time in Economics*, Amsterdam: North-Holland Publishing Co.

—— (1965) 'Comment (on V. Mukerji's "Two Papers on Time in Economics")', *Artha Vijnana* 7(4), December, 308.

—— (1966) *The Nature of Economic Thought. Selected Papers 1955–1964*, Cambridge: Cambridge University Press.

—— (1969) *Decision, Order and Time in Human Affairs*, second edition, Cambridge: Cambridge University Press. First edition 1961.

—— (1970) *Expectation, Enterprise and Profit. The Theory of the Firm*, Chicago, Ill.: Aldine Publishing Co.

—— (1972) *Epistemics and Economics. A Critique of Economic Doctrines*, Cambridge: Cambridge University Press.

—— (1973) *An Economic 'Querist'*, Cambridge: Cambridge University Press.

—— (1979a) *Imagination and the Nature of Choice*, Edinburgh: Edinburgh University Press.

—— (1979b) 'Imagination, Formalism and Choice', in Rizzo (1979b), 19–31.

Shahan, R.W. and Swoyer, C. (eds) (1979) *Essays on the Philosophy of W. V. Quine*, Norman, Okla.: University of Oklahoma Press.

Shand, A.H. (1984) *The Capitalist Alternative: An Introduction to Neo-Austrian Economics*, New York: New York University Press.

Shapere, D. (1964) 'The Structure of Scientific Revolutions', *Philosophical Review* 73, 383–394.

—— (1966) 'Meaning and Scientific Change', in Colodny (1966), 41–85.

—— (1971) 'The Paradigm Concept', *Science* 172, 706–709.

Shapero, A. (1975) 'The Displaced, Uncomfortable Entrepreneur', *Psychology Today*, November, 83–133.

Shapiro, C. (1989) 'Theories of Oligopoly Behavior', in Schmalensee and Willig (1989), 329–414.

Sharma, S. and Mahajan, V. (1980) 'Early Warning Indicators of Business Failure', *Journal of Marketing* 44, Fall, 80–89.

Shocker, A.D. and Srinivasan, V. (1974) 'A Consumer-Based Methodology for the Identification of New Product Ideas', *Management Science* 20, February, 921–937.

Siegel, S. (1956) *Nonparametric Statistics for the Behavioral Sciences*, New York: McGraw-Hill Book Co.

Siegel, S. and Castellan, Jr., N.J. (1988) *Nonparametric Statistics for the Behavioral Sciences*, second edition, New York: McGraw-Hill Book Co.

Simon, H.A. (1957a) *Administrative Behavior*, second edition, New York: the Macmillan Company. First edition 1947.

—— (1957b) *Models of Man*, New York: John Wiley & Sons.

—— (1962a) 'The Architecture of Complexity', *Proceedings of the American Philosopical Society* 106, December, 467–482.

—— (1962b) 'New Developments in the Theory of the Firm', *American Economic Review* 52, May, 1–15.

—— (1965) *The Shape of Automation for Men and Management*, New York: Harper & Row.

—— (1969) *The Sciences of the Artificial*, Cambridge, Mass.: MIT Press.

—— (1972) 'Theories of Bounded Rationality', in C.B. McGuire and R. Radner (eds), *Decision and Organization: A Volume in Honor of Jacob Marschak*, Amsterdam: North Holland, 161–176.

—— (1976) 'From Substantive to Procedural Rationality', in Latsis (1976b), 129–148.

—— (1982) *Models of Bounded Rationality*, two volumes, Cambridge, Mass.: MIT Press.

Simons, P.M. (1983) 'Time and Action', Paper presented at the Liberty Fund Symposium on *Perception, Opportunity, and Profit*, Vienna, August, 1–4.

Sklair, L. (1973) *Organized Knowledge. A Sociological View of Science and Technology*, St. Albans: Paladin.

Smart, J.J.C. (1949) 'The River of Time', *Mind* 58, 483–494.

—— (1955) 'Spatialising Time', *Mind* 64, 239–241.

—— (1967) 'Time', in Edwards (1967), Volume 8, 126–134.

Sommers, W.P. (1982) 'Product Development: New Approaches in the

1980s', in Tushman and Moore (1982), 51–59. Reprinted from Booz-Allen and Hamilton, Inc. (1979) *Product Development: New Approaches in the 1980s*, New York: Booz-Allen and Hamilton, Inc.

Soros, G. (1987) *The Alchemy of Finance: Reading the Mind of the Market*, New York: Simon & Schuster.

—— (1992) 'Introduction', in W.H. Newton-Smith and J. Tianji (eds), *Popper in China*, London: Routledge, 1–11.

Spadaro, L.M. (ed.) (1978a) *New Directions in Austrian Economics*, Kansas City, Kan.: Sheed, Andrews and McMeel.

—— (ed.) (1978b) 'Toward a Program of Research and Development for Austrian Economics', in Spadaro (1978a), 205–228.

Sprent, P. (1989) *Applied Nonparametric Statistical Methods*, London: Chapman & Hall.

Starbuck, W.H., Greve, A., and Hedberg, B.L.T. (1980) 'Responding to Crisis', *Journal of Business Administration* 9(2), 111–137.

Staw, B.M. (1976) 'Knee-Deep in the Big Muddy: Study of Escalating Commitment to a Chosen Course of Action', *Organizational Behavior and Human Performance* 16(1), June, 27–44.

Staw, B.M. and Ross, J. (1987a) 'Knowing When to Pull the Plug', *Harvard Business Review*, March–April, 68–74.

—— (1987b) 'Understanding Escalation Situations: Antecedents, Prototypes and Solutions', in L.L. Cummings and B.M. Staw (eds) *Research in Organizational Behavior*, Greenwich, Conn.: JAI Press.

Steinbruner, J.D. (1974) *The Cybernetic Theory of Decision: New Dimensions of Political Analysis*, Princeton, N.J.: Princeton University Press.

Steiner, G.A. (1979) *Strategic Planning: What Every Manager Must Know*, New York: Free Press.

Stephen, F.H. (ed.) (1984) *Firms, Organization and Labour. Approaches to the Economics of Work Organization*, London: Macmillan.

Stewart, I.M.T. (1979) *Reasoning and Method in Economics: An Introduction to Economic Methodology*, London: McGraw-Hill.

Stewart, J. (1976) *Understanding Econometrics*, London: Hutchinson.

Stigler, G.J. (1961) 'The Economics of Information', *Journal of Political Economy* 69(3), 213–225.

—— (1983) 'Nobel Lecture: The Process and Progress of Economics', *Journal of Political Economy* 91(4), 529–545.

Stiglitz, J.E. (1985) 'Information and Economic Analysis: A Perspective', *Economic Journal* 95, 21–41.

—— (1989) 'Imperfect Information in the Product Market', in Schmalensee and Willig (1989), 771–848.

Stuart, R.W. and Abetti, P.A. (1987) 'Start-up Ventures: Towards the Prediction of Initial Success', *Journal of Business Venturing* 2(3), 215–230.

Suppe, F. (1977a) 'Afterword –1977', in Suppe (1977c), 615–730.

—— (1977b) 'The Search for Philosophic Understanding of Scientific Theories', in Suppe (1977c), 3–241.

—— (ed.) (1977c) *The Structure of Scientific Theories*, Second Edition, Urbana,,Ill.: University of Illinois Press.

Tang, A.M., Westfield, F.M., and Worley, J.S. (eds) (1976) *Evolution,*

Welfare, and Time in Economics, Essays in Honor of Nicholas Georgescu-Roegen, Lexington, Mass.: Lexington Books, D.C. Heath & Co.

Tauber, E.M. (1972) 'What is Measured by Concept Testing?', *Journal of Advertising Research*, December, 35–37.

Teece, D.J. (1980) 'Economies of Scope and the Scope of the Enterprise', *Journal of Economic Behavior and Organisation* 1(3), 223–247.

—— (1982a) 'Some Efficiency Properties of the Modern Corporation. Theory and Evidence', manuscript, University of California, Berkeley.

—— (1982b) 'Towards an Economic Theory of the Multiproduct Firm', *Journal of Economic Behavior and Organisation* 3, 39–63.

—— (1986) 'Firm Boundaries, Technological Innovation, and Strategic Management', in L.G. Thomas (ed.) *The Economics of Strategic Planning: Essays in Honor of Joel Dean*, Lexington, Mass.: Lexington Books.

Tegar, A. (1980) *Too Much Invested to Quit*, New York: Pergamon Press.

Thaler, R. (1980) 'Toward a Positive Theory of Consumer Choice', *Journal of Economic Behavior and Organization* 1, 39–60.

Thompson, A.A. and Strickland, A.J. (1978) *Strategy and Policy: Concepts and Cases*, Dallas, Tex.: Business Publications, Inc.

Thompson, J.D. (1967) *Organizations in Action: Social Science Bases of Administrative Theory*, New York: McGraw Hill Book Co.

Thomsen, E.F. (1992) *Prices and Knowledge: A Market-Process Perspective*, London: Routledge.

Timmons, J.A. (1980) 'A Business Plan is More Than a Financing Device', *Harvard Business Review*, March–April, 28–34.

—— (1981) 'Venture Capital Investors in the US: A Survey of the Most Active Investors', in Vesper (1981), 199–216.

Timmons, J.A. and Bygrave, W.D. (1986) 'Venture Capital's Role in Financing Innovation for Economic Growth', *Journal of Business Venturing* 1(2), 161–176.

Timmons, J.A. and Gumpert, D.E. (1982) 'Discard Many Old Rules about Getting Venture Capital', *Harvard Business Review*, January–February, 152–156.

Timmons, J.A., Smollen, L.E., and Dingee, A.L.M. (1977) *New Venture Creation: A Guide to Small Business Development*, Homewood, Ill.: Richard D. Irwin, Inc.

—— (1990) *New Venture Creation: Entrepreneurship in the 1990s*, third edition, Homewood, Ill.: Irwin.

Toulmin, S. (1953) *The Philosophy of Science: An Introduction*, London: Hutchinson.

—— (1961) *Foresight and Understanding*, London: Hutchinson.

—— (1970) 'Does the Distinction between Normal and Revolutionary Science Hold Water', in Lakatos and Musgrave (1970), 39–48.

—— (1972) *Human Understanding*, Volume One, Princeton, N.J.: Princeton University Press.

Townsend, R.M. (1978) 'Market Anticipations, Rational Expectations and Bayesian Analysis', *International Economic Review* 19, 481–494.

—— (1983) 'Forecasting the Forecasts of Others', *Journal of Political Economy* 91(4), August, 546–588.

Tunstall, W.B. (1986) 'The Breakup of the Bell System: A Case Study in Cultural Transformation', *California Management Review* 28(2), Winter, 110–124.

Turner, G. (1971) *The Leyland Papers*, London: Eyre & Spottiswoode.

Tushman, M.L. and Moore, W.L. (1982) *Readings in the Management of Innovation*, Boston, Mass.: Pitman.

Tyebjee, T.T. and Bruno, A.V. (1984a) 'A Model of Venture Capitalist Investment Activity', *Management Science* 30(9), September, 1051–1066.

—— (1984b) 'Venture Capital: Investor and Investee Perspectives', *Technovation* 2, 185–208.

Ullmann-Margalit, E. (1978) 'Invisible-Hand Explanations', *Synthese* 39, 263–291.

Urbach, P. (1978) 'The Objective Promise of a Research Programme', in Radnitzsky and Andersson (1978b), 99–113.

Uzawa, H. (1962) 'On the Stability of Edgeworth's Barter Process', *International Economic Review* 3, May, 218–232.

Van de Ven, A.H., Hudson, R., and Schroeder, D.M. (1984) 'Designing New Business Start Ups: Entrepreneurial, Organizational, and Ecological Considerations', *Journal of Management* 10(1), 87–108.

Vaughn, K.I. (1980) 'Does it Matter that Costs are Subjective?', *Southern Economic Journal*, March, 702–715.

—— (1983) 'Review of Mark Casson's (1982) "The Entrepreneur: An Economic Theory"', *Journal of Economic Literature* 21, September, 991–992.

—— (1992) 'The Problem of Order in Austrian Economics: Kirzner vs. Lachmann', *Review of Political Economy* 4(3), 251–274.

—— (1994) *Austrian Economics in America: The Migration of a Tradition*, Cambridge: Cambridge University Press.

Venkatesan, M. and Holloway, R.J. (1971) *An Introduction to Marketing Experimentation: Methods, Applications and Problems*, New York: Free Press.

Verrechia, R.E. (1986) 'Managerial Discretion in the Choice Among Financial Reporting Alternatives', *Journal of Accounting and Economics*, October, 8(3), 175–195.

Vesper, K.H. (1981) *Frontiers of Entrepreneurship Research 1981*, Proceedings of the 1981 Babson College Entrepreneurship Research Conference, Wellesley, Mass.: Center for Entrepreneurial Studies Babson College.

—— (1982) *Frontiers of Entrepreneurship Research 1982*, Proceedings of the 1982 Babson College Entrepreneurship Research Conference, Wellesley, Mass.: Center for Entrepreneurial Studies Babson College.

Waite, C.P. (1982) 'The Presentation and Other Key Elements', in Pratt (1982), 121–126.

Walker, D.A. (1986) 'Walras's Theory of the Entrepreneur', *De Economist* 134(1), 1–24.

Walker, G. and Weber, D. (1984) 'A Transaction Cost Approach to Make-or-Buy Decisions', *Administrative Science Quarterly* 29, September, 373–391.

Wartofsky, M.W. (1976) 'The Relation Between Philosophy of Science and History of Science', in Cohen, Feyerabend and Wartofsky (1976), 716–737.

Watkins, J.W.N. (1955) 'Decisions and Uncertainty', *British Journal for the Philosophy of Science* 6(21), May, 66–78.

—— (1968a) 'Hume, Carnap and Popper', in Lakatos (1986b), 271–282.

—— (1968b) 'Non-Inductive Corroboration', in Lakatos (1968b), 61–66.

—— (1970) 'Against "Normal Science"', in Lakatos and Musgrave (1970), 25–38.

—— (1978a) 'Corroboration and the Problem of Content-Comparison', in Radnitzky and Andersson (1978b), 339–378.

—— (1978b) 'The Popperian Approach to Scientific Knowledge', in Radnitzky and Andersson (1978b), 23–43.

Wegenhenkel, L. (1980a) *Coase-Theorem und Marktsystem*, Tübingen, Mohr (Paul Siebeck).

—— (1980b) *Transaktionskosten, Wirtschaftssystem und Unternehmertum*, Tübingen, Mohr (Paul Siebeck).

—— (1981) *Gleichgewicht, Transaktionskosten und Evolution. Eine Analyse der Koordinierungseffizienz unterschiedlicher Wirtschaftssysteme*, Tübingen, Mohr (Paul Siebeck).

—— (1983) 'Property Rights and Entrepreneurial Motivation', Paper presented at the Liberty Fund Symposium on *Perception, Opportunity, and Profit*, Vienna, August 1–4, 1983.

Weimer, W.B. (1974a) 'The History of Psychology and Its Retrieval From Historiography I: The Problematic Nature of History', *Science Studies* 4, 235–258.

—— (1974b) 'The History of Psychology and Its Retrieval From Historiography II: Some Lessons for the Methodology of Scientific Research', *Science Studies* 4, 367–396.

—— (1979) *Notes on the Methodology of Scientific Research*, Hillsdale, N.J.: Laurence Erlbaum Associates.

Weiner, B. (1974) 'Achievement Motivation as Conceptualized by an Attribution Theorist', in B. Weiner (ed.) *Achievement Motivation and Attribution Theory*, Morristown, N.J.: General Learning Press.

Weintraub, E.R. (1979) *Microfoundations. The Compatibility of Micro-economics and Macroeconomics*, Cambridge: Cambridge University Press.

—— (1985a) 'Appraising General Equilibrium Analysis', *Economics and Philosophy* 1, 23–37.

—— (1985b) *General Equilibrium Analysis. Studies in Appraisal*, Cambridge: Cambridge University Press.

—— (1988) 'The Neo-Walrasian Program is Empirically Progressive', in de Marchi (1988c), 213–227.

Weiss, L.A. (1981) 'Start-Up Business: A Comparison of Performance'. *Sloan Management Review*, Fall, 37–53.

Welsh, J.A. and White, J.F. (1977) 'Conditions for the Successful Exploitation of a New Idea', *APLA Bulletin*, April–May, 294–304.

—— (1978) 'Recognizing and Dealing with the Entrepreneur', *S.A.M. Advanced Management Journal*, Spring, 21–31.

—— (1981) 'Converging on the Characteristics of Entrepreneurs', in Vesper (1981), 504–515.

Wheelen, T.L. and Hunger, J.D. (1989) *Strategic Management and Business Policy*, third edition, Reading, Mass.: Addison-Wesley.

White, L.H. (1976) 'Entrepreneurship, Imagination, and the Question of Equilibrium', unpublished paper.

—— (1978) 'Entrepreneurial Price Adjustment', paper presented at the session on Entrepreneurship and Economic Activity at the Southern Economic Association meetings, Washington D.C., November, 1978.

—— (1984) *The Methodology of the Austrian School of Economists*, revised edition, Auburn, Ala.: The Ludwig von Mises Insitute of Auburn University. First edition 1977.

Whyte, R.R. (1975) *Engineering Progress Through Trouble: Case Histories Drawn Largely From the Proceedings of the Institution of Mechanical Engineers Which Illustrate the Wisdom, Experience and High Professional Skills Demanded by Creative Engineering and Something of the Exhilaration, Excitement, and Agony Which Goes With Engineering Creation*, London: Institution of Mechanical Engineers.

Wible, J.R. (1982–83) 'The Rational Expectations Tautologies', *Journal of Post Keynesian Economics* 5, Winter, 199–207.

—— (1984) 'Towards a Process Conception of Rationality in Economics and Science', *Review of Social Economy* 42(2), October, 89–104.

—— (1984–85) 'An Epistemic Critique of Rational Expectations and the Neoclassical Macroeconomic Research Program', *Journal of Post Keynesian Economics* 7, 269–281.

Wiener, N. (1948) *Cybernetics: Or Control and Communication in the Animal and the Machine*, New York: John Wiley & Sons.

Wilber, C.K., and Harrison, R.S. (1978) 'The Methodological Basis of Institutional Economics: Pattern Model, Storytelling, and Holism', *Journal of Economic Issues* 12(1), 61–89.

Wilcoxon, F. (1945) 'Individual Comparisons By Ranking Methods', *Biometrics* 1, 80–83.

Wiles, P. and Routh, G. (eds) (1984) *Economics in Disarray*, Oxford: Basil Blackwell.

Williams, B.R. and Scott, W.P. (1965) *Investment Proposals and Decisions*, London: George Allen & Unwin.

Williams, D.C. (1951) 'The Myth of Passage', *Journal of Philosophy* 48, 457–472.

Williamson, O.E. (1971) 'The Vertical Integration of Production: Market Failure Considerations', *American Economic Review* 61(May), 112–123. Reprinted in Williamson (1986a), 101–130.

—— (1975) *Markets and Hierarchies: Analysis and Antitrust Implications*, New York: Free Press.

—— (1979) 'Transaction Cost Economics: The Governance of Contractual Relations', *Journal of Law and Economics* 22(October), 233–261. Reprinted in Williamson (1986a), 101–130.

—— (1981a) 'The Economics of Organization: The Transaction Cost Approach', *American Journal of Sociology* 87(November), 548–577.

—— (1981b) 'The Modern Corporation: Origins, Evolution, Attributes',

Journal of Economic Literature, 19(December), 1537–1568. Reprinted in Williamson (1986a), 131–173.

—— (1981c) 'On the Nature of the Firm: Some Recent Developments', *Zeitschrift für die gesamte Staatswissenschaft/Journal of Institutional and Theoretical Economics* 137(4), 675–680.

—— (1983a) 'Credible Commitments: Using Hostages to Support Exchange', *American Economic Review* 73(September), 519–540.

—— (1983b) 'Organizational Form, Residual Claimants, and Corporate Control', *Journal of Law and Economics* 26(June), 351–366.

—— (1983c) 'Organizational Innovation: The Transaction Cost Approach', in Ronen (1983a), 101–134.

—— (1984a) 'The Economics of Governance: Framework and Implications', *Journal of Theoretical Economics* 140(1), 195–223.

—— (1984b) 'Efficient Labour Organization', in Stephen (1984), 87–118.

—— (1984c) 'The Incentive Limits of Firms: A Comparative Institutional Assessment of Bureaucracy', *Weltwirtschaftliches Archiv* 120(4), 736–763.

—— (1984d) 'Perspectives on the Modern Corporation', *Quarterly Review of Economics and Business* 24(Winter), 64–71.

—— (1985a) *The Economic Institutions of Capitalism: Firms, Markets, Relational Contracting*, New York: The Free Press.

—— (1985b) 'Reflections on the New Institutional Economics', *Zeitschrift für die gesamte Staatswissenschaft/Journal of Institutional and Theoretical Economics* 141(1), 187–195.

—— (1986a) *Economic Organization: Firms, Markets and Policy Control*, Brighton: Wheatsheaf Books.

—— (1986b) 'The Economics of Governance: Framework and Implications', in Langlois (1986b), 171–202.

—— (1986c) 'Transforming Merger Policy: The Pound of New Perspectives', American Economic Review, *American Economic Association Papers and Proceedings* 76(2), 114–119.

—— (1986d) *Vertical Integration*, Working Paper Series D, Economics of Organization, 19, Yale University.

—— (1986e) 'Vertical Integration and Related Variations on a Transaction-Cost Theme', in J.E. Stiglitz and G.F. Mathewson (eds), *New Developments in the Anaylsis of Market Structure. Proceedings of a Conference held by the International Economic Association in Ottowa, Canada*, Cambridge, Mass.: MIT Press.

Williamson, O. and Bhargava, N. (1972) 'Assessing and Classifying the Internal Structure and Control Apparatus of the Modern Corporation', in K. Cowling (ed.), *Market Structure and Corporate Behaviour Theory and Empirical Analysis of the Firm*, London: Gray-Mills Publishing, 125–148. Reprinted in Williamson (1986a), 54–80.

Wilson, A. (1971) *The Art and Practice of Marketing: A Decade of Experimentation*, London: Hutchinson.

Winter, S.G. (1986) 'The Research Program of the Behavioral Theory of the Firm: Orthodox Critique and Evolutionary Perspective', in Gilad and Kaish (1986), Volume A, 151–188.

Wiseman, J. (1980) 'Costs and Decisions', in Currie and Peters (1980), 473–490.

—— (1983a) 'Beyond Positive Economics – Dream and Reality', in Wiseman (1983b), 1–12.

—— (ed.) (1983b) *Beyond Positive Economics? Proceedings of Section F (Economics) of the British Association for the Advancement of Science, York 1981*, New York: St. Martin's Press.

—— (1989) *Cost, Choice and Political Economy*, Aldershot: Edward Elgar.

Witt, U. (1987a) 'How Transaction Rights are Shaped to Channel Innovativeness', *Journal of Institutional and Theoretical Economics*, 143(1), 180–195.

—— (1987b) *Individualistische Grundlagen der evolutorischen Ökonomik*, Die Einheit der Gesellschaftswissenshcaften, Studien in den Grenzbereichen der Wirtschafts- und Sozialwissenschaften, Band 47, Tübingen, Mohr (Paul Siebeck).

Wittgenstein, L. (1953) *Philosophical Investigations*, Oxford: Blackwell.

Wolf, C., Jr. (1970) 'The Present Value of the Past', *Journal of Political Economy* 78, July–August, 783–792.

—— (1973) 'Heresies about Time: Wasted Time, Double-Duty Time, and Past Time', *Quarterly Journal of Economics* 87(4), November, 661–667.

Wolk, S. and DuCette, J. (1974) 'International Performance of Incidental Learning as a Function of Personality and Task Dimensions', *Journal of Personality and Social Psychology* 29(1), 90–101.

Woodruff, R.B. (1976) 'A Systematic Approach to Market Opportunity Analyses', *Business Horizons* 19(4), August, 55–65.

Worchester, R.M. (ed.) (1972) *Consumer Market Research Handbook*, London: McGraw-Hill Book Company.

Worrall, J. (1978) 'The Ways in Which the Methodology of Scientific Research Programmes Improves on Popper's Methodology', in Radnitzky and Andersson (1978b), 45–70.

Wu, S.-Y. (1989) *Production, Entrepreneurship and Profits*, Oxford: Basil Blackwell.

Yoshino, M.Y. (1968) *Japan's Managerial System: Tradition and Innovation*, Cambridge, Mass.: MIT Press.

Yu, B. (1981) 'Potential Competition and Contracting in Innovation', *Journal of Law and Economics* 24(2), 215–238.

INDEX

403

Printed in Great Britain
by Amazon

79703582R00251